RISKY BUSINESS:
CANADA'S CHANGING SCIENCE-BASED POLICY AND REGULATORY REGIME

Risky Business is a comprehensive look at Canada's science-based policy and regulatory regime. It asks what risks Canadians might be exposed to as fiscal pressures strain the capacity of regulators in areas such as food, drugs, pesticides, fisheries, and the environment.

The essays in part 1 raise diverse and major themes pervading science-based regulatory regimes today through discussions of a range of topics including eco-labelling, BSE (Mad Cow Disease), and raspberry imports. The second set of essays suggest a framework for analysis and endeavour to present both sympathetic and critical perspectives on the inner-workings of regulatory departments and agencies dealing with the protection of human and environmental health and safety.

Covering areas such as the organizational evolution of regulatory agencies, regulatory bodies' changing sources and levels of funding, a review of the independence of science, and the increased potential for realization of risk, these essays point to the need for regulators to operate with openness and accessibility in order to maintain public confidence. Indeed, the contributors argue that this openness is crucial to both democratic governance and the development of innovative knowledge economies.

(Studies in Comparative Political Economy and Public Policy)

G. BRUCE DOERN is a professor in the School of Public Administration at Carleton University, and holds a joint chair in Public Policy in the Department of Politics at Exeter University. At present he is involved in the Carleton Research Unit on Innovation, Science, and Environment (CRUISE).

TED REED is a research fellow in the Carleton Research Unit on Innovation, Science, and Environment (CRUISE) at Carleton University and is also a lecturer with the Department of Environmental Studies and Geography at Carleton. He was formerly Assistant Secretariat in the Department of Continuing Education of the Government of Saskatchewan.

Studies in Comparative Political Economy and Public Policy

Editors: MICHAEL HOWLETT, DAVID LAYCOCK, STEPHEN MCBRIDE, Simon
Fraser University

Studies in Comparative Political Economy and Public Policy is designed to
showcase innovative approaches to political economy and public policy from
a comparative perspective. While originating in Canada, the series will
provide attractive offerings to a wide international audience, featuring
studies with local, sub-national, cross-national, and international empirical
bases and theoretical frameworks.

(Series list on page 387)

G. BRUCE DOERN and TED REED,
Editors

RISKY BUSINESS

*Canada's Changing Science-Based Policy
and Regulatory Regime*

UNIVERSITY OF TORONTO PRESS
Toronto Buffalo London

© University of Toronto Press Incorporated 2000
Toronto Buffalo London
Printed in Canada

ISBN 0-8020-4481-6 (cloth)
ISBN 0-8020-8262-9 (paper)

Printed on acid-free paper

Canadian Cataloguing in Publication Data

Main entry under title:

Risky business : Canada's changing science-based policy and regulatory
regime

(Studies in comparative political economy and public policy)
ISBN 0-8020-4481-6 (bound)   ISBN 0-8020-8262-9 (pbk.)

1. Science and state – Canada.   2. Administrative agencies – Canada.
I. Doern, G. Bruce, 1942–   .   II. Reed, Edward James, 1948–   .
III. Series.

Q127.C2R57 2000   338.9'26'0971   C00-930491-6

University of Toronto Press acknowledges the financial assistance to its
publishing program of the Canada Council for the Arts and the Ontario
Arts Council.

University of Toronto Press acknowledges the financial support for its
publishing activities of the Government of Canada through the Book
Publishing Industry Development Program (BPIDP).

Contents

Preface

This book is the product of a collaborative effort initiated by the editors and the Carleton Research Unit on Innovation, Science, and Environment (CRUISE) in the School of Public Administration at Carleton University. It also builds on earlier research work on comparative regulatory institutions (1998) and on Canadian regulatory institutions.

The task of examining Canada's science-based policy and regulatory regime is a 'risky business' in at least three senses. First, no two persons entering into such a debate or analysis possess the same knowledge base or value framework. Nor can any of them have full certainty about what they know or do not know about the science-based policy and regulatory regime being investigated. Second, to engage in the debate, or even to begin mapping the regime and its constituent institutions requires one to be almost perversely interdisciplinary in one's approach. Third, the debate about aspects of the science-based regime, including its independence, openness, inherent technical capacity, and performance, is increasingly influenced by a larger discussion of the nature of risk in society. It is also influenced by debate about the risks to the state of not understanding what its appropriate and feasible role might or should be in this area.

Initial drafts of the chapters were presented at the CRUISE Conference on Canada's Science-Based Regulatory Regime, held in Ottawa on 1–2 October 1998. We were also very fortunate in securing the involvement of leading practitioners and academics including Bill Doubleday of the Department of Fisheries and Oceans, Ron Doering of the Canadian Food Inspection Agency, Mary Measures of the Atomic Energy Control Board, Steve Hindle of the Professional Institute of the Public Service, Bob Ingratta of Monsanto, Peter Calamai of the *Toronto*

Star, Albert Teich of the American Association for the Advancement of Science, Tim Caulfield of the University of Alberta, John Carey of Environment Canada, Anne Mackenzie of CFIA, Beth Pieterson of Health Canada, Doug Russell who is an environmental consultant, and Keith Newton and Glen Toner of CRUISE. We are grateful to all these participants for their constructive comments, to other scientists and policy analysts who also attended the conference, and also to three anonymous reviewers of the manuscript who provided constructive commentary.

This enterprise would have been impossible without the generous financial assistance of several bodies, and we would like to thank CRUISE, the School of Public Administration at Carleton University, the Politics Department at the University of Exeter, the Social Science and Humanities Research Council of Canada, Industry Canada, Health Canada, Natural Resources Canada, Environment Canada, and the Canadian Food Inspection Agency.

G. BRUCE DOERN and TED REED
July 1999

Contributors

MARGARET BARKER is a consultant in the interrelated areas of science, technology, and industrial strategies and innovation, nationally and internationally. She is founder and principal consultant of Conseil Equilibrio Consulting, a 'virtual company' whose mission is to 'facilitate access to scientific and technical knowledge, and to support goals defined by communities for social and economic analysis.' She is the author of *The University-Industry Relationship in Science and Technology* (1995, with Jerôme Doutriaux).

DENNIS BROWNE is director of the Centre for Trade Policy and Law, which is jointly sponsored by the Norman Paterson School of International Affairs at Carleton University and the Faculty of Law of the University of Ottawa. During his earlier thirty-year career in the Canadian foreign service he held several managerial positions in trade and economic policy and trade development, in addition to seven foreign postings. He is editor of *The Culture/Trade Quandary: Policy Options for Canada* and has published articles on cultural trade and split-run magazines.

RAMESH CHAITOO is a research associate at the Centre for Trade Policy and Law. He has conducted commissioned research for UNCTAD, Foreign Affairs and International Trade, Industry Canada, Agriculture Canada, and various industry associations. He currently focuses on North American and Western Hemisphere trade issues.

JOHN DE LA MOTHE is professor in the Program of Research in International Management and Economy (PRIME) in the Faculty of

Administration at the University of Ottawa. He is the author and editor of numerous books and articles on Canadian and international science and technology policy including *Evolutionary Economics and the New International Political Economy* (with Gilles Paquet); *Science and Technology in Canada* (with Paul Dufour); and *Science, Technology and Governance*. The co-editor of the journal *Science and Public Policy*, he is also the editor of the Pinter (U.K.) series on *Science, Technology, and the International Political Economy*. He has also served as a consultant to several government departments and agencies such as Industry Canada as well as international agencies including the OECD and NATO.

G. BRUCE DOERN is professor in the School of Public Administration, Carleton University, and holds a joint chair in public policy in the politics department, University of Exeter. At present he is involved in the Carleton Research Unit on Innovation, Science, and Environment (CRUISE). His recent books include: *Canadian Intellectual Property: The Politics of Innovating Institutions and Interests* (2000, with Markus Sharaput); *Global Change and Intellectual Property Agencies* (Pinter, 1999); *Changing the Rules: Canada's Regulatory Regimes and Institutions* (1999, with Margaret Hill, Michael Prince, and Richard Schultz); *Free Trade Federalism* (1999, with Mark MacDonald); *Changing Regulatory Institutions in Britain and North America* (1998, with Stephen Wilks); *Comparative Competition Policy* (1996, co-edited with Stephen Wilks); *Crossing Borders: The Internationalization of Canadian Public Policy* (1996, co-edited with Brian Tomlin and Leslie Pal), and *The Greening of Canada* (1994, co-written with Tom Conway).

MICHAEL HART is professor of international affairs at the Norman Paterson School of International Affairs and senior associate at the Centre for Trade Policy and Law. He is also visiting professor of trade and commercial diplomacy at the Monterey Insitute of International Studies at Monterey, California. An experienced federal trade negotiator, he has published widely in trade policy, including recent books such as *Fifty Years of Canadian Tradecraft: Canada at the GATT 1947–1997* (1999); *Finding Middle Ground: Reforming the Antidumping Laws in North America* (1998); and *What's Next? Canada, the Global Economy and the New Trade Policy* (1998).

BILL JARVIS is director, special projects, of the Public Policy Forum where he is heading a research program on science and government.

He is the author of *The Role and Responsibilities of the Scientist in Public Policy* (1998). An economist, he was formerly an economic forecaster with Informetrica Limited and then served from 1982 to 1998 as a senior official in Energy, Mines and Resources Canada (now Natural Resources Canada). His responsibilities there included a lead involvement with the deregulation of oil and gas markets. He was in 1998–9 on an executive interchange from Natural Resources Canada with the Public Policy Forum, but has recently joined Environment Canada, where he is leading a policy research program.

IVO KRUPKA is president of the consulting firm, Public Policy and Management Inc established after his thirty-year public service career. He was assistant secretary to the Privy Council Committee on Scientific and Industrial Research as well as to various other Cabinet committees, including the Cabinet Committee on the Public Service, chaired by the prime minister. Towards the end of his career he led the establishment of Health Canada's Pest Management Regulatory Agency. He is co-editor of the proceedings of a series of international conferences on Science, Statistics, and Public Policy held annually at Herstmonceux Castle in the United Kingdom.

DANIEL E. LANE is professor and currently vice-dean and associate dean (research) at the Faculty of Administration of the University of Ottawa. He is the author of numerous articles on fisheries management. His continuing research interests are in systems modelling and decision-making processes as applied to the management of fisheries. He has been involved as peer reviewer and working group member for the Department of Fisheries and Oceans, and he has ongoing research initiatives on the evaluation and performance of fisheries with the International Council for the Exploration of the Sea (ICES) and the Fisheries Committee of the Organization for Economic Cooperation and Development (OECD). He is currently a member of the Fisheries Resource Conservation Council.

WILLIAM LEISS, FRSC, is president of the Royal Society of Canada. He is a professor in the Faculty of Management at the University of Calgary and holds there the NSERC/SSHRC research chair in Risk Communication and Public Policy; he is also visiting fellow in the School of Policy Studies at Queen's University. He is the author or co-author of numerous books, the most recent of which are *Risk Issue*

Management: A New Approach to Risk Controversies (2000); *Mad Cows and Mother's Milk: The Perils of Poor Risk Communication* (1997, with Douglas Powell); and *Risk and Responsibility* (1994).

EVERT A. LINDQUIST is director of the School of Public Administration at the University of Victoria. He has written on government transitions, Cabinet decision making, budgetary processes, consultation, capacity for policy innovation, government restructuring, think tanks, policy communities, alternative service delivery, business planning, and performance reporting. Recent research has focused on alternative recruitment strategies for improving policy capacity, the management of overlap and duplication, and a comparative study of central agencies.

MARK R. MACDONALD is an SSHRC postdoctoral fellow in the department of political science, McMaster University, where he is currently completing research on a transaction cost theory of policy networks. He has also done work on Canadian federalism and internal trade, and is co-author of *Free-Trade Federalism* (1999, with Bruce Doern). He has a PhD in public policy from Carleton University.

ERIK MILLSTONE is a senior faculty member at the Science Policy Research Unit (SPRU) at the University of Sussex. Dr Millstone is a physicist whose research work has focused in the past decade on food safety and regulation and who was instrumental in advising the British government on the reform of food regulation in the wake of the BSE crisis. He is the author of numerous articles and studies on food safety and is currently engaged in research on risk regulation in the European Union.

DOUGLAS POWELL is assistant professor and director of the Agri-Food Risk Management and Communication project in the department of plant agriculture at the University of Guelph. He is the co-author of *Mad Cows and Mother's Milk* (1997, with William Leiss).

MICHAEL J. PRINCE is Lansdowne professor of social policy, University of Victoria. He is the author or editor of several books on Canadian public policy including: *The Changing Politics of Canadian Social Policy* (2000, with Jim Rice); *Changing the Rules: Canada's Regulatory Institutions and Regimes* (1999, with Bruce Doern, Margaret Hill, and Richard Schultz); *How Ottawa Spends* (1986; 1987); *Federal and Provincial Budgeting* (1985, with Allan Maslove and Bruce Doern); *Public Budgeting in Canada* (1988, with Allan Maslove and Bruce Doern); and *The Origins of Public Enterprise in the Canadian Mineral Sector* (1985, with Bruce Doern).

TED REED is a research fellow in the Carleton Research Unit on Innovation, Science, and Environment (CRUISE) at Carleton University and is also a lecturer with the department of environmental studies and geography at Carleton. He is completing a PhD in public policy at the School of Public Administration at Carleton. He was formerly assistant secretary, Saskatchewan Science Council, and assistant director, Science Policy Secretariat in the Department of Continuing Education of the Government of Saskatchewan. In addition to public service, he has experience in risk management as a derivatives trader with Merrill Lynch Canada Inc. and Nesbitt Burns Inc.

PATRICK VAN ZWANENBERG is a research fellow at the Science Policy Research Unit (SPRU) at the University of Sussex. He is currently working on a European Commission funded project on the history of BSE policy making. He has a first degree in environmental sciences and an MSc and a DPhil in science and technology policy studies.

RISKY BUSINESS:
CANADA'S CHANGING SCIENCE-BASED POLICY
AND REGULATORY REGIME

1 Canada's Changing Science-Based Policy and Regulatory Regime: Issues and Framework

G. BRUCE DOERN and TED REED

As a century ends and a new millennium begins, a series of episodes and controversies, both Canadian and global, have brought the issues of science in the formation of government policy and regulations to the fore in ways that are in many respects unprecedented. In Canada these have centred on controversies surrounding the collapse of fish stocks in the Atlantic fishery and the issue of tainted blood and the failure of the country's blood regulatory system. Concerns have been raised about the independence of science in the Health Protection Branch at Health Canada and about the nuclear reactors used to generate electricity in Ontario. These controversies have developed alongside global concerns that have included the debacle over bovine spongiform encephalopathy (BSE) or 'mad cow' disease in the United Kingdom, the cloning of Dolly the sheep, and the new technical and ethical imperatives of what one author has referred to as the 'biotechnology century' (Rifkin, 1998). Previous decades saw periodic episodes where science-based controversy emerged on the Canadian political and economic agenda (Doern, 1981; Salter, 1988). What is different about the turn of the millennium cluster of controversies and concerns is that they raise deeper issues about the entire science-based policy and regulatory regime of government and its ability to grapple with the issues, bringing into question how risk itself is assessed, managed, and communicated in government (Powell and Leiss, 1997).

This book has two main purposes. The first is to examine key macro-issues concerning the new challenges of science in governmental policy making and regulation. The second is to suggest a framework through which Canada's science-based policy and regulatory regime can be understood as a complex functional system of agencies and key sub-

Table 1.1 Key elements of the dual conceptual focus

Macro science-based policy issues and influences
(mainly set forth in Part 1 of the book)

- Government science, the public interest, and the science deficit
- Changing paradigms of risk and the independence of science
- Trade policy, science, and innovation
- Macro-pressures from hallmark cases: interests and transparency

Science-based regime subprocesses, pathways, and relations
(explored in more depth in Part 2 of the book)

- Regulation making, policy, and standard setting
- Product and case review and approval
- Overall compliance and enforcement
- Postmarket and/or general monitoring and reporting
- Financial and human resource management

---

processes that exhibits a rich variety of relations between science and government and among scientists and other players. We look in particular at five science-based agencies as institutional actors in this larger regime: the Therapeutic Products Program (TPP) of Health Canada, the Canadian Food Inspection Agency (CFIA), the Pest Management Regulatory Agency (PMRA), Fisheries and Oceans Canada, and Environment Canada. Table 1.1 conveys at a glance the basic elements of the dual conceptual focus of the book being introduced in the main sections of this chapter.

Before presenting a fuller elaboration of our dual framework, we first need to set out some key features of definitional scope and also of limits to the analysis.

What Is 'Science-Based' Policy and Regulation? Definition, Scope, and Limits

Governments throughout the world 'are becoming increasingly dependent on scientists for expert advice to inform policy on a wide range of issues ... particularly in sensitive areas affecting people's health and safety, biotechnology, animal and plant protection, transport and the environment' (Office of Science and Technology, 1998: 1). This growing dependence of governance on science, particularly in the presence of scientific uncertainty and fiscal limitation, is demanding a more principled, efficient, and effective use of science in governmental decision making, including policy and regulation making (Jarvis, 1998).

'Science-based' policy and regulation can be defined as policy and regulatory decision making where scientific knowledge and personnel constitute significant or effective inputs into, or are distinctive features of, the relevant decision-making process. The science base as a complex of activities underlying or underpinning the formation of policy and regulations involves the work of science proper, as well as related science-based activities, and includes such diverse tasks as:

- Research, model building, and analysis
- Monitoring, data gathering, and assessment
- Technology and indicators for research and development
- Performance measurement and reporting activities
- Priority setting and foresight in science and technology – early identification of issues for which scientific advice or research will be needed, particularly where potentially significant risks may be involved
- Acquisition of best available scientific advice drawing upon a wide range of expert sources and institutional arrangements both within and outside government
- Publication of scientific advice and analysis underlying policy and regulatory decisions as well as the associated research findings of scientists. (Government of Canada, 1997; Office of Science and Technology, 1998)

The conduct and use of science in government is thus not something homogeneous, but rather a complex set of activities. The practical decision context is predominantly one in which science is an important, and possibly decisive, but not the only *base* for policy and regulation making.

The science-based policy and regulatory regime must somehow be differentiated from other policy and regulatory realms or phases of decision making that are dependent upon other types of *expertise* or on other kinds of information such as those provided through market pricing or democratic voting systems (Schooler, 1971). In short, there is a spectrum or continuum of expertise in which other policy makers and regulators display legal, economic, or some other expertise or simply knowledge specific to the policy field. One example would be the Canadian Radio and Telecommunications Commission (CRTC) with legal, economic, and cultural expertise and Industry Canada with scientific and technical expertise, both in relation to the assignment and use of the radio spectrum.

We make no attempt in this book to cover science-based policy making in all of its macro-realms and senses. Nevertheless, they must be kept fully in mind since this book ultimately is about a subset of policy making and regulation that is reliant upon science, functioning within a far larger policy-making system. Part 1 of the book, however, does address some key macro-issues that derive from the macro-policy environment, hence our reference to Canada's science-based *policy* and regulatory regime. Science-based *regulation* is the other half of the book's main defining focus. As we see later, regulation involves making rules that in one sense flow from macro-policy. Regulation can involve a confluence of activity that includes delegated legislation, guidelines, voluntary codes, and complex compliance processes (Doern et al., 1999). But before being immersed in the substance of science-based regulation, we need to examine some key issues that emerge from the first half of this two-part volume. The discussion of definition and scope has placed some boundaries around the concept of a science-based policy and regulatory regime. It also suggests the presence of inexact continuums and categories of ideas and behaviour about which we have no choice but to be conscious and cautious.

Macro-Science-Based Policy Issues and Influences

The chapters in Part 1 and other relevant literature suggest that there are four macro-science-based issues and influences of importance regarding Canada's science-based policy and regulatory regime. These are: (1) government science and the public interest, including the idea of the state having a 'science deficit' analogous to the fiscal deficit; (2) changing paradigms of risk and issues of the independence of science, including the question of appropriate locations or institutional venues for various components of the science base; (3) the impact of trade policy and pressures for harmonization in a global economy where innovation is a new policy mantra and competitive reality; and (4) particular hallmark controversies which, when pushed onto the agenda raise or expose macro-policy issues of a substantive kind. These controversies may also serve to crystallize key institutional issues having to do with the roles of players such as the media and, often unexpected, policy communities and interest coalitions that are still in the process of formation.

Government Science, the Public Interest, and the 'Science Deficit'

The broadest macro-question to pose is, 'What is the role of the federal government in the conduct of science in its own laboratories and facilities, and how have the public interest rationales for such activity changed?' John de la Mothe's analysis in Chapter 2 addresses some key aspects of this question in a historical and contemporary context. He concludes that, over time, the federal science effort has been continuously adaptive as our collective development itself went through nation-building and then capacity-building phases. This effort is still evolving to meet the current cycle of globalization challenges with creative responses in the form of national systems of innovation. Such a broad and positive portrait of change is essential to keep in mind, but it also needs to be textured by a more particular set of concerns, which as editors, we pose under the rubric of a real or potential 'science deficit.'

Ultimately science in government is tied closely to regulating and managing risks, and this aspect will be explored further below. But there is another sense in which risk must be examined, namely, in relation to the systemic risks to the legitimacy and capacity of the state if it does *not invest* in or make adequate provision for its own science capacity, thereby incurring a science deficit. This can be likened to the problems posed by the federal financial deficit. It took at least a decade (virtually all of the 1980s) to develop a recognition, politically, that the protracted running of financial deficits was a serious and cumulative problem and a growing risk to the state and society. It has taken much of the 1990s to gather the force of will required to begin dealing with it. This two-decade-long saga of the financial deficit belies a profound democratic weakness and institutional inertia. The deficit has posed a threat to the legitimacy and financial integrity of the state and to democratic institutions, and a heavy political price was paid in the form of a marked growth in voter and citizen mistrust of government and lack of confidence in its institutions (Swimmer, 1996). Thus, the costs and risks of the accumulated deficits have spilled over from the financial into other aspects of our system of governance.

There is another sense in which the financial deficit has metaphorical and practical utility in thinking about a science deficit. Less known to Canadians is the underlying need for government to manage increasing costs and risks associated with managing a portfolio of direct market debt and other public liabilities, by trading off various costs and risks inherent to the short-, medium-, and long-term financial obligations and choices. With larger exponential growth in the public debt came greater fiscal instability arising from higher levels of cost and risk, since the levels of both were rising even as debt managers sought to make increasingly difficult trade-offs between the two.

The notion of a science deficit, with analogous risk-benefit and risk-cost decision challenges in the science-based regime, is a useful concept. Like the fiscal deficit it too is a manifestation of institutional inertia and democratic weakness, because, to this point at least, the analogy between trading off cost and risk in government science capacity and the trade-off in the context of debt management has not been fully appreciated. A government can reduce the cost of its existing science base but, other things remaining equal, it is thereby increasing the risk to the government, taxpayers, and citizens from a budgetary policy of short-term cost minimization.

Through a policy of cost recovery that is not matched by improved efficiency in regulatory performance, government will also be increasing the costs, and hence the risks of loss of market share, of regulated entities. In consequence, there is a reduced 'capacity for action,' a science deficit, or a diminution in the 'science reserve' that may previously have been available to cope with sustained exposure to risk or to combinations of multiple risks. Learning about policy making from an awareness of the cumulative risks and costs of protracted deficits can alert us to, and help us to take seriously, the concerns expressed about the science deficit. Finally, the fiscal analogy points us to the need to treat science management as a portfolio selection problem. In such a treatment, the diversification and weighting of investment in the science base would come as a result of assessing and trading off costs, risks, and benefits as well as being prudent by hedging our risks and bets.

Science budgets and the number of scientists supporting federal policy and regulatory functions have been cut in the past fifteen years overall, while selected science budgets have grown or been rekindled in various ways. For example, the granting councils initially experienced cuts, followed by partial restoration and some commitment to more stable funding. Other amounts of science funding have been moved some distance from the federal bureaucracy into 'third-party trusts' such as the Canadian Foundation for Innovation (in the 1997 and 1999 federal budgets) and a new network of health science research institutes (in the 1999 budget).

While federal ministers have not 'gutted' science establishments, the best that can be said is that they have treated this aspect of the science portfolio generally with benign neglect. This reveals that they are not at all sure about the place of science in government, although credible observers elsewhere have attested to the increasing dependence of government upon science (Office of Science and Technology, 1998).

There is also little to indicate from the 1993–4 Program Review (Swimmer, 1996) that ministers had any special appreciation that citizens perceived health, safety, and environmental regulation as a crucial task for the federal and other governments to undertake. This area of concern is largely coincident with Canada's regime of science-based regulation. Overall, Canadians have been prepared to support federal privatization, harmonization, and deregulation initiatives generally, but not in the area of human and environmental health and safety. Thus, the concept of a science deficit also refers to a diminution in the capacity of the federal government to think through and to defend those areas where its long-term future legitimacy is at stake and where science provides crucial foundations. As has been argued elsewhere (Smol, 1998), 'Basic research is much like an investment in the bank – when you need it, you call upon it. *It is our foundation, our insurance.* Surely, the main difference between pure and applied research must simply be just a matter of time' (our italics). In short, Program Review reduced science capacity, thus increasing risks for the legitimacy of the state, quite apart from how it was or was not handling particular health and environmental risks or promoting an innovative economy.

As with the analogy to the fiscal deficit and debt management, there are problems and dangers in not consciously managing the costs and risks of the federal science portfolio. An unduly expensive base for science regulation shared with regulated entities may render industry non-competitive, while minimization of the cost of the science base may expose citizens to inappropriate and avoidable levels of risk. This means at one level that the aggregate size of science budgets is not itself an indicator of whether one is doing well. The composition and mix of scientists employed, their capacity to keep up to date in their knowledge, and their ability to link with outside networks of other scientists are all a part of the portfolio management challenge. Science portfolio thinking also implies being able to make or buy science in more flexible ways, with greater speed, precision, and purpose than has been possible in the past. However, the concept of the science deficit can only be taken so far. This is because it immediately begins to intersect with other general forces to be discussed below.

Changing Paradigms of Risk and the Independence of Science

The chapters by Leiss and by Millstone and Van Zwanenberg each address the changing paradigms of risk and the issue of the locational independence of science. Both are prescriptive chapters but in quite different ways. On the one hand, Leiss's more general analysis argues that all or most science should *not* be done in government and needs to be undertaken in locales outside the state (excluding industry). That is where it can be 'most true to itself,' as Leiss puts it, and therefore useful to democratic governance. This is because, in Leiss's view, the old bureaucratic model of science in government is not capable of dealing with the new paradigms of risk management. The Millstone and Van Zwanenberg chapter, on the other hand, documents the catastrophic and total failure of U.K. regulators to deal with the United Kingdom's BSE or 'mad-cow disease' controversy. These authors see a need for adherence to independent science, but they believe that such science can emanate, if allowed, from both inside and outside the state. The BSE chapter certainly anticipates new kinds of risk emerging in food production chains but opts for more traditional regimes of accountability, backed by good science combined with effective enforcement. We examine other issues inherent in the question of the 'independence' of science in our conclusions in Chapter 15.

One aspect of the changing paradigm of risk can be found in the debate or discussion about *objective* risk versus *perceived* risk. In the United Kingdom and United States, these differences emerged in early major studies in the 1980s by the Royal Society and National Research Council, the voices of the scientific establishment, in each country respectively. *Objective* risk is risk that experts know about and can measure and is the preserve of the formal sector. *Perceived* risk is identified and handled informally by the freelance risk managers. The latter notions of risk came to be cast around a theory or view that risk is *culturally* determined or constructed. In the case of the U.K. debate, Adams (1995: 9) observes that by the time that a 1992 Royal Society report on risk was published, the view that one could separate the two kinds of risk was no longer a mainstream position; but the physical scientists found it 'variously maddening and frustrating' that risk might be culturally determined. Risk was constructed in a variety of ways because reality was fashioned from different experiences and judgments of risk and benefit. To quote one of Adam's examples, 'Young people slipping and sliding on the ice, and old people striving to avoid doing the same, belong to separate and distinct cultures' (ibid.).

Such general debates about risk can be linked to other realms of intellectual and political debate (Breyer, 1993; Harrison and Hoberg, 1994), such as the postmodernist attack on science and rational thought itself. A cultural theory of risk, however, is also presented by its advocates as being empirically valid and hence itself rational (Douglas and Wildavsky, 1983). These ideas can be related to debates about the role of government and the nature of intervention into people's lives. Hence consideration of the nature of risk raises debate 'beyond the welfare state' to even broader attacks on the regulatory state (Skidelsky, 1997). In the United Kindgom, for example, this has led simultaneously to attacks against the 'nanny state' but also, in the wake of the death of a child in care, to demands for the greater regulation of nannies!

The wide-ranging debate about risk is a growing part of the climate and content of science-based policy and regulation, particularly when risk-based regulation takes a central place in the context of budgetary constraints. Experienced health and safety regulators recoil at the thought that this is a new paradigm, justifiably in one sense because risk-benefit and risk-cost trade-offs have always existed and will always exist. But there is also evidence of a shift towards broader risk-benefit concepts that are penetrating particular regulatory realms in different ways. This expands with the growth of our knowledge and technical capacity for the conceptualization, identification, measurement, and management of risk.

The new paradigm also means that, more and more, regulators have to deal analytically, organizationally, and politically with risk assessment, risk management proper, and risk communication. For drug regulators, for example, *risk assessment* involves scientific analysis of the probable severity of adverse health effects, the size of the population at risk, and other related factors. *Risk management* involves analysis and positive actions to reduce, avoid, hedge, and insure against risks, as well as forbearance or decisions not to act. Such actions are determined by statutory responsibilities, commitments and partnerships, public perceptions, public health benefits relative to risks, and available resources including staff, expertise, money, and political capital. *Risk communication* could be defined as 'any purposeful exchange of information about health or environmental risks,' but it can also extend to communication that 'seeks to change attitudes and behaviour in light of knowledge about health risks' (Health Protection Branch, 1997: 34). The communication of science-based risk information by government regulatory bodies to those potentially affected is important for the efficient allocation and consumption of risk in a manner analogous to the role played by price information in the efficient allocation of resources by the market mechanism.

It is the complexity, fluidity, and uncertainty of the overall risk analysis, management, and communication tasks that prompts Leiss to discuss the issue of the independence of science in this new paradigm. The concluding analysis in Chapter 15 in Part 2 of the book counsels empirically and otherwise against the extreme thrust of the Leiss argument. However, the BSE case, along with some of the other chapters dealing with the institutions, do show the need to come to terms with the issue of the independence and uncertainty of science in the institutional world of regulation. We reserve further comment on this topic until Chapter 15 in order to give the reader the opportunity to develop a better picture of science-based regulators as real institutions.

Trade Policy, Science, and Innovation

The chapter by Browne (with Chaitoo and Hart) examines arguably the most overt macro-policy influence of the past decade on science-based policy and regulation, namely, the impact of liberalized trade policy in general and the World Trade Organization and the North American Free Trade Agreement in particular (Trebilcock and Howse, 1995). The key features of these agreements are set out in Chapter 5, along with the ways they create an even greater dependence on science to underpin international regulation and standard setting. Science-based regulation is seen to be crucial to ensuring that health, safety, and environmental rules do not distort trade and thus become the new guise for protectionism. Browne and his colleagues link these changes in the trade regime to the question of eco-labelling and to whether campaigns led by environmentalists involving competitive informal standard setting undermine official science-based standards sanctioned through trade agreements. The authors of Chapter 5 see this latter type of activity as a threat to democratic, formalized, international science-based regulation and harmonization, whereas many other groups and environmentalist coalitions see it as a necessary democratic counterweight to the institutionalized or official trade system.

Liberalized trade policies may be the most manifest set of changes or determinants that affect science in government. Behind them lie the forces of globalization, the quickening of the knowledge economy, the rapid growth of the Internet, and the general movement of governments to recast earlier industrial policies into innovation policy, the new mantra of micro-economic orthodoxy.

Canada has been portrayed as a laggard in innovation, falling behind its competitor countries in terms of productivity. This picture has been derived from a variety of scenes of Canada's economic past and from selective policy indicators. At the broadest level, one view is forged around the fact that Canada has lived off its natural resources and has not, until recently, been forced to 'live off its wits.' The Royal Commission on the Economic Union and Development Prospects for Canada (Macdonald Commission) of the mid-1980s conveyed this picture, but it was hardly the first to do so (Canada, 1985). Another element arises because Canada has permitted extensive foreign ownership of its economy, resulting in a branch plant economy with limited research and development performed domestically by firms. Canada's lower than average R&D spending as a percentage of gross domestic product was a commonly cited aspect of its portrayal as a laggard industrial economy. To this indicator could be added that some 80 per cent of patent filings in Canada are by foreigners.

With the fuller emergence of the knowledge economy, some economists are turning their attention to a re-examination of growth theory with a focus on *endogenous* growth. This is because earlier simpler aggregate growth theory treated knowledge or technology as if they were 'just another good, capable of being accumulated like capital and aggregated with the same precision (or lack of precision) as capital' (Howitt, 1996: 9). Endogenous growth theory has questioned and researched the way in which knowledge is different from physical goods, and therefore should be thought about differently in market exchange.

Endogenous growth theory thus implies that there is a new form of knowledge-based competition (Best, 1990; Rubinstein, 1994; Webster, 1991), one aspect of which could involve the relative performance of national science-based regulatory regimes. Thus, if Canada wishes to be an innovative leader in emerging sectors like biotechnology, it will have to evolve more efficient and effective science-based regulatory capacity capable of fostering industrial competitiveness in global markets while protecting its citizens from avoidable risks (Centre for Medicines Research International, 1997).

The whole notion of innovation policy thus flows from a complex set of factors, but one of its key features is that it breaks down many traditional policy fields. Indeed, within the federal government as a whole, one implication is that all departments have to rely more and more on various kinds of emergent knowledge – scientific and otherwise. In this sense, internal science and knowledge capacities are ever *more* important, provided one thinks of science and knowledge capacity not only as a portfolio with cost-risk trade-offs, but also as innovating institutions (private and public) with the potential to contribute to the creation of national wealth.

Macro-Pressures from Hallmark Cases: Interests and Transparency

The chapter case studies that end Part 1 of the book raise an interesting puzzle that occurs in all realms of policy making. How much do political systems learn from single cases or episodes that become publicly contentious and which, as hallmark cases, begin to drive policy or institutional change? Another question that such cases pose is: 'How much of science-based institutional design should be determined by abnormal cases as opposed to normal or routine ones?' This is of no small import in that Cabinet ministers who head up science-based regulatory departments are concerned in any given time period with an array of potential policy issues and case situations in which particular interests and stakeholders are involved and where conflicting notions of transparency are involved.

The case study by Douglas Powell centres on raspberries from Guatemala imported into Canada and the United States but which, when persons became ill from their consumption, elicited differing regulatory responses. In essence, Powell argues that the regulatory response of the United States was better than that of Canada. Although the cases did not gain particular notoriety, Powell's account does focus on the more open processes of exposure and debate about these incidents in the United States. His analysis is centred at the level of both institutional openness (on the part of several different regulators), but even more so at the level of the mass media and public debate. Powell's analysis is also tied to international trade issues and the increased complexity of regulation and risk management. Indeed, Powell sees institutional failure occurring in part because Canadian authorities did not systematically and openly go through some of the key stages of risk assessment, management, and communication. Thus, the lessons and pressures from this kind of case relate to a lack of systemic transparency in what might conceivably be quite normal everyday health risk situations in the global trade in food. The difference in national regulatory responses may reflect a more mature, formalized, and open system of administrative regulatory processes in the United States as compared with Canada. It is essential to be cautious about such potentially broad conclusions, however, because U.S. advantages in openness at the regulatory agency level may be offset by the incredibly litigious nature of U.S regulatory systems, particularly in the realms of health, environment, and safety.

The case study of the use of recombinant bovine somatotrophin (rbST) in the Canadian dairy industry, by Mark MacDonald, deals with one biotechnology product and its controversial passage through the federal regulatory process in the 1990s. While as a class of products, biotechnology is quite controversial, there is no particular reason, other than that it involved milk, why rbST should gain more notoriety as a test case than any other biotechnology products that had already gained regulatory approval. But it did. MacDonald's analysis focuses on the structure of interest groups and policy networks and on the interaction between the formal and informal regulatory systems. It was this political interplay, in part, that made the rbST case a 'controversy,' and generated a demand for special or novel institutional responses, eventually leading to the decision in January 1999 to deny it a licence. Concerns about transparency and scientific independence were present, and the rbST case makes clear that regulatory systems, perhaps especially for biotechnology products where genetic modification is involved, have to be capable of handling both normal and abnormal cases.

Some controversial cases do in fact become pivotal in reshaping science-based regulatory debate. The far larger case of the U.K.'s BSE controversy, analysed by Millstone and Van Zwanenberg, has been included in this volume because it has become a hallmark case globally. Although it has had significant effects on policy and regulation making, smaller cases may also have an effect. This is because it may be easier for citizens, the media, and Cabinet ministers to understand issues through the 'morality tale' of the case rather than through aggregate trend data, even where the latter supply evidence of normality and possibly even regulatory efficacy.

In sum, science-based policy and regulatory regimes can be seen to be subject to general pressures and influences such as the public interest and the science deficit, trade and innovation, and changes in the risk-management paradigm as examined above. These pressures are revealed in controversies that take on macro-implications either because key interests elevate them to the level of national or international consciousness, or because some interest conflict captures the imagination of an interested public.

Characteristics of the Science-Based Regulatory Regime

While such macro-issues and influences are important, they are at best only half the story. Accordingly, Part 2 looks at the characteristics of the science-based regulatory regime as revealed through the set of five chapters about departments or agencies as well as the cross-governmental chapters provided by Jarvis and Lindquist and Barker. Each of the case studies of the S&T-based agencies presents key features of the mandate, structure, and evolution of the institution concerned and examines selected aspects of the editors' framework set out below. The framework builds on other literature on regulatory governance into which is incorporated the notion of different or diverse potential science paths or the ways in which scientists and non-scientists are likely to interact.

The science-based regulatory regime, as seen at the multi-agency level, must be mapped as the multifaceted entity that it is. It is above all a mistake to think even for one minute that there is only one overall cycle or pattern of science input in the science-based regulatory regime. Its key characteristics include five subprocesses and related pathways where science is fed into decision making within the regime as a whole or in and around its individual regulatory agencies and bodies. As set out in Table 1.2, these subprocesses are: the regulation-making, policy-making, and standard-setting process; the product or case approval process; the overall compliance and enforcement process; the broader monitoring and information provision process; and the government-wide budgetary and personnel management system that affects 'make or buy' science choices. These are each profiled briefly below in terms of observed characteristics about the nature of the science input and the interactions between scientists and other kinds of participants. All subprocesses are present to some extent as part of the operating reality of any science-based regulatory agency,

Table 1.2 Regime subprocesses and potential science paths

Regime subprocesses	Science paths and relations
1. Regulation-making, policy-making, and standard-setting process(es)	• Periodic, lower volume, but more complex multi-stakeholder decision making • Likelihood of highly pluralistic science presence
2. Product or case review and approval process(es)	• Direct, more micro-relations between the firm's scientists and the regulator's science reviewers • Higher volume of activity and pressure for internationally competitive approval processes • More likely to raise issues of commercial secrecy and privacy
3. Overall compliance and enforcement process(es)	• Diverse tasks and therefore regulatory load but in situation where spatial and geographic sites are numerous • Greater reliance on inspections and visits by qualified inspectors, but can never cover it all; need to rely on networks of scientists, professionals, and generalists • Difficult choices regarding whether to respond to non-compliance cases *when* they become known and *in the order* in which they become known, as opposed to setting priorities about which non-compliance cases or issues to deal with as significant precedents
4. Postmarket and/or general monitoring and reporting process(es)	• The newer/broader realm of expanded focus, especially under the ethos of the risk-benefit model of regulatory management • Extremely broad networks of scientists and technical persons involved, as well as lay public (patients, users, citizens) • Particularly enabled by digital and information technologies • But considerable variation by regulatory sector
5. Financial and human resource management processes (within the state and in the agency)	• Mix of user fee versus state-financed regulation • New organizational forms (SOAs etc.) and make or buy choices regarding science • Education and upgrading of personnel

but there are of course differences in the particular ways they are manifested in domains such as fisheries, food, health, or the environment. While presenting the framework below, we also draw attention to these sectoral features as revealed in our authors' chapters about departments or agencies.

Regulation Making, Policy Making, and Standard Setting

The regulation-making, policy-making, and standard-setting process extends to the statutory base of the regulatory system. The concerns here are not only the actual statutory terms and the regulatory compromises enshrined therein, but also how open and consultative the regulation-making process is or seems to be. Statutes and regulations are less frequently reviewed and altered than the processes for product approvals and for compliance, two of the other regime subprocesses examined below. The development of guidelines and codes is part of this first process and may be seen as a part of regulation per se or indeed as a policy-making exercise. In other words, there is a hierarchy of norm or goal-setting modes that descends from law or statutory expressions and policies, continues into regulations (delegated legislation passed through the Regulatory Impact Assessment or RIAS–*Canada Gazette*-centred review processes), and moves down to guidelines and codes (Stanbury, 1992).

The role of science and of scientists in this pathway is part of a broader process where many stakeholders are involved. Practices range from formal procedural requirements to periodic task force undertakings and the role of advisory committees. The more that such approaches are informed by the risk-benefit ideas traced earlier, the more that scientists, perhaps paradoxically, will occupy a smaller part of a larger policy and regulatory space. This process is also increasingly tied to intricate international protocols and processes, both bilateral and multilateral. The more critical the science component is to regulatory decision making in such broad evaluative processes, the greater is the risk of not heeding the science input. Somehow, the relative importance of the science must influence the pecking order of the norms, information, and professional expertise. However, it is a simple fact of governance that the higher up the government and bureaucracy that one goes, the fewer scientists one finds. Canada's ministers, deputy ministers, and senior officials above a director general or equivalent level are far more likely to be generalists or possess other non-scientific expertise.

The analysis of Fisheries and Oceans Canada in Chapter 11 brings out some of these key features of regulation making in a stark fashion. Regulation making in fisheries is predicated on a determination of what would constitute an allowable sustainable catch for a given species or area. But the collapse of the Atlantic fishery has brought out the new challenges of managing and structuring scientific advice. Lane's account of the fisheries crisis shows the growing complexity of the science base itself as it moves from a reliance on biology to a greater need for interdisciplinary research on ecosystems. Simultaneously, the relations between scientists in the Department of Fisheries and Oceans and fishery interests and stakeholders become more multifaceted and greatly complicate institutional management of the scientific peer review process. Lane also links recent problems to the discipline-based structure through which science is organized in the fisheries bureaucracy.

The Product and/or Case Approval Process

A second element of an operational regulatory system is the product or case approval process. We use the word *product* to refer to situations found in drugs or pesticide regulation where actual products are involved and *cases* to convey other situations where the regulator has to handle a core case load (for example, an environmental regulator's responsibility for ensuring that numerous environmental assessments are conducted). Science as an input into this second type of subprocess is different from the regulation-making process, first because of the inherently larger *volume* of decisions required, and second because of the need to bring science to bear at the specific product level. There is a different level, flow, and volume to this aspect of the risky business and hence the relations between scientists and non-scientists are different in this subprocess.

The analyses of the Pest Management Regulatory Agency (PMRA) in Chapter 10 and of the Therapeutic Products Programme (TPP) in Chapter 8 serve to bring out some of these different dynamics. In both pesticide and drug product approvals, the crucial relationships of scientific exchange take place between the firm's scientific personnel and the regulator's qualified reviewers as the formal approval process begins. Indeed, there are likely to have been discussions well before any formal application arrives.

The early phase of the case-handling process involves preliminary discussions and perhaps even negotiations between the proponent or applicant and the regulators. Such discussions are encouraged by the regulator to avoid future problems and to potentially save time, as concerns about regulatory lag times are central in the case-handling process. Global comparisons here are crucial since multinational firms in particular are aware of the relative regulatory performance and are applying pressure to speed up the process.

It is easy to underestimate the importance of the firm's internal review processes. But the product-centred risk regulatory system is crucially dependent on it. Firms have their own concerns and disciplines that centre on profit and return on investment. They are equally concerned, however, with producing an efficacious and safe drug or pesticide, that enhances the reputation and market position (product market integrity) of the firm, and that does not subject it to unwanted liabilities and costly litigation. At this stage, the firm is in many respects 'policing itself,' both because it knows there is a regulatory system it must eventually satisfy, but also because of enlightened self-interest concerning product efficacy and quality (Dewees, 1983). Many cases never reach the starting line because of these early and anticipatory stages of self-regulation and are 'non-events.' While these do not get counted in regulatory statistics (Sparrow, 1994), they nevertheless constitute a very healthy aspect of effective regulatory regimes.

The regulatory reviewer's science role emerges as the application for approval arrives, but here some sectoral differences become apparent in product approvals. Doern's analysis of the drug approval process in the TPP stresses that the pre-1992 regime was focused on *de novo* review, a legacy of the late 1960s thalidomide debacle. This kind of review process was predicated upon the assumption that reviewers should trust no one else's judgment, neither the sponsoring firms' nor other countries' regulators. Chapter 8 also reveals that this model was unsustainable, given the number of new drugs, their greater complexity and interaction in use, as well as the new patterns of regulatory reform and scientific peer exchange becoming evident in Europe and elsewhere in the early 1990s. Meanwhile in the pesticides sector, as Krupka's analysis in Chapter 10 shows, the premarket process was somewhat different. It still relied on close scientist-to-scientist relations between the firm and the regulator, but *within* the pesticide regulator a more dispersed sharing of science advice was necessary. This more varied science input was interdepartmental in nature involving both health and environmental scientists, largely because pesticides are products that produce involuntary risks when used in the environment. Such risks can produce harmful effects in people who are likely to be unaware that they may be exposed to such actual or potential adverse effects.

Another feature of science in product approval or case approval processes is that scientists and other players are far more likely to

encounter laws or other regulatory strictures designed to protect commercial secrets and uphold privacy provisions. Here science operates
in a much more intensive decision-making space with greater volumes of activity compared with policy, regulation, and standard-setting processes.

Overall Compliance and Enforcement

A third subprocess of any regulatory system is that of compliance and
enforcement. In most regulatory systems, compliance and enforcement
would include all of the previously mentioned aspects of the product
approval and case-handling process (Sparrow, 1994; Grabosky, 1995).
After all, such products are at the centre of implementing laws, regulations, and guidelines. However, if implementation embraces softer
compliance activities and approaches, as well as harder enforcement
actions (Hood, 1986), then it goes beyond case handling per se. This
third element of regulation deserves separate mention and attention
because of the impact of 'new public management' and 'reinvented
government' (Aucoin, 1997; Grabosky, 1995). These two concepts have
induced regulators to see compliance in much broader terms than
before, and to see themselves as providing services to customers and
clients rather than just dealing with 'regulated' industries or entities
(Doern et al., 1999).

One key aspect of science in compliance and enforcement can be
found in the inspection function and in the determination of certification and best practices. This requires the engagement of the regional
or field structures of regulatory agencies or departments. There is
always a spatial or geographical dimension to regulatory compliance
and enforcement and a set of choices as to how science or technical
inspectors will function. They cannot be present at all potential sites
where non-compliance may occur, such as border points, factory sites,
transportation systems, laboratories and clinical test sites in hospitals
and universities, farms, and government laboratories. These are far
too numerous for anything but periodic visits or the implementation
of auditing systems based on sampling procedures. The front line
science inspector must engage in many forms of cooperative information and intelligence sharing with persons in these places and locations, including the scientists and technical people employed there.

Compliance activities can pose a common intellectual and practical
dilemma, whether seen as a generic problem of implementation or as
a problem inherent in risk-benefit management. Do regulators have a

duty to respond to all compliance episodes and cases *when* they come in the agency door and *in the order* in which they come in the door? Or do they have an obligation to set priorities to act upon, on the grounds that priority selections will be more cost effective, will deter more unacceptable behaviour, and will help to set significant precedents? In the end, most regulators do a little of both kinds of responding and choosing, but the broad thrust of recent compliance thinking and strategy is to lean strongly towards the latter strategic concept. And this concept takes us into precisely the same realm of choice as do theories of risk and risk-benefit management. In other words, not all risks are equal or are perceived to be so: accordingly, the regulator and its scientists, interacting with non-scientists, must somehow set priorities that will almost always be disputed.

The analysis of the Canadian Food Inspection Agency (CFIA) in Chapter 9 highlights many of these spatial and compliance realities. Although Prince's treatment of the CFIA stresses that it is far more than just an 'inspection' agency, it starkly reveals the numerous ways in which science input emerges in compliance activity and the varied relations between scientists and non-scientists. Study of the CFIA also shows concretely how the current regulatory system, partly under the impetus of trade regimes, is evolving towards a system of auditing, and away from one of detailed inspection as the main approach to compliance.

Postmarket and/or General Monitoring and Reporting

Actual monitoring and reporting activities are normally subsumed in the compliance function discussed above. But with increasing reliance being placed upon the postmarket and general monitoring aspects of regulation, and the science base it implies, an important separate sub-process can be seen to be emerging. This is because several of the macro-forces examined all point in the direction of increased reliance on science-based postmarket monitoring and reporting as a growing complement to premarket product review and approval processes. This is in part a consequence of the expanding consumption of the products of bioscience and technology and of the resulting increased potential for interactions that may only be revealed through the monitoring of postmarket data.

The language of pre- and postmarket has its greatest resonance in a sector such as drug regulation, whereas in the broader environmental field or in the fisheries the notion of pre- and postmarkets may be more blurred: broader systems of continuous reporting and information provision may therefore prevail. As Chapter 8 shows, postmarket monitoring and surveillance, or 'pharmacovigilance,' is a central concept in the area of drug regulation. This subprocess is intended to ensure that legally approved drugs are also further evaluated in the postmarket on the scientific grounds that this environment provide a more realistic basis for risk-benefit assessment.

Postmarket monitoring is also a feature of pesticide regulation, although institutionalized to a greater extent than in the regulation of therapeutic products. Krupka's analysis of the PMRA in Chapter 10 points out that in pesticide regulation, there has always been the recognition that registered products need to be re-evaluated *systematically by the regulator* to determine whether they should remain on the market. The regulator is obliged to determine whether older registered products meet contemporary standards. This is quite apart from reports of adverse effects and other problems that would trigger and be handled by 'special reviews.' Internationally, pesticide regulators have collaborated to divide the labour in the monumental task of reviewing older pesticides. This process can be much more labour intensive for the regulator, and to some extent the producer, since new studies, not required in past approvals, may currently need to be conducted and evaluated.

In the environmental field, as revealed in Chapter 12, monitoring and reporting activity is linked to the whole notion of green reporting writ large and to particular initiatives such as conservation of biodiversity. This kind of activity can be found in overall 'state of the environment reports,' or it can take more specific forms such as reporting systems on particular water basins, transboundary problems, or industries such as pulp and paper. In the latter case they may be tied to the enforcement of particular standards and regulations. Such reporting activity is also linked to environmental indicators, and to departmental accountability based on performance in respect of key commitments to achieve results, as in the case of sustainable development frameworks. The analysis of the fisheries in Chapter 11 also reveals complex networks of science and scientists engaged in this vital ongoing function.

Overall Fiscal and Human Resource Management Processes

The last of the subprocesses in the regime is the overall fiscal and human resource management process. Clearly this is partly a process that occurs *within* a given science-based regulatory agency or department, and it partly extends to the central management of financial and human resources, since it involves budgetary allocation for science activity and scientific personnel choices. As such it is subject to the many pressures and factors that prompted our earlier discussion of the federal science deficit.

One such pressure centres on normal budgeting and, in recent years, on cutbacks and Program Review (Swimmer, 1996). As suggested earlier, neither normal budgeting nor cutback budgeting can be said to have had a focused concern for the federal regulatory science base. Recent budgeting has been largely driven by the problems of deficits and debt management. A related second facet is the central pressure in the 1990s to increase the use of user fees as a way of funding regulators. As the agency chapters in Part 2 show, this funding imperative has made inroads into several of the science-based regulatory bodies. It is a practice that is also linked to the selective encouragement of alternative delivery mechanisms such as special operating agencies (SOAs) or related hybrids. These are intended to provide some federal agencies or subunits with greater managerial and operational autonomy in terms of finance and personnel (Ford and Zussman, 1997).

Personnel aspects of the science-based regime are entwined in the federal merit system that still seeks to ensure that system-wide merit criteria and procedures are applied in the recruitment, promotion, pay, and career processes. These principles and procedures often, but not always, collide with the need for particular regulators to attract, pay, and maintain the kinds of scientists they need for the front-line regulatory and risk-benefit analytical tasks. As the agency chapters in Part 2 show, these issues are linked to new organizational forms and to issues of how independent a particular science-based regulatory body is or should be allowed to be. They also relate to Leiss's discussion of the best venue for science activity in the macro-discussions of Part 1.

Chapters 13 and 14 focus on these regime issues in two different ways. In Chapter 13 Jarvis looks at new approaches to the organization and funding of science-based regulators including the issues of public goods science and tax financing versus private benefit science and user-fee funding. Broadly speaking Jarvis sees value in this new mix and in the use of alternative service delivery modes of organization, provided that their use is accompanied by good analysis and understanding of institutional forces and incentives and that a sense of balance is achieved through accountable institutions.

A different but complementary examination of regime-wide features is supplied by the analysis by Lindquist and Barker in Chapter 14, as to how the federal government and central agencies have attempted to manage, coordinate, and report on S&T policy and implementation across government. This S&T analysis is linked to broader problems of horizontal coordination in any major policy field. Lindquist and Barker see some progress in recent years tied to budgetary review but consider the S&T area (and other horizontal matters as well) to be being accompanied by 'precarious values.' These are characterized as values that are insufficiently entrenched or easily shunted aside as newer horizontal matters occupy the limited political space at the centre of the state.

Each of the five itemized characteristics and subprocesses of the science-based regulatory regime can only supply glimpses of how the science paths enter and interact within such a system. This chapter cannot do justice to the full complexity of regulatory institutions or to the ways that subprocesses interact in different sectors such as food or the fisheries. What it does suggest is that there cannot be any simple single path or view by anyone seeking to generalize about science in the regulatory process. The agency chapters of Part 2 will bring these realities out more concretely and in the context of actual legal and policy mandates.

Conclusions

More systematic attention needs to be given to Canada's science-based policy and regulatory regime that for too long has been subject to benign neglect. This chapter, and the book as a whole, contributes to such a process of public scrutiny and examination. Although there have been some important signs of renewed interest and commitment in recent years, a more concentrated focus is needed in the name of both public interest regulation and industrial prosperity and innovation. The dual conceptual focus of the book is intended to facilitate such an examination.

This chapter has described how the science-based policy regime encompasses an array of entities that depend significantly on science and scientists in the conduct of their statutory mandates. It is important to deal with it as a regime because, whether it is seen as the subset of agencies and departments examined in this book or as a larger cluster of bodies, it has common features and is responding to similar macro-pressures for change.

We have highlighted four macro-influences that separately and interactively are affecting the regime. The notion of public interest science combined with the idea of a science deficit as a parallel to the fiscal deficit is important because it suggests the need to squarely address the science deficit as both an aggregate issue and as a portfolio problem. This latter involves a set of cost-and-benefit decisions about risk, including decisions about 'make or buy' in the realm of science. Globalization, the knowledge economy, and the emergence of innovation policies, as opposed to earlier industrial policies, are also undoubtedly important. They mean not only that the science-based regulatory regime is crucial to dynamic sectors such as pharmaceuticals and biotechnology, but also that such a regime is a key part of the broader cultural and economic systems of innovation.

Paradigms of safety and risk have changed, with greater emphasis now being placed upon concepts of risk-benefit management. While earlier systems sought to manage risk, there has been an evident shift in thinking and in the financing mix, albeit with sectoral emphasis and manifestations within the overall science-based regulatory regime. The chapter has also shown how hallmark cases or controversies have become macro-influences as citizens learn more about the changing world of risks and benefits in which they live.

In the second part of our dual conceptual framework, we have argued that the appraisal of the science-based regime means looking within it to identify the main subprocesses and different pathways for science and scientists to enter into policy making and regulation. We have observed that science and scientist-generalist relations are likely to be different in each of the five key subprocesses, namely, regulation making, product approval, compliance and enforcement, postmarket monitoring and reporting, and financial and human resource management. But there is much more to learn about the nature of these pathways and the inner workings of the regime that can be gleaned from the chapters to follow. With the agency chapters in place, Chapter 15 then examines, from the editors' perspective, four important aspects of Canadian science-based institutional reform and prospects for further institutional change.

References

Adams, John. (1995). *Risk*. London: UCL Press.

Aucoin, Peter. (1997). *The New Public Management: Canada in Comparative Perspective*. Montreal: McGill-Queen's University Press.

Best, Michael. (1990). *The New Competition: Institutions of Industrial Restructuring*. Cambridge: Polity Press.

Breyer, Stephen G. (1993). *Breaking the Vicious Cycle: Toward Effective Risk Regulation*. Cambridge: Harvard University Press.

Canada. (1985). Royal Commission on the Economic Union and Development Prospects for Canada, *Final Report*. (Macdonald Commission). Ottawa: Minister of Supply and Services.

Centre for Medicines Research International. (1997). *1997 Annual Report*. Carshalton, Surrey: Centre for Medicines Research International.

Dewees, Donald, ed. (1983). *The Regulation of Quality*. Toronto: Butterworths.

Doern, G. Bruce. (1981). *The Peripheral Nature of Scientific and Technological Controversy in Federal Policy Formation*. Ottawa: Science Council of Canada.

Doern, G. Bruce, Margaret Hill, Michael J. Prince, and Richard Schultz, eds. (1999). *Changing the Rules: Canadian Regulatory Regimes and Institutions*. Toronto: University of Toronto Press.

Douglas, M., and A. Wildavsky. (1983). *Risk and Culture*. Berkeley: University of California Press.

Ford, Robin, and David Zussman, eds. (1997). *Alternative Service Delivery: Sharing Governance in Canada*. Toronto: Institute of Public Administration of Canada.

Government of Canada. (1997). *Minding Our Future: A Report on Federal Science and Technology – 1997*. Ottawa: Industry Canada.

Grabosky, Peter N. (1995). 'Using Non-governmental Resources to Foster Compliance.' *Governance*, 8(4): 527–50.

Harrison, K., and G. Hoberg. (1994). *Risk, Science and Politics: Regulating Toxic Substances in Canada and the United States*. Montreal: McGill-Queen's University Press.

Health Protection Branch. (1997). *Draft Risk Management in Health Protection: Revised HPB Risk Management Framework, Phase II Report*. Ottawa: Health Canada.

Hood, Christopher. (1986). *Administrative Analysis*. London: Harvester Wheatsheaf.

Howitt, Peter, ed. (1996). *The Implications of Knowledge-Based Growth for Micro-Economic Policies*. Calgary: University of Calgary Press.

Jarvis, Bill. (1998). *The Role and Responsibilities of the Scientist in Public Policy.* Ottawa: Public Policy Forum.

Office of Science and Technology. (1998). *The Use of Scientific Advice in Policy Making: Implementation of the Guidelines.* London: Office of Science and Technology, Department of Trade and Industry.

Powell, Douglas, and William Leiss. (1997). *Mad Cows and Mother's Milk.* Montreal: McGill-Queen's University Press.

Rifkin, Jeremy. (1998). *The Biotechnology Century.* (New York: Tarcher/Putnam Books.

Rubenstein, Albert. (1994). 'At the Front End of R&D/Innovation Process: Idea Development and Entrepreneurship.' *International Journal of Technology Management,* 9(5–7): 652–77.

Salter, Liora. (1988). *Mandated Science: Science and the Making of Standards.* Amsterdam: Kluwer.

Schooler, Dean. (1971). *Science, Scientists and Public Policy.* New York: Free Press.

Skidelsky, Robert. (1997). *Beyond the Welfare State.* London: Social Market Foundation.

Smol, John P. (1999). 'Convocation Address.' *Queen's Alumni Review,* 73(3): 34–5.

Sparrow, Malcolm K. (1994). *Imposing Duties: Government's Changing Approach to Compliance.* London: Praeger.

Stanbury, William T. (1992). *Reforming the Federal Regulatory Process in Canada, 1971–1992.* Published as Appendix to House of Commons, Standing Committee on Finance, Subcommittee on Regulations and Competitiveness. Issue No. 23. Ottawa: Supply and Services Canada.

Swimmer, Gene, ed. (1996). *How Ottawa Spends 1995–96: Life under the Knife.* Ottawa: Carleton University Press.

Trebilcock, Michael, and Robert Howse. (1995). *The Regulation of International Trade.* London: Routledge.

Webster, A. (1991). *Science, Technology and Society: New Directions.* London: Macmillan.

PART 1:
MACRO-ISSUES AND POLICY CONTROVERSIES

2 Government Science and the Public Interest

JOHN DE LA MOTHE

What is the role of the federal government in conducting science and technology[1] within its own laboratories and facilities? Within the context of the emerging knowledge-based economy, and within the current period of government restructuring, this question is very timely. The tensions are clear. Despite the strong activity in science by several provincial governments, the performance of science and technology by national governments in a number of advanced industrial economies, including Canada, has fallen since the early 1980s.[2] The number of non-traditional science-performing nation states – many of which are becoming Canada's trading partners – has risen. Science-based issues are on the rise in both complexity and number on the public's agenda. And, with an increasingly interdependent economy like Canada's, the roles and missions of private and public sector institutions in performing science have become overlapped and, in the process, have become increasingly complex.

Within this very demanding environment, the underlying logic from which once irrefutable public goods – such as the provision of basic infrastructure, support of policy goals, strengthening of regulatory mandates, and the protection of society – were derived has come in danger of being lost. Indeed these logics have been partially obscured by a view of economic growth and development, ascendant in the early 1980s and widely dominant until recently, which was strongly led by research and development and technology, and which celebrated private sector practices over public sector logics, particularly in terms of efficiency and cost management. One subtle implication of this view was that the importance of non-R&D-related scientific activities, which are absolutely critical to closing the innovation gap and in which government is – of necessity – heavily engaged to deliver science in the public interest, has been diminished. It is against this broad background that this chapter's interest in retrieving the proper contemporary role of Canada's federal government in performing science and technology can be understood.

To be sure, the question of government science raises an array of issues that are by no means new. In 1973 Maurice Lamontagne's Senate Committee on Science Policy, for example, dedicated a complete volume of its report, *A Science Policy for Canada*, to it (Canada, 1973). This was in recognition of the fact that while, over the course of its history, the Government of Canada had put in place an impressive knowledge infrastructure consisting of a network of federal laboratories, testing establishments, survey groups, and the like, at the same time there was a growing question of how best to organize for science given the available resources. This formulation is popular today but it reduces the issue to a question of balance. In so doing it implicitly presumes that there is a 'right balance.' The search therefore becomes an elusive one for the 'right' micro-policy and management levers instead of one that clarifies and focuses on the reasons why government should conduct science.

A more useful way of putting this important question may be in terms of searching for the appropriate amount of flexibility and capacity of our government knowledge infrastructure. Directed in this way, it quickly can be seen that throughout the long history since the federal science capabilities have been put in place, the government has *continually* responded to contemporary demands, has helped to build capabilities in industry, universities, and communities, and has adjusted its operations to maintain service, relevancy, and preparedness. In so doing, the scientists, engineers, and technicians working within the federal science-based departments and agencies (SBDAs) have continued to identify and protect the public interests of Canadians. In other words, the government SBDAs – considerable institutions though they are, with considerable responsibilities – have a long history of flexibility and innovating in the public service.

Yet challenges remain. Whereas in the past the government has used its scientific capabilities to build the nation and then to build its capabilities, today the challenges facing government science and the public interest in terms of structural pressures – globalization, innovation, and governance – are historically unique. It is no longer simply a question of 'science' in 'government' (Dupré and Lakoff, 1962). Indeed together these new challenges demand a renewed clarification of the core *raison d'être* behind the government's performance of science.

Challenging Contexts

The new environment for government science and the public interest can be sketched succinctly as follows.

Globalization has increased both the interdependency between Canada and other economies as well as the pace of information, technology, and other knowledge flows. This has been accelerated by an internationalization of research and development in the private sector and an increase in the number of science and technology performers or service providers (de la Mothe and Dufour, 1995). At the same time, international cooperation in science between governments on a range of issues has risen.[3] The new context is perhaps best typified, *au fond*, by an increase in complexity and diversity. Globalization has thus resulted in increased competitive pressures, particularly in new research-intensive technologies such as in energy (for example, hydrogen fuel cell technology), earth sciences (remote sensing and geographical information systems), and next generation informatics (CA*Net3) in which Canada has particular interests. It has increased potential challenges to security, through such areas as population health (for example, the rapid spread of infectious diseases through tourism and the re-emergence of virulent, antibiotic-resistant illnesses), environment (as with the transboundary flow of persistent organic pollutants), and multilateral benchmarking (as with state-of-the-environment indicators). Globalization has critically decreased response times available to firms and governments. In short, it can be said that the science and technology challenges to our economy, our environment, and our security will only increase in scale and in scope, thus challenging institutions dramatically – augmenting the need for our science-based departments and agencies.

A second related challenge stems from how well Canada produces and uses knowledge. Here again the government SBDAs have an important role, and this issue is really at the core of government's concern over the 'innovation gap' in which both codified and tacit knowledge are critical. 'Knowledge' is the key to achieving high value-added growth and sustainable development as well as to protecting the health of Canadians and promoting viable social communities. 'Knowledge' refers not only to research and development in the natural sciences and engineering; it also includes related scientific activities (for example, surveys, statistics, and mapping) as well as a full range of technical, managerial, and social skills. Organizations and economies alike remain competitive through continual knowledge-based adjustment and innovation. The way through which they can identify, appropriate, apply, and diffuse knowledge (particularly in science and technology) is through acting as part of an innovation system (Lundvall, 1992; Nelson, 1993; Edquist, 1997; de la Mothe and Paquet, 1998; Niosi, 1999).

This *innovation system challenge* reflects an important shift in how the government is now (properly) conceiving Canada in the twenty-first century (Liberal Party of Canada, 1993; Industry Canada, 1994). Such a lens importantly allows us to reframe our 'mental maps' of how science and technology actually become useful knowledge and to move away from the highly stylized (and unrealistic) linear models of innovation in which firms, universities, and government were imagined as having a clear and separate social division of labour in performing and funding science and technology, and in which R&D reliably led to technological progress and commercialization (all appropriable here in Canada). An 'innovation system' approach allows us to move towards more accurate depictions of how knowledge actually leads to growth, underpins our economic and social union, and how institutions adapt to rapidly changing circumstances. This embraces the reality that no institution – firm, research lab, or government agency – can 'know it all' or 'do it all.'

This means understanding that the benefits of an innovation system emerge, not only from more R&D but, from strong partnerships, networks, and linkages, through improved information flows and communications within and across sectors, through better coordination mechanisms, and by bringing decision-making responsibilities down to the most appropriate (and most responsive) level in an organization. Indeed, not only has much of the language and imagery of 'the innovation system' already been adopted by government policy, but much of the logic of 'the innovation system' has also been cast in both the Program Review and the Science and Technology Review exercises which called for more transparency and greater horizontal coordination.

By recasting sectoral roles in terms of innovation systems or in terms of networks of innovators, not only are responsibilities reconceived and redistributed, but the system as a whole becomes capable of developing a greater capacity to scan and process the massive amounts of data and information that are emerging from a fast-moving globalized context and then to develop, delegate, and implement appropriate responses. In such a picture, the role of government SBDAs can therefore be clarified and strengthened.

The twin processes of globalization and innovation of course challenge the strategic vision and management of any complex organization. But this is even more true for government SBDAs which, like the Canadian federal government as a whole, not only rival the largest multinationals in size but which must also continually respond to, and serve, multiple domestic objectives at the same time. Managerially, the demands placed on the federal science-based departments and agencies and on federal civil servants are daunting. The current move across government towards considerations of 'alternative service delivery' is one major response to these managerial issues. Strategically, however, SBDAs face a higher *governance challenge*. It is a challenge – not of reacting and micro-social engineering but of steering and positioning complex organizations in turbulent waters. It is a matter of leadership, responsibility, and vision, not only on the part of the science-based departments and agencies but also on the part of government as a whole in dealing with its science. It requires the SBDAs to become, as they have shown a facility to before, highly adaptive organizations, to shift from being fat ocean liners to a connected and streamlined team of speed boats. It requires becoming good signal processors, good learning organizations, and good strategists. Of course, this requires a clear view of what the job is.

While the goal of good management is to achieve near term and (more or less) well-defined objectives, the goal of good governance in a systems context is more complicated. Unlike an isolated actor working alone in an environment, in a system we can never just do one thing. System effects are everywhere. In addition to the direct effects of an action, the interconnections within a system produce indirect and delayed effects.[4] Second, in a system in which there are more than two actors, the relationship between any two will be determined not just by how they act towards each other but also by the interactions among the other members of the system. Third, relations in a system are interactive rather than additive. Actions may not lead directly to an intended result because the outcome also depends on how the other elements in the system respond. These traits are particularly important for the governance of government science-based departments and agencies.

Taken together, the information explosion and interdependencies of *globalization*, the surprise-generating mechanisms of science-based *innovation* systems, and the strategy and leadership challenges of the new *governance* create a bundled context for today's science-based departments and agencies as well as the public interest. Managerially, the government has succeeded in laying out the appropriate principles of good management, capturing the benefits of partnership, increasing effectiveness, value for money, and so on. The civil service is also actively building better information networks, positioning for international markets, and extending linkages – both across government and between government and its clients. But strategically, the question remains: What is the role of the federal government in conducting science and technology?

A Commitment to Public Service

The above sketch, of course, represents only a glimpse of the contemporary context. But in the most general of terms, we know that science-based issues will become more – not less – important. One need only think of the implications of encryption or xenotransplants. Canada's fortune will rest on how well we marshal and deploy our intellectual resources. This will require the continued express involvement of the federal government, as well as of every other player. There will be opportunities for Canada and for government laboratories (through technical advancements in telecommunications, computing, robotics, biomedical devices, and cold ocean drilling). There will be threats (through the transborder migration of pollutants, the transmission of infectious diseases, and rise of new terrorist capabilities in chemical and biological form). And there will always be responsibilities (for health, safety, security, intergenerational trusts, emergency preparedness, and support of policy initiatives). The role of government SBDAs is crucial in all of these areas.

In somewhat more specific terms, this role will continue to entail a commitment to technical assistance to small and medium-sized firms, exploration in nascent technology areas of interest to Canada, continued participation in international standards setting and harmonization, heightened involvement in testing and approval, environmental monitoring and benchmarking, emergency preparedness, policy support, public information and service, and basic research (both to stay on top of new developments and opportunities and to attract new talent into government science).

The nature of governance is changing. Nevertheless, Canadians continue to rightly expect the government to be custodian, partner, and leader. In science-based issues, Canadians have come to rely on a government science capacity that is innovative, adaptive, and reliably responsive. This demonstrated capacity has generated remarkable benefits for Canada. It is poised and willing to continue in this tradition. But in order to do so, government science must be thought of in strategic, not reactive, terms. As such, the role of government science must not be allowed to fall between the logical stools of the private sector science and university research, nor is it to be diverted by casual notions of privatization and alternative service delivery. While contracting out, cost reductions, and cost recovery are attractive short-cuts to good management, real innovative organizational arrangements are needed for the medium and long term.[5] Canada's SBDAs have proven to be long-standing innovators and to have continuously matched science to the public interest. Historical accounts of developments in geology, agriculture, the fisheries, and astronomy have borne this out and need not be surveyed here.[6]

Emerging Roles

In response to rising public demands for security and industry, the period between the two world wars saw a rapid growth in government scientific establishments and budgets. However, this was not a seamless development. Indeed, differing models of science policy, organization, and coordination that were offered from various corners of government at times were at odds with the views of other science-based departments. Typical differences, which are still debated today, pivoted around questions regarding the right balance between exploratory research, project research, practical research, and the division of labour among SBDAs. Debates notwithstanding, the developments of the past fifty years reflect, not a series of tensions but, a series of innovative institutional adjustments to rapidly shifting demands, contexts, and capabilities.

For example, prior to 1939 Canada did not have much in the way of *scientific infrastructure*. The federal government, in the spirit of nation building, deliberately put one in place, leading and linking with the industrial and university sectors and transmitting the idea that science would be a powerful force as Canada developed. Similarly, as government science grew, its capabilities were marshalled in *support of public policy goals* (ranging from economic and technological development to the promotion of trade). At the same time, increased public attentiveness to community and social risk led to a strong role for government science in *support of new regulatory frameworks* (from construction and consumer product standards to nuclear safety guidelines). And, of course, the full range of services for public *protection and preparedness* (e.g., defence, health, emergency detection and response, and protection of the commons) also came to demand the dedicated engagement of government science-based departments and agencies.

The growing recognition by government of the importance of science can be seen in budget growth. For example, by 1963 the annual R&D expenditures of the federal government on agriculture had grown to roughly $35 million; those for environment and fisheries to about $20 million, with $17 million for energy, mines, and resources and $8 million for health and welfare (Hayes, 1973: 28). By 1973 they had continued to rise significantly: with environment at $110 million, agriculture at $90 million; energy, mines, and resources at $40 million, and so on.

To many the drive to such growth in science expenditures was to be encouraged, either for security reasons (given the rise of science-based weapons) or for economic reasons (given that Canada's industrial structure was still narrow and weak in terms of R&D). By the late 1960s broader public concerns with the environment, food, safety, and health, as well as the need for science as a *sine qua non* for advanced nation status and standard of living, had all begun to emerge. In any case, there was a clear acceptance that there was a role for the federal government in science.

By 1971 government funded 44 per cent of Canada's gross expenditure on R&D and performed 28 per cent of it. But during the 1980s, recognizing the overburdening of government science and that wealth creation was a phenomenon led by the private sector, a major policy focus was to increase the level of industrial R&D and to rebalance the Canadian science system to contribute to economic competitiveness. By 1997 this balance had been addressed by government through a variety of programs, mechanisms, incentives, and policies so that business now performs 64 per cent of Canada's total R&D. However, government performance of science and technology activities has fallen to 11 per cent, raising concerns that the current level has not only resulted in a real reduction in both R&D and RSA but has resulted in an even deeper erosion of the government's monitoring capabilities and preparedness than the numbers might suggest, as the government's knowledge workers have shifted their orientation away from science itself and towards science management. This is an important question that can only be addressed by people in the know, but – for our purposes – this transition of the science system has revealed two prevalent, but inappropriate, models in considering government science.

Markets for Science and the Public Interest

As science policy – defined by the OECD as 'science for policy and policy for science' – became a much more deliberate government activity, particularly since the early 1980s, government asked two related questions: (1) What is the relationship between science, technology, and the economy (in terms of growth, competitiveness, total factor productivity, investment, and job creation)? (2) Based on this understanding, what are the appropriate roles of the various sectors of the economy?

The Poverty of Linear Models

In answer to the first question, governments and researchers across the OECD developed highly stylized views of the innovation process, often referred to as 'linear models.' Most simply put, linear models came in three variations: science push, technology push/pull, and market pull. In the science push variation, and put most bluntly, scientists working in university laboratories conduct exploratory basic research and publish it in the peer-reviewed, open, literature; engineers working in industry but trained in applied sciences read the open literature, occasionally see a result, method, or approach that is of use to the firm; it is then applied in the industrial context and commercialized. In the case of the technology push/pull variation, the problem starts when the engineer in industry comes to a technical bottleneck that requires fundamental inquiry, a university scientist is contracted, the answer is developed and passed back to the client, and commer-

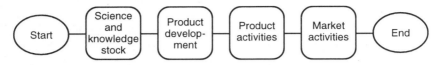

FIGURE 2.1 A traditional linear model of innovation

cialization or improved production proceeds. In the market pull variant, the research problem and idea originate with the final customer (see Figure 2.1).

Seen in this light, a number of important problems are discernible in linear models, not the least of which is that such a framework hardly begins to capture the complexity of the innovation process. Nonetheless, using a simple but popular view of 'innovation' as 'the first commercial application of an idea or invention' (Freeman and Soete, 1997) such approaches tended to reduce the driver of economic activity to R&D, ignoring all the tacit skills and RSA that are required for useful science or technology development to flourish. This creates a caricature of the mandates, roles, and functions of university laboratories and technology-intensive firms. And it leaves no room whatsoever for government, except possibly in terms of monetary and macro-economic policy. (Of course, this should not be surprising given that neoclassical economics, which still exerts a powerful hold on policy thinking, tends to promote a view of economic growth in which technological change is either static or exogenous.) Finally, it reduces the purpose of innovation to purely economic functions – ignoring social or environmental roles, except in a market-failure sense, ignoring important make or buy types of questions, and ignoring free rider questions which are especially important for advanced small open economies like Canada. But as the influential economist Nathan Rosenberg (1990: 253), has put it, 'The linear model is dead (in terms of its explanatory powers) but it won't lie down.'

What such linear models miss is that the knowledge-based economy places great importance on the diffusion and use of information and knowledge, as well as its creation (R&D). They miss that innovation is not just about commercialization but is critically important to new products, processes, markets, sources of material, and new forms of social organization – each of which has great applicability in government agencies. They miss that knowledge as an economic input tends to become very specific, depending on the context of application (based on where it is applied, how it is applied, and so on). Thus, specialization in the creation, diffusion, and use of knowledge (which is defined not only by the kind of information, but also by the type of actors using it), gives rise to interdependencies between different agents. Similar knowledge will display differing characteristics in a firm, in a government laboratory, or in a university). All this is missed by linear models (de la Mothe, 1994).

The Poverty of Market Failure

In attempting to answer their first question about the relationship between science and the economy, and in trying to stimulate technoeconomic competitiveness, governments tacitly inferred from both the linear logic and its policy imperative of strengthening the technoeconomic performance of the country at a time of government restructuring and deficit reduction, an allure for private sector notions of markets and market failure.[7] Given the multidimensional imperatives of government, such rationales can of course find some legitimate utility for government activities in some areas such as technical assistance to firms or the provision of medical isotopes at market prices. But as a broad rationale, it falls short.

The market as a concept does help to explain resource exchanges – the buying and selling of goods, services, and factors of production (such as labour and capital). The essence of this view is that, first, production of goods and services takes place as much because of the pressure of consumer demands as because of the desire on the part of producers to earn income. In turn, demand for goods exists because goods possess utility (defined typically as the ability to satisfy wants). Exchange takes place in markets where the price of any commodity reflects the strength of influences on both the supply and demand sides. In this stylized view, markets are never inherently unstable because every market has the tendency to seek equilibrium, where the demand for and supply of the commodity in question is exactly equal. Quite apart from questions of how to describe the market for universal health care and the like, intervention by the government in an economy is, in this view, often seen as being an unwanted distortion of the market.

In the context of science and government, the market failure argument attempts to reduce public policy decisions to a limited number of levers and to reduce the Canadian socioeconomy to little more than a series of economic exchanges. It also bravely attempts to ascribe a value, that is, a price, to such factors as research and knowledge (Clark, 1985; Stoneman, 1987). But there are problems from this perspective *vis-à-vis* government science.

First, knowledge as a factor of production has a number of features that make it unique. It is reuseable without losing value (unlike, for example, spent fuel). It can be applied time and time again in new contexts, thus creating new value across sectors and among actors over time. It can be transmitted in a variety of forms. It can be codified in blueprints, patent applications, or design drawings; it can be downloaded and imported to an organization; it can be in tacit form in the experience of researchers; and so on.

Second, firms tend to invest suboptimally in research, ever aware that they can always acquire publicly funded research or skills. Third, and consistently, there is a greater social rate of return on public, rather than private, research. And fourth, stylized economic theory would be at a loss to explain some things, for example, the exploratory work of the Geological Survey in the 1850s, for which there was no market and no price, just non-linear public utility, and it tends to be unable to explain Canada's involvement in space exploration and research except in terms of the public cost / Canadian industrial contract ratio.

Neither linear models nor market notions are capable of providing a sound understanding or basis for undertaking a government role in science. Nevertheless, the role is critical.

Roles and Responsibilities Revisited

In part the allure of the linear model and of market arguments can be understood in terms of an inattention to sectoral mandates and imperatives. To be sure, moving towards a view in which government services are provided to clients (that is, Canadians) has the benefit of promoting a commitment to responsiveness, value for money, and effective cost management. But to carry this to the next step, and to assume that the mandates of all sectors can only be legitimately defined in terms of costs, profits, and so on, is to entirely misappreciate institutional responsibilities and roles in Canadian society.

In an innovation system, every institutional player has a role in promoting economic opportunity, social cohesion, and political stability. This includes firms, universities and colleges, not-for-profit agencies, and governments. For example, one clear reason that the Ottawa area is strong in telecommunications and information technologies is because of the numerous linkages that exist among the universities and colleges (producing both new technologies and well-trained graduates), federal laboratories (which offer technical assistance to firms, testing, and survey support), banks that understand the financial requirements of the information and communications technology (ICT) sectors, supplier firms, major manufacturers, industry associations, and networking organizations (such as the Ottawa Centre for Research and Innovation [OCRI] that organizes technology marketing breakfasts and so on). Similar complex synergies can be found across all of Canada's 'smart' cities, from Saint John and Sherbrooke to Kitchener-Waterloo, Calgary, Saskatoon, and Vancouver. Every institution must itself innovate to stay relevant, and in so doing it is inevitable that roles will overlap. This is how a strong national fabric is woven. This is not to say that roles and responsibilities are interchangeable.

Firms are at the centre of wealth and job creation. They compete with other firms and are, by definition, profit driven. This means that any activity that a firm engages in must be rationalized by management in terms of returns to its shareholders and in terms of its long-term viability as a firm. The firm's time frame for measuring performance is the business quarter. If a firm undertakes the performance of any science and technology activities – and only 0.4 per cent of firms in Canada do so – then it undertakes these activities in the belief that this will lead to, or support, profits. Research has shown that even in advanced technology areas, firms tend to invest suboptimally in science and technology because (a) they can acquire needed know-how or information more cheaply off the public shelf, and (b) in so doing they retain a degree of flexibility enabling them to take advantage of new, unforeseen developments in science. Thus, firms are ill-prepared to undertake science in the public interest – for example, in terms of emergency preparedness, regulatory support (which would be an area fraught with possible conflicts of interest), policy support, or infrastructure support.

Similarly, universities are terribly important institutions in the conduct of science and technology. However, again, their role and responsibility are specific. Society charges them with the twin mandates (a) to educate and to train tomorrow's citizens and workers, and (b) to advance – or provide access to – knowledge. Thus, university researchers carry out both exploratory research and (increasingly) project research. The former, usually defined in fundamental terms with an unspecified application or timeframe, can be done solo or in collaboration with colleagues in Canada or around the world. The latter typically is done in collaboration with industry, with a determined outcome and timeline in mind. In either case, though, the *raison d'être* is education and the advancement or transfer of knowledge. These are public goods, but the universities' role and responsibility are different from those of the private sector or government. In the case of firms and universities, given the current climate for knowledge and innovation, it is not surprising that there would be functional overlaps between them and government science activities. But science in the public interest is uniquely the business of government.

Whereas firms have a principal responsibility – the long-term viability of the firm evaluated in short-term steps – and whereas universities have a few responsibilities, governments have multiple responsibilities, ranging from supporting the economic union to ensuring the social union and protecting the commons. The government is thus custodian, partner, and leader. To be sure, alternative service delivery mechanisms such as contracting out research services can be valid is certain circumstances, but they do not provide a blanket solution for performing government science, technology, and related activities. Seen in more concrete terms, the government carries out science and technology activities in order to:

- Provide *technical assistance* to small and medium-sized Canadian businesses that are working in a technology-intensive area and that do not have the needed in-house expertise or equipment. This important role for government has enabled thousands of firms to grow, compete, and in turn create new value-added jobs. No firm or university could easily provide this service.
- Pursue *development of new technology* in areas such as data encryption, where there is both a security issue for Canada (in privacy, for example) that will involve government regulatory functions and an economic issue (in CA*Net3, for example), where the future technology can be stimulated in concert with universities and consortia for example, the Canadian Network for the Advancement of Research, Industry, and Education (CANARIE), and in which no one firm could afford solo development in Canada.
- *Establish and negotiate* standards in order to harmonize Canadian and international regimes to protect Canadians and provide a

favourable business climate. Again, state-to-state negotiations cannot be done by firms, and government science in the public interest is needed to ensure level playing fields and to avoid conflicts of interest.

- Undertake *testing and approval* in areas related to drugs, biomedical devices, vaccines, blood products, and the like, which clearly require government involvement as well as a research capability in order to evaluate and verify outside results for the protection of Canadians.
- Undertake *environmental monitoring* for the protection of Canada's ecosystem and commons (in support of existing environmental standards and in anticipation of the identification of new environmental threats). The capacity of the government to carry out such work is critical as ecological threats emerge and as the government commits to meeting negotiated international treaty levels that would be difficult to contract out. Moreover, the capacity to conduct *survey work and stock assessments* in order to understand changes in the ecological systems of Canada (including the fisheries), geological transitions, and so on are key and germane to government – not industry – goals and mandates.
- Support *emergency preparedness* for disasters, for example, earthquakes and floods. Again, firms operating for profit would be hard-pressed to undertake earthquake modelling and monitoring over the long haul, and Canadians would rightly wonder if emergency preparedness, operated by the private sector, would provide the responsiveness, warning, and universality that Canadians require.
- *Support policy* in the science-based departments and agencies as well as in industry, heritage, foreign affairs, international trade, defence, and transportation. To farm all these responsibilities out to academic or private sector concerns would not only create a government contract monitoring and management nightmare, but it could also lead to breaches of security, a decoupling of government science from government policy, and a lack of assurance that government and the public interest were 'in synch.'
- *Regulate and monitor compliance activities*, including the monitoring and regulatory control of food, drugs, consumer product safety, transportation safety, and the like.
- Conduct *basic research*, not because government researchers should be expected to contribute to the international open

literature, but because basic research will (a) keep government researchers sharp and aware of the latest developments, findings, and techniques; (b) keep vibrant an external research network that can be called upon in support of government science; and (c) promote an attractive career path for researchers in which valuable scientific and technical work can be carried out – thus ensuring the revitalization of government science. These are but a few concrete examples.

Conclusions

This chapter sketched a series of arguments in support of the federal performance of research, development, and related scientific activities. In so doing it has advanced a number of lines of argument. First, it argued that the issue is not one of balance between sectors but of responsibility. Second, it demonstrated that the federal science system has been evolving over time, to the great benefit of Canada and Canadians, innovating and adapting all the while to a wide variety of demanding conditions. Third, it critically inspected two logics that had become quietly influential in the restructuring of government science over the past decade – namely, linear models of innovation and markets – arguing that although alluring, they are inappropriate logics. Fourth, it revisited the roles and responsibilities of firms, universities, and government in science.

In an overall sense this chapter has argued by example that government science is of critical importance to the public interest and that it will become more so as the knowledge-based economy and the information society continue to unfold. Nowhere did it argue, depending on the task at hand and the need for innovative institutions or responses, that government science must not be done in partnership. Indeed, such possibilities are very promising and can strengthen the Canadian system. As we approach the twenty-first century, however, we cannot allow ourselves to be seduced into thinking that government science can be more efficiently done elsewhere. To walk down this path is to lose sight of the very purpose of government itself.

Notes

1 It is important to remember that throughout this chapter, the term 'science and technology' in government refers to an important balance between

'research and development' (R&D) and 'related scientific activities' (RSA).

2 Canada's government-funded gross expenditure on science and technology has fallen, as a percentage of GDP, from 0.7% in 1982 to less than 0.5% in 1996, compared with 0.9% in the U.S. and Germany, 0.7% in the U.K., 1% in France, and 1.2% in Sweden. Moreover, Canada's government performance of science and technology has fallen since the 1970s from 28% to 11%. See Eric Arnett, 'Letters,' *Science*, 281, 18 Sept. (1998), 1807.

3 Note Canada's involvement, e.g., in the October 1998 Science and Technology Ministerial Meeting of the APEC on 'Knowledge, Partnership, and Cooperation.'

4 For example, altering the federal tax code has a direct effect on government revenues, and it also has a direct effect on investment decisions, consumer spending, and so on.

5 As an example, the idea of 'collaboratories' (in which central labs equipped with the latest of informatics technologies are able to test mineral samples from, say, the University of British Columbia or air quality samples from Montreal and be on-line in real time nationally sharing the results and allowing a variety of applications and uses for the information) is currently favoured.

6 The history of science in Canada is extremely rich and well documented. See Doern, 1972; Dufour and de la Mothe, 1993a, 1993b; Harrison, 1975; Hayes, 1973; Vodden, 1992; and Zaslow, 1975.

7 Markets can be thought of as embodying exclusivity, rivalry, and transparency. In economic terms, 'market failure' is sometimes referred to as 'negative externalities' or 'missing markets' (as, e.g., when a firm pollutes and there is no 'market' to meet the created demand, hence forcing the government to step in.

References

Canada, Senate Committee on Science Policy. (1973). *A Science Policy for Canada: Report of the Senate Special Committee on Science Policy*, Vol. 3: *A Government Organization for the Seventies*. Ottawa: Government of Canada.

Clark, Norman. (1985). *The Political Economy of Science and Technology*. London: Macmillan.

de la Mothe, John. (1994). 'Canada and National Innovation Systems.' In J.A.D. Holbrook, ed., *Science and Technology Resource Handbook*. Ottawa: Government of Canada.

de la Mothe, John, and Paul Dufour. (1995). 'Techno-Globalism and the Challenge to Science and Technology Policy.' *Daedalus*, 124(3): 22–33.

de la Mothe, John, and Gilles Paquet, eds. (1998). *Local and Regional Systems of Innovation*. Boston: Kluwer.

Doern, G. Bruce. (1972). *Science and Politics in Canada*. Montreal: McGill-Queen's University Press.

Dufour, Paul, and John de la Mothe. (1993a). 'The Historical Conditioning of Science and Technology,' in Paul R. Dufour and John de la Mothe, eds., *Science and Technology in Canada*. London: Longman.

– eds. (1993b). *Science and Technology in Canada*. London: Longman.

Dupré, J. Stefan, and Sanford A. Lakoff. (1962). *Science and the Nation*. Englewood Cliffs, NJ: Prentice-Hall.

Edquist, Charles, ed. (1997). *Systems of Innovation: Technologies, Institutions and Organizations*. London: Pinter, 1997.

Freeman, Chris, and Luc Soete. (1997). *The Economics of Industrial Innovation*. London: Pinter.

Harrison, J.M. (1975). 'The Geological Survey of Canada.' *Canada Year Book*. Ottawa, Supply and Services Canada, 68–81.

Hayes, F. Ronald. (1973). *The Chaining of Prometheus: Evolution of a Power Structure for Canadian Science*. Toronto: University of Toronto Press.

Industry Canada. (1994). *Building a More Innovative Economy*. Ottawa: Industry Canada.

Liberal Party of Canada. (1993). *Creating Opportunity: The Liberal Plan for Canada*. Ottawa: Liberal Party of Canada.

Lundvall, B.A., ed. (1992). *National Innovation Systems*. London: Pinter.

Nelson, Richard, ed. (1993). *National Innovation Systems: A Comparative Analysis*. New York: Oxford University Press.

Niosi, Jorge. (1999). *Canada's National System of Innovation*. Toronto: Oxford University Press.

Rosenberg, Nathan. (1990). 'Emergent Issues in Science Policy.' *Science and Public Policy*, June/July, 101–5.

Stoneman, Paul. (1987). *The Economic Analysis of Technology Policy*. Oxford: Oxford University Press.

Vodden, Christy. (1992). *No Stone Unturned: The First 150 Years of the Geological Survey of Canada*. Ottawa: Energy, Mines and Resources Canada.

Zaslow, Morris. (1975). *Reading the Rocks: The Story of the Geological Survey of Canada 1842–1972*. Toronto: Macmillan.

3 Between Expertise and Bureaucracy: Risk Management Trapped at the Science-Policy Interface

WILLIAM LEISS

Recent experience in Canada indicates that there is some serious misalignment in the interplay between science and public policy. Indeed, one might conclude that the two appear to be fundamentally incompatible with each other, so much so that their respective outcomes could be expected to dovetail only by pure chance. This experience is useful, for it tells us that an old pattern – where government departments directly do scientific work which is then applied to policy choices – is obsolete. This chapter argues the case for a new paradigm, where governments *manage* health and environmental risks, and draw upon independent scientific bodies for the risk assessment expertise they need in order to effectively carry out their risk management mandate. The strict institutional separation of science and policy is good for both of them. Science is only useful to policy when it is completely true to itself, which requires autonomy in the setting of research questions and an unconstrained peer-review and publications process, with its often brutal questioning of methods, experimental procedures, and findings. Nevertheless, even in the area of health and environmental risk management, where scientific research is indispensable to sensible decision making, good policy does not and cannot flow automatically from the science itself.

In what I call the older model, governments thought it wise to provide for in-house science expertise so as to translate risk assessments into policy choices for everything from food safety to wildlife conservation. Like everything else in the civil service bureaucracy, the scientific advice was given in secret and was thus not open to challenge by the public, which was especially useful for covering up the existence of huge uncertainties and the lack of essential data to support a preferred policy choice. Although the risk management decisions emanating from this model had some successes as well as spectacular failures, other changes in society now have rendered it obsolete.

The newer and still-emerging model requires that governments should concentrate on being accountable for managing risks, especially where the risk factors are publicly controversial – a duty that is generally discharged poorly these days – and leave the provisioning of science relevant to those risk factors to independent institutions. In fact until the realization dawns about where the real duty of governments lie in the area of health and environmental risk management, we will continue to waste scarce resources on suboptimal risk reduction ventures. Until governments are able to focus their attention on their inescapable duty to carry out credible risk management, and to staff their professional ranks with the requisite skills for this purpose (which a training in the sciences alone cannot provide), they will not have resolved the real nature of the dilemmas that exist for them at this zone of the science–policy interface.

Three fisheries scientists created a stir in 1997 when they published a journal article entitled, 'Is Scientific Inquiry Incompatible with Government Information Control?' (Hutchings et al., 1997). What was perhaps most surprising about the ensuing *contretemps* was that anyone thought that the question itself was scandalous – or that the answer to it was less than obvious. The answer to the question they posed is 'Yes': Of course scientific inquiry is incompatible with the management of information within government bureaucracies. The fact that the question even had to be posed provides the backdrop for this chapter.

Perhaps the source of misunderstanding lies not in some uncertainty about the nature of scientific inquiry, but rather in a lack of familiarity with the needs of governments as they pertain to the use of information, including scientific research findings, in the formation of public policy. In this latter domain there is no question whatsoever that good government practice requires the bureaucracies that serve ministers to manage the flow of policy-relevant information.[1] A look at any major policy issue in the broad area of health and environmental risk management will confirm the truth of this contention.[2] If we consider, for the moment, only the aspect of uncertainty in risk analysis, and ignore all other dimensions of risk management, we can see why the process of developing policy must include the management of information.

In most cases where public concern about risk factors leads to demands for government action, there are insufficiently definitive results in the risk analysis to justify a single path of risk control at any particular time. (This uncertainty can persist for decades, even where expensive, large-scale research programs are under way; some illustrations of this are given later.) In other words, reasonable persons legitimately can and will disagree on the type of policies and control measures (including none at all) that are called for, on the basis of the perceived facts or the evidence at hand, to protect human health and the environment.[3] To make intelligent policy choices under such circumstances, Cabinet ministers and their senior advisers should hear vigorous arguments in favour of various interpretations of both the scientific data and the risk assessment assumptions, as well as the full range of risk control options and their likely impacts – economic, social, political, and institutional. Many risk issue domains are extremely contentious, where interested parties of all kinds have strongly opposed viewpoints and proferred solutions which they are desirous of impressing upon governments. A sane policy development process must to some extent insulate itself from the rough play of social interests. To this end the flow of policy-relevant information must be managed, by which I mean that confidentiality is needed during the policy deliberation period.[4]

That said, should these same policy advisers be running down the hallway to the offices of the government's own staff, in order to get a quick-and-dirty version of what the state of science is? No: at least, not any more. For it is naïve in the extreme to think that the institutional system of official bureaucracy, which has over the centuries raised the craft of information control to the level of high art, would shrink from doing everything in its power to shape and channel what it hears from its servants, whether they be scientists or janitorial staff.[5] Neither governments nor anyone else can do health and environmental risk management without the aid of science. However, in all risk management domains it is clearly in the interest of governments today, as well as of scientists, for that assistance to be provided *in every instance* at arm's length (and governments these days need scientists primarily for risk management). Science can serve policy best – indeed, can only serve it at all – in our era by coming to policy with expert advice from an independent standpoint.[6]

This was not necessarily always the case, for things have changed over the past thirty years or so, and there is a specific explanation as to why in our own era, and hereafter, only independent science can serve the needs of policy in risk management. There are two reasons for this transition: one has to do with the different type of risk management challenges we face, and the other with the changing role of the public and interest groups, including their access to expertise in risk matters.[7]

The Older Model: Science in the (Secret) Service of Policy

In the older model, beginning in the early twentieth century and continuing through the 1980s, government-employed scientists in both regulatory and non-regulatory matters produced confidential risk assessments that became the basis of policy choices.[8] In the cases of ministries responsible for natural resources, such as agriculture, forestry, fisheries, mining, and wildlife, the government-owned scientific research establishments could be (and sometimes still are) substantial indeed. These establishments generally worked in applied science areas, ultimately in the service of economic development; their specific tasks covered such areas as occupational health and safety, control of environmental factors (for example, insect pests), and yield management.

The public health services were perhaps the only science-based government units that did not have primarily an economic development function under the older model. But there as elsewhere the refrain was and is the same, when public queries are raised: 'Trust us, we (as scientists) have the necessary expertise and we also (as civil servants) have your best interests at heart. It is unnecessary for you to trouble yourselves about the messy details of scientific investigation or risk assessment – besides, you would be utterly unable to understand all this even if we tried to explain it. We can assure you that you are "perfectly safe"' (to use the line about British beef fed to politicians by their advisers during the bovine spongiform encephalopathy, or BSE, crisis).

The only other institution that had complementary resources invested in applied science, as well as some basic science, was private industry. Thus, in practice both the risk assessments and the risk control strategies – in the many cases where industry and government interests overlapped – were negotiated behind closed doors between these two parties. The innate secrecy of government bureaucracies was reinforced by industry's insistence that commercial confidentiality also was at stake in many cases. With respect to all health and environmental risk factors related to economic activity, which covers a huge range of such factors, there was and is a direct relationship between choices among risk control options, which for human health are primarily a matter of controlling exposures, and 'the bottom line' for industry: generally speaking, the more stringent the risk control, the higher the monetary cost.

This direct relationship between risk and economic interest has had a number of consequences. First, there has been a strong urge not to know if unacceptable occupational or other risks are present. This urge was satisfied first by simple denial that evidence of harm existed; second, by demands for proof of cause-and-effect relations (and a legal standard of proof at that), where any sort of proof was difficult or impossible to obtain; or third, by blaming the victim (for carelessness at work or immoral behaviour at leisure). So the scope of the damage usually has only emerged after the fact, when the body count could be tracked in epidemiological data. Typical of this pattern was the finding of a significant correlation between vinyl chloride and liver cancer in rubber-plant workers; after the studies were done, the exposure limits were lowered. Most of the effective standards for occupational exposure to both natural and industrially created hazards that we have today came about in this way.[9]

The older model remains strong. Within the past decade there is no better example than the mismanagement of the risk of 'mad cow disease' (BSE) by the U.K. Ministry of Agriculture, Fisheries, and Food. The new type of pathogen that is implicated in this disease remains a great challenge for scientific research itself. But the public risk management of the disease was fatally compromised by other agents entirely, namely, the pathological secretiveness of the British bureaucracy, aided and abetted by the farm lobby, which feared for its livelihood and conspired to bring down ruin upon itself (Powell and Leiss, 1997, chapter 1).[10] Every stage of the work of British government scientists over the decade 1986–96 was tainted by the overriding 'policy' need for information control, accompanied by completely ineffective animal disease control measures, blockage of access to information for external researchers, misuse of uncertainties, and, above all, provision of false reassurances of 'safety' to the public.

It is perhaps too easy to list the high-profile events of a similar nature in Canada during the preceding two decades: the catastrophic contamination of the blood supply from the viruses that cause AIDS and hepatitis C; the vanishing of the North Atlantic cod, originally a natural resource of prodigious abundance; the imperilled state of the equally prodigious Pacific salmon fishery; and the fact that the safety and performance status of Ontario Hydro's nuclear power system appears to have been a mystery to the engineers who ran it. In all of these cases government-controlled science had some role to play, if not as the author of the tragedy, then at least in failing to prevent it. In some of these cases a noisy cabal made up of provincial governments, industry, and labour also sought to ensure that no one looked too closely at the uncertainties in the risk assessments.

A bitter controversy surrounds the case of the Atlantic fishery, but in my opinion a strong and plausible case has been made for the view that fisheries science was abused over a long period as a result of short-sighted economic and political considerations (Hutchings et al., 1997; Hutchings, 1997). In the case of the Atlantic cod fishery the indictment is severe: 'Nonscientific influences on fisheries research incompatible with normal scientific inquiry included: (i) government denunciation of independent work, (ii) misrepresentation of alternative hypotheses, (iii) interference in scientific conclusions, (iv) disciplining of scientists who communicated publicly the results of peer-reviewed research, and (v) misrepresentation of the scientific basis of public reports and government statements' (Hutchings et al., 1997: 1204). None of the replies published to date seriously challenge the evidentiary basis of this indictment, and those taking the contrary position are content to make light of the complainants' alleged belief in a right to do 'pure science' while being supported from the public purse.[11] While the Atlantic cod fishery debacle has garnered most of the attention to date, many are perhaps unaware that Hutchings et al. examine another case in their article, namely, the fate of fisheries science over a period of more than a decade during Alcan's ill-fated 'Kemano Completion Project' in British Columbia. Here the evidence of bureaucratic interference with scientific evaluation is, if anything, even stronger than in the case of the Atlantic cod fishery – indeed, the political pressures on government fisheries scientists in this case displayed unrelenting contempt for the work of science (ibid.: 1204–6).[12]

Sometimes the failings under the older model take a tragicomic form, although the show still can be expensive for the public to watch, as the notorious case of methylcyclopentadienyl manganese tricarbonyl (MMT) demonstrates well (McCarthy, 1998b). MMT is a gasoline additive that came into use in Canada as tetraethyl lead was being phased out. What the public heard was that the Canadian federal government was passing a law to force MMT off the market because its use entailed unacceptable health and environmental risks – a rationale hotly disputed by its sole manufacturer, Ethyl Corporation. (The public also heard a more muted message from the auto industry, claiming that MMT did serious harm to the emissions control systems in cars.) When a senior Environment Canada official had appeared before the Senate to defend the bill dealing with MMT, he acknowledged that no formal risk assessment had been done, because there were insufficient scientific resources in his department to carry out this task. At the same time the manufacturer was taking out advertisements in newspapers, pointing out that another department of the same government, Health Canada, had declared some time ago that MMT did not pose an unacceptable health risk. A year later Canada's federal government was forced to undergo a very public humiliation, issuing an apology and a twenty-million-dollar compensation payment to the manufacturer and affirming publicly that it did not have conclusive evidence of unacceptable risk (Hill and Leiss, 1999). What is worse, the sideshow – continued sniping between the government and the auto industry – went on, with the government publicly disputing the industry's contention that the numerous 'scientific' studies that it had supplied adequately supported its claim of damage to the emissions control systems. All in all, a very ugly business. What if the government simply had asked two different and equally independent scientific panels – one on health and environmental risk issues, the other on risk to the emissions systems – to review the scientific basis of the various positions? And what if it had done so sometime before making up its mind to pass legislation in this area?

The most significant failure of the older model, however, is in occupational health and safety, and no case illustrates this better than risk from asbestos. As it developed under the older model, asbestos is an appalling story of deceit and cover-up for a lethal occupational risk, as awful diseases took their toll on thousands of workers and their families. When the full history of this tragedy finally emerged into the light of day, largely as a result of class-action litigation in the United States, we understood how industry science had concealed what it knew and feared, and how governments committed to economic and technological benefits had turned a blind eye to the human health costs. In the area of environmental risks, pesticides regulation provides the best example: until the early 1980s decisions emerged from a secretive and cozy relationship between industry and government scientists, and those who dared to dissent, such as Rachel Carson, were subjected to frenetic attack. And, of course, the long march of the tobacco industry's prevarication, helped along by legions of politicians, shows best the uses to which a science crafted in secrecy can be put.

It would be churlish not to concede that the older model was – and is – capable of achieving outstanding results and of serving the public interest. An excellent example of this in recent times is the work of Environment Canada scientists on the environmental impacts of pulp mill effluent (for the full story see VanNijnatten et al., 1997). Strong initiatives by that department beginning in the late 1980s concentrated on ensuring sharp reductions in dioxins and furans residues in the effluent, and the departmental scientists came to the conclusion that their approach in this matter provided a wide range of environmental benefits, especially in controlling the production and release of chlorinated organic compounds generally. By the early 1990s they had decided that further attention to chlorinated organics derived from industrial sources alone – the so-called AOX parameter – was unwise, and they turned their attention to other substances (including natural sources) in the effluent that were still giving rise to unacceptable levels of adverse impacts on aquatic organisms. This stance proved unpopular with those who believe that industrial chemicals alone are the root of all evils, and some nasty confrontations ensued, during which the integrity of the government scientists unfairly was called into question. These scientists stood their ground, however, and in subsequent years the consensus of expert opinion supported their position.

So there were notable successes as well as failures in the older model, bringing gradual and important improvements in managing risks. There were many dedicated scientists and regulators in both government and industry who waged campaigns for more enlightened practices out of public view. Especially notable have been the conservation biologists in the fish and game departments, who often were leaders in the fight for the protection of wildlife and its habitat. That this older model is obsolete is not the result of its high-profile failures, all of which simply illustrate its inadequacies without proving its inherent unworkability. The need for a new model is grounded elsewhere: in the changing capabilities of the public and public interest groups with respect to expertise; in the nature of the specific risk management challenges that we face now and will face even more in the future; in the merging of disparate risk issue domains into a unified sequence of both opportunities and resource constraints for optimal risk reduction programs; and, finally, in our relation to the environment and its resources itself. In every one of these four dimensions – in the zone where science and policy meet – an independent science is more useful and indeed necessary than is a government-employed science.

Transition to the New Model

We face *utterly different* risk management challenges now as compared with the past. This changes the roles of both science and government, and the relationship between them, at the science–policy interface. I shall explain this change with reference to the four dimensions listed above.

The Public and Public Interest Groups

With few exceptions (notably in the area of public health) neither individual members of the general public nor public interest advocacy groups can or did interfere with the secret service of science to policy under the older model. This began to change in the late 1970s, beginning in the United States, although it will be some time yet before that change is complete. One of the notable steps, for example, was the victory in 1984 by the U.S. Natural Resources Defense Council, when it persuaded the federal courts to crack open the long-standing, secretive process of pesticides registration (Leiss and Chociolko, 1994, chapter 6).[13] Now in the United States major advocacy groups regularly take on both industry and governments over health and environmental risk management, and some like Greenpeace operate on a global scale.

The effective newer players have the resources to bring their own staff scientists to the table and to confront the original participants on equal terms. Industry has adapted to the new rules but, by and large, governments have not, for they are caught between their original mandate and their new one. In the former (which has evaporated) governments were the sole players with scientific competence representing the public interest; in the new one governments must act as brokers in risk controversies (including brokering the different representations of science offered by other players), a role that requires a completely different set of professional skills. These skills are not now widely available in the ranks of civil servants, alas.

Over the past few decades university-based scientists have taken on intervenor roles in risk controversies, both as members of panels of independent experts and also as individuals with strong views on appropriate risk management. New journal publications also try to bring science to a broader public. But as well, and increasingly, individual members of the public who do not necessarily have scientific expertise, but who have concerns about risk issues, use Internet resources to gather information, establish contact with like-minded people everywhere on the globe, ask questions of experts, and prepare themselves to become skilled intervenors in risk controversies (Leiss, 1998). The information-search, document-retrieval, and networking facilities of the Internet have huge advantages over earlier resources available to the general public, and these advantages will grow steadily in future years. From now on, all controversies over risk management decision making will be played out on a public stage with an international cast and audience.

The game is up for the older model. Today the only response that makes sense to the public's demands for a full accounting of the risk management decision making is to put all the science and the risk assessments on the table.[14] As a practical matter, in all countries except the United States, government is the only party which can be accountable to the public for risk management decisions in the final analysis (because only in the United States is it feasible for private groups to take on industry in the courts). But then governments cannot do the science itself, because today they will be perceived – and rightly so, in my opinion – to be an interested party in that regard.[15] Because they are still staffed to carry out the older mandate rather than the newer one, they have not been able to deliver – in many high-profile cases – credible risk management decisions to the public. (A number of such cases will be presented later.)

The Changing Nature of Risk Management Challenges

In Western industrial societies, with respect to the intrinsic difficulties of carrying out credible risk management decision making itself, all of the low-hanging fruit has been picked, so to speak: The easier victories have been won, and the harder ones remain. These victories amounted to drawing firm conclusions from toxicology and epidemiology that unacceptable levels of risk exist, that exposures should be reduced, and that either governments or industry should pay the costs for risk reduction without further ado. Again, occupational risks provide the best illustration: for workplace accidents and for exposures to metals, hydrocarbons, minerals, heat, particulates, gases, and industrial chemicals of all kinds, as well as unsafe conditions tolerated earlier by workers (primarily because they had no choice but to do so) and social institutions that are no longer acceptable. Exposure to most of these same substances and new ones as well still occurs in industrial plants, but at levels many, many times lower than in the past.

These were relatively easy victories for risk management but not in terms of the institutional battles that had to be waged to secure them. The direct relation between risk reduction and incremental cost was apparent to every industrial corporation. In the worst cases, such as the dye industry earlier and asbestos later on, every conceivable obstacle to risk reduction measures – advocated by labour unions and independent medical scientists – that could be devised by the industry's own scientists and lawyers was employed (Leiss, 1995). But the struggle was actually about the balance of power in society, not about competing risk assessment methodologies (although the latter could become implicated indirectly in it). The same was true in the case of public health: Huge risk reductions and increments in human welfare were achieved at relatively low cost in the battle against infectious diseases.

Now our risk management battles are almost entirely different, sometimes because the risk reduction gains are purchased at much higher prices, but even more importantly because the reasons for carrying on the battles themselves are so much murkier.[16] This is a complex and contentious matter, so two examples must suffice.

The first is asbestos. Although the earlier occupational risk battles have been won, in the sense that industrial exposures in Western countries are now at levels considered to be appropriate, there remains much controversy over the risks to the general public posed by the continued marketing of asbestos products (which have many highly desirable and useful properties) and by the fact that the nearly indestructible asbestos fibres are found ubiquitously in our environment from past uses. It is not at all clear that anyone should worry about this level of risk, or that measures such as the removal of intact asbestos insulation from buildings is warranted, but the expert disagreement can be furious on these and other points (Royal Society of Canada, 1996).[17] It is also most unclear whether there are substitutes for asbestos that present lower levels of risk. Canadian governments have a high stake in these disputes, since Canada is one of the two largest exporters of asbestos in the world, and some countries have instituted total bans on the importation of asbestos products. Nevertheless, one lesson is already very clear: Governments should stay out of direct involvement in the scientific research on asbestos hazards and allow the further studies by independent scientists to take their own course, wherever they may lead. Governments should confine their involvement to the risk management of asbestos, which takes the balance of expert opinion on acceptable risk into account, and factors in economics, relative risk, evaluation of substitutes, and so forth. In other words, governments are accountable for deciding whether further risk reduction measures for asbestos are or are not warranted, and they can safely leave the ongoing scientific investigation of the health risk factors themselves to university-based experts.

Then there is the case of dioxin (Powell and Leiss, 1997, chapter 3). Publicly labelled 'by far the most toxic compound known to mankind' by a U.S. Environmental Protection Agency scientist in 1974, dioxin (the shorthand name for several families of organochlorine compounds) became thereafter an emblem for the concerns about risks associated with industrially produced chemicals felt by many people, and especially about the potential adverse health effects from toxins at extremely low doses. As is often the case, industry first learned about dioxin as a result of relatively high occupational exposures in chemical plants, often as a result of accidents; later there were other terrible accidents affecting the public, notably two in Asia involving contaminated rice oil, where thousands became ill. After a decade of new research in the 1970s, industry and governments began to act relatively quickly (compared with similar episodes in the past) to lower dioxin emissions from industrial facilities. For example, dioxin in pulp-mill effluent became a public issue in 1987, and by 1995 Canadian mills in British Columbia had lowered such emissions by about 95 per cent. The North American chemical industry has taken similar steps. Scientific research has demonstrated that the total environmental burden of dioxinlike compounds, which had risen steadily around the world during most of the twentieth century, had begun a slow but uninterrupted decline around 1980.

No one cheered, however, and the reason for this tells us a great deal about the systematic failure of governments to develop publicly credible risk management frameworks.[18] The absence of cheering can be explained thus: For something that is 'by far the most toxic compound known to mankind,' 95 per cent reductions in emissions arguably are not good enough, and only 100 per cent will do; on this reasoning if entire industries (pulp mills or PVC plastic producers, say) must be shut down, no matter how many useful products they market, so be it. Yet there is no credible evidence at hand to suggest that either worker or public exposures to dioxin after 1980 represent an unacceptable level of risk. So why does the dioxin issue still have such a high profile on the public's risk agenda? The answer is this: The scientific characterization of dioxinlike compounds (which by now must fill whole libraries) is exceedingly complex. Beginning around 1970 governments allocated substantial budgets to this scientific area, including their own expert staff resources. They allocated *no* resources whatsoever to an attempt to credibly explain dioxin science and risk assessment to the public or to engage the public in a dialogue about dioxin risk.

So the controversy goes on, apparently indefinitely, now accompanied by a related one, involving what are called 'endocrine-modulating substances,' where there are also widespread fears of serious adverse health effects that may result from exposures to these substances at extremely low doses (Kavlock and Ankley, 1996). These can be expensive as well as frustrating episodes, because the costs for risk reduction rise exponentially as environmental concentrations of the targeted substances fall.[19] We seem condemned to go on along this path unless and until governments recognize that their real duty in this regard is to facilitate the public dialogue on risk rather than to help in doing the science.

The Synthetic Nature of Risk Management Today

Traditionally government departments have been watertight compartments where ministers vigorously defend their allotted turf. Responsibility for risk management has been no exception to this rule.[20] This allocation of discrete mandates under the older model worked equally well for the political order and the public interest, insofar as there were (as indicated earlier) notable successes in risk management. But although it still may provide comfort to civil servants and their political masters, it no longer serves the public interest at all, for reasons advanced in the preceding section: The nature of the most important risk management challenges facing governments has changed dramatically and permanently in the meantime.

During the first half of this century, the great victories that were won for risk reduction – in occupational health and safety, public health, air pollution, even environmental risks – were achieved initially by dealing with each of them separately.[21] There are many reasons for this, for example, in each case the skills for characterizing very diverse types of hazards and for identifying sometimes convoluted routes of exposure (that is, the toxicology and epidemiology) were still in their infancy. In addition, although governments had accepted responsibility for some types of hazards early on, such as food safety and infectious disease, other mandates – especially for environmental risks – were added much later, layer by layer, down to the present. Now there is no significant risk factor in the lives of the population for which government cannot be expected to be called upon for a policy response.

The shift in the pattern of dominant risk factors themselves, as noted earlier, comes into play here. Now with far broader sets of responsibilities for risk management, with ever-increasing public expectations for risk control, and faced with the iron law of exponentially mounting costs for incremental risk reduction, in principle governments should look at risk factors synthetically, that is, from the standpoint of comparative efficiencies in resource allocations for risk reduction opportunities. But by and large they are paralyzed, prevented from doing so both by the legacy of bureaucratic turf allotments and by their unwillingness to confront an apparently resistant public – who, to be fair, have not yet been introduced to the idea by their governments.[22]

The costs for reducing risks vary by many orders of magnitude. It is not uncommon for policy choices requiring risk reduction actions to be made in one area of government responsibility, while other areas under the jurisdiction of the same government are relatively neglected. The important costs are in lost opportunities for enhanced health benefits.[23] With every advance our society makes in collective risk reduction there are distinctive benefits to be reaped, both in terms of enhanced quality of life and longevity. But in most cases the marginal costs for risk reduction inexorably keep rising, so that with each passing day it becomes increasingly more important to allocate risk reduction resources wisely. This must mean, quite simply, that some public alarms would be addressed with dollars, while other concerns, however loudly expressed, would be answered only with explanations as to why the expenditures would not be made. Addressing this awkward state of affairs is such an enormous challenge for the government policy domain that it is unsurprising that no one wants to be first in line to do so. Sooner or later, however, it must and will be done.

Society's Relation to the Natural Environment and Its Resources

Earlier I referred to the mismatch of science and policy in the older model: Science usually couches its answers to cause-and-effect questions in 'maybe' (probability) terms, whereas policy demands a 'yes or no.' Over time the dilemma posed by this mismatch becomes increasingly onerous. This is because, with relentless population growth and resource-intensive lifestyles, we inevitably erode the margins of safety between our demands on natural resources and the recuperative powers (sustainable carrying capacity) of natural ecosystems. The disaster in the East Coast fishery is the most dramatic illustration, but quite apart from its singular meaning, it is also a metaphor for the more general category. A risk management approach informed by modern applied sciences is, in the case of (once) renewable resources such as fish or forests, designed to maximize long-term sustained resource yield indefinitely, but it can only do so by giving estimates, ranges, or scenarios with various probabilities attached to them.

At the same time, in a country such as Canada, where the state has a huge and continuing role in natural resource policy, pressure builds at various times to maximize short-term yield, which exploits the inevitable element of uncertainty in the probabilistic scenarios. In the West Coast forests (and now soon perhaps in its salmon fishery), as in the East Coast fishery, the modern science of yield management has been crushed at least in part by policies of overcutting and overfishing, as the necessarily cautious voices of at least some resource managers were drowned out by the loud cheers of all interest groups – politicians, business, and labour.

It is now generally recognized that the relentless growth of human populations and their economic systems challenges the sustainability of natural ecosystems – insofar as the capacity of those ecosystems to serve human interests is concerned.[24] Another way of phrasing this point is to say that humanity has eroded the once-substantial margin of error it had, *vis-à-vis* the natural environment, with respect to the extractive technologies it employs in the service of its needs. For example, the long-term fluctuations in the populations of North Atlantic cod and Pacific salmon species certainly respond to purely natural forces, such as food supply and ocean temperatures (Glavin, 1998), but almost certainly the technological power of the modern commercial fisheries also had a major part to play in their recent collapse. The margin of error in agriculture has to do with how much fertile land we can afford to convert to other uses, and also allow to erode and deteriorate, before the food supply is imperilled – no matter what manipulations of industrial technology or genetic engineering we can deploy. The debate about global climate change is based on the presumption that, in highly complex natural phenomena such as global weather patterns, a relatively small incremental impact from anthropogenic greenhouse gas emissions might be sufficient to trigger alterations in those patterns, which otherwise might not have occurred (at least within the same time frame), which can have adverse consequences of enormous scope for human societies.

Modern scientifically based risk management rests on the idea that we can derive significant new human benefits by becoming increasingly cunning in shaving the margin of error in our manipulations of nature. Chemotherapy regimes, for example, depend on fine-tuning the medicinal dose so that aggressive cancers can be destroyed without an unacceptable level of risk of collateral damage (killing the patient). In general, since everything we encounter in nature is toxic at some dose, but so many of those same things are also extremely useful to us, we try to find the dose at which some limited exposure is 'safe' while we use them.[25] But we will not tolerate now the level of human costs for our technological manipulations that obtained in the past, when, as mentioned earlier, we did the body counts retrospectively and adjusted the exposure limits after the data were in. At least, not on the same scale.

So with decreasing margins of error the risk *management* exercises – the inescapable responsibility of governments – demand much more exacting attention than was bestowed on them earlier. In part just because the assumptions, data quality, risk control options, and evaluative judgments brought to bear in risk management decision making are more complex and nuanced than they used to be, and become progressively more so with each passing year, they all must also be presented and defended to the citizenry, in a never-ending public dialogue. A truly daunting task, to be sure, but an equally inescapable duty – as yet unacknowledged.

The New Model: Science, Government, and the Public Dialogue on Risk Management

In the absence of this ongoing public risk dialogue we face obstacles to sensible risk management that simply cannot be overcome. One is what I call 'the tyranny of small and unfamiliar risks.' One of the surest findings in the risk perception research is that we underestimate the probability and consequences of familiar risks and overestimate those same dimensions for unfamiliar ones. The thought that miniscule doses of obscure chemicals called 'endocrine modulators' (EM) may be having devastating effects on reproductive and immune systems of both humans and wildlife is very worrying to many people now. There is a huge, worldwide research program under way to test the relevant hypotheses; in the meantime, while we are awaiting the results, the most responsible provisional conclusion might be that EM risk factors are *unlikely* to turn out to be as significant for us as are many others with which we are quite familiar.[26] But if, for the sake of argument, that is indeed the appropriate message from a risk manager, it cannot be just tossed off in a press release.

To be credible such a message must be accompanied by an elaborate translation of the current state of good science into publicly understandable terms; by a framework that relates possible outcomes from the scientific research programs to a set of feasible risk control options; and by a decision matrix in which various probabilities of adverse health effects are arrayed against achievable risk reduction scenarios and their costs. These are some of the nuts-and-bolts components in the foundations of sensible policy choices in risk management domains. And all of this must be done over and over again, because it is also unlikely that we will be in a position to make definitive judgments about EM risk management strategies for another ten, twenty, or more years.

To be sure, the most secure part of those foundations is the painstaking assembly of scientific research findings through which the nature of the hazards in question are characterized with precision. But for every risk domain that is now or may become controversial, the scientific research enterprise itself is clouded in suspicion – simply because basic and applied scientific research is the source of that technological innovation, past, present, and future, that gives rise to many risk factors. The rising level of public awareness of and participation in risk controversies means that there is simply no reasonable expectation that governments that are directly involved in doing or even promoting that research in terms of its economic development potential can be regarded as credible sources of information about it.[27]

Another obstacle is what I call 'premature policy closure,' and there is no better illustration of this one than the conduct to date of the public conversation on global climate change issues. Long before the public was afforded the opportunity to grasp the nature of the exceedingly complex risk factors at stake here, or the implications for their future lifestyles of the kind of greenhouse gas emissions reductions agreed to at Kyoto, they have been asked just to believe that the government that negotiated at Kyoto on their behalf knew what it was doing.[28] Public opinion polls show that two-thirds of Canadians apparently are convinced that Canada should have insisted on even further reductions for ourselves and other nations. Perhaps so, although it would have been nice if the pollsters had gone on to inquire what these same citizen respondents thought this would mean for their expected lifestyles.

Since we are unable as yet even to assign any reliable probability numbers to the potential adverse effects implicit in global climate change scenarios, would it not be kinder to the public for the government to engage citizens first in a comprehensive dialogue about the relevant risk factors, risk control options, and risk reduction scenarios? The Kyoto conference had been scheduled years in advance. Why did the impenetrable policy fog lift only briefly at the penultimate moment, when the hapless citizenry learned that we had to 'beat the Americans'?

Clearly we have a long way to go. But at least – so I have argued – we have the right map in hand that indicates the path we need to follow. If we do so we will forget about doing science in the public sector and concentrate instead on taking the steps that will enable governments to deliver credible risk management decisions to a public that will eventually be grateful for the gift.

A recent internal review of these matters within the federal government considered whether the science capacity now resident in government departments should be transferred to independent organizations; it answered in the negative, on the grounds that, if it were, research would become irrelevant to the policy process (Treasury Board, 1998). That incorrect answer is based on an elementary mistake in the analysis. The relevance of scientific research to the policy process in risk management is in no respect whatsoever a function of its organizational proximity. Rather, the continuing policy relevance of science and indeed its indispensability is grounded simply in the fact that governments must manage risks and that health and environmental risk management cannot be done without science. Period.

In the reference to 'independent organizations' we should have in mind primarily universities or other entities that draw on the independent expertise resident in universities.[29] One well-established way of organizing this expertise for risk-related issues is the convening of expert panels; this is done in many parts of the world but nowhere more systematically than in the United States, under procedures administered by the National Academy of Sciences and its related institutions (Leiss and Cairney, 1995; Smith, 1997). The Royal Society of Canada set up comparable procedures in 1995, and it has carried out expert panel reviews regarding asbestos, the future of the primate colony at Health Canada, health risks associated with radiofrequency fields, and in other areas (Royal Society of Canada, 1996, 1997, 1999).

Another outstanding recent example is the *Report of the Federal Environmental Assessment Panel on the Nuclear Fuel Waste Management and Disposal Concept* (Canadian Environmental Assessment Agency, 1998). This panel first generated a thorough and credible technical review using independent scientific experts, but it also argued that the waste management framework must meet 'social' as well as 'technical' criteria, and it explicitly included ethical and equity dimensions in the former. Its conclusions are: 'From a technical perspective, safety of the Atomic Energy of Canada Ltd. (AECL) concept has been on balance adequately demonstrated for a conceptual stage of development, but from a social perspective, it has not. As it stands, the AECL concept for deep geological disposal has not been demonstrated to have broad public support. The concept in its current form does not have the required level of acceptability to be adopted as Canada's approach for managing nuclear fuel wastes.' These conclusions are supported in the report by careful and sophisticated reasoning, making this arguably the most balanced environmental assessment document produced in Canada since the famous 1977 Royal Commission report by Thomas Berger on northern pipeline development. Its main recommendations have been accepted (Government of Canada, 1998).

To return to my main theme: Governments could still insist on cloaking in unnecessary secrecy the applied scientific studies they might purchase as contract research from universities under the new model. But they would run a number of risks in doing so. First, most senior researchers, who have the best access to unrestricted grant monies, would have nothing to do with them. Second, it would defeat the basic purpose, because it would not be responding to the changed nature of the challenges in risk management decision making, as outlined above. Under today's conditions the science itself should be thrown on the table for everyone to see as soon as it comes out of the peer-review process, every time, without exception. Even when a particular study result is subsequently found wanting and is superseded or withdrawn, the credibility of the entire scientific enterprise is enhanced. This credibility will also be transferred to the risk management process within which such science is utilized – if only the civil service and its political masters can be persuaded that the obsessive secretiveness which, they believe, serves them well does not do so here.

The other side of the coin is that the public will have to get used to the fact – through persistent persuasion from the new breed of risk managers – that *no* scientific study finding in itself, however dramatic or unexpected the results might be, can dictate a policy choice in and of itself. This message must be repeated ad nauseum, if necessary, until the disbelievers surrender.

The large scientific research establishments that still exist in governments represent an awkward intrusion of reality into the otherwise untroubled logic of this chapter. But, after all, we are told that we are at the cusp of a 'renewal' of the public service, which will be a long-term venture. So we should start now to change the relation in Canada between science and policy in the field of risk management and hope to complete the project over the next thirty years or so.

Notes

1 I have deliberately changed 'control' to 'management' with respect to the use of information by governments. There is far too much (attempted) information control, and far too little intelligent information management, in today's government practices. The need for confidentiality should be restricted to a tightly circumscribed sphere of 'advice to ministers' for policy formation and implementation. Most of the other policy-oriented information circulating in governments – so much of which is of dubious quality anyway – should be available to the public without the need to invoke access-to-information legislation, which is far too weak in Canada in any case.

2 My policy expertise is in the area of health and environmental risk management, and in this chapter I will be confining my illustrations to this area.

3 On 2 February 1998 the University of Ottawa hosted a panel discussion on the role of scientists in government. A discussant who was formerly a senior government scientist took the position that science differed from policy in that the former was based on 'fact,' whereas the latter includes a large dose of opinion. This is a surprising notion and, in my view, a most imprecise characterization of the relation between the two.

4 By the same token, this confidentiality should be relaxed when a period of policy development has been completed; the ministerial advisers would benefit from external, critical reviews of the advice they have been given by their experts.

5 Not to mention the exercise of police authority to inhibit spontaneous disclosures to the public.

6 I distinguish between the always evolving scientific characterization of hazards, on the one hand, and risk assessment on the other. The latter takes the former into account, along with exposure information, and applies complex models for estimating probabilities of harm. The very nature of risk assessment methods, and their direct bearing on the setting up of choices among risk management options, means that governments must have competent risk assessment expertise among their staff resources. But none of the basic science needs to be done in-house.

7 One of the main challenges undermines the very basis of the older model, which was based on expertise arrayed in watertight bureaucratic compartments: Today sensible risk management requires that we do relative risk comparisons across the domains that separate departments and agencies (food, transportation, chemicals, drugs, infectious disease, and so forth). More on this later.

8 The older model is still resilient today, but it is beginning to break down.

9 The same is true for industrially generated environmental hazards as they affect other species. The best study of the relation of science to policy in risk management under the older model is Salter, 1988, and for the more general relation between the two in Canada, see the early works of Bruce Doern.

10 See Chapter 4 in this volume by Millstone and Van Zwanenberg, which comes to a similar conclusion.

11 References to those replies and a criticism of this belief will be found towards the end of Chapter 11 by Lane in this volume; however, that chapter contains no rebuttal of the substantial case made by Hutchings et al.

12 Indeed it seems that the older model is unravelling completely in a very public fashion at the federal level. Newspaper coverage during the fall of 1998 was filled with stories of disarray among the science staff in the Health Protection Branch at Health Canada, including allegations of destruction of documents and suppression of evidence in the evaluation of rBST, a product to increase milk production in cows (Powell and Leiss, 1997, chap. 6; McIlroy, 1998; see also Chapter 7 by MacDonald in this volume).

13 At about the same time the Canadian regulatory system for pesticides at Agriculture Canada began voluntarily to transform its original, equally secretive process (where only industry sat down at the table with governments) and reach out to a broader set of stakeholders.

14 Governments will still protect the commercial confidentiality of scientific studies undertaken in support of new products in those cases where regulatory approval is required prior to marketing – primarily in the cases of pesticides and prescription drugs. But even in these cases good ways can be found to permit (under confidentiality rules) disinterested parties to review the scientific studies and report their findings to the public.

15 In the current case about health risks associated with the radio-frequency fields that are generated by the operation of wireless communications technologies (Royal Society, 1999), national governments sell to industry the permits to construct the wireless networks, getting a nice financial windfall in the process. These same governments are the risk regulators who set the exposure limits for those fields. It is no longer acceptable for them to conduct in secret the evaluations of the scientific studies on which the health risk assessments are made. It would be better still if they were to offload completely – to credible independent bodies – the making of those evaluations.

16 As a general rule, the type of risk factors that are most significant for the average person in industrial societies has shifted, over the course of the preceding 150 years, from occupational and public health domains to that of individual lifestyle choices. (It has also shifted because of the huge rise in average income or standard of living.) This shift is so difficult and complex a matter for societal intervention, however, that an adequate exposition of it cannot be undertaken here.

17 See also the article on asbestos and lung cancer by three Canadian scientists (Camus, 1998), which says that the U.S. EPA's risk assessment methodology overstates the risk of lung cancer for some populations by a factor of 10 – a contention that was not at all well received by some of the best-known experts in the United States.

18 The same is true for another notorious group of substances, PCBs (Powell and Leiss, 1997, chap. 8).

19 Frustrating because one is never done: Dioxins are now regulated at the picogram (parts per trillion) level and detected at even lower (nanogram) levels; but if there were to be a campaign launched to 'virtually eliminate' dioxins at the nanogram level, those compounds would still be among us, somewhere, to be detected and virtually eliminated once again, in an endless hunt for the last molecule on earth.

20 During the recent internal federal government discussions of the role of science in the public sector, the idea of a government-wide 'science adviser' position was floated; this notion quickly floundered on the shoals of departmental autonomy.

21 Even the first generation of modern chemical pesticides developed during the 1940s, which were later deemed to engender unacceptable levels of risk, represented a huge advance over the compounds they replaced, such as arsenic.

22 In government departments, which are responsible for sets of risk factors that are both extensive and varied in nature, such as food-borne pathogens or industrial chemicals, the question about efficiency in the allocation of resources is also an internal matter.

23 In principle it might be possible to calculate the lost health benefits to Canadians that resulted, e.g., from the fact that, within a specific span of time, the federal minister of environment chose to focus on MMT rather than on sulphur in gasoline. There are many who will not like the implications of this example, for quite different reasons, but such is the nature of risk management.

24 Natural ecosystems are always changing irrespective of human impacts. The reference here is to the type of impacts implied in the sustainable development concept – namely, those that might impair fatally the ability of humans to create a desirable quality of life indefinitely into the future.

25 The word 'safe' is the simple expression for the more accurate phrase, 'not an unacceptable probability of harm.'

26 Of course one has the solemn duty to be as clear and careful as is humanly possible in carrying out responsible risk communication: The word 'unlikely' indicates that *every* risk factor is a matter of probabilities and ranges of uncertainties. This must be stated openly and repeatedly. The statements 'There is no risk' and 'The public is perfectly safe' must be banished from our lexicon.

27 The best example is the federal government's 'national biotechnology strategy.' Why anyone thinks that the same government that is supposed

to regulate dispassionately the relevant risks should become a huckster for the industry is a profound mystery – especially when it is abundantly clear that private industry is doing a perfectly adequate job of promotion all by itself. The authors of this mistake will regret doing so when it is too late to repair the damage.

28 There is some as yet unspecifiable probability that the Canadian government's risk reduction strategy, implied in its commitments at Kyoto, will turn out to have been exactly the right response to the nature of the relevant risk factors; however, if it comes to pass this would be a purely accidental phenomenon. The nasty exchanges among some scientists in this debate are all the more reason for governments to 'let it all hang out' so far as the science is concerned. Some of the oil industry majors have been rather bull-headed on the issue, while others have been calmer and more reasonable, which is helpful. And some scientists themselves seem to have fallen victim to others' political agendas. A brief glimpse into this big story is contained in Strauss, 1998.

29 The perceived conflict of interest that governments have with respect to risk-relevant science is not dissolved by creating new crown agencies that have presidents rather than deputy ministers. There may be many administrative advantages to be realized from such creations, but no one will believe, nor should they, that they are qualitatively different from government departments.

References

Camus, Michel, J. Siemiatycki, and B. Meek. (1998). 'Nonoccupational Exposure to Chrysotile Asbestos and the Risk of Lung Cancer.' *New England Journal of Medicine*, 338(22): 1565.

Canadian Environmental Assessment Agency. (1998). 'Nuclear Fuel Waste Management and Disposal Concept: Report of the Nuclear Fuel Waste Management and Disposal Concept Environmental Assessment Panel.' Ottawa: February. http://www.ceaa.gc.ca/panels/nuclear/reports/report_e.htm

Glavin, Terry. (1998). 'Salmon's Sea Change.' *Globe and Mail*, 18 July, D1.

Government of Canada. (1998). 'Government of Canada Response to Recommendations of the Nuclear Fuel Waste Management and Disposal Concept Environmental Assessment Panel.' Ottawa: author.

Hill, Stephen, and William Leiss. (1999). 'MMT, A Risk Management Masquerade.' Unpublished paper, Faculty of Management, University of Calgary. September.

Hutchings, J.A. (1997). 'Presentation to the House of Commons Standing Committee on Fisheries.' 4 December.

Hutchings, J.A., C. Walters, and R.L. Haedrich. (1997). 'Is Scientific Inquiry Incompatible with Government Information Control?' *Canadian Journal of Fisheries and Aquatic Sciences*, 54: 1198–1348.

Kavlock, Robert, and Gerald Ankley. (1996). 'A Perspective on the Risk Assessment Process for Endocrine-Disruptive Effects on Wildlife and Human Health.' *Risk Analysis*, 16(6): 731–40.

Leiss, William. (1995). '"Down and Dirty": The Use and Abuse of Public Trust in Risk Communication.' *Risk Analysis*, 15(6): 685.

– (1998). 'The Internet as a Public Information Resource: A Canadian Controversy over Radio-Frequency Fields as a Case Study.' Paper presented for delivery at the International Seminar on EMF Risk Perception and Communication, sponsored by WHO, Ottawa, September.

Leiss, William, and John Cairney (1995). 'Feasibility Study on Expert Panels: Credibility in Risk-Based Decision Making.' Working Paper 95–3, Environmental Policy Unit, Queen's University, October.

Leiss, William, and Christina Chociolko. (1994). *Risk and Responsibility.* Montreal: McGill-Queen's University Press.

McCarthy, Shawn (1998a). 'Threat of NAFTA Case Kills Canada's MMT Ban.' *Globe and Mail*, 20 July, A1.

– (1998b). 'Gas War: The Fall and Rise of MMT.' *Globe and Mail*, 24 July, A1.

McIlroy, Anne. (1998). 'Approval for Bovine Growth Hormone Hits Roadblocks.' *Globe and Mail*, 4 December, A4.

Powell, Douglas, and William Leiss. (1997). *Mad Cows and Mother's Milk: The Perils of Poor Risk Communication.* Montreal: McGill-Queen's University Press.

Royal Society of Canada. (1996). *A Review of the INSERM Report on the Health Effects of Exposure to Asbestos.* Ottawa: author.

– (1997). *Recommendations for the Disposition of the Health Canada Primate Colony.* Ottawa: author.

– (1999). Report on Potential Health Risks of Radio-Frequency Fields from Wireless Telecommunications Devices.' http://www.rsc.ca/english/Rfreport.html

Salter, Liora. (1988). *Mandated Science.* Boston: Kluwer.

Smith, Willie. (1997). 'Review of Expert Panels for Provision of Scientific and Technological Advice for Development of Public Policy.' Auckland, NZ: Ministry of Research, Science and Technology.

Strauss, Stephen. (1998). 'Discrepancy Cools Down Climate Debate.' *Globe and Mail*, 13 August, A3.

Treasury Board Secretariat, Research and Analysis, Public Affairs. (1998). 'Getting Science Right in the Public Sector (Working Draft).' Ottawa: author.

VanNijnatten, Debora, W. Leiss, and P. Hodson. (1997). 'Environment's X-File: Pulp Mill Effluent Regulation in Canada.' Working Paper 97–1, Environmental Policy Unit, Queen's University, September.

4 Bovine Spongiform Encephalopathy (Mad Cow Disease): Lessons for Public Policy

ERIK MILLSTONE and PATRICK VAN ZWANENBERG

The bovine spongiform encephalopathy (BSE) saga is generally, and rightly, regarded as having constituted the largest single failure in U.K. public policy since the Suez Crisis of 1956. It almost certainly did more damage to Britain's public finances, and to the United Kingdom's international reputation and relationships than did the perfidious events of 1956. That fact alone might suggest that an account of BSE could interest policy analysts in other countries, but when seen from a North American perspective two issues come into particularly sharp focus. First, an analysis of the history of BSE policy making, and its consequences, might cast some light on the extent to which a market-based approach could contribute to regulatory policy making. Second, it might highlight some important features of the role that scientific evidence and expertise can, and cannot, play in the policy-making process.

This chapter therefore, first, provides a description and analysis of the history of BSE from the early 1980s to the late 1990s, as an example of public food-safety policy making, and, second, highlights the implications of that analysis for two of the central themes of this book, namely, that policy can and should be based on sound science and the increasingly made suggestion that science-based regulatory functions might be better organized if they were to become more market based, and less a matter of command and control.

The BSE Saga: Crisis and Consequences

Preamble

The BSE crisis that began in the United Kingdom on 20 March 1996 represented the culmination of a seventeen-year-long saga. The events which led to that crisis can, however, be traced back to policies and decisions which were set and taken during the early years of the Conservative party's eighteen years of government (1979–83, 1983–7, 1987–92, and 1992–7), but which can also be attributed, in large measure, to key structural characteristics of Britain's policy-making system. While the British government did not make every one of the mistakes it might have made, it made every available *type* of mistake.

The analysis we shall be providing, therefore, will in part take the form of a catalogue of errors; it will not be an exhaustive list but it will indicate the kinds of mistakes made and the scale of the government's follies. The task of assembling all the evidence with which to document each and every mistake would be too great for this chapter. Indeed, Tony Blair has allowed Lord Justice Philips and his well-staffed public inquiry team eighteen months before a report is expected; and you can already fill numerous diskettes by downloading text files of statements, evidence, and cross-examination, from the public inquiry's website (The BSE Inquiry). In this context, we shall only be able to highlight a few of the most important mistakes, and we will outline those follies in a sequence that will be partly chronological and partly analytical. But first a brief technical summary is provided.

A Brief Technical Summary

The most reliable evidence suggests that the first animal that was diagnosed officially with symptoms of BSE became ill in (or shortly before) 1985. The Central Veterinary Laboratory (CVL) of the U.K. Ministry of Agriculture, Fisheries and Food (MAFF) learned of the occurrence of an unusual disease later that year and officially acknowledged BSE to be a new disease in November of 1986.

BSE is primarily a disease of cattle, although it has also afflicted, for example, domestic cats, zoo cats, and various species of antelope that were fed cattle rations or cattle remains. BSE is a member of a class of diseases known as 'transmissible spongiform encephalopathies,' or TSEs. TSEs are untreatable and invariably fatal. Pathological examination of animals and humans who have died from TSEs reveals characteristic features. Their brains exhibit spongy structures, with vacant spaces, while the tissue that remains contains clusters of aberrant material known as plaques consisting of an abnormal type of protein known as a 'prion.' The most widely held theory about the cause of TSEs is that these prions or rogue proteins are the pathogenic agents.

Not all prions are pathogenic. There is evidence that prions are normal constituents of healthy tissue. The theory is that prions become pathogenic only once their structural conformations have been transformed, but that once aberrant proteins have developed, they can trigger similar transformations in the structural conformations of otherwise innocuous molecules, producing a cascade effect, until the aberrant proteins overwhelm the victims' brains. That plausible theory has, however, the disadvantage that it is profoundly inconsistent with orthodox molecular biology. Since prions are, as far as we can tell, proteins devoid of any DNA, this would entail that DNA is not essential for all biological reproduction – that a pathogenic agent can reproduce without possessing any DNA. Although the prion (or 'protein only') hypothesis is the dominant explanatory model, it is not the only theory. Other competing theories suggest that the pathogenic agents might be so-called slow viruses. Perhaps not surprisingly that approach is favoured mainly by virologists. The most familiar TSE is scrapie, which afflicts sheep, but there are also human TSEs such as Creutzfeld-Jakob disease (CJD).

It is widely believed that the BSE pathogen is found in its most concentrated form in brain and nervous tissue, but it is not necessarily confined to those tissues. When cattle are incubating the pathogen we do not know whether or not some tissues are pathogen free. It may be that the pathogen is confined exclusively to some tissues, or it may be that all and any tissue will contain some of the pathogenic agent, though at varying concentrations. That is a topic on which we are profoundly ignorant, but it is enormously important for public health, for public policy, and for the meat trade.

Beliefs about the identity of the BSE pathogen are speculative, but we do possess some reliable information about some of the characteristics of TSE pathogens. We know that TSE pathogens are remarkably tough and extremely hard to destroy. Several unfortunate individuals have been inadvertently contaminated with Creutzfeld-Jakob disease after having been operated upon with surgical instruments that had previously been used on patients infected with CJD, despite those instruments having been thoroughly autoclaved (Ironside, 1996).

When BSE was first drawn to the attention of the British government's scientists at the CVL, a team of veterinary epidemiologists did some excellent detective work which indicated that the most probable route of transmission was through contaminated feed, and the evidence suggested that the pathogen managed to enter and survive the animals' feed chain as a consequence of changes that had taken place in the rendering industry.

In terms of the symptoms of diseased animals and post-mortem pathology, BSE in cattle closely resembles scrapie in sheep – a TSE which is endemic in British flocks, and has been for several hundred years. The CVL team concluded that the BSE pathogen derives from the scrapie pathogen and that changes in the rendering process had allowed pathogenic material, which had previously been de-activated, to survive (Wilesmith et al., 1988). The remains of both sheep and cattle were routinely rendered down, and the animal protein residue from the rendering process (known as meat and bonemeal, or MBM) was routinely incorporated into animal feedstuffs. Some scientists have more recently suggested that BSE might not have derived from scrapie, but that a spontaneous case of a sporadic TSE occurred in cattle (just as sporadic CJD occurs in humans) and that the infected animals were then recycled though the rendering plants and the animal food chain, reproducing and amplifying the disease.

Traditionally, rendering was accomplished using a technology based on a batch process that involved loading the material into a retort, and then heating it thoroughly. There were then several methods for separating the resulting fat from the protein residue. One of the traditional methods for separating fat from MBM involved the use of organic solvents such as cyclohexane. During a period which began in the mid-1970s and which continued into the mid-1980s, a wave of technical change transformed the U.K. rendering industry. The batch processing plant was replaced with continuous flow-process equipment, and the use of organic solvents was phased out. Flow processes substantially raised the through-put of the rendering plants, but the material was not heated to such high temperatures, and the temperatures that were reached were not maintained for such long periods. The evidence strongly suggests that changes in rendering technology enabled the pathogenic agent(s) responsible for BSE to survive the process while it (or they) had not been able to do so when the previous methods had been used.

In 1986 the British government enthusiastically embraced the hypothesis that BSE derived from scrapie, and it has remained wedded to that explanation ever since because it enabled the government to provide a reassuring and optimistic narrative along the following lines: 'BSE comes from scrapie. It will behave (we hope, in most ways) just like scrapie. Britons have been eating sheep meat from scrapie-infected flocks for at least 200 years, and there is no evidence that it has caused any human TSE.' The obvious counter to that argument is: 'Scrapie had never previously crossed the species barrier to cattle, and the fact that it has crossed once suggests that it might cross again.' That rejoinder was vigorously expressed by several critics of government policy. In the event, it emerged that BSE was able to *passage* naturally into several other species, including domestic cats, and several unfortunate non-indigenous species kept at British zoos that received cattle rations, and experimentally into mice, pigs, marmosets, and mink. In the spring of 1996 it emerged that, despite repeated assertions to the contrary, humans had succumbed to a new variant of CJD (nv-CJD), almost certainly as a consequence of having consumed BSE-contaminated foodstuffs.

BSE Policy: A Taxonomy and Chronological Catalogue of Policy Failures

A Failure to Regulate Process Conditions in the Rendering Industry

The most crucial type of mistake was the repeated failure of the British government to set adequate regulations. If the policy had been a genuinely precautionary one, and the central objective had been to protect public health from any hazard which exposure to the BSE pathogen might cause, then the government should have set a strict framework of regulations designed to eradicate, as far as possible, the BSE pathogen (and pathogens from other TSEs) from the food supply to both people and animals. At the same time it would also have been investing in scientific research designed to diminish, as rapidly as possible, the crucial scientific uncertainties.

The problem with that policy, as seen from the perspective of the U.K. government, was that there was no proof that BSE could cause CJD in humans, and that if it had taken such steps its statements and actions would, in the short term at any rate, have seriously undermined confidence in the safety of British beef. The government believed that if it followed that policy, consumer confidence and demand for British beef would have declined abruptly and that the profitability of most farming and the meat industry would have declined concomitantly. Moreover, if the government had tried to eradicate BSE and TSE pathogens from the food supply it would also have necessitated increasing public expenditure, at least in the short run.

The government would have been expected to have provided farmers and traders with financial compensation for much of their losses, until stability had been re-established in the marketplace.

The U.K. government gambled (with public health and public money) that the risks to human health from BSE-contaminated food were vanishingly slight. Their political judgment was that the investment of public resources to eliminate the pathogen from the food supply would be disproportionate to any foreseeable benefit. The government therefore chose to assert repeatedly that all materials derived from U.K. herds were entirely safe, despite the fact that evidence to sustain their position did not exist and that their expert advisers made sure that policy makers knew that (Dorrell, 1995).

To be (a little bit) on the safe side they did establish a regulatory regime that set some restrictions. Those regulations governed, for example, the composition of animal feedstuffs, the materials that should not enter the human food supply, and the disposal of the contaminated animal remains. The U.K. government's regulatory regime was not, however, designed to eradicate the BSE pathogen. It was designed to provide the customers of the British beef and dairy industries, both in the United Kingdom and overseas, with sufficient confidence in the safety of their products that they continued to purchase them, at the lowest possible cost to both the exchequer and the food industry.

Through a multistage process, the details of which are being disclosed at the public inquiry chaired by Lord Justice Philips, the British government took steps to remove from the food supply much of the most BSE-contaminated materials, but the policy was never one of eradicating TSE pathogens from the herds or from the food supply. The policy of the government was to subordinate consumer protection in favour of supporting the private sector and its short-term market interests and to avoid increasing public expenditure. The government's policy was, in that sense, a market-oriented policy.

It was not, however, quite that simple, because while the U.K. government could initially provide the reassuring narrative that 'BSE comes from scrapie and is essentially no different from scrapie,' the scientific wishful thinking upon which that narrative was constructed was always fragile, and it kept unravelling as new evidence emerged. For example, transmission experiments with rodents, published in 1987, indicated that it was impossible to predict what the properties of a given strain of scrapie would be once it had *passaged* to another species (Kimberlin, et al., 1987; Kimberlin, 1998). Furthermore, if it was assumed that the BSE pathogen would behave just like the scrapie agent, then it would follow that BSE would be transmissible both vertically from cow to calf, as scrapie is from ewe to lamb, and horizontally within herds, but that conclusion contradicted the British government's chosen narrative. The government initially claimed, and continued to claim, that while the risks from the BSE agent to human health were remote (on the basis of the analogy with scrapie), there would also be no vertical or horizontal transmission between cattle (unlike with scrapie).

The official narrative repeatedly unravelled between 1988 and 1996. It did so partly as a consequence of its own internal contradictions, but mainly because evidence kept emerging indicating that BSE was significantly different from scrapie. For example, the BSE pathogen can infect cats but not hamsters, whereas with the scrapie pathogen the reverse applies, and studies conducted in the United States have indicated that cows experimentally infected with scrapie do not contract BSE. In due course, BSE-derived TSEs were found in cats, mink, pigs, mice, monkeys, ostrich, and antelope.

When the 1996 crisis broke, the government's narrative had completely disintegrated. The most reassuring account that the British government could then offer was to accept that BSE-contaminated material had entered the food supply, and probably had made a few people very ill, but that contamination had taken place almost entirely prior to 1989, from which time a regulatory regime had been in place and was being strengthened, which meant that all British beef and dairy products were then entirely safe, even if they may not have been so eight years earlier.

Protecting Public Health – a Regulatory Template

If U.K. public policy had been primarily about the protection of public health, then the government would have established a regulatory regime which would, at least, have required the slaughter of all animals that had been exposed to feedstuffs known, or suspected, to have been contaminated with TSE pathogens. All materials from those slaughtered animals should then have been excluded from the food chain for all species. The government would also have needed to identify, isolate, and destroy all animal feeds known to be, or suspected of being, contaminated. It would also have decontaminated all feed chains, including storage and delivery vessels. Steps should also have been taken to ensure that farmers had no incentive to conceal from public officials any suspicion that their animals might be incubating or exhibiting BSE or scrapie. Once the use of rendered animal remains in feedstuffs ceased, the government should have been trying to identify and utilize safe means for their disposal.

British policy has never approximated that template. It is not that the government failed even to contemplate such actions, rather what happened was that Cabinet ministers and senior civil servants considered, discussed, but then rejected those courses of action because their political judgment was that policy was first and foremost (notwithstanding their rhetoric to the contrary) designed to maintain consumer confidence and market conditions, while imposing the least draconian regime possible on the relevant industries and costing the exchequer as little as possible.

As the BSE saga unfolded, and as the government's reassuring narratives unravelled, consumer confidence required that the government was seen to be taking some action, and consequently proposals marginally to tighten regulations emerged rather like thinly sliced salami. On most occasions ministers tried to represent regulatory reforms as being, on the one hand, justified solely by reference to considerations of a scientific nature, while at the same time they were appropriate to reassure the public that the food supply was entirely and completely safe. Occasionally, exasperated officials in closed meetings would argue that the regulations were determined solely by political considerations and were not supported by scientific considerations, but only by presuming that BSE posed no risk whatsoever to human health (Bradley, 1990; European Parliament, 1997: 10, par. 4). When compared with the benchmark of acting to protect public health, each of the government's regulatory decisions can be seen, and were even then widely seen, as providing too little too late.

The Chronology of Regulatory Policy Making

The first BSE-specific mistake made in the United Kingdom occurred when the incoming Conservative government, under Margaret Thatcher, decided not to implement a set of draft regulations to control the rendering industry. In a report entitled *Agriculture and Pollution*, published in September 1979, the Royal Commission on Environmental Pollution (RCEP) discussed the possibility that changes to the technology of rendering might entail that pathogens that previously had not been able to survive the more severe processing methods might be able to survive the newer and less severe processes (Royal Commission on Environmental Pollution, 1979). The RCEP said: 'The major problem encountered in this recycling process is the risk of transmitting disease-bearing pathogens to stock and thence to humans' (ibid.: 149–50, par. 5.63). In the government's defence, some commentators have suggested that that comment was intended to refer only to *salmonella* and other familiar bacteria, not to pathogens such as those responsible for scrapie or BSE. That interpretation, however, is hard to sustain (ibid.: 150, par. 5.63). In response to the RCEP, the Labour government, under James Callaghan, had instructed civil servants in the Ministry of Agriculture, Fisheries and Food to draft regulations setting minimum standards on process conditions in the rendering industry. Labour ministers decided to impose those regulations, but before that decision could be implemented the 1979 general election occurred, and the new Conservative government took a different approach.

Once ministers had taken up office, their attention was drawn to the warning and advice that the RCEP had provided, and the previously drafted regulations were presented to ministers. Ministers chose to disregard the RCEP's warning and decided not to implement those regulations. Instead, ministers decided to 'leave it to the market.' On 16 April 1980, ministers issued proposals for a Protein Processing Order, but those regulations did not set restrictions on conditions within the rendering process. A government statement explained: The 'proposals reflect the wish of Ministers that in the *present economic climate* the *industry should itself determine how best to produce a high-quality product*, and that the role of Government should be restricted to prescribing a standard for the product and to enforcing observance of that standard' (emphases added; Barclay, 1996: 8).

Ministers took the view that the draft regulations were unnecessarily burdensome and that an optimal solution might be achieved by allowing firms to make their own decisions concerning process conditions and by relying on such discipline as the market could provide. Consequently, they did set some relatively weak restrictions on the output of the rendering industry, supposedly to reduce bacterial contamination, but no restrictions were set on the process with which that output was generated.

A strong case can be made for the thesis that if the regulations governing the conditions in rendering plants that had previously been

accepted by Labour ministers had been established by their succes-
sors, and if they had been fully complied with, then BSE might never
have arisen. If the new ministers had established such a regime, and if
as a consequence BSE had never emerged, then some protagonists
could have argued that the regulators must have imposed unnecessary restraints on corporate freedom, and their choice of technology.
They could have argued that an overrestrictive regime had been established without sufficient scientific evidence indicating that it was necessary. Subsequent events, however, demonstrate the fragility of such
opportunistic arguments.

It might now be interesting to establish experimentally whether or
not implementing the draft regulations would have prevented the development of BSE. That question could have been settled experimentally before now had the government chosen to initiate a suitable
series of experiments. If two groups of cattle were kept in identical
conditions, and if both had received a feed containing MBM derived
from sheep carcasses contaminated with scrapie but rendered by
different methods, one of which did, and the other of which did
not, comply with the regulations drafted at the end of the 1970s,
we might get a clear answer. Unfortunately, that is one line of
research that the British government chose not to fund. (Other
examples will be discussed later.)

Once animals started to fall ill and a new disease was identified,
ministers eventually, though reluctantly, started to set regulations; the
earliest regulatory action was not taken until nineteen months after
ministers were first told that the disease had emerged. The regulations
were repeatedly revised, and on each occasion those revisions represented a marginal tightening of the controls. All the regulatory revisions were reactions to problems, occasioned by the emergence of
information or evidence that undermined the government's reassuring narrative. None of the regulatory amendments can be counted as
having been anticipatory – they were all reactive.

When BSE first emerged, the private sector in the form of farmers,
the vets whom they employed, and those managing the meat trade
did not know how to cope with this disease, nor what risks it posed to
animals, farm workers, public health, or the food industry. The only
institution with any effective responsibility for responding to BSE was
the government. Only the government could take and exercise the
relevant powers, and only it could mobilize the scientific resources
needed to address the problem. BSE presented scientific problems that

the private sector was neither capable of addressing, nor had any incentive to address. The failure of the government in those regards was therefore crucial.

Regulating the Animal Feed Chain

The first set of regulations imposed by the British government was introduced on 14 June 1988 and came into force in August of that year (the Bovine Spongiform Encephalopathy Order of 1988). That first piece of legislation was a ruminant feed ban which required only that ruminant protein should no longer be incorporated into feed for ruminants (that is, cattle, sheep, and deer). Its use in feed for other species remained lawful. Since the CVL team had told ministers at the end of 1987 that BSE had occurred because the animal feed chain was contaminated, one might ask why they waited until the following summer before introducing any regulatory controls.

When the government initially announced the regulation, ministers suggested that it would be temporary, and last only until December of that year, while a (presumably rather quick) review of rendering took place. A period of two months was also allowed between the time at which the regulations were announced and the time at which they came into force, so as to allow renderers to clear existing stocks of ruminant feed (Lawrence, 1998: 9, par. 47). Furthermore, the regulation did not apply to ruminant feed destined for export, even though civil servants expected the domestic ban to divert ruminant feedstuffs overseas (ibid.: 24, par. 135). Those regulations were subsequently amended at least six times.

At the end of 1988 the duration of the ruminant feed ban was extended (under pressure from scientific advisers) and its scope enlarged to include prohibitions on the use of milk from cows suspected of having BSE, although their milk could still be used to feed calves from infected cows. It was not until January 1989 that the provisions of the ruminant feed ban were applied to Northern Ireland. It was not until September 1990 that MAFF banned the use of what came to be known as specified bovine offals (or SBOs) from the feed chain of all mammalian and four-legged animals after evidence emerged showing that BSE had been transmitted to pigs under experimental conditions. Even then some potentially contaminated materials were allowed to remain in feedstuffs intended for poultry. Initially the banned SBOs were defined as including the brain, spinal cord, spleen, thymus, tonsils, and intestines from sheep and cattle that were more than six months old. Four years later, in November 1994, ministers widened the scope of the SBO regulations to cover thymus and intestines from animals killed between the ages of two and six months.

When in 1996 the BSE crisis eventually erupted, a ban was placed on the incorporation of all mammalian MBM from the food supply of all farm animals, irrespective of whether or not they were ruminants. It was, moreover, not until the summer of 1996 that an attempt was made to clean out and de-contaminate the animal feed chain. It appears that, during the preceding ten years, old cattle feed remaining in feed hoppers had repeatedly contaminated the newer feed, and also that non-ruminant feed had contaminated feed for ruminants.

Regulating the Human Food Supply

In the early stages of the saga, MAFF sought advice only from the experts at the CVL, but several of the CVL's veterinary experts were uncomfortable with this arrangement because as veterinarians they emphasized that they were not adequately qualified or equipped to make informed judgments about the risks to human health that BSE might pose. At the insistence of officials, including staff at the CVL and the Department of Health's chief medical officer, MAFF decided in the spring of 1988 to convene what they insisted on referring to as an 'independent' expert advisory committee under the chairmanship of Professor Richard Southwood.

The Southwood Committee was formed in April 1988 and was asked to advise on 'any possible hazard' that BSE might pose to human health. In 1996, after the crisis had erupted, it emerged that the members of the committee had wanted to call in 1988 for a complete ban on the use of all cattle brains in the human food supply. In 1996 Southwood acknowledged that his committee had failed publicly to issue the advice that they had thought prudent because they knew it would be politically unwelcome to the government. Southwood explained: 'We felt it was a no-goer. They [MAFF] already thought our proposals were pretty revolutionary' (Pearce, 1996). The scientists on the Southwood Committee therefore allowed their supposedly scientific judgment to be undermined by political pressure from ministers. A ban on selected offals was introduced in 1989, but even then ministers claimed that they agreed with the committee that the action was not necessary on scientific grounds, but was required rather to reassure the public on political grounds (House of Commons Agriculture Committee, 1990; Meldrum, 1989).

In August 1988 MAFF introduced regulations making BSE a 'notifiable' disease, requiring the compulsory slaughter and destruction of animals affected with BSE. That only meant, however, that animals exhibiting conspicuous clinical symptoms of BSE would have been slaughtered and excluded from the food chain. It did not require the slaughter, or exclusion from the food chain, of all the animals that had received feed known, or believed, to have been contaminated with the BSE pathogen; it only applied to those animals at a late stage in the development of the disease that were overtly ill. Animals that were incubating the disease, but that had not yet reached the stage at which symptoms became overt, were still allowed to enter the food supply. The policy was therefore not about eradicating contaminated material, just about reducing the quantities of pathogenic material being consumed.

When ministers first decided that farmers were to be required to hand over to the government all cattle showing overt symptoms of BSE, they announced that farmers would be compensated, but that they would receive only 50 per cent of the value the animals would have fetched had they been healthy. That decision was vigorously opposed by farmers, vets, and public health professionals, including the government's chief medical officer (Metters, 1998).

Several of the government's advisers argued that providing only 50 per cent gave farmers a strong disincentive to report BSE cases. The government's chief veterinary officer, Keith Meldrum, suggested that full compensation would discourage good husbandry, but that was unconvincing because animals that were well cared for were no less vulnerable to BSE than those kept less well. One retired former MAFF chief scientist has claimed that MAFF had wanted to give farmers 100 per cent compensation, but that the Treasury vetoed it, even though MAFF had the evidence from previous crises to show that offering less than full compensation would result in underreporting. In the event, ministers had to relent, and in February 1990 they agreed to provide compensation at the full market rate. When 100 per cent compensation was introduced, on 14 February 1990, the numbers of animals notified doubled from one week to the next. As late as May 1990 the British government's policy was still that decisions about breeding from offspring of affected cows should be left to farmers and vets and need not be subject to regulation (House of Commons Agriculture and Health Select Committees, 1996: 3).

Using several plausible assumptions, an estimated 446,000 infected animals entered the human food chain before the specified bovine offal ban at the end of 1989, and approximately 283,000 between 1990 and 1995 (Anderson et al., 1996). It was estimated that almost 750,000 BSE-infected animals entered the U.K.'s food supply (ibid.) – which corresponds to just over 80 per cent of all those that are suspected of having carried the infection. It is difficult to reconcile those figures with the claim of the British government that they acted promptly and properly to protect public health.

MAFF's refusal to adopt a precautionary approach is evident from numerous official statements. For example, according to the science correspondent of the *Times*, Meldrum had suggested in 1990 'that the elimination of the disease might take some years and eventually require tougher control measures. He [Meldrum] said he would not be surprised if research now [i.e., in 1990] under way showed that BSE could be transmitted from cattle to their calves, in the same way that the related brain disease, scrapie, can be inherited in sheep. Mr Meldrum also insisted that British beef was safe, and that the Government's measures were more than adequate to remove what was "probably a zero risk" to consumers ... "There are so many unknowns with BSE that research is absolutely crucial, and we must demonstrate without any doubt that BSE behaves exactly the same way in cattle that it does in sheep and goats. We believe it does; we have now to demonstrate that it does"' (Prentice, 1990: 7). In relation to research into the possibility of vertical transmission of BSE in cattle, Meldrum remarked: 'It would be bad news if it did, because it would show that more cattle have been exposed, not from eating meat or bone meal, but from their mothers. We would have to consider *then* adapting our own control programme' (ibid.). Those quotations indicate that MAFF was not following a precautionary approach, and also display MAFF's view of the character and function of scientific research.

MAFF civil servants have disclosed that when the regulations on SBOs were first established, no systematic risk analysis was conducted. It was, even in those days, commonplace for MAFF officials to talk of the importance of conducting so-called HACCPs or 'hazard analysis and critical control point assessments.' In the event, nothing resembling a HACCP approach was taken, but instead the regulations were almost 'scribbled on the back of an envelope' during a discussion about what could be achieved at lowest costs and with least disruption. For example, the liver had been shown to be infective for several TSEs, in every species tested except cattle, but it was not included in the SBO restrictions (Dealler, 1996).

As the Institute of Environmental Health Officers asked in February 1990: 'If the spinal cord is deemed as SBO and is to be removed from the carcass, should not the tail, from which it is almost impossible to remove the spinal cord, be regarded as prohibited offal? Why also are the main nerves of the carcass not included?' (Corbally, 1990). Those tissues selected for inclusion on the list of SBOs were chosen on the assumption that only they harboured the infectious agent; but, perhaps coincidentally, they were also the offals of lowest commercial value. It was not until 1991 that it became unlawful to spread SBOs on agricultural land (House of Commons Agriculture and Health Select Committees, 1996: 4).

The regulations therefore fell far short of what would have been appropriate to protect public health. Regulatory developments constituted a succession of inadequate and unconvincing public relations exercises, but then as Meldrum explained in 1989 to the European Community's Standing Veterinary Committee, U.K. public policy was 'more an issue of consumer confidence than consumer protection' (European Parliament, 1997: 10, par. 4).

The Failure to Enforce the Regulations That Had Been Set

The next major category of mistakes made by the British authorities was their repeated failure to enforce those regulations that had been set. When the 1996 BSE crisis erupted, the chief medical officer insisted that new variant Creutzfeld-Jakob disease (nv-CJD) had arisen only because the regulations had not been enforced. It is clear why that line of analysis might have been attractive, because it absolved his department from any blame and avoided the question of whether the regulations would have been sufficient had they been fully enforced (Meikle, 1998). Nonetheless, the failure to enforce was important, and almost certainly accounts for a significant proportion of the cases of BSE that occurred in cattle born after the animal feeding regulations were established.

As early as 1990 MAFF officials were told in detail about numerous failures to observe the SBO regulations in particular in abattoirs, but also in rendering plants. A letter dated 1 February 1990 was sent by

Mike Corbally, head of professional and technical services at the Institute of Environmental Health Officers, to the Animal Health Division at MAFF (Corbally, 1990). That eleven-page letter included the results of a survey of local authority Environmental Health officers and it asked for answers to specific questions, as well as assurances and a meeting. MAFF never responded.

A member of the Spongiform Encephalopathy Advisory Committee (SEAC) has explained that a failure to observe the relevant regulations was occurring not just at abattoirs, but also in rendering plants, at the animal feed producers and on the farms (J. Almond, personal communication, 18 June 1997). The standard arrangement at abattoirs, once the SBO regulations has been introduced, was to use two adjacent bins – one for the SBOs and one for the material that could be recycled into the feed chain. Regular checks were made at abattoirs, but since the owners had to pay to have the SBOs removed, they were tempted to discard some SBOs into the bins designated for the legitimate material.

Senior officials in MAFF knew that the regulations were not being properly observed, but that fact did not especially trouble some of them because they presumed that the removal of the offals was necessary only for public reassurance, not for the protection of human health (European Parliament, 1997: 10, par. 4). That helps to explain several other facts that might otherwise seem bizarre. For example, MAFF officials knew that the method being used to enable abattoirs to comply (at least partly) with the regulations might provide a route for recontamination. The approved method for removing the animals' spinal column involved sawing through the backbone for its full length using a high-powered saw. The use of those tools inevitably dispersed onto the material designated for human consumption the very offals that they were supposed to be removing. Officials realized that if the abattoir workers were to use a different but safer method, new equipment and training would have been required, and at some cost. Slaughterhouses would have needed to utilize different ways of hanging the carcasses, namely, ones that did not rely on the spine to hold the carcass together.

MAFF was well aware that the SBO regulations were not being observed because the department regularly collected and analysed figures revealing substantial divergences between the quantities of SBOs recorded as destroyed at incinerators and the amounts supposedly removed from animals in abattoirs. In 1995, during unannounced visits by enforcement officers to British abattoirs, some 48 per cent were found to be failing to comply with the regulations (House of Commons Agriculture and Health Select Committees, 1996: 10). Even in April 1996 BSE officials found that there were routes of cross-contamination between different feed streams. In June 1996, when the United Kingdom had just six rendering plants, it emerged that only four had been visited by enforcement officers during the previous twelve months, and of those three were violating the regulations (*Newsnight*, 1996).

Believing Their Own Rhetoric

One mistake, made both by senior officials and ministers, was that they came to believe their own rhetoric at least some of the time. They kept asserting that British beef was perfectly safe to eat, and while they were never entirely successful at reassuring the British public, there are indications that they succeeded in persuading themselves.

One of the clearest indications that Cabinet ministers and senior officials believed their own rhetoric was the fact that British government had made no contingency plan whatsoever for responding to the emergence of evidence that BSE had infected humans. When the crisis broke in March 1996 the government simply did not know what to do. When the facts, which contradicted the government's previous reassurances, became inescapable, ministers retreated into chauvinism and sought a scapegoat, which turned out to be 'foreigners,' in particular other EU member states, especially Germany, which insisted that it was not prepared to buy British beef. When the United States had imposed similar restrictions in July 1989, the British government made no public complaint (MAFF, 1990a; Barclay, 1996).

The British Government's Failure to Commission Sufficient or Appropriate Research

Between 1989 and 1996 the British government spent approximately £50 million on scientific research into BSE. Yet when the government published its BSE research agenda in late 1996 it was virtually indistinguishable from that set out in 1989; the only difference was that the 1996 agenda contained one extra item, namely, research to develop effective treatment for CJD (Tyrrell Report 1989; Department of Health, 1996). That implies that the £50 million which the British government spent on BSE research accomplished very little. Several factors might account for that lack of progress.

First, the scientists were confronted by enormous technical difficulties. No one has yet conclusively identified the pathogenic agent, nor provided an adequate account of how it operates. No one has (or had) developed a reliable test with which to detect the presence of the pathogen, let along establish its absence. Those difficulties are, however, part of the problem, and it is therefore unhelpful to focus on them as if they provided an explanation for the lack of scientific progress. Second, MAFF has been remarkably incompetent at commissioning research and at ensuring that the research coupled effectively to the main elements of the government's nominal research agenda (House of Lords Select Committee on Science and Technology, 1998–9; Millstone, 1995a, 1995b; Baker, 1997; House of Commons Science and Technology Committee, 1997: 20, xi par.). Notwithstanding those factors, a third set of considerations may also have been at play.

Given that MAFF repeatedly insisted that BSE posed no hazard to human health, and that BSE would not cross any further interspecies barriers, ministers had very little incentive to invest in research that might have provided evidence that would undermine their reassurances. Ministers were understandably reluctant to invest in research that might cause their optimistic narratives to unravel or disintegrate. It will, therefore, be important to examine the record of BSE research in the United Kingdom to establish which factors influenced the decisions taken regarding the lines of investigation that were funded and those that were avoided.

As long ago as the 1970s discussions among U.K. government officials reached the stage at which 'experiments were planned to test the theory that scrapie might be transmissible experimentally to cattle' (Consumers in Europe Group, 1994: 19). We have subsequently learned, however, that 'insufficient funds were made available for what was considered an unnecessary experiment' (ibid.). In June 1988, immediately after his committee's first meeting, Southwood wrote to the MAFF permanent secretary asking that an experiment be undertaken to test if meal infected with scrapie could cause BSE in cattle (Southwood et al., 1989: 3–4, par. 11). Similarly, the government's first BSE research advisory committee, under the chairmanship of Dr David Tyrrell, had argued in 1989 that 'we need to be sure that the disease really came from sheep' (Tyrell Report, 1989: 5, par. 33). These are just some of the many pieces of sound scientific advice that ministers chose not to follow.

The Southwood and Tyrrell committees also emphasized the importance of trying to develop a test with which to detect the presence of the BSE pathogen. The Tyrrell Committee assigned the highest priority to that work, but there is no evidence that the government invested in the development of tests until 1992, and even then the amount spent was relatively slight, and also the commissioning policy was problematic.

The secretary of state was asked in April 1990 in the House of Commons for his 'reasons for refusing to grant aid ... for a project for the development of a routine diagnostic test for BSE as an alternative to histopathology' (Hansard, 1990: col. 628). He replied: 'Research to find a diagnostic test *in the live animal* was considered a high priority ... and funds have already been made available for this work. A proposal was made under the open contracting and strategy fund for a post-mortem test. *A technique for post-mortem confirmation of BSE already exists* and, while this [particular] project was examined carefully, when compared with other project applications under the fund, it was not considered to be of sufficient merit to warrant funding on this occasion' (emphasis added; ibid.). The minister's answer was, however, unconvincing. No evidence can be found that the government was treating the problem as a high priority. Funds may have 'been made available,' but there is no evidence that any were being spent. That pathologists were able to confirm a diagnosis of BSE post-mortem was entirely beside the point.

Two projects were eventually commissioned at the CVL for biochemical investigations of the BSE pathogen, but not until 1992, when £45,000 was spent on the 'diagnostic potential of the pharmacological manipulation of clinical signs of BSE,' and a sum twice that size was devoted to the 'Electrophoretic analysis of body fluids to identify diagnostic markers in BSE and scrapie.' That latter project was eventually extended to three years. Three years worth of funding was also devoted to trying to identify BSE- and scrapie-infected animals by scrutinizing urinary metabolites, but that too was unsuccessful.

The evidence shows not that MAFF did nothing, but that it did too little and too late. The potential usefulness of an *ante-mortem* test had been obvious to all the scientists involved. After all, the great triumph of the government's veterinary service had been achieved in the mid-

1960s when it controlled and eradicated a serious outbreak of foot-and-mouth disease. That achievement had depended on the availability of a reliable, quick, and cheap test which enabled robust decisions to be taken.

MAFF's approach to commissioning work on developing an *ante-mortem* test took its most puzzling twist in 1995, when MAFF signed a one-year collaborative agreement with a company called Electrophoretics International (EI) to try and develop techniques for the diagnosis of BSE. There were two noteworthy features to that arrangement. First, EI was owned by a Conservative MP, Sir Michael Grylls ('The Other BSE Scandal,' 1997: p 25–6). Second, and more worryingly, the agreement was 'exclusive' because MAFF undertook to ensure that, for the duration of the agreement, MAFF would not cooperate with any other laboratory or company that might also be trying to develop electrophoretic detection methods. The agreement also specified that MAFF would not provide EI's competitors with the pathogenic materials that they would require for their work. In the event, even EI complained that MAFF failed to provide all the pathogenic samples requested.

Ministers have never explained why they signed such an agreement, given that there was most to be gained from competition among research teams. One might have expected that a government that endlessly preached the virtues of competition would have appreciated its relevance to BSE research. Since the eruption of the BSE crisis of 1996, venture capital has been flowing into small start-up biotechnology companies that are trying to develop technologically and economically effective tests. There will be a huge market for a successful test, especially from farmers and retailers wanting their meat certified as BSE-free.

A Failure to Establish a Centralized Animal Identification and Record-Keeping System

In 1989 the Tyrrell Committee called for the establishment of a centralized and computerized animal identification record-keeping system of the sort that had already been established in most EC continental member states. An integrated identification and record-keeping system could perform several important functions. It would support research in veterinary epidemiology, but perhaps more importantly, in the event that evidence emerged that BSE could be transmitted vertically (that is, from cow to calf), it would be possible to trace the offspring of any cow that developed BSE, so that such offspring could be withdrawn from the human food supply. In the event, a decision fully to establish such a system was not finally made until December 1996, and data were not finally entered into the official database until the autumn of 1998. The importance of establishing that database was repeatedly emphasized by authoritative advisers, and ministers repeatedly suggested that they were getting closer to delivering what they had promised, but in practice this precautionary measure has been subject to the most consistent and lengthy delay (European Parliament, 1990: 11; House of Commons Agriculture Committee, 1990: par. 60; Durham, 1994: 8; Brown, 1996: 6).

Conclusions

In the period 1980 to 1997 BSE public policy makers in the United Kingdom made just about every type of mistake open to them. The BSE saga, and the policy decisions that produced it, need to be understood in both their specific and general contexts. While the pro-market ideology of the Thatcher and Major governments contributed to the introduction and spread of BSE, those governments sowed the seeds of their terrible harvest in the fertile ground of traditional British political practice.

The tradition of locating within single government departments responsibility for both promoting the commercial interests of particular industrial sectors and for regulating those sectors long predates Mrs Thatcher's premiership, but it created the conditions in which the Ministry of Agriculture could covertly protect the short-term interests of the dairy and meat industries, while pretending to the general public that the protection of public health was paramount. The Official Secrets Act, which helped to sustain the policy until unwelcome facts overwhelmed the rhetoric and torpedoed the reassuring narrative, dates back to the 1911 espionage panic that fuelled nationalistic fervour in the run-up to the First World War.

The culture of selective disclosure is very strong in Whitehall. Even after March 1996 it took the threat of a public rebuke from the leadership of the Royal Society to persuade MAFF to allow a team of independent epidemiologists (led by Roy Anderson of Oxford University) to have access to the government's data on the BSE epidemic (Anderson et al., 1996). Whitehall departments have also been skilled at avoiding commissioning research projects that might yield unwelcome results.

In the particular circumstances of the period 1979 to 1996 ministers and their senior officials saw themselves as confronted by the dilemma of whether to take steps effectively to protect public health from the possible hazard which BSE might pose or to gamble with public health and public money by insisting that there could be no possible risk and by taking only those steps thought necessary to maintain consumer confidence and buoyant markets. The policy was, in this particular respect, consistent. Whenever there was a choice, ministers chose to subordinate consumer protection to support for agricultural markets. If they had not done so the BSE saga would either never have happened, or rapid steps would have been taken in the mid-1980s to eradicate the disease from the human food chain.

BSE is the type of problem, therefore, that can be solved only by following a robust regulatory strategy that is distinct from, and independent of, policy to support agricultural markets. It is difficult to conceive of any useful contribution that market-based instruments could make to the solution of problems posed by BSE. The public will never accept tradable quotas for pathogenic material. Taxes to discourage the use of contaminated feed would be insufficient. Consumers want their animals fed from uncontaminated sources. They are not asking for the freedom to choose between cheap burger patties that may contain BSE-contaminated material and more expensive brands that are likely to be uncontaminated. They want *all* their burger patties to be BSE-free, at all price points. The political obligations that confront policy makers dealing with BSE are not ones that can be fulfilled by leaving it to the market or by relying upon market-based instruments. Furthermore, a market-oriented policy approach was largely responsible for the occurrence of the problem in the first place, and so it would not help solve the policy challenge of BSE, and the continuation of such an approach would be counterproductive.

It is also noteworthy that in the ten-year period that began in 1985, BSE was seen, and rightly so, as just one in a lengthy series of food-safety policy crises that afflicted MAFF. When ranked alongside the debates on the safety of food additives or pesticides, and the hazards posed by bacterial contamination and technological innovations such as food irradiation and genetically engineered products such as bovine somatotropin, the debate on (and level of concern) about BSE was unexceptional (London Food Commission, 1998; Millstone, 1991). The structural features of British policy making and the distinctive ideological stand of the Thatcher and Major governments contributed to numerous other food safety policy problems and failures among which BSE, until March 1996 at any rate, did not particularly stand out.

If, therefore, institutional arrangements had been in place to ensure that any one of those food-safety problems had been properly addressed, then those arrangements would almost certainly have dealt more effectively with the others too. The conclusion about the irrelevance of a market-based approach to the problems posed by BSE would apply equally to a very wide range of other food-safety issues, and what is true for food-safety policy making also applies analogously to a very wide range of other public health and environmental protection issues.

Market-oriented policy instruments can make almost no contribution whatsoever to helping policy makers meet their responsibilities in respect of the protection of environmental and public health. They are at best of marginal relevance and at worst counter-productive. From the point of view of public health and environmental policy making, the discussion of market mechanisms is a red herring. Rather than focusing on what role the market can play, and what role the state should play, we should just concentrate on helping governments, and international governance bodies, to discharge their regulatory responsibilities more effectively.

The role of scientific evidence and scientific expertise in these events was especially important. Some might try to argue that the BSE fiasco occurred precisely because policy was not guided by sound scientific advice. If the government had made all the evidence available to independent experts, and had been willing to take seriously the concerns being expressed, the government would have had to recognize that there was no evidence that BSE would be innocuous for human consumers.

The contention that policy should be based on sound science risks neglecting the fact that the perceived soundness of science can vary with the perspective of different protagonists. Perceptions often depend, in part, upon the policy objectives to which those protagonists are committed. Because the objective of policy was the maintenance of consumer confidence, and not the protection of public health, the government set about gathering and promoting scientific evidence and statements that could be represented as reassuring; but they also set about concealing evidence that conflicted with their optimistic message, and deliberately denigated those scientists who acknowledged the dangers, especially if they tried to draw the public's attention to those dangers.

The demand that policy should be based on sound science is often used by those in industry and government who want to disguise their reluctance to interpret evidence in a precautionary fashion. They imply that until the science has become sound, that is, until a hazard has been proved, restrictions would be premature.

The contention that policy should be based on sound science can also mislead people into forgetting that scientific considerations are never by themselves sufficient to settle policy issues. However sound the science, policy cannot be left to the scientists, and scientific advisers should not be excused from democratic accountability.

To the extent that it did, the British government only contrived to sustain the illusion that its policy was based on sound science by following a strict policy of selective disclosure of information and by repeatedly (though discreetly) trying to circumscribe the independence of those scientists who were used to provide a scientific legitimation for policies that had previously been decided by reference to economic and political considerations. Since science can all too readily be used to misrepresent the underlying objectives that are driving policy, the policy objectives that frame the scientific agenda are at least as important as the subsequent science.

Policy should of course be based on sound science rather than on *shoddy* science. Misconstruing the absence of evidence as evidence of absence is bad science and bad policy. Open democratic scrutiny of policy makers and their scientific advisers has an important role to play in maintaining the quality of public science. One of the most effective ways of making science less unsound is to ensure that all the uncertainties are fully and publicly acknowledged and consequently that research designed to diminish those uncertainties is commissioned. Recognizing this point also entails appreciating that, however sound the science may be, it can never provide conclusive grounds for policy judgments. The BSE saga shows how crucial the policy framing of the scientific agenda can be for the soundness of both the scientific judgments and policy judgments that follow. If the policy is sound, it is so much easier for the science to be generated and interpreted in a prudent, responsible, and sound fashion.

References

Anderson, R.M. (1996). 'Transmission Dynamics and Epidemiology of BSE in British Cattle.' *Nature*, 382 (29 August): 779–88.

Baker, R. (1997). House of Commons Science and Technology Committee, Fourth Report, *The Research Council System: Issues for the Future*, vol. 2, *Minutes of Proceedings and Appendixes*, HC 309–II, 18 March, 27-39. London: Her Majesty's Stationery Office.

Barclay, C. (1996). *Bovine Spongiform Encephalopathy*. House of Commons Library Research Paper No 96/62, 15 May, Section II B, 13.

Bradley, R. (1990). CVL Pathologist to House of Common Agriculture Select Committee, see *Bovine Spongiform Encephalopathy*, Committee Fifth Report, 10 July, 71. London: Her Majesty's Stationery Office.

Brown, P. (1996). 'Cattle to Be Barcoded.' *Guardian*, 11 December, 6.

BSE Inquiry. To see the Inquiry website go to http://www.bse.org.uk/

Consumers in Europe Group. (1994). *Meat and Medicine: Human Health, Safety and Animal Pharmaceuticals*. London: author, 19.

Corbally, M. (1990). Letter to Animal Health Division of MAFF, from Institute of Environmental Health Officers, 1 February, 3. (The IEHO is now the Chartered Institute of Environmental Health.)

Dealler, S. (1996). Commons Agriculture and Health Select Committee, 17 April, 51. London: Department of Health.

Department of Health. (1996). *Strategy for Research and Development Relating to the Human Aspects of Transmissible Spongiform Encephalopathies*, November. London: Department of Health.

Dorrell, S. (1995). Independent Television, 4 December 1995, in conversation with Jonathan Dimbleby.

Durham, M. (1994). 'BSE Database Ban Adds to Troubles of Beef Farmers.' *Observer*, 7 August, 8.

European Parliament. (1990). *Bovine Spongiform Encephalopathy (BSE)*. Research and Documentation Papers Agriculture-Forestry-Fisheries, No. 20, December, 11. Brussels: European Parliament.

– (1997). *Report on Alleged Contravention or Maladministration in the Implementation of Community Law in Relation to BSE, without Prejudice to the Jurisdiction of the Community and National Courts*. Doc. EN\RR\319\319544 A4-0020/97A. Brussells: European Parliament.

Hansard. (1990). 4 April, col. 628.

House of Commons, Agriculture Committee. (1990). *Bovine Spongiform Encephalopathy (BSE)*, Fifth report, 10 July. London: Her Majesty's Stationery Office.

100   Erik Millstone and Patrick Van Zwanenberg

– Agriculture and Health Select Committees. (1996). *Bovine Spongiform Encephalopathy (BSE) and Creutzfeldt-Jakob Disease (CJD) Recent Developments*. Minutes of Evidence, HC-331. London: Her Majesty's Stationery Office.
– Science and Technology Committee (1997). Fourth Report. *The Research Council System: Issues for the Future*, vol. 1. Report HC-309-I. London: Her Majesty's Stationery Office.
House of Lords, Select Committee on Science and Technology. (1988–9). HL (1988–9)13. London: Her Majesty's Stationery Office.
Ironside, J. (1996). BBC, *Horizon*, 18 November.
Kimberlin, R. (1998). Statement No. 95 to the BSE Inquiry. Unpublished paper issued 1 July 1998 by the BSE Inquiry, London. Available at http://www.bse.org.uk.
– S. Cole and C.A. Walker. (1987). 'Temporary and Permanent Modifications to a Single Strain of Mouse Scrapie on Transmission to Rats and Hamsters.' *Journal of General Virology*, 68: 1875–81.
Lawrence, A. (1998). Statement No. 76 to BSE Inquiry. Unpublished paper issued 12 June 1998 by the BSE Inquiry, London. Available at http://www.bse.org.uk.
London Food Commission. (1988). *Food Adulteration and How to Fight It*. London: Unwin Hyman.
Meikle, J. (1998). 'Tories Panicked over BSE Chaos, Inquiry Reveals.' *Guardian*, 1 August, 10.
Meldrum, K. (1989). Cited in European Parliament, *Report on Alleged Contravention or Maladministration in the Implementation of Community Law in Relation to BSE, without Prejudice to the Jurisdiction of the Community and National Courts*, Doc_EN\RR\319\319544 A4-0020/97A, 7 February 1997. Brussels: European Parliament.
Metters, J. (1998). Statement no. 116 to the BSE Inquiry. Unpublished paper issued 14 July 1998 by the BSE Inquiry, London. Available at http://www.bse.org.uk.
Millstone, E. (1991). 'How to Involve Consumer Organisations in the Agricultural Policy and International Relations Debate?' *Comment Nourrir Le Monde? Les politiques alimentaires face à la libéralisation des économies et des échanges*, SOLAGRAL, Montpelier, December.
– (1995a). 'Fishing for Coherence in MAFF's Drifting Research.' *Research Fortnight*, 1(12): 12.
– (1995b). 'MAFF Brief Still Muddled.' *Research Fortnight*, 1(21): 3.
Ministry of Agriculture, Fisheries and Food (MAFF). (1990a). Memorandum to House of Commons Select Committee on Agriculture, *Bovine Spongiform Encephalopathy (BSE)*, June. London: MAFF.

–   (1990b). 'British Beef Is Safe, Gummer.' News Release 185/90, 15 May.
Newsnight. (1996). BBC 2 TV, 19 June.
'The Other BSE Scandal.' (1997). *Economist*, 22 February, 25–6.
Pearce, F. (1996). 'Ministers Hostile to Advice on BSE.' *New Scientist*,
    30 March, 4.
Prentice, T. (1990). 'Mad Cow Disease Could Have Been Avoided.' *Times*,
    22 January, 7.
Royal Commission on Environmental Pollution (RCEP). (1979). 7th report,
    Agriculture and Pollution, September. London: Her Majesty's Stationery
    Office.
Southwood, R. (1989). Statement No 1 to BSE Inquiry, par. 11, pp. 3–4.
    Unpublished paper issued March 11, 1998, by the BSE Inquiry, London.
    Available at http://www.bse.org.uk.
–   et al. (1989). *Report of the Working Party on Bovine Spongiform Encephalopa-
    thy*. London: Department of Health and Ministry of Agriculture, Fisheries
    and Food.
Tyrell Report. (1989). *Consultative Committee on Research into Spongiform
    Encephalopathies*. Interim report, dated June 1989. London: Ministry of
    Agriculture Fisheries and Food.
Wilesmith, J.W., G. Wells, M. Cranwell, and J. Ryan. (1988). 'Bovine
    Spongiform Encephalopathy: Epidemiological Studies.' *Veterinary Record*,
    123: 638–44.

5 Can Eco-Labelling Undermine International Agreement on Science-Based Standards?

DENNIS BROWNE (with RAMESH CHAITOO and MICHAEL HART)

The major issues in this book concern the capacity of Canada's regulatory institutions to regulate their various sectors on a sound scientific basis, the possible impact of such regulation on the competitiveness of Canadian industries whose activities are being regulated, and the level of public trust in the scientific and technical abilities of the regulatory agencies themselves. This chapter focuses mainly on the last area – the question of public trust – and considers whether that public trust can be manipulated in such a way that the relevance of the scientific basis of regulation is undermined. In short, can the science be made irrelevant by creating market demand for product standards that are not based on science?

To get to the nub of that question, however, we should briefly consider the international framework developed by governments to ensure, through trade regulations, that regulatory requirements are actually science-based and not put in place principally to protect domestic producers from international competition.

In his formal address to the World Trade Organization's (WTO) ministerial meeting in Geneva in May 1998, Canada's trade minister, Sergio Marchi, set out a number of questions which, in Canada's view, must be addressed to ensure that 'trade and investment liberalization meets the key needs and interests of all our peoples.' Two sets of Marchi's questions related to matters under consideration in this book:

- How can we guard against the erosion of rights to regulate for reasons of public health, consumer safety, social policy, and other public interests?

- In the sale of goods and services abroad, what steps can we take to reduce impediments caused by the arbitrary application of standards and regulations? How can we ensure that these standards and regulations are set at appropriately high levels, applied equitably, and based on science?

These questions nicely capture the tension that underlies much of the design of the international framework of rules embodied in the WTO agreements relating to the regulation of international trade. The agreements recognize that individual governments have the sovereign right to take measures to pursue their legitimate national interests, but they also recognize that the unfettered exercise of such sovereign rights could easily lead to significant reductions in global welfare through trade distortions and the resulting misallocations of productive resources. Thus, the framework of rules must constantly seek a balance between governments' rights to pursue national policies and the global benefits to be derived from greater market efficiencies.

The Main Features of Trade Regulation

Key Assumptions

An important economic assumption underpinning the General Agreement on Tariffs and Trade (GATT) and other WTO agreements is that all nations will gain from international trade and that such gains are optimized through a relatively open system that permits each economy to specialize in those things it does best.

Another important assumption is that international trade is conducted by firms, not by governments, and that the role of governments is to set an appropriate legal and regulatory framework that will be conducive to the establishment and maintenance of efficient international markets. Thus, international trade rules set out what governments should or should not do. The international rules do not directly regulate the activities of firms engaged in international trade or the activities of other private parties.

There is also an assumption that governments will always be faced with the challenge of finding an appropriate balance between policies that bring optimal longer-term economic benefits (that is, more openness) and policies that satisfy either short-term demands for economic stability (for example, protecting failing or fledgling industries) or political requirements to attain domestic social or political goals (for example, environmental and health standards). This means that governments must constantly seek an appropriate balance between more openness and more regulation.

Appropriately structured trade agreements can help governments find an optimal balance, as every international trade agreement contains provisions to reduce the scope for governments to intervene in the market in pursuit of national economic, social, or political goals and counterbalancing provisions to allow governments to take the measures that they deem appropriate to achieve these goals. The former provisions are generally referred to as the 'principles' of trade regulation, the latter are the 'exceptions' to these principles.

Main Principles

International trade agreements are based on four principles: most favoured nation (or MFN); national treatment; elimination of quantitative restrictions on imports and exports; and transparency. The first two, MFN and national treatment, simply mean that WTO members must extend the same treatment to imports of goods and services from all other WTO members and that they must treat imported products no less favourably in their domestic markets than they treat domestically produced goods or services. Elimination of quantitative restrictions, which would include any prohibition of imports or exports of specified products, removes unwarranted obstacles to international trade. The transparency principle requires that all regulations affecting trade be published and available, as markets can only function efficiently if the rules are clear.

Exceptions from the Principles

For the purposes of this discussion, the most important exceptions to these principles are found in GATT, Article XX, which sets out general exceptions giving governments possibilities to adopt or enforce measures for various objectives. Under this article, governments may, for example, take measures that are necessary to protect human, animal, or plant life or health (Article XXb), or that are related to the conservation of exhaustible natural resources provided, in the latter case, such measures are made effective in conjunction with restrictions on domestic production or consumption (Article XXg). The limitation on these exceptions is that the measures taken for these purposes must not be applied in a manner that would constitute a means of arbitrary or unjustifiable discrimination between countries where the same conditions prevail, or a disguised restriction on international trade.

These provisions of the original 1947 GATT are carried over into the WTO. Since the GATT first came into effect, a body of understandings and ancillary rules has developed through dispute settlements and through the work of various GATT committees and working parties. This experience is now largely codified in two WTO agreements: the Agreement on Technical Barriers to Trade and the Agreement on the Application of Sanitary and Phytosanitary Measures.

The Agreement on the Application of Sanitary and Phytosanitary Measures

This agreement, generally referred to as the SPS agreement, builds on the Article XXb exception by setting out the rights and obligations of WTO members taking measures to protect human, animal, or plant life or health from the spread of pests or diseases that may be brought into a country by contaminated fruits, vegetables, meat, other food products, or plants and earth stuck to their roots. Its aim is to prevent the use of such sanitary and phytosanitary measures as disguised barriers to trade or as means for unwarranted discrimination between like products from various trading partners. In short, a legitimate objective and purpose of an SPS measure would be to protect the country's population from genuine risks to health, not to protect domestic producers from import competition.

While SPS measures are defined broadly enough to encompass measures whose objectives go beyond farm-based activities to protect wild animals and plants, including fish and forests, their definition is not broad enough to include measures intended to protect the environment per se or to address concerns about animal rights.

Agricultural and agri-food products subject to sanitary and phytosanitary measures may also be subject to other technical regulations and standards, the use of which would be governed by the Agreement on Technical Barriers to Trade. For example, tinned or frozen vegetables in consumer packages would normally be subject to phytosanitary regulations to ensure their safety and to technical regulations or standards concerning the size of their packages and the language and/or content of their labels.

If every country were independently to set its own SPS standards and certification procedures without reference to any others, international trade in agricultural and agri-food products would be unnecessarily difficult. Thus, to facilitate international trade, WTO members are required to base their SPS measures on international standards where they exist.

Individual WTO members may adopt standards that are higher than those established by international organizations, provided such higher levels of protection are scientifically justified on the basis of appropriate risk assessment. Levels of protection set higher than international standards would reflect unique characteristics of the country adopting them rather than simply a public attitude that they might be desirable. Nonetheless, if relevant scientific evidence is insufficient, a WTO member may adopt provisional measures on the basis of available information, with a view to obtaining the necessary information within a reasonable period of time.

A WTO member intending to adopt an SPS measure that is different from existing international standards or for which international standards do not exist must follow notification procedures set out in the SPS agreement. Basically, in such case, a member government must publish its intention, notify product coverage, provide copies of draft regulations upon request, and allow reasonable time for other members to provide comments and other inputs. If requested, the regulating member is to discuss comments of other members with them and take their comments and the results of any discussions into account when formulating measures to be put in place.

All SPS measures must be published, and, except in urgent circumstances, there must be a reasonable interval between publication and implementation so as to allow producers in exporting member countries to adapt to the new requirements. Each member government must establish an enquiry point from which all other members may obtain answers to their reasonable questions, as well as documentation relating to SPS regulations, control and inspection procedures, risk assessment procedures, and the participation of the member and/ or bodies within its territory in various international organizations or agreements relating to SPS matters.

If internationally agreed SPS standards do not exist, WTO members are encouraged to recognize the equivalency of their trading partners' standards and certification procedures so that they need not be identical as long as they provide equivalent levels of protection. The agreement places the onus on the exporting member to demonstrate objectively that its standards and certification procedures provide equivalent levels of protection to those in effect in the importing member country.

The SPS agreement also sets out detailed requirements for control, inspection, and approval procedures so that such procedures are not unduly burdensome to exporters and so that they, in effect, ensure national treatment to foreign suppliers without discriminating unduly among them.

The Agreement on Technical Barriers to Trade

This agreement also builds on the Article XXb exception and recognizes that all countries set at least some mandatory technical standards specifying some property, quality, dimension, or other characteristic that must be met by both domestic and imported products to protect the health and safety of their populations or their domestic environment, or to prevent deceptive practices. A simple example: all electric appliances sold in Canada must have plugs of certain size, shape, and conductive capacity so that users may safely plug them into standard electrical outlets. Other common technical regulations would include such things as emissions controls on automobiles, prohibitions on the use of lead-based paint on toys for small children, and labelling requirements to clearly indicate the quality and quantity of foodstuffs contained in retail packages.

Technical standards may impede market access if they are developed in ways that make it difficult for foreign suppliers to participate in the standard-setting process, or to get information about the standard or about compliance testing, or to comply with unusual local product characteristics. Thus, the goal of the TBT agreement is to ensure that these circumstances do not arise, that is, that technical standards are not used as disguised barriers to trade and that legitimate standards restrict trade as little as possible.

The TBT agreement distinguishes between 'technical regulations' as mandatory and 'standards' as not mandatory (that is, voluntary). *Technical regulations* set out mandatory product characteristics or their related processes and production methods. They may also deal with terminology, symbols, packaging, marking, or labelling requirements. They may be set by central governments, local governments, or designated non-governmental bodies.

Standards, which may be set by recognized bodies, provide – for common and repeated use – rules, guidelines, or characteristics for products or related processes and production methods with which compliance is not mandatory. Like technical regulations, they may also deal with terminology, symbols, packaging, marking, or labelling requirements.

While meeting mandatory technical regulations is a legal prerequisite to market access, complying with voluntary standards is not. Nonetheless, failure to comply with a voluntary standard may effectively exclude a product from the market or significantly reduce the product supplier's ability to contest the market if buyers insist, as a commercial matter, that the standard be met. For example, the ISO 9000 standards covering manufacturing processes are voluntary, but many large manufacturers refuse to buy parts or components from suppliers whose plants are not ISO 9000 certified. Similarly, a retailer may insist that all products in a certain category qualify for eco-labelling, or some public agencies might seek to use only recycled paper in their publications.

The TBT agreement addresses technical regulations and standards as they apply to products. Although they may be cast in terms of production processes or methods, to be covered by the provisions of this agreement, their aim must relate to some characteristic of the product. For example, high-quality process regulations for the production of medical equipment will ensure that the resulting products are safe for their intended uses.

By regulating the quality or other characteristics of a product, relevant authorities are protecting the health and safety of their population and their environment within their own jurisdiction. On the other hand, process regulations or standards intended to protect the environment in overseas jurisdictions would not be condoned by the TBT agreement. The quality and usefulness of newsprint, for example, would not likely be affected by the amount of effluent the mill that produces it releases into neighbouring waterways. Setting a technical regulation for paper products based on the environmental impact of production processes in the country of export would amount to extraterritorial regulation, something which is not provided for directly in the WTO agreements.

Like the SPS agreement, the TBT agreement incorporates the usual GATT principles of MFN, national treatment, and transparency, so that imports from all WTO member countries will be treated equally; the same rules will apply to imports and domestically produced products; and the rules will be published and available to governments and to businesses engaged in international trade. The exception is the elimination of quantitative restrictions.

Procedural provisions of the TBT agreement relating to technical regulations are similar to those of the SPS agreement, but are, in some respects, somewhat less stringent so that governments have more room for discretion when formulating technical regulations than they do for sanitary and phytosanitary measures. For example, a requirement that motor vehicles be suitable for driving on the left side of the road in some countries is based on established practice rather than science, and, although it is an obstacle to trade in motor vehicles, it may be maintained as the costs of changing related infrastructure would be very high.

The TBT agreement also contains a Code of Good Practice for the Preparation, Adoption, and Application of Standards, which sets out similar provisions for standards. Central governmental standardizing bodies must adhere to the code and members must 'take such reasonable steps as may be available to them' to ensure their subnational governments and non-governmental standardizing bodies also accept and comply with the code.

Measures Relating to the Conservation of Exhaustible Natural Resources

As noted above, GATT Article XXg permits WTO members to take measures 'relating to the conservation of exhaustible natural resources if such measures are made effective in conjunction with restrictions on domestic production and consumption.' Such measures would normally be export or import controls that would otherwise be disallowed under the principle prohibiting the use of quantitative restrictions on trade.

The meaning of the words 'relating to ... conservation' was considered by two GATT panels, one considering Canadian export restrictions on salmon and herring (GATT, 1988), the other considering American import restrictions on tuna (GATT, 1991). The earlier of the two panels, on Canadian export restrictions, found that for a trade measure to qualify under this provision, it had to be primarily aimed at the conservation of an exhaustible natural resource, and its objective must be to make the restrictions on domestic production or consumption effective.

The later panel, on U.S. tuna import controls, confirmed the above interpretations and went on to find that 'a country can effectively

control the production or consumption of an exhaustible natural resource only to the extent that the production or consumption is under its
jurisdiction.' The panel also noted that the U.S. harvesting regulations,
which were intended to prevent the collateral drowning of dolphins,
had no effect on the quality of the tuna that were caught. There is
therefore no legitimate basis for trade measures to discriminate between
tuna products on the basis of catching techniques that may or may not
have collateral effects on other species. Thus, trade measures taken to
force other countries to change their domestic environmental or health
and safety regulations cannot be justified under GATT Article XXg.

A more recent WTO panel considered the efficacy of U.S. trade
regulations requiring imported gasoline to meet U.S. environmental
regulations and found that clean air is an exhaustible natural resource
that can be protected through appropriately structured trade regulations to control domestic use of polluting products (WTO, 1996). As
this ruling distinguishes between the exhaustible natural resource that
is being conserved and the product whose production or consumption
is being restricted and whose trade is being constrained, the case introduces a new perspective that has considerable potential to allow
the use of appropriately balanced trade measures in support of domestic environmental rules.

The Impact of Trade Rules

It follows from the above that environmental laws or regulations that
discriminate against imported products on the basis of their production methods are not consistent with the international framework of
rules for the regulation of trade. Imports must not be restricted or
prohibited because harvesting or production methods practised in foreign jurisdictions are disallowed or disapproved of at home. It also
follows that any technical regulations or standards that are applied to
goods within a given market must be applied equally to domestic and
imported goods and must relate to the characteristics or qualities of
the goods themselves. Additionally, all SPS measures, technical regulations, and standards should be based on internationally agreed measures, regulations, and standards or on scientifically based assessments
of risk of non-compliance.

We must recognize, however, that the rules embodied in international trade agreements apply only to the members of the agreements,
that is, national governments, not non-governmental organizations.
While member governments are required to take 'such reasonable mea-

sures as may be available to them' to secure compliance with WTO provisions by non-governmental bodies that set standards, these disciplines only apply to measures that are recognized by central governments and/or enforceable under domestic law. They would not apply to voluntary standards set by private actors, standards that are not enforceable but may have commercial impacts. It is to this grey area that we now turn our attention.

Quality Labels: A Long-Standing Tradition

The practice of including certifications of quality on the labels of consumer goods is generations old. From our own recollections and observations it is evident that the European practice of publishing labels including the manufacturer's claim to be purveyors of high-quality goods to various royal courts extends back at least into the nineteenth century. While this claim is to no objective standard other than to having been selected by the court's purchasing authority, the clear intention is to convey the impression that goods so labelled are superior to those whose manufacturer cannot make similar claims.

More recently, the wool industry developed the 'woolmark' to certify that a product is made from pure wool rather than a synthetic substitute. This is a clear indication of product content intending to assert the higher qualities claimed for wool. There is also a clear indication that a specific content standard has to be met before the mark can be used.

Another popular label that has appeared on garments for many years is 'Union Made.' This label has a double purpose. On the one hand, it implies that union workers are likely more highly qualified than non-union workers and therefore the garment is of better quality. On the other, it informs the consumer that the garment was not made under conditions unduly oppressive to the workers who made it. Thus, we see social values being expressed and attributed to consumer products through labels.

Eco-labelling has become increasingly popular in recent decades. Labels on cosmetics claim 'no animal testing' to appeal to those who are concerned about cruelty to animals. Many foods carry an 'organically grown' label which suggests more wholesomeness in the product and more environmentally friendly growing practices. A 'recycled' seal is increasingly found on consumer paper products, again to suggest more environmentally friendly production of the materials from which the final product is made.

Products bearing each of the above labels may or may not meet some objectively set and demonstrable standard. Each label is, nonetheless, intended to appeal to some belief held by many consumers that will differentiate the product and establish market preference. The use of any of these labels is voluntary and based on commercial calculations as to their value. This distinguishes them from labelling requirements to demonstrate that a product meets certain standards as a precondition of its being offered for sale. For example, household electrical appliances offered for sale in Canada traditionally required a CSA stamp of approval, while household fire extinguishers required a ULC mark; under the NAFTA, many products requiring such certification prior to being offered for sale in Canada may now bear either the Canadian seal or that of its U.S. counterpart. These marks are, of course, intended to provide assurances of product safety by certifying that the products have met officially sanctioned standards of quality.

Government regulations may also require products to carry marks of origin. Such requirement is presumably imposed on the assumption that an informed consumer would prefer to purchase a local product rather than one that is imported. While marks of origin requirements are permitted under the GATT, they must be applied on an MFN basis and should be minimally disruptive of trade (GATT, Article IX).

Whether a label is voluntary or required, its intent is to inform the consumer about the nature or quality of the product bearing the label. Problems arise when the actual meaning of the label is unclear or when there is a proliferation of labels for the same categories of products such that consumers become confused as to their various meanings. Problems also arise if labelling requirements or practices unduly burden international commerce.

This latter circumstance is of special interest to the theme of this chapter. As we shall see below, it may well be possible for a 'voluntary' labelling scheme to limit market access in a way that substitutes value-driven criteria for science-based criteria, thereby undermining the latter by calling their relevance into question.

The Impact of Environmental Activists on Science-Based Regulation

Before turning to a consideration of environmentally based labelling, it will be helpful to set the stage by considering some other tactics that have been used by environmental activists and which, in our view, led to the development of the certification and labelling scheme we wish to consider in more detail.

In some sectors, mainstream environmental groups traditionally worked cooperatively with appropriate authorities to ensure that regulatory frameworks served environmental goals. The regulatory process in industrialized countries has tended to be heavily influenced by interest groups most affected by specific regulations. Regulation of resource use in such sectors as mining and forestry, for example, has traditionally taken account of the needs of the resource companies, labour unions, local communities, and, more recently, the indigenous populations who might be affected, as well as other interested parties sufficiently concerned to make their views known. This last category includes environmental organizations such as the Canadian Wildlife Federation and the Sierra Club, who worked for many years within the regulatory framework. The objective of each of the participants was to have the government develop regulations and management plans that satisfied their specific interests in the context of society's more general needs.

Practices changed, however, in the late 1970s and into the 1980s as more militant environmental interest groups arose in conjunction with increasing public awareness of and concern about environmental issues. The more militant groups did not seek to find common ground with other interests, as had been traditionally done. They believed that environmental concerns should take precedence over all others, especially commercial considerations. They therefore tended to prefer dramatic public gestures to reasoned negotiation, and they became very skilful in capturing public attention with a view to changing government policies and regulatory frameworks. While their early demonstrations were aimed to achieve direct changes to government policies, for example, with relation to nuclear power, they soon learned that influencing market behaviour could be more powerful than direct pressure on government.

The Anti–Seal Hunt Campaign

One of the activists' more dramatic successes in Canada was the cancellation of the white-coat seal hunt.[1] The well-established annual taking of seal pups was closely regulated by the federal government, with regulations based on scientific principles such as those used to establish appropriate harvest levels to prevent depletion of the seal population and the established principle that taking young members of a population has a less damaging impact on the species than does the taking of adults, especially females. It could also be demonstrated that skilled use of the hakapik was less cruel than other killing techniques since it delivered almost instant death.

Notwithstanding these rational bases for regulating the hunt, it was relatively easy for concerned environmentalists to depict it as barbarous; to assert that killing pups was not rational population management, but simply opportunistic killing of readily available victims. What is more, the pups were babies and they and their mothers were easy to photograph looking distressed. The twitching of the pups muscles in the period shortly after death made it appear that, far from being humanely killed, they were being skinned alive. And, of course, the abundance of bright red blood on the sparkling white ice provided shocking television footage. The activists were able to stage dramatic acts of civil disobedience, getting in the way of the hunters and their ships to produce forceful images of determined cruelty on the part of those engaged in the annual harvest.

These images were not used only in Canada, directly against the regulators. They were also taken to Europe with the objective of destroying the market. The activists' reasoning was that if there was no market for the seal pup skins, the hunt would collapse whether Canadian regulations were changed or not. Lots of street theatre and the broadcasting of dramatic images through European media generated an enormous flow of mail to European parliamentarians demanding an end to the cruelty and barbarism off the coast of Newfoundland. For the European parliamentarians, reacting to this pressure was a cost-free way to show solidarity with the voters since no EC economic interests were at stake. Accordingly, legislation was introduced into the European Parliament to ban imports of white-coat pelts, effectively removing the commercial incentive to continue the hunt. Although the import ban was almost certainly contrary to GATT rules, the dispute settlement provisions then in place were not effective enough for Canada to challenge them successfully. Even in the absence of an import ban, however, the market had been badly damaged, as the wearing of sealskin had become socially unacceptable in many circles in several countries in Europe.

The hunt was eventually officially ended in Canada when the government acted on a Royal Commission's recommendations to do so.

The commission's recommendations did not claim that the regulation of the hunt was based on flawed science. In fact, the validity of the science was recognized. Its recommendations were based on the perceived barbarity of the hunt itself, a perception of a level of barbarity that was deemed to be unacceptable in a civilized society. In short, social values overruled science-based regulation and made it irrelevant.

The Anti-Fur Campaign

A similar success was almost achieved when activists turned their attention to trapping animals for furs.[2] The killing of wild animals to make fur coats was easily depicted to many as frivolous and cruel. But fur trapping is an integral part of many indigenous Canadian cultures and an important source of income for Native communities with very few alternatives, especially in the north. The government was therefore under pressure to retain fur-trapping opportunities while seeking to address the legitimate concerns raised by the anti-trapping movement.

As the anti-fur activists focused initially on the cruelty of trapping, government regulators sought to develop and implement scientifically based, humane, trapping methods. A research centre was established at Vegreville, and Canada became the world leader in research into trapping and its effect on its victims. A humane killing technique was defined as one that promptly renders the animal unconscious and causes it to subside into death without regaining consciousness. A humane trap would either do this or hold the animal without undue injury or distress until such a humane death could be effected. Considerable progress has been made in developing humane trapping techniques for various species and in training trappers to use them, including modified versions of the much vilified leg-hold trap.

It soon became apparent however that most activists were not interested in humane trapping methods per se. They wanted the killing to stop. Similar tactics to those used so successfully against the seal hunt were used against trapping. Dramatic imagery was assembled and taken to the market. Antipathy towards the wearing of furs was engendered, and European parliamentarians were called upon to ban imports. Again, such a move could be relatively cost-free as the vast majority of European fur was farmed, and there were no indigenous populations dependent on trapping; these circumstances changed somewhat with the entry of Sweden and Finland into the European Union, but not for the majority of European parliamentarians. Legislation that would ban the import of furs taken with leg-hold traps was accordingly introduced into the European Parliament. But this time the Europeans could not act with impunity, as the intended ban could be challenged under the new TBT agreement. The measure was therefore changed to a labelling requirement for furs made from animals caught with leg-hold traps. This measure could also be challenged under the TBT agreement, and Canada has moved to protect its fur-trapping interests. Rather than pursue the lengthy WTO dispute-settlement procedures, an agreement has been reached between the EU and Canada (with a possibility that Russia will also sign on) to jointly define humane trapping methods for which market access will not be impeded. This should at least move the discussion to a more science-based context.

Campaigns against Canadian Forestry Practices

Through successive campaigns, the activists have honed their skills and developed new techniques to achieve their objectives.[3] While civil disobedience continues to be used to attract attention, more sophisticated and legal techniques are being developed. Campaigns against Canadian forestry practices provide some good examples of the various measures being used.

The early stages of campaigns against forest practices in British Columbia focused public attention through dramatic demonstrations culminating in a large 'camp-in' at Clayoquot Sound. International celebrities were brought in, regulations were broken, arrests were made, and allegations of police brutality were hurled about. It was great theatre, and it captured the public's imagination. It also put in place serious political efforts to re-evaluate the province's forest regulatory and management structure, with the eventual result that British Columbia adopted what may well be one of the most enlightened and forward-looking codes of forest management practices. Those who care about sustainable and balanced use of B.C.'s forest resources can be thankful for the determined efforts of the activists.

As might have been expected, however, many of the activists could not take 'yes' for an answer. They do not want sustained harvesting of B.C.'s rainforest. They want all logging in the rainforests stopped. What is more, if they were to declare a victory, the campaign would be over, and many of their supporters would see no reason to continue making financial contributions. Consequently, the campaign must continue, albeit with a shift in focus.

Efforts continue to disrupt the market for B.C. forest products. For example, a very large consumer of B.C. paper is Pacific Telesis, a San Francisco-based company that prints telephone directories for most of the southwestern United States. Environmental organizations have bought shares in the company and regularly appear at its annual meetings to propose resolutions that would stop the company's purchases of B.C. paper. At the same time, street theatre is used to encourage the press to vilify the company for allegedly encouraging environmental irresponsibility. Meanwhile resolutions are sought and obtained from California municipal councils calling upon their administrators to refuse to buy any products using paper from Canada's ancient forests. All of this has had a public relations effect, but it has not noticeably reduced the market for B.C. and Canadian forest products in California and the neighbouring states.

A much more sophisticated operation is being pursued on a much wider basis to influence forestry practices around the globe. In implementing this new approach, environmental groups are building on the experience they have accumulated in past campaigns, especially those that have sought to change government practices by causing difficulties in the markets for products produced under government regulations that, in their view, fail to address important environmental values. The brilliance of this new approach is that, if it succeeds, it will make government regulations irrelevant as keys to market access, and it has the potential to generate very large revenues for environmental groups, thereby reducing their dependency on continuous fund-raising campaigns.

The Forest Stewardship Council's Certification System

The Forestry Stewardship Council (FSC) is an international coalition of organizations and individuals concerned about perceived weak government forestry policies and poor industry practices.[4] Its mission is to support environmentally appropriate, socially beneficial, and economically viable stewardship of the world's forests. The FSC seeks to accomplish this goal by evaluating, accrediting, and monitoring certification bodies and by strengthening national certification and forest management capacity through training, education, and the development of national certification initiatives. Products derived from certified forests are entitled to the FSC eco-label to assure consumers of sound forestry practices and to distinguish them from non-certified products.

To obtain FSC approval, forest certifiers must adhere to the FSC's principles, criteria, and guidelines, which apply to all types of forests (see Table 5.1). They are designed to allow flexibility in their application through the development of national and regional standards that fit ecological, social, and economic circumstances. The principles and criteria are intended to provide consistency among certifiers and their standards by providing an overall framework for developing and evaluating local and national forest management standards. They are, however, social principles, not scientific principles.

The FSC stipulates that the development of local standards based on their principles must be an open, consensus-based, and participatory process that involves consultations with affected stakeholder groups. To this end it encourages the formation of local, national, and regional working groups to develop forest management standards based on realistic and locally defined forest management practices. To date, local initiatives have been established in about twenty countries, including Brazil, Bolivia, Papua New Guinea, Sweden, Switzerland, and the United Kingdom. By the end of March 1998 the total amount of FSC certified forest area was 6.279 million hectares in nineteen countries, comprising sixty-three forest properties covering tropical, temperate, and boreal forests[5] (International Tropical Timber Organization, 1998).

The FSC is strongly endorsed and supported by the World Wide Fund for Nature (WWF) through its Global Forests for Life Campaign. The campaign seeks to (1) promote the certification of ten million hectares of forests by the end of 1998, and (2) establish a network of protected areas covering at least 10 per cent of the world's forests by the year 2000.

In order to 'promote and accelerate sustainable forest management,' the WWF has formed buyers' groups of retailers in several countries, particularly in Europe, and there are concerted attempts to replicate the process all over the world. The first group (formed in 1991) of approximately a dozen retailers and suppliers in the United Kingdom pledged to purchase all of their wood and paper products from certified sources by 1995 (referred to as the Group of 1995). However, increased membership and insufficient supplies of certified products led to a name change to the '1995 Plus Group' with a target of 100 per

Table 5.1 Principles of the Forestry Stewardship Council (FSC)

Principle 1: Compliance with Laws and FSC Principles
Forest management shall respect all applicable laws of the country in which they occur, and international treaties and agreements to which the country is a signatory, and comply with all FSC Principles and Criteria.

Principle 2: Tenure and Use Rights and Responsibilities
Long-term tenure and use rights to the land and forest resources shall be clearly defined, documented, and legally established.

Principle 3: Indigenous Peoples' Rights
The legal and customary rights of indigenous peoples to own, use, and manage their lands, territories, and resources shall be recognized and respected.

Principle 4: Community Relations and Workers' Rights
Forest management operations shall maintain or enhance the long-term social and economic well-being of forest workers and local communities.

Principle 5: Benefits from the Forest
Forest management operations shall encourage the efficient use of the forest's multiple products and services to ensure economic viability and a wide range of environmental and social benefits.

Principle 6: Environmental Impact
Forest management shall conserve biological diversity and its associated values, water resources, soils, and unique and fragile ecosystems and landscapes, and, by so doing, maintain the ecological functions and the integrity of the forest.

Principle 7: Management Plan
A management plan – appropriate to the scale and intensity of the operations – shall be written, implemented, and kept up to date. The long-term objectives of manage-ment, and the means of achieving them, shall be clearly stated.

Principle 8: Monitoring and Assessment
Monitoring shall be conducted – appropriate to the scale and intensity of forest management – to assess the condition of the forest, yields of forest products, chain of custody, management activities, and their social and environmental impacts.

Principle 9: Maintenance of Natural Forests
Primary forests, well-developed secondary forests, and sites of major environmental, social, or cultural significance shall be conserved. Such areas shall not be replaced by tree plantations or other land uses.

Principle 10: Plantations
Plantations shall be planned and managed in accordance with Principles and Criteria 1–9, and Principle 10 and its Criteria. While plantations can provide an array of social and economic benefits, and can contribute to satisfying the world's needs for forest products, they should complement the management of, reduce pressures on, and promote the restoration and conservation of natural forests.

cent certified wood and paper by the year 2000. The group, consisting of about eighty companies, accounts for about 25 per cent of U.K. wood and paper products sales; companies such as Sainsbury's, Boots the Chemist, and B&Y, belong to the group and exert considerable market power, which is a major concern for companies trying to supply the mainly consumer-oriented U.K. market.

Another phenomenon that has direct implications on market access for exporters of wood and wood products to the European market is the decisions by some municipal governments to purchase primarily FSC-certified lumber and wood products. In the Netherlands, for example, the municipalities of Apeldoorn, Gouda, and Uithoorn entered into contracts with housing associations and project developers stating that FSC-certified lumber is to be used in building activities as much as possible.[6] In the United Kingdom, the city of Edinburgh developed similar policies, as did some municipalities in England.[7] More recently, BBC Publishing decided to purchase only FSC-certified paper for its magazines as soon as it becomes available.

Problems with the FSC and Its Certification System

There are numerous criticisms of the FSC, ranging from its composition to various aspects of its principles and criteria. At its inception, the composition of the FSC was predominantly environmental non-government organizations (ENGOs), but since 1996 commercial interests comprise one-third of its membership, and social and environmental interests each account for a further third. The list of FSC members in February 1998 totalled 243, of which ninety-seven were considered to represent 'economic' stakeholders, but the vast majority of these members are individuals, particularly consultants and certifiers, not major forestry companies. There is greater representation by distributors or retailers than by forest product manufacturers; notable members are Home Depot (U.S.), Assi Domän (Sweden), and B&Q and Boots the Chemist (U.K.). As a result, critics have focused on the potential for conflicts of interest.

The FSC endorses a single criterion label, that is, forest management, rather than a multicriteria system based on life-cycle analysis of the product, as in conventional eco-labelling schemes. A major shortcoming of this approach is that forest products that involve manufacturing processes that are environmentally harmful can bear the label if the forest from which the raw material originated was certified. Also, in seeking to be environmentally sensitive, the FSC principles are perhaps too idealistic. By excluding wood obtained from old growth forests that are then replanted, and emphasizing 'natural' forestry, the FSC discriminates against renewable resources and encourages forestry companies to pursue less intensive practices.[8] The preferred practical management option is to encourage greater forest productivity on the best lands and take pressure off the less productive and ecologically fragile lands. However, if overall management intensity decreases, production will have to spread over more forest land with greater annual disturbance.

One of the greatest shortcomings of the FSC approach is that there is no government participation in the process, as FSC members continue to mistrust or avoid government involvement. Excluding governments that own, control, and manage forests or grant usage rights in most areas of the world is a suboptimal approach at best. Additionally, there is the thorny issue of seeking to impose standards on government forests that are different from those developed by governments. Some critics argue that third-party certification is redundant or unjustifiable when governments' existing supervision and control mechanisms are already in place. They stress that from a democratic perspective, governments are best placed to regulate and manage forests in the public interest because they represent all the stakeholders. Except for the United States and some parts of Europe, most forests are publicly owned and, hence, governments are generally better placed to address the externalities involved in exploiting public goods.

Forest companies in the United States have criticized the FSC for (1) maintaining principles that are not scientifically based and do not represent good forestry practices; (2) insisting on the chain of custody approach, which is almost impossible to implement in the U.S. context; (3) ignoring lack of consumer support for labelling of products; and (4) discriminating against renewable wood and paper products. There are similar concerns in Canada. Furthermore, U.S. forest companies complain that the FSC considers government laws and regulations to be inadequate and incompatible with FSC principles that are intended to go beyond regulatory compliance. They argue that the FSC scheme bypasses and negates established processes and duplicates the role performed by state or provincial forestry and other regulatory agencies.[9]

The FSC also gains rents from the use of its label. If the FSC succeeds in its plan to operate globally, it stands to earn considerable profits from certification fees, and some critics wonder how this money will be used.

Forestry Management in Canada

Canada is the world's largest exporter of forest products, accounting for approximately 19 per cent of the total value of world exports. Forests are an integral part of the historical development of the Canadian economy and hold an important position in the Canadian psyche. Furthermore, the vast majority of forests in Canada are publicly owned. According to Statistics Canada, the forestry sector (pulp, paper, wood, and wood products) accounted for $38.3 billion in exports in 1996. The sector involves about 3,500 companies and is responsible for more than 280,000 jobs.

Slightly more than 50 per cent of Canada's forest land (2.44 million square kilometres) is designated as commercial or 'timber productive.' An estimated 7.6 per cent (317,000 square kilometres) of Canada's forests are formally protected by legislation. In addition, approximately 5 per cent of forests on steep slopes or along waterways are protected from harvesting by provincial policy, and a further 38 per cent of Canada's forests are considered open forests in which no commercial harvesting takes place because the trees are either too small or of poor commercial value. Less than one half of one per cent of Canada's commercial forest is harvested each year (WTO, 1998).

In 1992 the Canadian Council of Forest Ministers (CCFM), in conjunction with organizations representing the interests of naturalists, wildlife, Native peoples, foresters, labour, private forest landowners, academics, and forest industries, released a national strategy to manage and protect Canada's forests in a sustainable manner (CCFM, 1996). The objective of the strategy is to ensure that Canada's approach to forest management includes both timber and non-timber values, while protecting the integrity, health, and diversity of the Canadian forest ecosystem. The strategy was reviewed in 1997; the analysis revealed that significant progress had been made towards achieving sustainable development but that further work is required. Following consultations with interested parties, the CCFM is in the process of designing a new strategy.

At the international level, Canada has participated actively in the Montreal Process to develop criteria for defining sustainable forestry. This forum involves twelve countries representing 90 per cent of the world's boreal and temperate forests. In 1993, based on international discussions pursuant to the U.N. Commission on Environmental Development (UNCED), the CCFM sought to define, measure, and report on the forest sector for *all* Canadians. The CCFM consulted extensively with officials and scientists from the federal, provincial, and territorial governments, as well as with experts from academia, industry, NGOs, Aboriginal communities, and various other interest groups. This was distilled in the document entitled *Defining Sustainable Forest Management: A Canadian Approach to Criteria and Indicators*, released in 1995.

Given the political sensitivity surrounding forest preservation and use today, it is difficult to achieve full consensus on approaches to the sustainable management of forests. The best option is to seek as broad a representation as possible, as well as a democratic and open process of consultation regarding the formulation of policies for forest use. To a large extent, the Canadian national regulatory framework for forest management meets these conditions, with the provincial governments playing the central role. As societal values change, forest policy and management practices will follow. As forestry policy and management practices adapt to changing values, however, it is important to distinguish between those driven by scientific findings and those that are limited to social value preferences alone.

The CSA Sustainable Forestry Management Standard

The Canadian Standards Association has developed a standard for sustainable forest management (CSA Z808/Z809) that is based on the ISO 14001 environmental management system. It includes several requirements specific to the Canadian forest management situation. Six criteria and twenty-one critical elements for sustainable forest management approved by the CCFM were written into the standard (see Figure 5.1). The eighty-three national indicators are included in the annex for information and guidance in the development of a suitable mix of indicators for any specific forest. Furthermore, CSA Z808/Z809 includes a requirement for public input into the development of policy, forest planning management objectives, and programs to achieve them.

Unlike the FSC, the CSA standard does not mandate a 'chain of custody' requirement, nor does it result in a product label. It is an environmental management system based on respect for nationally developed criteria (by the CCFM), federal and provincial regulations, and requirements for public consultations and input. In other words, it operates in a specific regulatory context. CSA's sustainable forestry management standard does have performance objectives that are stated

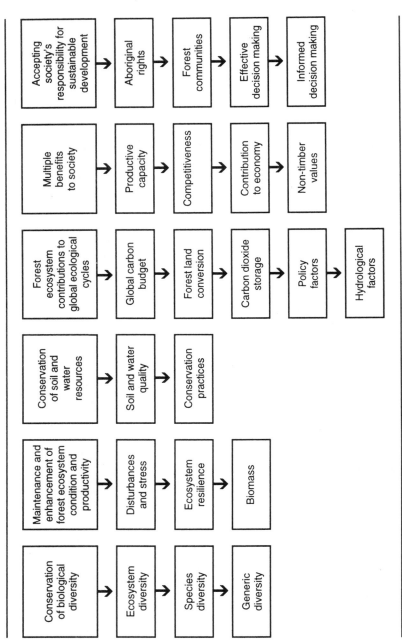

Figure 5.1 Sustainable forest management criteria and critical elements

in regulations and further developed through public consultations. CSA Z808/Z809 was approved by the Standards Council of Canada (SCC), the independent national body responsible for the development of standards. The SCC accepts and complies with the Code of Good Practice set out in the WTO Agreement on Technical Barriers to Trade.

To date, no Canadian companies have been certified as meeting the CSA sustainable forestry management standard. The Canadian Pulp and Paper Association (CPPA) reported in the autumn of 1997 that twenty-one companies were in the process of interpreting and applying the standard before applying to registrars certified by the SCC. The first registration of a company occurred in 1999.

Given the above, and the vast infrastructure of municipal, provincial, and federal regulations and processes regarding the management of forest lands, it is somewhat ironic that an externally based, non-scientific organization purports to determine that Canada's forests will not qualify as sustainably managed because they do not meet some of the criteria decided upon in a process that excludes governments and pays scant attention to economic interests.

Conclusions

As noted at the beginning of this chapter, governments share a dual concern regarding the need, on the one hand, to ensure that appropriate measures are in place to protect public health and safety and to address genuine environmental concerns and, on the other hand, to ensure that such measures do not unduly distort economies and reduce opportunities for rational development and growth. Because these concerns are widely shared, governments have gone to considerable lengths to put in place an international regulatory framework that preserves the right of governments to regulate for reasons of public health and safety and other legitimate societal goals, while also seeking to ensure such regulations are based on science, are applied equitably, and are minimally distortive. Product certification and labelling requirements are an integral part of health and safety regulation, and, thus, certification processes for governments and agencies accredited by them are also constrained by internationally agreed rules.

Voluntary certification claiming preferred product characteristics and production processes are, however, largely a marketing issue outside the framework for regulatory requirements. The purpose of such certification and its associated labels is to attract consumer preference by informing consumers about some allegedly superior characteristic of a product or about the environmental impact of producing it. This type of certification and labelling generally falls outside of international rules and, in most cases, it would be inappropriate for governments to engage in such activities as distinctions must be maintained between market-driven claims and the responsibilities of governments as regulators, promoters of public policy, and, in some cases, owners of public resources.

The true market impact for environmentally certified forest products is not clear. Surveys indicate that while consumers may be interested in reduced environmental impacts, they are seldom willing to pay more for certified products (Ramsteiner et al. 1998: 5; Carter and Murray, 1998: 23–8). In light of the uncertainty of consumer demand, the FSC network of supporters has concentrated its efforts on corporate buyers who could be vulnerable to charges of environmental irresponsibility. Through the potential use of traditional street theatre and other coercive tactics, Greenpeace and the WWF have persuaded senior managers of large corporations to join their buyers' clubs and to pledge exclusive purchase, use, or resale of FSC-certified products as they become available. Related public relations campaigns aimed at establishing the FSC standard as the primary standard for minimizing deleterious environmental impacts will reward buyers' club members by identifying them as environmentally concerned businesses.

Forming buyers' clubs of large industrial users, wholesalers, and retailers of a broad category of forest-based products is a brilliant strategy that could, if successful, close large segments of the market to products that do not qualify for FSC certification. As discussed above, Canadian authorities have gone to great lengths to develop and implement a regulatory system for Canadian forests that meets the balance of Canadian interests and requirements, including environmental concerns. The FSC's overriding concerns with environmental issues and the public stance taken by major FSC players, such as Greenpeace, that all logging activities should cease in the coastal rainforests of British Columbia, suggest that major portions of B.C.'s forest industries may not qualify for FSC certification no matter what balance of interests form the basis of government regulation of forest management and use. In short, the highly sophisticated tactics now being used by environmental activists are intended to render science-based regulations irrelevant. If they are able to certify sufficient forests in other jurisdictions to satisfy the needs of their U.K. buyers' clubs, success there could spread. This would likely result in increased demands for certification on the part of B.C.'s competitors, as they seek to ensure their continuing market access, thereby eliminating B.C. forest products from competition for major sectors of the international market.

Such use of certification is a disguised barrier to trade that would clearly be contrary to WTO rules if the certifiers fell within their ambit. The FSC, however, is a non-governmental body that does not have the legal power to enforce its measures, and is not a recognized body in the sense of the TBT agreement. Thus, it does not fall within the ambit of WTO rules.

Canada has argued in the WTO that voluntary labelling schemes are subject to the TBT's notification requirements set out in the Code of Good Practice, regardless of the kind of information provided on the label. Canada has also argued that bodies that develop and run eco-labelling programs should be considered as standardizing bodies (WTO, 1996). But WTO rules are enforceable only against WTO members, hence, any complaint about the trade-distorting activities of the FSC would have to be directed against the WTO member (national government) responsible for it. As no government takes responsibility for FSC actions, there is no basis for a claim under WTO dispute-settlement procedures.

To the extent that the FSC actually uses coercive tactics to recruit members to its buyers' clubs, it may be liable to prosecution under national competition laws. My colleague's consultations with U.K. and EU competition authorities, however, indicate that prosecution would not appear to be appropriate at least for the time being as, while the operation of buyers' groups may have the effect of distorting the market, they are not necessarily anti-competitive. In this respect the FSC is playing very close to the line, and it may be that they could run up against Articles 85 and 86 of the EU Treaty if their efforts to recruit wide membership in buyers' groups are hugely successful.[10] In any event, this aspect of FSC activities will not be clarified unless someone with the necessary standing brings a case before the European Court.

The FSC certification system is not yet sufficiently widely implemented to actually exclude Canadian forest products from major markets. It could, however, pose a serious threat to Canada's forest industry if it gains widespread popularity and becomes the label of choice for firms accounting for the majority of forest product purchases in a given market – as would be the case if enough FSC-certified products were available to meet the purchasing requirements of the current members of the U.K. buyers' club. Thus, it cannot be lightly dismissed. If it is able to certify enough temperate forests outside Canada, it could effectively dictate the terms of entry for all but the fringes of the U.K. market. Because the Canadian forest industry is so heavily dependent on exports for its commercial viability, Canada's regulatory structure for the industry and the resource would become commercially irrelevant if market entry were to be dependent upon a different certifying (and hence regulating) system. In such circumstances, Canada's science-based regulatory system would, indeed, be undermined.

Is the FSC a result of unique circumstances such that this approach will not be replicated with respect to other Canadian resources? Not necessarily. As noted above, environmental activists are highly adept at learning from their experience and applying successful techniques to other areas. Another example is already beginning to emerge. The WWF and Unilever launched the Marine Stewardship Council in 1997. Its aim is to work for sustainable marine fisheries by promoting responsible, environmentally appropriate, socially beneficial, and economically viable fisheries practices, while maintaining the biodiversity, productivity, and ecological processes of the marine environment. The MSC is in the process of developing and refining its principles and criteria which would operate in a similar manner to those of the FSC. The first official MSC National Working Group was established in the United Kingdom in December 1997 (Marine Stewardship Council, 1998). Consultation workshops with fisheries' stakeholders have been held in Canada, the United States, South Africa, Scotland, Germany, Australia, New Zealand, and Norway.

It is not clear, however, that establishment of the MSC is part of a wider trend towards such certifying bodies. Fisheries is a special case. The success of government regulation of the resource is highly debatable, as is witnessed by the current circumstances of the commercial fisheries off Canada's east and west coasts. ENGOs, by their nature, will be most attracted to areas where they believe government policies have failed. While it is doubtful that the FSC template will be widely replicated, it is clear that civil society is playing a greater part in policy making and that international coordination of single-interest and other niche groups is greatly facilitated by their increasing use of the Internet and its various electronic fora. Even if not widely replicable, the as yet immature FSC and the nascent MSC suggest there will be need for greater efforts by governments to incorporate the views of special interests into the regulatory process. The process has never been entirely science-based. Societal interests have always played a role. But societal interests are frequently fragmented, and it is difficult, if not impossible, to take account of all of them. Nonetheless, if a single-interest constituency is able to organize itself into a cohesive force as potentially powerful as the FSC may be, the regulatory process will have to find a way to accommodate it or risk having non-accountable groups undermine the more formal processes.

Notes

1 This summary of events is based on the writer's personal involvement in the final stage of the seal hunt and the establishment of the Royal Commission that led to its termination.

2 This summary of events is based on the writer's personal involvement in federal government activities relating to international actions against Canada's fur-trapping practices and to the fur industry per se.

3 The examples in this section of the paper are drawn from the writer's personal experiences in seeking to defend Canadian forestry management practices from activist attacks.

4 This and the following three sections of this chapter are adapted from an as yet unpublished paper prepared by two of my colleagues, Ramesh Chaitoo and Professor Michael Hart.

5 Some FSC-accredited certifications have been publicly challenged for a number of reasons including (1) the quality of assessment work (Costa Rica); (2) contradictory and ambiguous information and interpretations presented by stakeholders (Gabon); (3) participatory issues in defining the standards and consultations with interested parties (Poland).

6 Communication from Hilde Stroot of the Heart for Wood Campaign of Friends of the Earth, Netherlands.

7 Correspondence from the mentioned municipalities.

8 The FSC has indicated that it will address this in the near future.

9 The American Forest and Paper Association has made adherence to a set of sustainable forestry principles and implementation guidelines a condition of its membership. However, the environmental community holds the opposite view. A 1998 study *At the Cutting Edge* published by the Sierra Club argues that government management of Canadian forests

130   Dennis Browne (with Ramesh Chaitoo and Michael Hart)

is inadequate and biased towards the commercial forest products industry.
10 Based on correspondence with the U.K. Office of Fair Trading.

References

Canadian Council of Forestry Ministers. (1996). *Sustainable Forests: A Canadian Commitment.* Ottawa: Canadian Council of Foresty Ministers.

Carter, Douglas, and Frank Murray. (1998). 'The Nature and Status of Certification in the United States.' *Forest Products Journal*, 48(2): 23–8.

GATT. (1988). *GATT Panel Report on 'Measures Affecting Exports of Unprocessed Herring and Salmon'* L/6268, adopted on 22 March. 35S/98. Geneva: GATT.

– (1991). *GATT Panel Report on 'United States Restrictions on Imports of Tuna.'* DS21/R (unadopted), 9 September. 39S/155. Geneva: GATT.

International Tropical Timber Organization. (1998). 'Timber Certification: Progress and Issues.' March. Http://www.itto.org.jp/pds/199803.html

Kiekens, Jean-Pierre. (1997). *Certification: International Trends and Forestry and Trade Implications.* Study Prepared for Environmental Strategies Europe for the Ministry of the Environment, Natural Resources and Agriculture of the Walloon Region.

Marine Stewardship Council. (1998). *Newsletter* 4. January.

Ramsteiner, Ewald. (1998). 'Potential Markets for Certified Forest Products in Europe.' European Forest Institute. Discussion Paper. March.

Reynolds, Michael. (1997). 'EU Competition Policy in the Aftermath of Central Planning.' *International Business Lawyer*. November, 453–5.

WTO. (1996). *United States-Standards for Reformulated and Conventional Gasoline.* World Trade Organization Panel (17/01/96) and Appelate (22/04/96) Reports. Geneva: World Trade Organization.

WTO. (1998). WTO Committee on Trade and the Environment, 'Forests: A National Experience (Contribution by Canada).' WT/CTE/W/G/TBT/W (March). Geneva: WTO.

6 Risk-Based Regulatory Responses in Global Food Trade: A Case Study of Guatemalan Raspberry Imports into the United States and Canada, 1996–1998

DOUGLAS POWELL

On 11 June 1998, the associate medical officer of health for the City of Toronto, Dr Barbara Yaffe, announced that health officials were investigating more than sixty cases of cyclospora in people who had consumed contaminated food between 7 May and 15 May 1998 at seven different private dinners and catered events around the city (Canadian Press, 1998; Robertson, 1998a). While health officials were understandably reluctant to implicate any specific food, others immediately observed that in the previous two years, approximately 2,500 North Americans had been stricken with cyclospora, almost exclusively linked to the consumption of fresh raspberries from Guatemala, and at almost the exact same time of year (Robertson, 1998b).

But something was different in the 1998 case. In the past, cases tended to be clustered in large urban centres throughout North America. In 1998, however, only people in and around Toronto were getting sick; people in the United States had apparently been spared the painful and persistent diarrhoea associated with cyclospora infection.

As one U.S. epidemiologist noted, 'Canada's got some explaining to do' (Douglas Powell, 1998a, and personal communication). That is because officials from the U.S. Food and Drug Administration (FDA) had previously visited raspberry farms in Guatemala and decided to place a ban on the importation of fresh raspberries from Guatemala into the United States because of concerns about sanitary conditions. The ban was publicly announced and even the topic of widely covered U.S. Senate hearings.

To date, there has been no public explanation of why Canada allowed importation of Guatemalan raspberries in 1998, even though several journalists have directly asked health authorities, even though cyclospora is a serious and persistent parasitic infection, and even though it is known that Canadian officials visited Guatemalan farms in late March 1998 (Douglas Powell, 1998b, and personal communication). What was it that made FDA regulators conclude that Guatemalan raspberries should be banned from the United States, while Canada decided to continue importation? While the answer may never publicly be known, the question raises fundamental issues about the nature of food-borne risk, the interpretation of scientific data in an era of international trade, and serious questions about the Canadian government's commitment to regulatory transparency and public accountability. At the very least, the 305 people who were eventually confirmed to have been infected with cyclospora in the 1998 Toronto outbreak would probably appreciate an answer.

This chapter explores the differences in risk-based regulatory responses in global food trade by Canada compared with the United States as reflected in the case study of imported Guatemalan raspberries. Some key facts about the case have already been highlighted above, but before proceeding further on the case itself we need to locate the case against the larger backdrop of changing international regimes of global food trade and debate about the nature of risk assessment, risk management, and risk communication. Accordingly, the first three sections of the chapter deal respectively with food safety in the global trade system, the nature of risk assessment in food safety, and debates about the integration of risk assessment, risk management, and risk communication. The fourth and fifth sections of the chapter then return to the case study itself, showing its trajectory of development in the United States and Canada and the relative failure of the Canadian regime to respond appropriately. Conclusions then follow.

The purpose of the chapter is not to follow the case in a detailed way as it was handled *within* specific regulatory bodies, but rather to examine it in a broader manner by seeing risk analysis and regulation in terms of a larger set of players, including the media and the scientific community and how broader interests can engage in the process in a transparent way. These larger features become ever more important as global food trade increases under the auspices of new trade laws.

Food Safety and Global Trade

Lammerding and Paoli (1998) note that the changing epidemiology of food-borne diseases is a result of complex interactions and changes in pathogens, foods, food distribution, food consumption, and population immunity. Predicting the impact of a trend in one part of the food continuum presupposes an understanding of the whole system. Aspects of the food-processing and -distribution system can amplify or attenuate the trend as it grows into a potential health hazard. While a full understanding of pathogen contamination, infection, and survival is difficult, a systematic approach to assessing the impact of the pathogen on health may improve the quality of public health decisions (Rodricks, 1994; Foegeding et al., 1994).

Cyclospora in fresh produce is one of many examples of food-related trade disputes, albeit one that focuses more on levels of bureaucratic accountability than on international trade and interpretations of risk assessment. From a domestic perspective, science-based arguments of excess risk associated with an imported product may be the only means to protect public health. From an exporter's perspective, science-based arguments of decreased or equivalent risk may be the only defence against arbitrarily applied restrictions in international trade (Smith and Fratamico, 1996). The problem becomes then: What is a science-based argument?

The World Trade Organization (WTO, formerly GATT) agreement contains subagreements dealing with sanitary and phytosanitary (SPS) measures. These agreements came into effect on 1 January 1995 and are designed to curb the use of unjustified sanitary measures for the purposes of trade protection. For the purpose of the SPS, 'a sanitary measure is defined as a measure applied to protect human or animal life or health within the territory of the member from risks arising from food additives, contaminants, toxins or disease-causing organisms in food, beverages and feedstuff' (World Health Organization, 1995).

The agreements apply to all regulations and procedures including end-product specifications, processing and production methods, sampling procedures and risk assessment methods, and packaging and labelling requirements directly related to food safety. The basic principles espoused in the WTO SPS agreement state that sanitary and phytosanitary measures:

- Must be the least trade-restrictive in accomplishing their objectives
- Must be subjected to risk assessment to demonstrate that the measure does not exceed an appropriate and consistent national level of protection
- Cannot be more stringent for imports than for agricultural goods and food products of domestic origin. (ibid.)

Scientific standards, guidelines, and recommendations for some SPS measures are established by the Codex Alimentarius Commission (food safety), the International Office of Epizootics (animal health), the International Plant Protection Convention (plant health), and other international organizations identified by the WTO Committee on Sanitary and Phytosanitary Measures.

More concretely, there is an explicit linkage between the standards, guidelines, and recommendations of the Codex Alimentarius Commission and the WTO SPS agreements. In effect, if a member nation of the WTO complies with a relevant Codex standard, guideline, or recommendation, the product shall be presumed to have met its health and safety obligations and should not be denied market access. The SPS agreement preserves the rights of sovereign nations to set their own level of protection which may be more stringent than that of the Codex. However, the specific requirements that stem from this raised level of protection can be challenged on the basis of their scientific justification, or if a lesser standard is applied to domestic products.

Nations have the right to protect their agricultural systems, the health and well-being of their citizens, and their physical environments, but these protective measures can be interpreted as non-tariff trade barriers. The SPS agreement focuses on science and risk assessments as central to SPS decision making. A key feature for meeting this goal is a notion of establishing safety equivalency among signatory nations. But what constitutes an appropriate risk assessment can often be thrown into question.

Risk Assessment and Food Safety

Risk assessment is a component of risk analysis which was first formalized by the U.S. National Academy of Sciences – through its U.S. National Research Council – in 1983, in a publication commonly referred to as, *The Red Book*. Covello and Merkhofer (1994) define risk as a combination of something that is undesirable and uncertain. More specifically, 'the possibility of an adverse outcome, and uncertainty over the occurrence, timing or magnitude of that adverse outcome.' The 1983 NAS-NRC model explicitly distinguished between three stages of risk analysis: risk assessment, risk management, and risk communication. Risk assessment, it was argued, is a scientific assessment of the true risk; risk management allowed for the incorporation of non-scientific factors to reach a policy decision; and risk communication involved the communication of a policy decision. The limitations of risk assessment are discussed by the U.S. National Research Council Commission on Life Sciences Board on Environmental Studies and Toxicology Committee on Risk Assessment (U.S. National Research Council, 1983).

A risk assessment method is any self-contained systematic procedure conducted as part of a risk assessment that can be used to help generate a probability distribution for health or environmental consequences (Covello and Merkhofer, 1994). The NAS-NRC model of risk assessment consists of:

- Hazard identification – the determination of whether a particular chemical is or is not causally linked to particular health effects
- Dose-response assessment – the determination of the relation between the magnitude of exposure and the probability of occurrence of the health effects in question
- Exposure assessment – the determination of the extent of human exposure before or after application of regulatory controls
- Risk characterization – the description of the nature and often the magnitude of human risk, including attendant uncertainty.

These components of risk assessment have been endorsed and incorporated into the principles of risk assessment adopted by the U.S. National Advisory Committee on Microbiological Criteria for Foods (1998).

Lammerding and Paoli (1998) have summarized these four steps as applied to emerging food-borne pathogens. These include:

- Hazard identification – An association between disease and the presence of a pathogen in a food is documented. The information may describe conditions under which the pathogen survives, grows, causes infection, and dies. Epidemiological and surveillance data, challenge testing, and scientific studies of pathogenicity also contribute information. Data collected during hazard identification are later used in the assessment of exposure, where the impact of processing, distribution, preparation, and consumption of the food are incorporated.
- Exposure assessment – A description of the pathways through which a pathogen population is introduced, distributed, and challenged in the production, distribution, and consumption of

food. This step differs from hazard identification in that it describes a particular food-processing pathway. Depending on the scope of the risk assessment, exposure assessment can begin with the prevalence of the pathogen in raw materials or it can begin with the description of the population of the pathogen at subsequent steps such as input to a food-processing step.

- Dose-response assessment – A translation of the final exposure to a pathogen population into a health response in the population of consumers. The differences in response among various susceptible populations are important features in this step.
- Risk characterization – The integration of information gathered in the previous steps to estimate the risk to a population, or in some cases, to a particular type of consumer. In this step, by modifying the assumptions in the parameters of previous steps, the effects of these alternate assumptions on ultimate health risk can be evaluated and studied. Assumptions can be changed to study the impact of lack of knowledge and the potential gains through further research or to suggest the impact of a suspected trend. For this type of analysis, risk assessments are typically done in a computer environment to ease the computational burden and provide rapid responses to hypothetical questions using alternate assumptions and situations.

An alternative model of risk assessment presented by Covello and Merkhofer (1994) regards hazard identification as an altogether separate process that is necessarily conducted prior to risk assessment. These authors argue that treating hazard identification as merely one component of risk assessment underplays its importance. In a further conceptual difference, Covello and Merkhofer (1994) treat release assessment as a separate step because, for important types of risk such as industrial accidents or failures involving large technological systems, quantifying and describing the potential for a risk source to release risk agents into the environment consumes as much or more effort as the other steps of risk assessment.

Finally, while the last step of the Covello-Merkhofer model of risk assessment, like the NAS-NRC model, is one of integration, Covello and Merkhofer call it risk estimation to 'emphasize the view that risk is a characteristic of the world we live in and that the goal of risk assessment is to communicate that risk estimate in human terms, not to produce some abstract output from a risk assessment model.'

Beyond differences in risk assessment ideology, the NAS-NRC paradigm itself has recently been criticized as unworkable and unrealistic. Covello and Merkhofer (1994: 31) argue: 'The current state of the art of risk assessment does not permit questions of science to be clearly separated from questions of policy. In practice, assumptions that have potential policy implications enter into risk assessment at virtually every stage of the process. The ideal of a risk assessment that is free, or nearly free, of policy considerations is beyond the realm of possibility.'

Even the use of conservatism – the risk assessor errs on the side of safety – is a value judgment deliberately introduced into risk assessments to account for uncertainty. It can produce highly distorted risk assessments that affect the pattern of regulation and thus prevent limited resources for health and safety from being efficiently allocated.

Integrating Risk Assessment, Management, and Communication

Soby et al. (1993), in a review of risk communication research and its applicability for managing food-related risks, developed the concept of the risk management cycle. In this model, public and other stakeholder concerns are actively sought at each stage of the management process – including assessment. 'Unless the risk assessment procedure involves an element of interactive public participation and mutual questioning the decisions and conclusions reached may be more likely to be challenged' (Simpson, 1994). This integrative approach to risk analysis was endorsed by the U.S. National Academy of Sciences National Research Council Committee on Risk Characterization, which urged risk assessors to expand risk characterization beyond the current practice of translating the results of a risk analysis into non-technical terms. What was needed was an analytical-deliberative approach that involves stakeholders from the very inception of a risk assessment. Risk characterization needs to be reframed from an activity that happens at the end of the risk assessment process, as many people understand it, to a continuous, back-and-forth dialogue between risk assessors and stakeholders that allows the problem to be formulated properly, and depends on an iterative, analytic-deliberative process.

Similarly, the U.S. Presidential/Congressional Commission on Risk Assessment and Risk Management (1997) developed an integrative framework to help all types of risk managers – government officials, private sector businesses, and individual members of the public – make good risk management decisions. The framework has six stages (see Figure 6.1):

- Define the problem and put it in context.
- Analyse the risks associated with the problem in context.
- Examine options for addressing the risks.
- Make decisions about which options to implement.
- Take actions to implement the decisions.
- Conduct an evaluation of the action's results.

Of particular importance is that the framework is conducted in collaboration with stakeholders and using iterations if new information is developed that changes the need for, or nature of, risk management. Because of the inadequacy of scientific knowledge and the lack of public trust in government and in experts, risk regulators should be concerned with creating both institutional arrangements likely to foster trust and mechanisms for providing concerned individuals with credible reassurance.

In 1997, the United Nations Food and Agriculture Organization and the World Health Organization hosted a joint Expert Consultation on the Application of Risk Management to Food Safety Matters at which the ultimate objective of food safety standards were again reiterated: first, consumer protection; second, facilitation of global trade (World Health Organization, 1997).

Risk management is defined within Codex as the process of weighing policy alternatives in the light of the results of risk assessment and, if required, selecting and implementing appropriate control options, including regulatory measures. The outcome of the risk management process, as undertaken by committees within the Codex Alimentarius system, is the development of standards, guidelines, and other recommendations for food safety. In the national situation it is likely that different risk management decisions could be made according to different criteria and different ranges of risk management options. However, the resulting World Health Organization report seemed to move towards at least a recognition of the integrative model when it concluded that a review of current Codex standards and related texts suggested that in many cases there is insufficient quantitative information to translate requirements for 'safety and wholesomeness' into a definitive quantitative assessment of the risks to human health in consumer populations (World Health Organization, 1997).

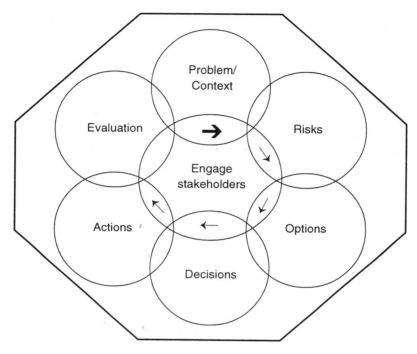

Figure 6.1 Integrated framework for risk assessment and risk management.

The inevitable default to more qualitative assessments of safe and wholesome is likely to be challenged as a basis for international trade restrictions, especially in an increasingly risk-based international trade environment. The development of Codex-wide principles and strategies for risk management requires that explicit attention be given to the concept of safe and wholesome. Further, the report concluded that although Codex standards and related texts are generally aimed at the reduction of risks in food, these risks can rarely be quantified, and any balancing of the risk reduction against other factors, such as costs and benefits of risk reduction, is normally a matter of judgment. Although industry and national regulators strive for production and processing systems that ensure that all food be safe and wholesome, complete freedom from risks is an unattainable goal. Safety and wholesomeness are related to a level of risk that society regards as reasonable in the context, and in comparison with other risks in everyday life.

There was also an explicit recognition in the report that risk assessment policy – the guidelines for value judgment and policy choices that may need to be applied at specific decision points in the risk assessment process – is a risk management responsibility, which should be carried out in full collaboration with risk assessors, and which serves to protect the scientific integrity of the risk assessment. The guidelines should be documented so as to ensure consistency and transparency. Examples of risk assessment policy setting are establishing the population(s) at risk, establishing criteria for ranking of hazards, and guidelines for application of safety factors (see the Appendix at the end of this chapter).

The committee also defined risk profiling as the process of describing a food safety problem and its context, in order to identify those elements of the hazard or risk relevant to various risk management decisions. The risk profile would include identifying aspects of hazards relevant to prioritizing and setting the risk assessment policy and aspects of the risk relevant to the choice of safety standards and management options. For example, the committee wrote that a typical risk profile might include a brief description of the situation, product, or commodity involved; the values expected to be placed at risk, (for example, human health or economic concerns); potential consequences; consumer perception of the risks; and the distribution of risks and benefits. When reviewing the complete details of the 1997 joint risk management framework, it becomes apparent that the model is much more similar to the integrative models incorporating risk assessment, management, and communication as a functional entity.

The Codex Alimentarius Commission (CAC) has concluded that the microbiological safety of foods is principally assured by control at the source, product design, and process control and the application of good hygienic practices during production, processing (including labelling), handling, distribution, storage, sale, preparation, and use, preferably in conjunction with the application of the Hazard Analysis and Critical Control Point (HACCP) system. This 'preventive' system offers more control than end-product testing, because the effectiveness of microbiological examination in assessing the safety of food is limited (FAO/WHO, 1996).

Quantitative risk assessment of microbiological hazards provides a focus for discussions among workers from diverse disciplines, including farmers, veterinarians, food-processing experts, microbiologists, and consumer behaviour experts. The model also allows for consideration and comparison of control strategies in a simulated environment (Lammerding and Paoli, 1998). Further, microbial risk assessment based on a model provides a repository of knowledge describing health risk outcomes and control strategies that can be iteratively updated and adapted. Nevertheless, the large amount of scientific uncertainty inherent in quantitative risk assessment means that an integrative approach incorporating management and communication considerations must be included in any policy about a particular food source, as well as a full and transparent accounting of the factors and uncertainties included in a specific risk assessment.

Cyclospora Strikes – Mistaken Identity

With these larger issues as context I can now return to the Guatemalan raspberry case study itself knowing that it was arriving on the risk agenda in the midst of developments and debates that were central to regulatory regimes in both the United States and Canada. The case itself is usefully divided into a two-part story, the first part of which is characterized as the emergence of cyclospora but with a mistaken identity.

Cyclospora cayetanensis is a recently characterized coccidian parasite. The first known cases of infection in humans were diagnosed in 1977, with sporadic reporting increasing through the 1980s, perhaps because of better detection. Before 1996 only three outbreaks of cyclospora infection had been reported in the United States. Cyclospora is normally associated with warm, Latin American countries with poor sanitation (Hofmann et al., 1996).

Cyclospora is transmitted through the fecal-oral route, such as the ingestion of food or water contaminated with human fecal material containing cyclospora. Cyclospora infects the small intestine (bowel) and usually causes watery diarrhoea, with frequent, sometimes explosive, bowel movements, usually about one week after exposure. Other symptoms can include loss of appetite, substantial loss of weight, bloating, increased gas, stomach cramps, nausea, vomiting, muscle aches, low-grade fever, and fatigue. Some people who are infected with cyclospora do not have any symptoms. The recommended treatment for infection with cyclospora is a combination of two antibiotics, trimethoprim-sulfamethoxazole, also known as Bactrim, Septra, or Cotrim. If not treated, the illness may last from a few days to a month or longer. Cyclospora needs days or even weeks after being passed in a bowel movement to become infectious. Therefore, it is unlikely that cyclospora is passed directly from one person to another. It is unknown whether animals can be infected and pass infection to people. People of all ages are at risk for infection.

Cyclospora was thrust to public attention in North America on 12 June 1996, when Ontario's chief medical officer, Dr Richard Schabas, issued a public health advisory on the presumed link between consumption of California strawberries and an outbreak of diarrhoeal illness among some forty people in the Metro Toronto area (Immen, 1996). The announcement followed a similar statement from the Department of Health and Human Services in Houston, Texas, who were investigating a cluster of eighteen cases of cyclospora illness among oil executives (United Press International, 1996).

Dr Schabas advised consumers to wash California berries very carefully before eating them, and he recommended that people with compromised immune systems avoid them entirely. He also stated that Ontario strawberries, which were just beginning to be harvested, were safe for consumption. Nevertheless, people in Ontario stopped buying strawberries (MacKinnon, 1996). Two supermarket chains took California berries off their shelves, in response to pressure from consumers. The market collapsed so thoroughly that newspapers reported truck drivers headed for Toronto with loads of berries being directed, by telephone, to other markets.

However, by 20 June 1996, discrepancies began to appear in the link between California strawberries and illness caused by cyclospora (Altman, 1996), even though the number of reported illnesses continued to increase across North America. Texas health officials strengthened their assertion that California strawberries were the cause of the outbreak, while scientists at the U.S. Centre for Disease Control and Prevention (CDC) and the U.S. Food and Drug Administration said they were not yet ready to identify a food vehicle for the outbreak (Drago, 1996). On 27 June 1996 the New York City Health Department became the first in North America to publicly state that raspberries were also suspected in the outbreak of cyclospora ('NYC,' 1996).

By 18 July 1996 the CDC declared that raspberries from Guatemala – which, it was subsequently postulated, had been sprayed with pesticides mixed with water that could have been contaminated with human sewage containing cyclospora – were the likely source of the cyclospora outbreak, which ultimately sickened about 1,000 people across North America (Meyer, 1996). Guatemalan health authorities and producers vigorously refuted the charges ('Guatemala,' 1996; *PRNewswire*, 1996).

The California Strawberry Commission estimated that it lost $20 to $40 million in reduced strawberry sales. Teresa Thorne, a spokeswoman for the commission was quoted as saying, 'We have a lot of extremely frustrated people in California. We were the victim of a food scare. You can take consumer confidence away in a day and it takes forever to restore.' That is why, according to Thorne, consumers should not stop eating raspberries. 'It would be a tragedy if another West Coast commodity was impacted from this food scare. People can continue to enjoy raspberries. Just remember to read the labels.'

In an assessment that followed the 1996 outbreak, Herwaldt and Ackers (1997) concluded in the *New England Journal of Medicine* that a total of 1,465 cases of cyclosporiasis were reported by twenty U.S. states, the District of Columbia, and two Canadian provinces in 1996. Of these cases, 978 (66.8 per cent) were laboratory confirmed and 725 (49.5 per cent) were associated with fifty-five events that were held from 3 May through 14 June. Raspberries were definitely served at fifty events and may have been served at four others. For twenty-seven of the forty-one events for which adequate data were available (65.8 per cent), the associations between the consumption of berries (raspberries with or without other berries) and cyclosporiasis were statistically significant ($P < .05$). For all twenty-nine events for which there were good data, the raspberries definitely came from Guatemala (twenty-one events, 72.4 per cent) or may have come from Guatemala (eight events, 27.6 per cent). As few as five Guatemalan farms could have accounted for the twenty-five events for which the raspberries could be traced to a single exporter per event. Herwaldt and Ackers noted that the mode of contamination of the raspberries remained unclear, but CDC officials were subsequently quoted as saying that water used in pesticide solutions was the likely source of the outbreak and recommended that growers use potable water in pesticide mixtures that are applied either to soil or plants throughout the growing and harvesting seasons. On three farms implicated in the outbreak, workers stored the water for pesticide mixtures in reservoirs, 'some of which were open and could easily become contaminated' ('CDC,' 1997).

The *NEJM* article appeared along with an accompanying editorial by Michael Osterholm of the Minnesota Department of Health on 29 May 1997. Osterholm pointed out that the investigation conducted by Herwaldt and Ackers illustrated the changing epidemiological characteristics of food-borne disease in the United States, especially substantial alterations in the American diet over the past two decades and the globalization of the food supply.

Osterholm added that although the promotion of a 'heart-healthy' diet (high consumption of fruits and vegetables and low consumption of fat) may be improving cardiovascular health, it has led to a new range of problems for the gastrointestinal tract, and that seasonally, up to 70 per cent of selected fruits and vegetables consumed in the United States come from developing countries. 'One does not need to leave home to contract traveler's diarrhoea caused by an exotic agent,' wrote Osterholm, adding, 'Although produce from U.S. growers is also a source of pathogens, fruits and vegetables from developing countries are cause for additional concern.'

Osterholm also noted that Herwaldt and Ackers emphasized the potential role of contaminated water but gave only limited consideration of the role that birds or other animals may have had in contaminating the berries as natural carriers. 'The use of high-quality water for irrigation and pesticide spraying and other good management practices will not solve the problem of *C. cayetanensis* contamination if birds play a major part in that contamination ... The seasonal migration of wild birds in Guatemala needs to be evaluated as a possible explanation for the patterns seen with berry shipments and outbreaks of disease in the United States. One test of this hypothesis will be whether there is another outbreak of cyclosporiasis associated with this year's spring shipment of raspberries from Guatemala' (Herwaldt and Ackers, 1997: 1550).

By the time the *NEJM* articles appeared, North America was once again in the midst of a cyclospora outbreak, and again, Guatemalan raspberries were identified as the most likely vehicle.

Cyclospora: A Public Response to a Scientific Puzzle (At Least in the United States)

In the second part of the case study story, it is evident that the U.S. regulatory regime, defined here to include a larger public interplay between regulatory authorities, the media, the public, and the science community, handled the raspberry and cyclospora case with greater transparency and efficacy than did Canada.

As early as 18 April 1997 two possible clusters of cases of cyclospora infection were being investigated in Florida (Division of Parasitic Diseases [DPD], NCID, CDC, 1997) and on 22 April 1998 the *Tallahassee Democrat*, a Florida newspaper, reported that seven area residents became ill with cyclospora after eating at Koolbeanz Cafe, described as a trendy eatery, on 19 and 20 March (Svingen, 1997).

Soon there were others. Don Willis of the Texas Department of Health wrote on ProMed, an Internet-based listserve containing information about outbreaks of infectious disease, that fifty-six out of eighty-nine patrons who attended a banquet at a Houston, Texas, hotel on 25 April 1997 developed symptoms resembling cyclospora infection, and as of 20 May 1997, fourteen had confirmed (by stool sample) cyclospora infection. Willis added that approximately eighty-five patrons completed questionnaires, and statistical information developed from those questionnaires indicated that there was a high probability that the infection resulted from eating a bavarian creme dessert that contained fresh strawberries, raspberries, blackberries, and blueberries, garnished with the same fruit items. By 22 May 1997 the story hit the national media, with the Associated Press wire service reporting that cyclospora had sickened eighty people in seven outbreaks across the United States. On 30 May 1997, the day after the *NEJM* papers appeared, which generated significant, national media attention, the *Fort Lauderdale Sun-Sentinel* in Florida reported two more additional outbreaks, one in New York City and one in Ontario, bringing the total number of cases in 1997 to more than 400.

In response, Guatemalan raspberry growers announced a temporary suspension of exports to the United States. Ricardo Santa Cruz, director of the Agricultural Commission of Exporters of Non-Traditional Products, said that the suspension of exports could affect more than 250 producers and 5,000 workers and could mean the loss of up to $10 million worth of income. On 12 June 1997 the FDA was cited as saying in a news report about the 1997 cyclospora outbreak that it would convene a public meeting in July to review the science on cyclospora on fresh produce and its control ('FDA,' 1997).

The cyclospora story then took an unexpected twist; uncertainty is, after all part of any risk analysis. On 7 July a company physician reported to the Alexandria Department of Health that most of the employees who attended a corporate luncheon on 26 June at the company's branch in Fairfax, Virginia, had developed gastrointestinal illness (Center for Disease Control, 1997). On 11 July the health department was notified that a stool specimen from one of the employees who attended the luncheon was positive for cyclospora oocysts. Many others subsequently tested positive. It was later revealed, in a

19 July 1997 story in the *Washington Post* citing local health department officials, that basil and pesto from four Sutton Place Gourmet
stores around Washington, DC, was the source of cyclospora for 126
people who attended at least nineteen separate events where Sutton
Place basil products were served, from small dinner parties and
baby showers to corporate gatherings (Masters, 1997a). Of the 126,
thirty members of the National Symphony Orchestra became sick after they ate box lunches provided by Sutton Place at Wolf Trap Farm
Park.

Food and Drug Administration spokesman Arthur Whitmore was
cited as saying that the chain buys basil from several sources, so FDA
investigators were trying to track the contaminated batch to a specific
producer, adding, 'It can be an incredibly difficult process, and it can
take weeks.' In addition to unsanitary water, basil or any other produce could become contaminated from contact with workers who may
be carrying the parasite without displaying symptoms, or through
contact with other infected produce.

A follow-up piece in the *Washington Post* (Masters, 1997b) stated
that if basil was the culprit, it could have been contaminated in the
Sutton Place Gourmet's warehouse or kitchen, or it could mean that
one of its suppliers – a wholesaler or farmer – sold contaminated basil.
Sutton Place spokeswoman Betsy Garside was cited as saying the company believed the basil must have arrived contaminated because there
were no documented cases in which food handlers were the source.
But officials at Rock Garden, a Washington- and Miami-based grower
and distributor that sells basil to Sutton and dozens of wholesalers
and caterers, were cited as saying they did not understand how bad
basil could have come through their warehouses and shown up only
at Sutton Place. Lolo Mengel, co-owner and general manager of the
Washington branch was quoted as saying, 'We sell probably 2,000 to
3,000 pounds [of basil] a week, and Sutton only gets 100 to 200 pounds.'
'It doesn't make scientific sense.' (Actually it could have made sense.
Most cases of food-borne illness are believed to be sporadic, only involving a single individual, and are rarely reported. Most people do
not go to the doctor in response to gastrointestinal upset, believing
erroneously that they have a touch of the flu. Outbreaks are much
easier to detect because clusters of people show up with the same
symptoms at the same time, upon which an attending physician may
order the appropriate tests.)

Farmers, meanwhile, were cited as saying they grow other herbs
right beside their basil, so it is unlikely that only one herb would

become contaminated on their property. A month later, CDC issued a preliminary report at the promised public meeting hosted by FDA, which estimated that more than 1,400 Americans may have been sickened with cyclospora in 1997 from outbreaks linked to Guatemalan raspberries, basil, and mesclun lettuce. Some of that increase undoubtedly came about through better tracking by physicians after the widespread publicity of the 1996 outbreak. In the fall of 1997, U.S. media coverage focused on the importation of fresh fruits and vegetables (Sanchez, 1997), with the occasional article in Canada. U.S. President Clinton announced an initiative to make imported fruits and vegetables safer, at the same time as the White House was trying to win 'fast track' authority to negotiate new trade agreements. Food industry experts said the initiative was aimed at countering critics who opposed the fast track and expanding the North American Free Trade Agreement (NAFTA) because of food safety concerns (Vorman, 1997). Under the new proposal, Clinton asked Congress to pass a law giving the FDA the authority to bar imports from any country with food safety standards not on a par with those of the United States.

A *Business Week* article ('Eating Scared,' 1997) correctly pointed out that domestic growers and food processors sometimes try to curb competition by calling attention to tainted foreign produce. One country's scientific standard is another's non-tariff trade barrier. However, other food scientists and regulators have repeatedly stated that there is no evidence that imported food is more dangerous than that produced domestically. Rather than comparing foods on the basis of country of origin, it is much more practical to compare foods based on safety. And everyone should do their part as a member of a farm-to-fork food safety system to reduce levels of food-related risk.

Nevertheless, several trends are merging. The North American food market is one of the most open in the world. Consumers are driving the demand for imports by seeking fresh fruits and vegetables year-round. From 1992 to 1997, U.S. food imports have doubled, to thirty billion tons, and are expected to keep rising. Increased travel and tourism, reduced immunity because of AIDS and cancer treatments, an aging population, and the evolution of pathogens into new and sometimes drug-resistant strains all add to potential problems.

By December 1997 the U.S. Food and Drug Administration publicly announced a decision made in late November (Powell, 1998b, and personal communication) that it was blocking imports of raspberries from Guatemala for 1998. The ban became effective on 15 March and continued through 15 August, the normal Guatemala raspberry exporting season. The FDA stressed that its objective was not to create trade barriers but to make U.S. food safer. Guatemalan industry and government officials saw the ban as unfair, because growers had invested in new equipment to make the berries safe. It was seen as unfair to accuse one product when it has been demonstrated that other products, such as lettuce and sprouts, have been related to outbreaks.

With the ban in place, outbreaks of cyclospora did not occur in 1998, in the United States. However, a U.S. General Accounting Office report, issued in May 1998 and again, widely reported, urged that the United States should stop importing food from nations that do not meet U.S. health and safety standards (Weiner, 1998). One solution advocated by the report was to demand that foreign nations create food-safety systems that meet U.S. standards. However, U.S. federal officials have not made this demand, fearing that it would disrupt trade.

The bottom line of all this public discussion: the U.S. public was reasonably informed through various media of efforts undertaken by U.S. health authorities to balance the sometimes competing goals of enhanced trade with public health. In Canada, almost no public discussion occurred, Guatemalan raspberries were imported, 305 people in the Toronto area got sick, and still, no public accounting has been provided by any federal authorities.

For Canadians, the 11 June 1998 announcement of a cyclospora outbreak seemed to come from nowhere. After the initial stories, a subsequent *Globe and Mail* story (Robertson, 1998b) raised the suggestion that, for the first time since cyclospora appeared in Canada in 1996, there were no reported outbreaks anywhere in the United States and that U.S. import restrictions on Guatemalan raspberries may have accounted for this. But the public questioning seemed to end there, with media coverage turning to irradiation as a possible solution (Strauss, 1998). There has been no public explanation or accounting.

Conclusions: Cyclospora and Risk Analysis

This chapter has examined the case of regulatory regime responses to Guatemalan raspberry imports by the United States in comparison with Canada. The central conclusion is that the Canadian food and health regulatory and risk management system failed to deal expeditiously, transparently, and effectively with the health risks involved. This failure is not specific to any particular agency as such, but rather to the regime seen broadly, including an array of bodies, the media, and interactions with the scientific community. The case also shows a failure to deal with some of the suggested steps and public processes in modern risk assessment, risk management, and risk communication. Such integrated steps and processes are all the more necessary given the realities of new trade rules and given the growth of the global food trade.

Indeed, other issues beyond those covered above are also important. Cyclospora is an example of emerging food- and water-borne illnesses. It has been responsible for outbreaks of human illness in North America in 1996 and 1997, and in Canada in 1998. Cyclospora has also been the centre of controversy since it was erroneously linked to California strawberries during the 1996 outbreaks in North America. One reason for the large amount of uncertainty in the 1996 cyclospora outbreak is the lack of effective testing procedures for this organism. To date, cyclospora oocysts have not been found on any strawberries, raspberries, or other fruit, either from North America or Guatemala. That does not mean that cyclospora was absent; it means the tests are unreliable and somewhat meaningless. FDA, CDC, and others are developing standardized methods for such testing and are currently evaluating their sensitivity.

The initial, and subsequent, links between cyclospora and strawberries or raspberries were therefore based on epidemiology, a statistical association between consumption of a particular food and the onset of disease. For example, the Toronto outbreak was first identified because some thirty-five guests attending a 11 May 1996 wedding reception developed the same severe, intestinal illness, seven to ten days after the wedding, and subsequently tested positive for cyclospora. Based on interviews with those stricken, health authorities in Toronto and Texas concluded that California strawberries were the most likely source. However, attempts to remember exactly what one ate two weeks earlier is an extremely difficult task; and larger foods, like strawberries, are recalled more frequently than smaller foods, like raspberries.

Once epidemiology identifies a probable link, health officials have to decide whether it makes sense to warn the public. In retrospect, the decision seems straightforward, but there are several possibilities that must be weighed at the time. For example, in the 1996 outbreak, when the Ontario Ministry of Health decided to warn people that eating imported strawberries might be connected to cyclospora infection, two outcomes were possible: if it turned out that strawberries were implicated, the ministry made a smart decision, warning people against something that could hurt them; if strawberries were not implicated, then the ministry made a bad decision, with the result that strawberry growers and sellers lost money and people stopped eating something that is nutritionally valuable.

If, however, the ministry had decided not to warn people, another two outcomes were possible: if strawberries were implicated, then the ministry would have made a bad decision and people may have contracted a parasitic infection that they would have avoided had they been given the information (lawsuits usually follow a situation like this); if strawberries were definitely not implicated then nothing would have happened, the industry would not suffer and the ministry would not get in trouble for not telling people. More research is needed to develop rigorous, scientifically tested guidelines for informing the public of uncertain risks.

It was subsequently revealed that Canadian officials decided not to ban the importation of Guatemalan raspberries in the spring of 1998 for two reasons: the 1997 Canadian outbreaks of cyclospora were not conclusively linked to Guatemalan raspberries, and Canadian officials had visited Guatemalan farms during the first week of April 1998 and concluded that berries could be imported from what were deemed low-risk farms (Powell, 1998b, and personal communication). However, there has been no accounting of the assumptions that entered into the risk assessments and decision making that were presumably conducted to conclude that Guatemalan raspberries could be imported into Canada in the spring of 1998. A comparison with U.S. decision-making and risk assessment assumptions could provide insight for future disputes involving microbial food safety and global trade. Further, Canadian officials have also stated that they intend to ban the importation of the fall 1998 harvest of Guatemalan raspberries because, as one official stated, 'We want to err on the side of safety' (Powell, 1998b, and personal communication). Such sentiments are clearly value judgments incorporated into the risk assessment process for what seem political rather than scientific or heath reasons, considering that the fall harvest of Guatemalan raspberries has not been linked with any outbreaks of cyclospora in North America. Most importantly, that Canadian officials have made no attempt to communicate with the Canadian public only serves to undermine confidence in the food supply to the detriment of consumers, producers, and retailers alike.

Appendix: General Principles of Food Safety Risk Management

Principle 1: Risk management should follow a structured approach.
The elements of a structured approach to risk management are Risk Evaluation, Risk Management Option Assessment, Implementation of Management Decision, and Monitoring and Review. In certain circumstances, not all of these elements will be included in risk management activities (e.g., standard setting by Codex, with implementation of control measures by national governments).

Principle 2: Protection of human health should be the primary consideration in risk management decisions.
Decisions on acceptable levels of risk should be determined primarily by human health considerations, and arbitrary or unjustified differences in the risk levels should be avoided. Consideration of other factors (e.g., economic costs, benefits, technical feasibility, and societal preferences) may be appropriate in some risk management contexts, particularly in the determination of measures to be taken. These considerations should not be arbitrary and should be made explicit.

Principle 3: Risk management decisions and practices should be transparent.
Risk management should include the identification and systematic documentation of all elements of the risk management process including decision making, so that the rationale is transparent to all interested parties.

Principle 4: Determination of risk assessment policy should be included as a specific component of risk management.
Risk assessment policy sets the guidelines for value judgments and policy choices which may need to be applied at specific decision points in the risk assessment process, and preferably should be determined in advance of risk assessment, in collaboration with risk assessors.

Principle 5: Risk management should ensure the scientific integrity of the risk assessment process by maintaining the functional separation of risk management and risk assessment.
Functional separation of risk management and risk assessment serves to ensure the scientific integrity of the risk assessment process and reduce any conflict of interest between risk assessment and risk management. However, it is recognized that risk analysis is an iterative process, and interactions between risk managers and risk assessors are essential for practical application.

Principle 6: Risk management decisions should take into account the uncertainty in the output of the risk assessment.
The risk estimate should, wherever possible, include a numerical expression of uncertainty, and this must be conveyed to risk managers in a readily understandable form so that the full implications of the range of uncertainty can be included in decision making. For example, if the risk estimate is highly uncertain the risk management decision might be more conservative.

Principle 7: Risk management should include clear, interactive communication with consumers and other interested parties in all aspects of the process.
Ongoing reciprocal communication among all interested parties is an integral part of the risk management process. Risk communication is more than the dissemination of information, and a major function is the process by which information and opinion essential to effective risk management is incorporated into the decision.

Principle 8: Risk management should be a continuing process that takes into account all newly generated data in the evaluation and review of risk management decisions.
Subsequent to the application of a risk management decision, periodic evaluation of the decision should be made to determine its effectiveness in meeting food safety objectives. Monitoring and other activities will likely be necessary to carry out the review effectively. (World Health Organization, 1997)

References

Altman, L.K. (1996). 'Outbreak of Intestinal Infection Baffles Health Experts.' *New York Times*, 20 June.

Canadian Press News Service, Ottawa. (1998). Parasite Outbreak. 11 June.

'CDC: Water in Pest Spray Likely Source of Cyclospora in Outbreak.' (1997). *Food Chemical News* 38(51): 24.

Center for Disease Control. (1997). 'Outbreak of Cyclosporiasis Northern Virginia–Washington, DC–Baltimore, Maryland, Metropolitan area.' *CDC MMWR*, 46(30).

Covello, V.T., and M.W. Merkhofer. (1994). *Risk Assessment Methods*. New York: Plenum Press.

Division of Parasitic Diseases (DPD), NCID, CDC. (1997). 'Preparations for the Possibility of Outbreaks of Cyclospora Infection in 1997.' ProMed. 18 April.

Drago, M. (1996). 'Fruit Likely Source of Illness.' Associated Press. 20 June.

'Eating Scared: Worries Go Far beyond Beef – and an Increasingly International Food Supply Is Expanding Everyone's Risk of Contamination.'(1997). *Business Week*. 8 September.

FAO/WHO. (1996). Report of the twenty-eighth session of the Codex Committee on Food Additives and Contaminants. Manila, 18–22 March. Rome: FAO.

'FDA Warns of Cyclosporiasis in Guatemalan Raspberries.' (1997). *U.S. News and World Report*, 12 June.

Foegeding, P.M., T. Roberts, J.M. Bennett, F.L. Bryan, D.O. Cliver, M.P. Doyle, et al. (1994). Foodborne Pathogens: Risks and Consequences. Council for Agricultural Science and Technology Task Force Report No. 122, Ames, Iowa.

'Guatemala Defends Its Raspberries.' (1996). Reuters. 19 July.

Herwaldt, B.L., and M.L. Ackers. (1997). 'An Outbreak in 1996 of Cyclosporiasis Associated with Imported Raspberries.' *New England Journal of Medicine*, 336(22): 1548–56.

Hofmann, J., Z. Liu, C. Genese, G. Wolf, W. Manley, K. Pilot, E. Dalley, and L. Finelli. (1996). 'Update: Outbreaks of Cyclospora Cayetanensis Infection – United States and Canada, 1996.' *CDC MMWR*, 45(28): 611.

Immen, W. (1996). 'Strawberries Leave 35 Ill.' *Globe and Mail*, 13 June, A12.

Lammerding, A.M. and G.M. Paoli. (1998). 'Quantitative Risk Assessment: An Emerging Tool for Emerging Foodborne Pathogens.' *Emerging Infectious Disease*.

MacKinnon, D.J. (1996). 'Buyers Scared Off, Berry Vendors Say.' *Toronto Star*, 30 June, A3.

Masters, B.A. (1997a). 'Food Poisoning Is Linked to Basil Products – 126 Fell Ill after Eating Dishes from Sutton Place, Officials Say.' *Washington Post*, 19 July, B1.

– (1997b). 'Tainted Basil Shows the Challenges of Tracking a Microbe.' *Washington Post*, 28 July, B1.

Meyer, T. (1996) 'CDC: Guatemala Cyclospora Link.' Associated Press, 18 July.

Osterholm, M.T. (1997). 'Cyclosporiasis and Raspberries – Lessons for the Future.' *New England Journal of Medicine*, 336(22): 22–6.

'NYC Officials Warn on Berries in Illness Outbreak.' (1996). *New York Times*, 27 June.

Powell, Douglas (1998a). This statement was made during a workshop at the annual meeting of the U.S. Council of State and Territorial Epidemiologists, Des Moines, Iowa, 7 June.

- (1998b). From comments made during a telephone interview with three officials from the Canadian Food Inspection Agency, Ottawa, 8 September.

PRNewswire. (1996). 'Raspberries and Cyclospora: Guatemala Cooperating Fully,' 20 July.

Robertson, G. (1998a). 'Tainted Food Cases Baffle Health Experts.' *Globe and Mail,* 12 June, A10.

- (1998b). 'Growing Cyclospora Outbreak Baffles Experts; Up to 130 Stricken by Parasite; Scientists Struggle to Figure Out which Food Carries the Bug and Why Problem Is Isolated to Southern Ontario.' *Globe and Mail,* 16 June, A12.

Rodricks, J.V. (1994). 'Risk Assessment, the Environment, and Public Health.' *Environmental Health Perspective,* 102: 258–64.

Sanchez, R. (1997). 'Sanitation in the Fields Falls Short.' *Newsday,* 13 October.

Simpson, A.C.D. (1994). *Integrating Public and Scientific Judgments into a Tool Kit for Managing Food-Related Risks, Stage 2: Development of the Software. A Report to the U.K. Ministry of Agriculture, Fisheries and Food.* ERAU Research Report No. 19, University of East Anglia, Norwich.

Smith, J.L., and P.M. Fratamico. (1996). 'Factors Involved in the Emergence and Persistence of Food-borne Diseases.' *Journal of Food Protection,* 58: 696–708.

Soby, B.A., A.C.D. Simpson, and D.P. Ives. *Integrating Public and Scientific Judgments into a Tool Kit for Managing Food-Related Risks, Stage 1: Literature Review and Feasibility Study. A Report to the U.K. Ministry of Agriculture, Fisheries and Food.* ERAU Research Report No. 16, University of East Anglia, Norwich.

Strauss, S. (1988). 'Save Stomachs: Zap Food, Canada Advised; Irradiation Would Inactivate Cyclospora Parasite, Lengthen Shelf Life, Scientist Says.' *Globe and Mail,* 17 June, A1.

Svingen, K. (1997). Untitled. *Knight-Ridder Tribune,* 22 April.

United Press International. (1996). 'Houston Investigates Parasite Illnesses,' 31 May.

U.S. Presidential/Congressional Commission on Risk Assessment and Risk Management. (1997). *Framework for Environmental Health Risk Management.* Washington: U.S. Government Printing Office.

U.S. National Advisory Committee on Microbiological Criteria for Foods (1998).

U.S. National Research Council. (1983). *Risk Assessment in the Federal Government: Managing the Process.* Washington: National Academy Press.

Vorman, J. (1997). 'In the Fall of 1997, U.S. President Clinton to Unveil Food Safety Plan.' *Reuters.* 25 September.

World Health Organization. (1997). *FAO/WHO Expert Consultation on the Application of Risk Management to Food Safety Matters.* Rome: World Health Organization.
– (1995). *Application of Risk Analysis to Food Standards Issues. Report of the Joint FAO/WHO Expert Consultation.* WHO/FNU/FOS/Report No. 95.3.
Weiner, T. (1998). 'Report Calls for Banning Food from Some Nations.' *New York Times,* 11 May.

7 Socioeconomic versus Science-Based Regulation: Informal Influences on the Formal Regulation of rbST in Canada

MARK R. MACDONALD

Over the past decade, the potential use of recombinant bovine somatotropin (rbST) in the Canadian dairy industry has stimulated vigorous policy debate. Battles were waged over the science of rbST, the socioeconomics of rbST, and the process by which rbST was to be regulated (Mills, 1996; Powell and Leiss, 1997). As one of the first veterinary drugs manufactured using biotechnology to enter the Canadian food regulatory process, rbST generated significant concern among a variety of actors with vested interests in the outcome of its regulation. This confronted regulators with the difficult task of balancing the formal scientific criteria by which rbST ultimately is to be judged, against the socioeconomic concerns of producers, dairy processors, and consumer advocates. The chapter was written during the debate about rbST licensing in Canada; subsequently, the application for licence has been denied (Canada, 1999). This turn of events, however, does not run counter to the arguments presented herein. In fact, as will become clear to the reader, the rejection of rbST on the basis of scientific advice from the Panel on Animal Health Safety can be interpreted as re-establishing public credibility, precisely because of the arm's-length market-based procurement.

From a regulatory perspective the rbST case is, on the face of it, a strictly scientific issue. The Bureau of Veterinary Drugs (BVD) at Health Canada is charged with the responsibility to govern the licensing of rbST under the Food and Drugs Act; Canada has an established, formal, science-based regulatory process. Thus, there appears to be little room for debate. Closer examination of the case, however, reveals that extra-scientific concerns – mainly socioeconomic – have had an informal effect on the debate. The chapter argues that this should come as no surprise. In fact, the rbST case may well have set the stage for a new comprehensive Canadian biotechnological regulatory strategy in which both science and socioeconomics play key and legitimate roles.

Bovine somatotropin (sometimes called bovine growth hormone) is a naturally occurring protein growth hormone that stimulates milk production in cows. Without it cows would be unable to produce milk at all (Peel and Bauman, 1987). Recombinant bST is a man-made, genetically engineered copy of the natural protein, and it represents one of a growing number of biotechnology products that can be produced efficiently, easily, and safely utilizing the well-established processes of recombinant DNA technology. These techniques are currently used in the manufacture of a wide variety of important human and animal health products, including insulin and calcitonin (Agriculture Canada 1993).

Recombinant bST leads to an increase of 10 per cent to 25 per cent in milk production from a corresponding 5 per cent to 15 per cent increase in feed. This increased efficiency in milk production could lead to as much as a 17.5 per cent boost in average annual returns on dairy quota values for Canadian farmers (Stennes et al., 1990). Proponents argue that rbST could thus play an important role as a new and efficient dairy-farm management tool. But critics worry about what effect 'genetically engineered milk' might have on the safety of the milk supply and on the economic viability of the Canadian dairy industry.

The licensing of rbST in Canada became a controversial issue for policy makers, mainly because of questions about the criteria by which rbST specifically, and biotechnology products in general, are deemed to be acceptable for introduction into the marketplace. While the current federal regulatory system has a well-defined testing process for new animal products based strictly on scientific analysis (Doern and Sheehy, 1997), the rbST issue has witnessed the introduction of extra-scientific concerns about the socioeconomic impact that biotechnology raises for consumers (Speller, 1994). At its base, the debate is about the extent to which scientific information alone is to be used as the standard to judge the public desirability of products like rbST.

rbST in a Policy Perspective

It is useful to bear in mind the chronology of regulatory events with respect to rbST in Canada. These are sketched in Table 7.1, in terms of

158   Mark R. MacDonald

Table 7.1 rbST policy chronology

rbST time frame	Major regulatory events
1990–3 The regulatory status quo	• Monsanto submits their rbST product for review by the Bureau of Veterinary Drugs (BVD) • Health Canada confirms human health safety of rbST • Formal regulatory process carried out by BVD and governed by the Food and Drugs Act proceeds • Growing public debate about rbST in the U.S.
1994–7 Emerging public debate: questioning the regulatory status quo	• rbST approved for sale in U.S. in Feb. 1994 with visible public concern both in U.S. and Canada by some groups • House of Commons Standing Committee on Agriculture and Agri-Food meets in March 1994 to discuss potential impact of rbST on dairy industry • rbST Task Force struck, membership includes Monsanto, Dairy Farmers of Canada, National Dairy Council, and Consumers' Association of Canada • Task Force Report in April 1994, recommendations include further scientific and socioeconomic review • One-year moratorium on rbST established (expired summer 1995) • Health Canada's formal regulatory review continues
1997–9 Informal influences and the rbST network: changing the formal regulatory process?	• May 1997, media reports of internal difficulties at BVD questioning the adequacy of the formal regulatory review • Emergence of rbST policy network: evidence of informal influence by the Dairy Farmers of Canada, National Dairy Council, and Consumers' Association of Canada introducing socioeconomic concerns to the regulatory policy process • Health Canada appoints two independent review panels to complete research on human and animal health safety of rbST • Senate Committee on Agriculture and Forestry holds meetings on rbST, questions legitimacy of formal regulatory review process
1999–2000 Rejection in the face of continuing debate	• Jan. 1999, independent Panel on Animal Health Safety recommends the rejection of rbST based on cow health safety • Health Canada immediately denies Monsanto licence • Senate Committee continues to review regulatory process; Monsanto indicates likelihood of resubmission

both formal and informal influence; it is to this chronology that the chapter speaks.

In brief, the chronology spans the 1990s beginning with Monsanto's initial application for approval of rbST and ending with Health Canada's denial of a licence in 1999. It also highlights political pressure and policy review in several settings, including House of Commons and Senate committees, as the rbST controversy heated up and refused to go away.

From a policy perspective, the rbST debate is particularly important given that using current analytical techniques it is impossible to detect differences between milk from treated and untreated cows. This means that there is no way to test for milk from rbST-treated and -untreated cows, which potentially impinges on freedom of choice in the market. Indeed, additional controversy over the labelling of milk and milk products has been led by industry and consumer advocates who claim a strong desire for freedom of choice. Exacerbating this difficulty is the fact that milk marketing in Canada is the jurisdiction of both the federal and provincial governments, and each province can legally have different requirements with respect to labelling, including mandatory labelling for rbST. Even voluntary labelling – either positive 'does contain' or negative 'does not contain' – is difficult to manage, given that there is no scientific technique to detect whether claims are legitimate. Some have suggested that an affidavit system might be developed whereby farmers and milk pools register their use of rbST; critics, however, argue that if an effective second market for milk and milk products from treated and untreated cows cannot be established, Canadians neither need nor want rbST.

The controversy about rbST in Canada boils down to three general concerns: (1) its safety for human and animal health; (2) freedom of industrial and consumer market choice; and (3) controversy about the regulatory process itself. Of these concerns, only one is science-based – safety. The broader context of the rbST controversy is over the regulatory system itself, which raises questions about institutional design. Primarily, I am interested in determining whether current, formal decision-making processes are suitable for conflict resolution, or, whether alternative or additional mechanisms are also required for controversial issues such as those that surround rbST. The rbST case is important because it has raised questions about the legitimate role of scientific and extra-scientific forms of information in the regulatory process. As a result, it presents an opportunity to examine institutional responses to controversy in science-based decision making.

The issue of institutional response can be illuminated by looking at the rbST issue through the lens of transaction cost theory – a theory particularly adept at questioning the alternative organizational arrangements available to governments as they respond to contentious issues. In this context, science-based decisions in public policy are viewed to have organizational implications, given that legislators increasingly require new and different sources of information in order to make comprehensive social choices. For the rbST case specifically, the sources of information are represented by the key actors who influence the debate, leading some researchers to suggest that rbST is 'lost in regulatory space' (Powell and Leiss, 1997). However, I argue that this apparent regulatory confusion can actually be viewed as a rational response on the part of legislators to allow *informal* influence over the *formal* regulatory process. Such a view suggests that similar responses may well become the norm in the organizational response to the science-based regulation of biotechnology in Canada.

Policy Making and Transaction Costs

The transaction cost framework was developed as a means to explain alternative forms of economic organization (Coase, 1960; Williamson, 1975, 1985, 1991, 1996). Its argument is that economic relationships can be viewed in contractual terms and that different organizational forms have different capacities in their ability to overcome the costs of contracting. In a world characterized by positive transaction costs – the economic equivalent of friction in physical systems (Williamson, 1985: 19) – the total cost of production is the sum of the costs of procurement plus the costs of exchange. In deciding how best to organize production, the rational economic actor must consider not only how much a given input costs, but also how best to *organize* procurement. This decision is characterized along a continuum of organizational mechanisms with formal responses such as the market and the hierarchy at either end, and informal arrangements such as networks in the middle. The choice that economic actors make is typified as the 'make' or 'buy' decision: inputs are bought when they are widely available and procurement can be organized easily and cheaply as on the market; inputs are made when they are specific to a given economic task and procurement is costly enough on the market such that economies of scale and scope can be established through hierarchical organization (Rubin 1990).

The application of this theory to the public sector reveals a similar choice between organizational forms for the procurement of inputs for policy making (MacDonald, 1998). If one considers that policy makers require inputs or resources to make public policy, it is reasonable to assume that they will procure such resources in a manner similar to their private sector brethren. That is, alternative organizational forms to govern exchange will be evident in the public sector. In other words, the actors ultimately responsible for policy making in a democracy – legislators – will face a make or buy decision for policy resources. Procuring resources such as computers, pencils, and opinion polls will be organized easily on the market; procuring resources such as experience with public health, education, or national defence will be organized by the public bureau. In addition, informal organizations such as the *policy network* will also be organized when the resources being procured are not marketable, or easily 'made' in the public sector (Hindmoor, 1998; MacDonald, 1998).

The trade-off between market, network, and bureaucratic organizational forms rests on the nature of the resources being procured, coupled with the manner in which contractual disturbances are resolved (Williamson, 1985). The market is used when resources are widely available from many sources (for example, computers) – that is, they are non-specific – and contractual disturbances can be dealt with by simply moving to an alternative source or by relying on court-enforced contracts. Hierarchies are adept at organizing the procurement or making of resources that are highly specific – that is, they are not easily secured from alternative sources (for example, national defence) – and contractual disturbances are dealt with by fiat. In both cases *formal* mechanisms exist to enforce *formal* contracts.

Networks are informal organizations that are instituted when resources are more specific than can be dealt with by the market, but less so than would require procurement by the hierarchical organization. Resolving disturbances rests on the ability of the trading partners to devise *informal* methods to deal with *informal* contracts. Mechanisms such as trust, reputation, tit-for-tat strategies, and embedded exchange relationships characterize the informal range of contractual relationships (Axelrod, 1984; Granovetter, 1985; Klein, 1997; Hindmoor, 1998).

The key research question for policy making becomes one of looking at the organizational response that legislators take in the design of appropriate mechanisms to procure the resources necessary to make public policy. Policy, writ large, is viewed in instrumental terms; legislators make policy to enhance their expectation of being re-elected. The instrumental view of policy making is a standard one in the literature on legislative responses to voting behaviour (Enelow and Hinich, 1984; Mueller, 1989; Coughlin, 1992). Under conditions of uncertainty about how voters will react on election day, it is argued that legislators design policies to enhance the expectation that voters will view them positively – opposition parties design their platforms in an attempt to overthrow incumbent parties. At its base then, the arena of policy making is viewed from the legislator's perspective as an expected vote-maximizing game. In this view, legislators strategically decide which set of policy resources is required to make a given policy. It is important to note, however, that no assertion is made about which set of resources this will be, only that the *form* of the response will be strategic – and rational. Transaction cost research looks at the organizational choices that legislators make for the procurement of vote-productive policy resources.

The fundamental nature of the policy process in a democracy is that it is predicated on collective choice. As such, when government actors set about to make decisions or formulate policy they do so with at least one eye focused on the effect that decisions or policies will have on voter preferences. To make 'good' policy – that is, vote-productive policy – decision makers appeal to a variety of sources, and the associated groups, for policy resources. Even under circumstances where formal, legal, ostensibly objective rules have been established to govern the decision-making process (such as is the case for rbST), good policy often still requires additional resources from groups who may or may not have a legal claim for consideration in decision making (again, such as is the case for rbST). Indeed, this is the underlying character of public decision making.

In terms of transaction costs, the rbST case is seen as one where contracting for multiple resources is required to make vote-productive policy which, in turn, requires alternative governance organizations. The dispute is between groups who support the legitimacy of relying only on scientific policy resources to judge the acceptability of rbST for the Canadian marketplace and those actors who argue that socio-economic concerns must also be key in the regulatory process. Legislators are faced with a difficult task in designing appropriate mechanisms to govern the procurement of all productive resources required to make vote-maximizing policy choices. One of the underlying reasons for this difficulty is, in large part, a function of the special nature of science-based decision making.

The Transaction Cost Nature of Science-Based Decision Making

Science-based policy making is rife with difficulties in resolving conflict between scientists, lay advocates, and politicians, particularly when 'scientific criteria of truth clash with legal standards of evidence and with political notions of what constitutes sufficient ground for action' (Majone, 1989: 4). These difficulties become crucial when the issue at hand is contentious or involves assessing the risk for human safety (Irwin, 1987; Throgmorton, 1991). In the regulatory process, organizational design is important in determining how debates over science and its implications are resolved. Issues regarding the appropriate design come to the fore as conceptual arguments are waged over the 'correct' criteria for reconciling debates. Essentially, the rbST battle is between those who view the public with some degree of contempt regarding its ability to understand or engage in rational decision making (Lewis, 1990), those who support the notion that the public will better understand decisions taken on their behalf if regulatory agencies undertake risk communication (Powell and Leiss, 1997), and those who share an increasingly accepted view that even though the nonexpert public might not fully understand the science of risk, to the extent that risk is also socially constructed the non-expert view must play a role in the decisions and policy on risk (Cutter, 1993). Essentially, what is happening is a pluralization of science-based decision making, in addition to what has earlier been observed to be the pluralization of science itself (Doern, 1998).

The significance of this pluralization of science-based decision making becomes apparent, given that legislators generally view the advice of experts as much, if not more, as political information rather than 'neutral' or 'objective' analysis: They 'do not understand analysis, policy studies, and other forms of expert information in isolation from their understanding of the people who have produced it' (Bimber, 1996: 5). In other words, science-based information is specific to groups. The implication of this is that as more groups make legitimate claims for entrance into the decision-making arena, more 'types' of information are likely to be introduced as well, with science potentially taking a back seat to other types. This will occur in fields such as biotechnology where science is only the enabling discipline behind the creation of technologies whose use is intended to be applied solely for economic gain, rather than as 'pure science.' Indeed, some argue that 'the creation of wealth through biotechnology firmly places [it] within the industrial sector and it is to the business community that one must then look to discern how [it] is to be applied and ultimately used' (Ratledge, 1992: 1). Thus, the organization of decision making must be judged primarily by looking at the manner in which different groups are seen to affect the nature of the resources that are required to draw appropriate conclusions for public policy.

In Canada, the organizational response to resolving conflict over science-based policy decisions in the case of products such as rbST is governed by the Food and Drugs Act (Section C.08.002), which stipulates that a drug manufacturer must submit information and materials to support claims of efficacy and effectiveness to the body in charge of governing the act. For rbST, the Bureau of Veterinary Drugs in the Health Protection Branch of Health Canada is responsible for the review. The drug company in question, Monsanto, must provide scientific information to demonstrate that its product is safe for animals, that milk and milk products from treated cows are safe for human consumption, and that all requirements for the safety of the manufacturing process have been met under the regulations set forth by the act. Once the review has been completed and all requirements of the act have been stipulated to, a notice of compliance (NOC) is given that can only be revoked by order of the minister (Health Canada, 1995). Other federal agencies including Agriculture and Agri-Food Canada, Industry Canada, and Revenue Canada also have interests in the rbST issue, and, in fact, it is plausible to suggest that legislators from these additional portfolios have been politically active in the rbST debate (witness the Standing Committee on Agriculture and Agri-Food). However, in order to simplify discussion for the current chapter, I treat Health Canada officials as the primary representative of the government position because they are legally responsible for rbST.

Legislators, in this case led by the minister of health, ostensibly rely solely on the formal regulatory process to resolve conflict. In other words, the procurement of resources is governed hierarchically; Health Canada scientists are charged with the responsibility to review industry submissions, and base their decisions only on science. From the perspective of transaction cost, this process is understood as one where legislators deem that public confidence is best guaranteed by hiring their own experts to determine the credibility of scientific information; in other words, science-based resources are highly specific and contracting for them is organized hierarchically.

The rationale for making scientific resources is uncovered by looking at the alternative arrangements – either buying the scientific information directly from the drug company on the market, or engaging in an informal exchange of information for approval. Either solution would require both that the legislator be able to determine the credibility of the submission himself or herself and that drug companies be willing to divulge valuable information about their products. Neither condition is likely to be met: legislators are rarely scientific experts (and even if they were, political questions about credibility would still arise), and drug companies jealously guard product information from the market to protect research investments (arguing strenuously for long-term patent protection). As a result, legislators who have an interest in science-based policies hire experts to interpret information for them, and they also write legislation that protects the confidentiality of drug company submissions to the regulatory process. The dual aspects of hiring bureaucrats to make scientific information by reviewing industry and secondary data, coupled with writing legislation to define specific limitations on the acceptable range of that information (that is, science only), indicates a formal contractual response to policy making for products like rbST. Of course, it is this formal contractual arrangement that is also seen to prevent the inclusion of extra-scientific concerns into the policy-making arena.

The formal regulatory process and its hierarchical organization is a legislative response to the costs of making a potentially 'bad decision' in science-based fields. The rbST example is a case in point. The minister of health, whoever it is at the time, is clearly interested in ensuring that the regulatory decisions made with respect to safety and health are the correct ones. The cost of making a bad decision, both in real safety terms and political ones, would be enormous. From the minister's perspective, the important questions are: 'How do I make decisions of this nature? Do I rely on the information presented to me by drug companies? Or, do I hire a group of scientists who essentially make my experience with the drug for me?' Clearly, the result is that the regulatory system is designed such that the minister effectively hires people to generate public scientific experience and information.

What happens, however, when *not all* vote-productive resources can be secured in a formal science-based regulatory process organized by hierarchical governance? That is, when extra-scientific concerns about a given product such as rbST arise – concerns that are also costly if the 'correct' decision is not made? How are they dealt with in a manner that both guarantees adherence to science-based regulation to determine the 'technical' viability of a product, while at the same time resolving conflicts about the extra-regulatory socioeconomic impacts of a given technology? The answer lies in determining the manner and extent to which additional legitimate policy resources are procured, a task that begins by analysing the positions of the key players in the game.

Main Actors in the rbST Case

The central question for policy makers in the rbST case is the extent to which groups other than Monsanto, the drug company that has made the submission to have its rbST product licensed, are allowed to affect the course of the regulatory process. Put another way, the fundamental concern of decision makers is to avoid making a bad decision. As a result, they must carefully gauge both the nature of the required resources and the identity of the groups who have access to them. It makes sense then, to give a brief outline of the positions of the key actors and analyse what it is about their organizational character and the nature of their resources that affords them an opportunity to enter the rbST process: Monsanto (industry); Dairy Farmers of Canada (producers); National Dairy Council (processors); Consumers' Association of Canada (consumers); and the Council of Canadians (activists).

Monsanto

The Monsanto Company is currently the only drug manufacturer with an rbST product before Health Canada. (Eli Lilly also had an rbST product before the review process but withdrew it in 1996 because of patent difficulties in the United States.) Since its submission to the Bureau of Veterinary Drugs in 1990, Monsanto's position has been consistent: the product should be approved based on the scientific evidence that rbST is effective and poses no health safety risks for animals or humans. In addition, Monsanto has been strongly supportive of the science-based regulatory process and has argued strenuously that it is the only legitimate process by which products like rbST can credibly be judged. As Ray Mowling, vice-president, government and public affairs, Monsanto, has stated: 'The science-based regulatory process must be allowed to continue until it reaches a science-based conclusion. Sound, extensive, in-depth research into the safety and efficacies of BST must be the basis for the decisions to be made by Canadian reviewers in deciding whether they will approve BST for sale and use in Canada. Should the product be registered, farmers and veterinarians can clearly voice their thoughts by either buying it or not. If there is no demand, the product will not be used. Any other approach may set an unacceptable precedent, implying that approval of human or animal products is not based on scientific findings' (Senate of Canada, 1998: 6).

The rationale for Monsanto's position is clear. First, it has a marketable product that it would like to sell for economic gain. Second, and perhaps more importantly, Monsanto has a vested interest in maintaining the current regulatory process whereby its products are judged only on scientific criteria. Not only does it have significant experience with the science-based system and designs its in-house development of new products accordingly, departures from science would effectively raise the cost of getting products approved by introducing a non-scientific 'fourth hurdle' to the regulatory process.

This fourth hurdle is understood by industry officials to be associated with the inherent economic, political, and social 'need' for products like rbST. Even though Monsanto has engaged in disseminating information about the potential benefit to the dairy sector that introducing rbST would have, it disregards notions put forth by other actors – most notably consumer advocates and dairy processors – that socioeconomic concerns are equally important as criteria by which rbST should be judged. Monsanto's bottom-line is that it is interested in creating a market for its product, and the most efficient way of doing this is to ensure that the regulatory process is strictly science-based.

This is not to say, however, that Monsanto is ignorant of consumer concerns about rbST. In fact, Monsanto has considerable experience with the important impact that scientific post-approval monitoring programs (PAMP) can play in alleviating consumer concerns about the continued safety of rbST. In Canada, Monsanto has offered to institute a similar voluntary PAMP as it has in the United States and to engage in consumer education about the health safety of milk and milk products from rbST-treated cows. After all, an approved product that nobody buys is as useful as a product that has not been approved. Monsanto does stress, however, that the ultimate worth of the product, given that it passes the formal regulatory tests for human and animal health safety, should be determined on the market.

Monsanto thus enters the decision-making process with clearly defined interests about rbST and the regulatory process. The strength of Monsanto's position rests on an ability to credibly maintain a purely science-based approach to the submission of its product for review before the BVD, and engaging in the dissemination of what it understands to be the scientific facts about rbST while at the same time rebuking the criticisms of other groups – both scientific and otherwise.

In a very real sense, Monsanto is situated most clearly among the other actors. At the same time, however, Monsanto maintains a unique actor position – it is the only group engaged in the formal regulatory process. It is not surprising then that Monsanto's stance on the rbST issue has always been couched in terms of the formal science-based requirements necessary for a licence. But this formal regulatory process also places restrictions on Monsanto's ability to engage in public debate about its product while it is before the review process. As a result, Monsanto has effectively steered clear of attempts to influence the informal debate about rbST. Still, its position is important, especially because it is a result of its efforts that the rbST issue perpetuates any additional group response at all.

Dairy Farmers of Canada

The Dairy Farmers of Canada (DFC) hold a more neutral position on rbST. In particular, the DFC supports the notion that individual farmers will ultimately be responsible for determining whether rbST is a suitable herd-management tool, and the DFC understands that some farmers would like access to cost-saving technologies. At the same time, however, the DFC is also concerned about the impact that rbST could have on consumer demand for milk, and it has a stake in ensuring that the product is approved only after sufficient scientific review. Its policy position reflects this attention to science-based regulation of rbST, but argues that Health Canada's credibility to complete the review is in question. The DFC's position was clearly stated in a press release: 'DFC is neither for nor against rbST. At this time, we simply want to ensure that rbST is approved for use *only* after the current credibility issue surrounding Health Canada's approval process is fully addressed' (DFC, 1997).

The Dairy Farmers of Canada are seeking a delay in the licensing of rbST in Canada until such time that an independent audit of the Health Canada process can be performed by the auditor general, that the United Nations Codex Alimentarius Commission rules on the safety of rbST, and that Health Canada publicly informs consumers about the risk assessment process and rationale that it will use in the evaluation and approval of rbST (DFC, 1998). (The Codex Alimentarius Commission is likely to rule favourably on the safety of rbST. A sister organization, the *Joint Food and Agriculture Organization of the United Nations and the World Health Organization Expert Committee on Food Additives*, recently concluded that rbST was safe for both human and animal health (JECFA, 1998).) The DFC's position is based on its concern for maintaining consumer trust in the Canadian dairy industry. As Barron Blois, president of the DFC, suggested: 'Canadians know that milk and dairy products they consume every day are pure, safe, and nutritious. Canadian dairy farmers have built a relationship of trust with the Canadian consumer that they do not wish to see jeopardized' (DFC, 1997).

There is a strong link between the livelihood of dairy farmers and consumer confidence and demand – a link that the DFC does not want weakened. As a result, the DFC, like Monsanto, has a stake in the credibility of the regulatory process. Ensuring a credible science-based decision is vital to the interests of farmers who rely heavily on the perception of complete safety in the milk industry. Credibility, from the DFC's position, therefore requires not only 'good science,' but a publicly transparent policy-making process.

The strength of the DFC's position as a legitimate voice in the rbST debate rests on two factors. First, rbST will be used by dairy farmers if it is licensed. It only stands to reason that if political actors are interested in assessing the potential impact that rbST might have on the dairy-producing sector in Canada, that the DFC would be the group approached for such information. Second, and perhaps even more importantly from the policy analysis perspective, the DFC has the ability to affect the positioning of the rbST debate at the political level.

As the national group representing some 25,000 dairy farmers in Canada, the DFC is in a credible position to threaten legislators with political protest should their views go unaccounted for – a threat that has been carried through in the past. In fact, as is shown below, it is this consideration that can be seen to have facilitated DFC's place as a legitimate influence over the informal aspects of the rbST case.

National Dairy Council of Canada

The National Dairy Council (NDC) has consistently been opposed to the use of rbST in Canada. As the representative of the dairy-producing industry, the NDC views the introduction of rbST as a significant threat to milk and milk product sales because of consumer concerns about health safety and the effect that changed perceptions about the natural production of milk might have on consumer demand. The NDC holds the view that there is no visible benefit for the processing industry or for consumers to the use of rbST in Canada, and it is worried that its processors will be held responsible for decisions that alter the manner in which milk is produced at the farm level. The NDC is steadfast in its position that rbST approval would be without the agreement of the dairy-processing industry (NDC, 1998).

The NDC's position is based on the potential effect that changes in consumer demand would have on the costs of milk processing. It is thought that consumers would demand a choice between milk from rbST-treated cows and -untreated cows, which would de facto require the creation of a segregated processing capacity to match the emergence of a dual market for milk. The NDC's concern is that it will have to bear the costs of the creation of new processing techniques that would rely on 'auditing procedures to ensure product integrity and both farmer and processor compliance with product segregation requirements' (ibid.). One of the reasons for this view is the simple fact that rbST labelling is such a difficult technical issue.

In principle, the NDC is opposed to the regulatory process that stipulates that the minister of health is required to issue a notice of compliance for rbST if the product meets the requirements of the Food and Drugs Act, without recourse to a legal ability to respond to consumer concerns. This is not to say that the NDC is opposed to science-based review of health safety, but rather that science is not the only measure of a product's viability for introduction to the market. Their policy response has been to appeal for protection from bearing what they expect to be increased processing costs as a result of consumer demand for two 'types' of milk. In particular, the NDC has requested that the milk marketing boards and milk control agencies make available a choice of milks, both from rbST-treated cows and those not treated, to ensure that processors can request at no additional cost that segregated milk is delivered along with appropriate guarantees and government-approved audits (ibid.).

The NDC enters the policy arena armed with two tools that are similar to the DFC's that make its position credible: it is the national voice for the dairy-processing industry, and it has a history of being able to influence politicians' views of the political landscape. In real terms, it is these organizational characteristics that have allowed NDC a place at the rbST table. However, as shown below, the NDC has found itself in a 'middle' position with respect to farmers and consumers regarding rbST and, as such, their influence over the informal side of the rbST debate has be accordingly limited.

Consumers' Association of Canada

The Consumers' Association of Canada (CAC) views the possible introduction of rbST to the Canadian marketplace primarily as a consumer issue. As the only national group representing Canadian consumer rights, the CAC's interest lies in the regulation of rbST such that human safety is secured, product quality, value, and choice are preserved, and that the consumer is represented in the decision-making process (CAC, 1994). The CAC's vision of the federal government's role in the regulatory process is not only to ensure that information about health safety is communicated fully, but that the composition and nutritional value of milk and milk products is not compromised and that guarantees against increased milk prices are established.

From the CAC's perspective, there is a dichotomous relationship between the safety of a product like rbST and consumers' acceptance of such products in the marketplace: safety and acceptability are not equivalent. The major issue, then, is the extent to which consumers will be able to distinguish between milk and milk products from rbST-treated and -untreated cows. The call is for the creation of a second market for milk in Canada if rbST is approved for use in the dairy industry, either through labelling or through an affidavit system. In a position that is similar to that of the National Dairy Council, the CAC views this second market as the only means by which consumers will have the freedom to demonstrate their demand for alternative products in the marketplace. With no direct or visible link between rbST use at the farm level and consumer benefit at the market level, the CAC is worried that rbST use in Canada will place an unnecessary restriction on consumer choice.

The rationale for this standpoint rests on the CAC's position as representative of consumer concerns in the broader policy-making process. The CAC itself has no direct interest in the regulation of rbST in the same way that Monsanto, the Dairy Farmers of Canada, and the National Dairy Council do; rather, the CAC's interest lies in protecting the credibility with which it can represent the voice of consumers in public decision making. Fundamentally, the CAC views itself as a protector of the Canadian consumer market. When issues such as rbST pose potential threats to the freedom of choice, the CAC positions itself to argue for the maintenance of markets, without necessarily taking a stand on the product itself. Indeed, for the rbST case, the CAC has maintained that as long as the health safety of Canadians is not jeopardized, the central concern for consumers is the right to market choice. Yet, even given the absence of a direct interest in the rbST case, the CAC is viewed as a credible player for similar reasons that the DFC and NDC are: they have a history of being able to affect the politics of consumer issues.

Council of Canadians

The Council of Canadians (COC) is the final group that can be seen to have had an impact on the issues surrounding the regulation of rbST in Canada, although as argued below, this impact is indirect. Still, the COC has played a significant role in couching the rbST debate in much broader terms about the legitimacy of introducing biotechnology to the Canadian food industry, and its position deserves some attention.

The COC takes what can only be described as a very negative view of the possible introduction to rbST in Canada. To some extent, this view rests on the perception that consumers reject biotechnology for religious or ethical reasons and that regulatory agencies disregard such concerns in the policy-making process. Perhaps more fundamentally though, the COC is opposed to the appearance that regulatory processes favour 'transnational drug companies who want to push recombinant bovine growth hormone onto Canadians' and that such a 'push' will have negative implications for the health of Canadians (COC, 1998a). In addition, the council is concerned that current decision making represents a step in the erosion of citizens' trust in democracy (COC, 1998b). As an activist group, the COC's rationale for its position is to 'keep big business out of Canadian milk' (COC, 1998a) and to protect democratic rights for an accessible regulatory process. While its role *vis-à-vis* any direct influence on the regulation of rbST is questionable, COC's has arguably been successful in raising some consumer concerns that can be seen to have had a secondary effect as mediated through other groups such as the DFC, NDC, and CAC.

Informal Responses to the Formal Regulation of rbST

The effect of informal contracting on the formal regulation of rbST in Canada is seen to be particularly important for three reasons. First, the delay in the review process can be attributed in part to political pressure placed on the office of the minister of health. Second, the appointment of independent panels to review the animal and health safety aspects of rbST can be seen as a response to credibility issues that have arisen at Health Canada as a result of the internal difficulties that have worked to add credence to some of the claims being made by external actors. Third, the broader impact of groups' calls for inclusion in the regulatory process can be seen to have influenced the federal government's recent launch of a new biotechnology strategy.

The rbST Policy Network

The rbST policy network consists of the Dairy Farmers of Canada, the National Dairy Council of Canada, the Consumers' Association of Canada, and the office of the minister of health. (I treat the office of the minister of health as the conduit of informal exchange in the policy network. The reason for this is based on information gathered through interviews with the associated groups who each indicated to me that while they are ultimately interested in affecting the minister's position on rbST, the minister's schedule is such that the vast majority of contact is actually with the office and not the minister per se. Still, the groups were certain that ministerial staff members were able to credibly represent the views of the minister to them, while at the same time credibly representing their views to the minister.) The Council of Canadians is as a secondary actor, that is, while it is not a member of the network itself, it has had an influence over the positions taken by the central participants. The key to uncovering the role that the rbST network has played is to look at *what* is being exchanged, at *how* the exchange has been organized, and at the *effect* that network exchange has had on the rbST decision-making process.

The rbST policy network emerged as a result of efforts on the part of the key players to have their interests accounted for. From the groups' perspective, the network is seen as the only mechanism available to them by which they can influence the rbST outcome, and they enter with a desire to have their individual interests guaranteed. From the minister's perspective, the network is seen as the mechanism by which extra-regulatory policy resources can be procured. The exchange, then, is predicated on the belief that gains from trade can be secured such that each actor is in a better position *vis-à-vis* its individual wants after the exchange than before it. Indeed, this is the central role of policy networks in policy making.

It is difficult to pinpoint the exact time at which the rbST network emerged; however, the groups indicate that it was during the summer of 1997 – at this time reports of internal difficulties at Health Canada were disclosed in the media, and these groups began to detect from the minister's office that their concerns about guaranteeing the safety of rbST were receiving attention. In a sense, conditions changed in the decision-making environment and opened up a new opportunity for groups to approach Health Canada. Whereas previous attempts to sway the policy process had been limited to participation in the rbST Task Force governed by Agriculture Canada, and to unrequited lobbying efforts to have extra-regulatory concerns addressed, public challenges about the legitimacy of the Health Canada review process afforded groups a stronger position on which to approach the minister.

The media reports questioning the credibility of the drug review process at Health Canada fundamentally changed the political position of the minister with regard to the rbST issue. With Health Canada legally bound by the Food and Drugs Act to offer a notice of compliance after a successful science-based review, the minister had previously had only one legitimate source for policy resources, the Bureau of Veterinary Drugs. However, with claims that the BVD was no longer credible, an opportunity presented itself for groups to approach the minister armed with new public concerns about Health Canada's position as a neutral regulator for rbST. From the minister's perspective, new policy resources were required to make a credible decision about rbST. Circumstances therefore emerged whereby the DFC, the NDC, and the CAC had a stronger bargaining position *vis-à-vis* getting Health Canada to effectively delay the licensing of rbST in Canada. Essentially, concerns about the internal review process presented the groups with the necessary ammunition to attack the rbST issue on science-based terms, even if those terms were used implicitly to mask additional socioeconomic concerns.

The groups approached the new decision-making environment with two important tools: the ability to credibly represent their constituents' views about rbST and the ability to credibly threaten the government's political position if group concerns were not addressed. Fundamentally, these tools are a function of group organizational capabilities and deserve further elaboration.

When a group approaches a legislator with a concern about a given policy issue, it does so successfully only if it can both demonstrate the legitimacy of its information and support its demonstration by its behaviour. In the rbST case, each of the groups' organizational characteristics facilitate such a demonstration – each is a national organization with a history of representing its constituents in the policy-making process (that is, if you want to know what dairy farmers are thinking you talk to the Dairy Farmers of Canada). Even more importantly, each of the groups also has a history of being able to enforce its positions, most notably by appealing to public protest either directly (for example, marching on Parliament Hill or engaging in public education campaigns) or through disclosures to the media. Effectively, it is the combination of a group's information credibility coupled to its ability to strategically enforce its position through politicians that allows it to potentially affect policy making. As Réjean Bouchard of the Dairy Farmers of Canada put it: 'Our organization represents the views of 25,000 dairy farmers in Canada – all of whom vote' (personal interview, 14 August 1998).

The complex dynamic of the rbST network pitted credible national organizations – the DFC, NDC, and CAC – both against each other and against the office of the minister of health, with three results. First, none of the groups has been able to secure a policy response that can be viewed to correspond directly to its desired position. In large part, this is because of restrictions placed on the minister with respect to affecting fundamental changes to the drug review process that would allow for socioeconomic variables to influence decisionmaking. For instance, the NDC's opposition to rbST based on economic concerns has not had an effect on the Health Canada position. What has been effectively achieved in the network, however, is an implicit 'bottom-line' for an *independent* assessment of the BVD's regulatory review to ensure the full public disclosure of the scientifically determined safety of rbST. Health Canada officials understand that interest group pressure at the political level was one of the major reasons for the creation of the external review panels. An employee of the Bureau of Veterinary Drugs suggested that the bureau is 'not ignorant' of the fact that interest group pressure at the political level 'certainly had a hand in' the decision to establish the review panels (personal interview, 18 August 1998). Essentially, network actors were able to secure this response by establishing that their membership would accept nothing less than a full safety guarantee for rbST and that they were willing to publicly enforce their position(s).

The second aspect of the Health Canada response to the network is the extent to which it is understood by the groups and some government officials that socioeconomic factors have played an important role in the continuing review of rbST. It is clearly apparent to all those concerned – particularly at the ministerial level – that the rbST issue is politically charged. The catch, of course, is that the politics of rbST do not 'jive' with the regulatory process and, in fact, contrast significantly with the currently available scientific information. Still, the extra-scientific concerns that are raised by the political aspects of rbST do appear to have had an effect on the length of time of the review, and Health Canada officials concede that one of the central reasons for this has been the continuing (and successful) call for delays by the DFC, NDC, and CAC.

Here, the position of the Council of Canadians has also been seen to play a role in creating a significant public confidence issue that is based primarily on the 'quantity' of the response in terms of letters to members of Parliament, rather than the 'quality' of the response. While none of the network actors acknowledge that the council's position is based on any legitimate claim for inclusion in the decision-making process, they all acknowledge that its 'scare tactics' have certainly played a role in determining the extent to which the public views rbST as a 'technical' versus an 'emotional' issue. Furthermore, each of the network members appealed to the COC's stance as a means to demonstrate that Canadians are truly concerned about rbST. As a result, it is important to consider that an indirect input from the COC does appear to have played at least a secondary role in the rbST network.

The COC, in conjunction with other activist groups including the Sierra Club and the National Farmers Union, has been active more recently in continuing to publicly propose that the internal difficulties at Health Canada are related to the 'corporatization' of the Health Protection Branch (HPB). Such allegations appear to have been similar to those levied against Health Canada management by their scientists in an appeal before the Public Service Staff Relations Board that suggests that management has put undue pressure on scientists to speed up regulatory reviews in response to industry pressure (Bueckert, 1998). However, the facts from Health Canada's perspective seem to suggest that perhaps the opposite is true. As Assistant Deputy Minister Joseph Losos has stated: 'The review has been going on for nine years. Certainly, it would be very difficult to ascertain that we have been putting pressure on to speed them up' (Senate of Canada, 1998: 34). Indeed, it is much more likely that external pressure to *delay* the licensing of rbST has been more central to the regulatory path taken. Each of the DFC, NDC, and CAC admit that Monsanto has been quite careful to avoid informal attempts to pressure the formal regulatory process.

Finally, the rbST network must be viewed in the broader context of what it indicates about the possible future of the science-based regulatory process in Canada. The case study reveals that extra-regulatory concerns can, and perhaps should, have a legitimate place in regulatory policy making. The argument here boils down to the analysis of the entire range of policy resources – both scientific and non-scientific – that are required to make publicly acceptable decisions about technologies such as rbST. It would appear that under conditions of uncertainty about the introduction of controversial products to the Canadian marketplace that science alone is insufficient as a basis on which to make decisions.

In organizational terms, this is really an argument that current formal regulatory processes are incomplete. What is required, then, is an appeal to all of the necessary and legitimate policy resources that go into making an acceptable decision. This suggests that while science is clearly the best criteria by which to judge human and animal health safety, health safety is apparently not the only criterion that determines product viability. Socioeconomic concerns also appear to play an important role, as witnessed by the evidence of informal influence over the formal regulation of rbST. This conclusion would seem to suggest that the key question is not so much whether rbST is 'lost in regulatory space,' but rather what the definition of the 'regulatory space' entails for public decision making.

Conclusion: A New Regulatory Status Quo

The current climate for regulatory review of biotechnological products has appeared to pit science *against* socioeconomics. One of the results of this has been the inability of the formal regulatory process to resolve public conflict over issues that arise when controversial products such as rbST appear for review. By focusing specifically on the rbST case, the chapter has examined why this is, and what the organizational response has been, showing that an opportunity for informal influence has emerged in response to an apparent void in the formal system. The key question for the future is whether this informal response is sufficient as a means to resolve the rbST conflict specifically, and controversy over biotechnology more generally.

Even in the face of the January 1999 rejection of a licence for rbST, this issue is doubtless to be of significant concern for the regulatory process. On the one hand, questions about when the status quo is insufficient to deal with important regulatory questions – potentially resulting in the appointment and subsequent effect of market-based arm's-length review panels – will continue to arise and act as challenges for regulators. On the other hand, specific issues about the use of rbST in Canada will also be of continuing importance, particularly as there are already indications that Monsanto will resubmit its application. The implication is that potential linkages, or even trade-offs between formal and informal responses are likely to extend the debate about regulatory governance well into the future.

It must be remembered that legislators view decisions about products like rbST in political terms. They have a vested interest in the design of credible mechanisms through which they can procure required policy resources in a manner that guarantees their own ends, while at the same time ensuring public confidence. Informal mechanisms are therefore likely to be formalized in an effort to establish public transparency in decision making.

The release of the federal *Canadian Biotechnology Strategy* appears to be a response to precisely this concern (Canada, 1998). It integrates social, ethical, health, economic, environmental, and regulatory considerations; addressing public information and participation; establishing a balanced, broad-based advisory committee; providing the context for strengthening the business, regulatory, and investment climate; and improving the government's ability to manage horizontal issues. While it is impossible to conclude that the rbST controversy is directly responsible for the design of the new strategy, it is reasonable to suggest that it had a key role in the government's desire to ensure that biotechnology regulation will guarantee that social and ethical considerations are fully addressed. Indeed, the legacy of rbST may well be that it initiated what could amount to a formal review process where science is viewed in *addition* to socioeconomics.

References

Agriculture Canada. (1993). *Biotechnology in Agriculture: General Information.* Ottawa: Minister of Supply and Services.

Axelrod, R. (1984). *The Evolution of Cooperation.* New York: Basic Books.

Bimber, B. (1996). *The Politics of Expertise in Congress.* Albany: State University of New York Press.

Bueckert, D. (1998). 'Scientists Claim Management Interference in Drug Reviews.' *Canadian Press.* 16 September, 21.

Canada. (1998). *The 1998 Canadian Biotechnology Strategy.* Ottawa: Industry Canada.

– (1999). News Release, 'Health Canada Rejects Bovine Growth Hormone in Canada,' 14 January. Ottawa: Health Canada.

Coase, R.C. (1960). 'The Problem of Social Cost.' *Journal of Law and Economics,* 3: 1–44.

Consumers' Association of Canada. (1994). 'Policy Position on Recombinant Bovine Somatotropin (rbST).' Ottawa: author, June.

Coughlin, P.J. (1992). *Probabilistic Voting Theory.* Cambridge: Cambridge University Press.

Council of Canadians. (1998a). 'Back off BGH: Keep Canadian Milk Safe.' Ottawa: author.

– (1998b). 'Genetically Engineered Food – Concealed and Dangerous.' Ottawa: author, 26 May.

Dairy Farmers of Canada. (1997). 'Dairy Farmers of Canada Seek Strong Government Assurances on Safety of rbST.' *Canada NewsWire,* 14 July.

– (1998). *1998 Dairy Policy: Adopted January 22, 1998.* Ottawa: author.

Doern, G.B. (1998). 'Risky Business: Canada's Changing Science-Based Regulatory Regime.' Paper presented at the Conference on Science, Government and Global Markets: The State of Canada's Science-Based Regulatory Institutions, Ottawa, October.

Doern, G.B., and H. Sheehy. (1997). 'The Federal Biotechnology Regulatory System: A Commentary on an Institutional Work in Progress.' Paper presented at the Conference on Biotechnology, the Consumer, and the Canadian Marketplace, Ottawa, September.

Enelow, J.M., and M.J. Hinich. (1984). *The Spacial Theory of Voting*. Cambridge: Cambridge University Press.

Food and Agriculture Organization. (1998). *Report of the Joint Food and Agriculture Organization of the United Nations and the World Health Organization Expert Committee on Food Additives, Fiftieth Meeting, Rome, 17–26 February 1998: Summary and Conclusions*. Rome: Food and Agricultural Organization.

Granovetter, M. (1985). 'Economic Action and Social Structure: The Problem of Embeddedness.' *American Journal of Sociology*, 91(3): 481–510.

Health Canada. (1995). 'Statement on Bovine Somatotropin,' in Agriculture Canada, *Review of the Potential Impact of Recombinant Bovine Somatotropin (rbST) in Canada, Report of the rbST Task Force*, May. Ottawa: author.

– (1998). 'The Safety and Efficacy of the Proposed Veterinary Drug Nutrilac (rbST).' Mimeo copy. Ottawa: Communications, Policy and Consultation Branch, Health Canada.

Hindmoor, A. (1998). 'The Importance of Being Trusted: Transaction Costs and Policy Network Theory.' *Public Administration*, 76: 25–43.

Industry Canada. (1998). 'Federal Government Releases New Biotechnology Strategy.' *News Release*, Ottawa, 6 August.

Irwin, A. (1987). 'Technical Expertise and Risk Conflict: An Institutional Study of the British Compulsory Seat Belt Debate.' *Policy Sciences*, 20: 339–64.

Klein, D.B., ed. (1997). *Reputation: Studies in the Voluntary Elicitation of Good Conduct*. Ann Arbor: University of Michigan Press.

Lewis, H.W. (1990). *Technological Risk*. New York: Norton.

MacDonald, Mark R. (1998). 'Governing Contracts for Productive Resources in Policy-Making: A Transaction Cost View of the Legislator's Choice to Govern by Policy Network.' Paper presented at the Annual General Meeting of the Canadian Political Science Association, Ottawa, 1 June.

Majone, G.(1989). *Evidence, Argument and Persuasion in the Policy Process*. New Haven: Yale University Press.

Mills, L. (1996). 'Scientific Knowledge and the Governance of Social Life – Biotechnology Regulation: The Case of Bovine Growth Hormone in the United States and Canada.' Paper presented at the Great Lakes Conference on Political Economy, York University, May.

Mueller, D.C. (1989). *Public Choice II*. Cambridge: Cambridge University Press.

National Dairy Council of Canada. (1998). 'Letter to the Minister of Health.' Ottawa, May.

Peel, C.J., and D.E. Bauman. (1987). 'Somatotropin and lactation.' *Journal of Dairy Science*, 70: 474–86.

Powell, D., and W. Leiss. (1997). *Mad Cows and Mother's Milk: The Perils of Poor Risk Communication*. Montreal/Kingston: McGill-Queen's University Press.

Ratledge, C. (1992). 'Biotechnology: The Socio-Economic revolution?' In E.J. DaSilva and C. Ratledge, eds., *Biotechnology: Economic and Social Aspects*, 1–22. Cambridge: Cambridge University Press.

Rubin, P.H. (1990). *Managing Business Transactions: Controlling the Cost of Coordinating, Communicating, and Decision-Making*. New York: Free Press.

Senate of Canada. (1998). *Proceeding of the Standing Senate Committee on Agriculture and Forestry: Issue 17 – Evidence*, 4 June.

Speller, R. (M.P., Chair of the Standing Committee on Agriculture and Agri-Food). (1994). *rBST in Canada: Report of the Standing Committee on Agriculture and Agri-Food*. Ottawa: House of Commons Canada.

Stennes, B.K., R.R. Barichello, and J.D. Graham. (1990). *Bovine Somatotropin and the Canadian Dairy Industry: An Economic Analysis*. Ottawa: Policy Branch, Agriculture Canada.

Throgmorton, J.A. (1991). 'The Rhetorics of Policy Analysis.' *Policy Sciences*, 24: 153–79.

Williamson, O.E. (1975). *Markets and Hierarchies: Analysis and Antitrust Implications*. New York: Free Press.

– (1985). *The Economic Institutions of Capitalism*. New York: Free Press.

– (1991). 'Comparative Economic Organization: The Analysis of Discrete Structural Alternatives.' Paper presented at Universitat des Saarlandes, Europa-Institut, May.

– (1996). *The Mechanisms of Governance*. New York: Oxford University Press.

PART 2:
SCIENCE IN REGULATORY AND
RISK MANAGEMENT INSTITUTIONS

8 The Therapeutic Products Programme: From Traditional Science-Based Regulator to Science-Based Risk-Benefit Manager?

G. BRUCE DOERN

Few areas of Canada's science-based regulatory system have faced the array of challenges and choices that are part of the routine of the Therapeutic Products Programme (TPP) of Health Canada. Embracing areas such as drug regulation, medical devices, biologicals such as vaccines and blood products, and complementary or natural medicines, the TPP is an organizational and regulatory amalgam with a daunting job to do. Though different in scope and form from its formerly separate predecessor bodies, the Drugs Directorate and the Medical Devices Bureau, the TPP is an entity whose essential rhythms of activity will be familiar to former ministers of health and those previously heading up its antecedent organizations. Particularly for the former Drugs Directorate, a key political and organizational reality was managing, both for its minister and for Canadians, the 'hazard of the week.' New drug products had to be reviewed for efficacy and safety and, quite literally in any given week, any one of these actual or potential hazards, could, if mishandled, land the minister and his or her regulatory scientists in serious political trouble (Doern, 1981). Like the incessant dripping of the tap on a prisoner's forehead, hazards, science, risk, and politics were a central part of the minister's job.

It is important to begin any analysis of the TPP with this ministerial focus. The minister of health is by statute the ultimate regulatory authority, and in Cabinet government and media politics, the ultimate focal point for accountability and blame when things go wrong. A minister will rarely get political credit for new drugs that are effective and safe but will get unbridled blame when products prove to be questionable or are even (for a few weeks or months) perceived to be so. Equally, however, one must go well beyond ministerial politics and the incessant rhythm of drug review approvals to understand the TPP or any other health regulator as a science-based regulatory institution (Abraham, 1995; Eastman, 1985). Both recent and current health ministers have faced controversies that included tainted blood and resulting compensation and moral issues (Canada, 1997; Picard, 1998), whole classes of new products such as biotechnology, and complex issues concerning AIDS and cancer where patients want rapid access to the latest drugs. Ministers also know on a daily basis that the drug industry is of crucial and growing importance to Canada's economy and to the health of Canadians in an increasingly borderless world (Mehta, 1996; Industry Canada, 1996a, 1996b).

This chapter examines the efforts to transform the Canadian therapeutic products regulatory regime from an older one characterized by traditional science-based regulation to a newer one infused more explicitly with broader concepts of risk-benefit management. Traditional science-based product regulation is centred upon a premarket approval process where the scientific and technical input is structured around the competence of internal scientists and medically trained personnel functioning as reviewers of proposals for new drugs. It tends also to review *de novo* all technical information from sponsoring firms and other countries rather than merely accepting it (Gagnon, 1992). The newer model of risk-benefit management places more, or much greater, complementary emphasis on postmarket surveillance and the provision of information to consumers, patients, and professionals. It also puts a far greater effort into ranking products or classes of products by means of a risk-benefit process of analysis and judgment. This process also relies more on technical resources and expertise from outside the regulatory body and outside national jurisdictions (Gagnon, 1992; TPP, 1997a).

These polar models are in fact more complex than sketched here so far and are examined further below. The older model obviously also dealt with risk but it was forged in a different historical period. The point to stress from the outset is that the focus of the chapter is ultimately on how the science and knowledge base and the science advisory process themselves both change as efforts are made to transform the system of regulatory therapeutic products from the older to the newer model. Thus, science-based regulation is our central concern but, as earlier chapters of this book have shown, it is clearly not the only reason that change is occurring.

The TPP is a regulatory and risk management body in the federal health portfolio. It is a complex and fast-changing institution, and this chapter can provide only a partial and necessarily selected examination. Some key features of overall change are examined, and the focus is on a review of drugs and medical devices. But many of the TPP's other aspects of regulation are not examined (such as biologics and radiopharmaceuticals, drug surveillance, compliance and field operations, and overall relations with the minister of health and the larger Health Protection Branch).

The chapter is organized into five sections. First, we outline the basic mandate and structure of the TPP, officially formed in 1997 but essentially in place since 1993–4. Second, we relate this mandate to the recent historical context of change, especially as reflected in two studies in the early 1990s. The third section examines the general nature of the science and risk aspects of the therapeutic products regulatory realm. The fourth section then looks at the more particular dynamics of science-based input into the TPP's drug review and medical devices regulatory realms. Section five takes brief note of several other organizational aspects of the management of science in the TPP. Conclusions follow about the state of the TPP's transformation, both successes and remaining problems and dilemmas, transitional as well as permanent.

TPP Mandate and Structure

The Therapeutic Products Programme was announced in 1997 as an amalgamation of the former Drugs Directorate and Medical Devices Bureau of Health Canada. A component of the larger Health Protection Branch at Health Canada, the TPP's mandate is derived from, and influenced by, nine statutes and five international agreements (TPP, 1997b). The key items of legislation are the Food and Drugs Act (and regulations regarding drugs and medical devices), the Department of Health Act, the Controlled Drugs and Substances Act (and regulations), and the Canadian Environmental Protection Act. But other laws also govern regulatory matters including those on financial administration, access to information, and privacy. The five international agreements, whose impacts are ever growing, include three conventions of the United Nations, as well as the North American Free Trade Agreement and the General Agreement on Tariffs and Trade and the World Trade Organization.

The TPP describes its overall mission as that of ensuring that 'the drugs, medical devices and other therapeutic products available in Canada are safe, effective, and of high quality (ibid.: 5). Its more specific strategic objectives are set out as follows.

They are:

1. To ensure Canadians:
   (a) Have a timely access to safe, effective, high quality therapeutic products
   (b) Are never put at undue risk by the use of therapeutic products available on the Canadian market
   (c) Are fully informed about the risks and benefits of those products.
2. To ensure the regulatory system in Canada:
   (a) Is innovative
   (b) Is developed with the full participation of clients, stakeholders, and the public
   (c) Is conducive to the introduction of effective therapeutic products into the Canadian market
   (d) Facilitates the competitiveness of Canadian industry in the world market.
3. To first set or adopt internationally competitive product and service standards in all aspects of our work, and then to meet and surpass them.
4. To contribute to an efficient and affordable health care system in Canada.
5. To provide national and international leadership in therapeutic product regulation from a science-based foundation of intelligent programming, constructive partnerships, full and open communications, and a productive organization. (ibid.: 5–6)

The definitions of a drug and a medical device are found in the Food and Drugs Act and cover a daunting range of therapeutic products which in turn help define key aspects of the regulatory scope of the TPP. At least nine categories of product are regulated and their risks and benefits managed: (1) pharmaceuticals (prescription and non-prescription); (2) complementary medicines (homeopathic, herbal); (3) biologicals (vaccines, blood and blood products, certain hormones and enzymes, allergic extracts, tissues and organs, biotherapeutics and genetic engineering); (4) radiopharmaceuticals; (5) medical devices (implants, test kits, contraceptive devices); (6) nutraceuticals; (7) disinfectants; (8) low-risk products (sunscreens, toothpaste); and (9) narcotics and controlled and restricted substances.

The TPP is structured around three 'product' groupings (pharmaceutical assessment, medical devices, and biologics and radio-pharmaceuticals), and three functional groupings (policy and coordination, compliance and enforcement, and drug surveillance, including postmarket monitoring). Underpinning the structure are the regional operations of the TPP located in five regional facilities. TPP has a staff of about 750 persons, including 575 scientists and professional staff.

While these are the skeletal features of the TPP as an organization, they are not coincident with the therapeutic products 'regulatory and risk management regime.' This larger array of ideas, institutions, clients, interests, businesses, as well as science-based professionals and experts (Canadian and international), will be introduced more gradually as the analysis proceeds. At the outset, however, it is important to have a sense of the broader agenda of Health Canada in which the TPP sees itself functioning. This action context is set out in Health Canada's 1998–9 Estimates to Parliament which set out the following challenges:

- Industry and stakeholder concern about and/or dissatisfaction with the department's performance in delivering its programs
- The Gagnon and Hearn reviews of drug and medical devices programs, which has led to extensive self-assessment and renewal of all facets of the programs
- The Krever Commission review of blood regulation and the Standing Committee on Health's review of natural health products
- Program Review, which has reduced appropriations and required implementation of cost recovery (now contributing 65.8 per cent of the budget)
- Increased media attention and public demands for transparency and involvement in the budgetary process
- New technologies and alternative health treatments
- Globalization of therapeutic product industries which requires regulatory harmonization and even regulatory globalization. (Canada, 1998: 42)

To these one could easily add both the demographic impact of an aging population making more demands on all aspects of the health care system and a greater proclivity to mistrust scientists, the medical profession, and the regulators (Foot, 1996).

Recent Historical and Political-Economic Context

The emergence of the TPP in 1997 and its transformed mandate is the product of at least a decade of dissatisfaction with and criticism of Canada's therapeutic products regulatory regime (Eastmann, 1985; Stein, 1987; Auditor General of Canada, 1987). This criticism was crystallized in two major review studies in the early 1990s, but the trail of dissatisfaction goes back further and was reflected in even earlier reports in the mid- and late 1980s. The report by Gagnon (1992) focused on the Canadian drug approval system and, as its name indicates, the 1992 Medical Devices Review Committee (the Hearn Committee) reported on medical devices. Both review processes included extensive stakeholder involvement, and the studies reported a broad consensus about the need for change and about the broad direction for change.

Gagnon's report was initially the result of industry pressure borne out of quite justified industry frustration with the failure of the government to carry out reforms advocated by the earlier report by Stein (1987). Key industry interest groups such the Canadian Drug Manufacturers Association (CDMA) had undertaken their own studies of the inefficiencies of the Canadian system. But the Gagnon deliberations quickly heard from other elements of the health lobby, some of whom were also concerned with the sluggishness of the Canadian drug approval process, a process that was denying some Canadians access to the latest drugs such as those for AIDS and cancer treatment (Kennedy, 1991). Gagnon made 152 recommendations for change. But the key argument of his report was that at the centre of its regulatory regime Canada was functioning within an out-of-date paradigm. This was cast by Gagnon as the traditional, post-thalidomide model of drug review 'based on *de novo* analysis of information submitted' (Gagnon, 1992: 1). Although this system had had considerable success in some respects, Gagnon argued that other countries and jurisdictions such as Australia, Sweden, and the European Union were already moving to another model. It was based on an 'expeditious review of medicines, using scientifically valid methods' but with a far greater 'sharing of expertise and responsibilities, and involving health professionals from outside their agencies' (ibid.: 1). The new paradigm centred on the need to strike a proper balance between pre- and post-marketing evaluations of drugs. As Gagnon stressed: 'This approach, which is scientifically indisputable, recognizes the fact that it is absolutely impossible to detect all eventual adverse effects of drugs through pre-market evaluation, no matter how extensive the process might be' (ibid.). He went on to explain that 'it is only when a drug has been widely used under different conditions and circumstances, that all of its effects become fully known to the health professionals and to the patients' (ibid.).

Gagnon focused on the then-existing Drugs Directorate of Health and Welfare Canada. The new leadership of the Drugs Directorate early in 1993 thus inherited a reform agenda that landed in an organizational and political environment characterized by three stark realities. First, relations with stakeholders were quite poor. Business interests saw the Drugs Directorate as the slowest approval system in the industrialized world (National Advisory Council on Pharmaceutical Research, 1992). Consumer interests were critical about the lack of proper information about risk and health for Canadians. Some analysts thought that business had too much influence in the combined drug approval and patent policy regime (Lexchin, 1992). But many health lobbies were also clamouring for a better and faster approval process. Second, the resources of the Drug Directorate were declining both under government-wide pressures to reduce the deficit and under Treasury Board sanctions to force adoption of cost-recovery practices that the directorate had been questioning and partially resisting largely on the grounds that it saw itself as a public interest regulator (Health and Welfare Canada, 1988, 1989). Third, the Canadian approval process was indeed among the slowest, with a heavy backlog of drugs needing review and with scientific review staff suffering from very low morale.

Though focused on the drug review process, Gagnon's report both explicitly and implicitly raised broader issues about the full therapeutic products regime. This included the area of medical devices, which in 1992 resided in a separate Environmental Health Directorate of Health and Welfare Canada. (Health and Welfare Canada became Health Canada in a 1993 reorganization). In January 1997, after considerable discussion, Health Canada was persuaded that the Medical Devices Bureau ought to join with the Drugs Directorate to form the new Therapeutic Products Programme. In the four-year period from

1993 to 1997, the journey to form the TPP and transform the old paradigm and its attendant organizational cultures involved several key steps and issues. Space does not allow a full account of these, but several features need to be highlighted. These are:

1 In 1993 a staff-centred 'renewal' exercise was begun involving sixty project teams, each headed by a staff member assigned to champion the reform area. By August 1995, fifty of these projects had been implemented, and most of the remaining ones had also led to partial reforms.

2 Debate and discussion occurred over the definition of a drug. This was because the legislation that defined drugs was quite old, and, moreover, the nature of scientific and technical change was blurring the boundary lines between what was a drug, a medical device, and even a tissue. These therapeutic products were also becoming increasingly blended in their use in treatment. The impact of the later 1997 Krever inquiry and report on the tainted blood issue affected this debate, but so also did emerging interests and industries supporting herbal medicines and so-called natural products which did not want such products to be defined as drugs. Indeed, in an overall sense this debate helped prompt the acceptance of the larger umbrella concept of 'therapeutic products' as the name of the new program or agency (Standing Committee on Health, 1998: 10–11).

3 The funding and resources of the eventual TPP had to be stabilized. This was inevitably linked to the implementation of cost recovery and was also affected by the internal governmental politics of the massive federal Program Review process of 1993–4. Business would not agree to pay new fees until the backlog was cleared and efficiencies were demonstrably proven. The TPP is now 50 to 75 per cent cost-recovery funded, depending on the area or activity. The average approval process for drugs has been reduced in half (see more below) but progress here has been far from ideal. The hard budget constraints of Program Review provided a key impetus for change, since the department offered up tax- or appropriations-financed areas of its activity if it could replace it with fee-based areas. Among the areas cut were parts of its laboratories. This produced the difficult-to-justify public image of a regulator 'cutting its science' just when its mandate

was expanding and health-risk controversies were pummelling its minister.

4 The TPP renewal process was occurring within the larger ambit of a renewal or transition effort for the Health Protection Branch of Health Canada. This was where legislative change ultimately resided, but also key decisions about the larger 'make-or-buy' decisions regarding the branch's scientific core. Also being debated were the new balances to be struck between the surveillance aspects of public health, the consistency of risk management approaches, and the structure of new programs, some arising from the transfer of the food inspection function to the new Canadian Food Inspection Agency. This larger process was proceeding much more slowly than the TPP renewal process and was sometimes supportive of TPP change, but at other times exerted an institutional drag on the reform process.

5 The TPP was actively and necessarily engaged in an elaborate process of international discussions, negotiations, and confidence-building measures to promote international harmonization, mutual recognition, and cooperation in the obviously globalized world of drug manufacture and distribution. This was occurring in the context of trade regimes and under the auspices of heath or sectoral processes as well.

Meanwhile, the 1992 Medical Devices Review Committee Report was also leaving its trail of influences and ideas. Some of these eventually show up in the new integrated TPP structure and philosophy. At this stage of the analysis, we simply highlight key findings and changes advocated for medical devices. In later sections on science in regulation we return to these points because the regulatory and risk politics, institutions, and cycles of activity in this sector are different from drug approvals.

The committee, composed of experts from several stakeholder sectors, drew attention to several key features of the medical devices regime, namely: (a) that most manufactured devices are *not* evaluated by the federal government before they enter the marketplace, a fact that few Canadians understood; (b) that the medical devices industry is largely foreign owned and 80 per cent of devices are imported, but that many small Canadian firms in the industry had the potential to succeed as science-and-technology-based industries; and (c) that a diverse community of health care professionals are at the centre of the delivery of the medical devices system, whose concerns, according to survey results, were more about the safety of medical devices than about their availability and efficacy (Medical Devices Review Committee, 1992: 2–3).

In the face of both technological change and numerous new devices, and the changing regulatory regimes of other countries, the committee argued that there was a serious lack of focus in the Canadian system. Its recommendations (forty-five in total) centred on a view that Canada should harmonize its system with key features of the U.S. regime, including 'the definition of a medical device, pre-market notification, a risk-based classification system and the concept of substantial equivalence' (ibid.: 5). Thus, the focus was on strengthening premarket review but in a targeted way based on risk. Again, as with Gagnon, the greater use of expert committees and contracted premarket submission evaluation was central. More postmarket surveillance was also advocated, including mandatory reporting of adverse incidents involving the use of devices. A third area of concern was the need to somehow clarify the legal definition of 'device,' so as to sort out, among the 450,000 products, those that have minimal impacts, such as bandages, from those that involve much greater risk. The MDR Committee also drew attention to the particular issue of devices for home use. In terms of regulatory agency finances, the committee somewhat cautiously recommended the selective use of cost recovery, provided it 'did not create an additional cost to the consumer' (ibid.: 7).

It is obvious that the immediate historical context for the formation of the TPP goes beyond, and is more complex than, the above two reports and their contents. Indeed, in the six years since there has been, as we will see, a convergence of regulatory philosophy regarding both drugs and medical devices. But for our purposes the two reports are a useful surrogate history and they certainly shaped, along with other factors, the cumulative institutional, regulatory, and risk-benefit agenda of the TPP.

Science and Risk in the TPP: General Issues

Several general issues about science and risk in the TPP warrant mention. The first general point to stress is that science and a science base of knowledge are central to both the older model of traditional science-based regulation and to the risk-benefit management model – the one into which many regulators are trying to transform themselves. As one regulatory scientist put it to me, in the older model, 'science was science was science,' whereas in the newer model science is 'paramount but not supreme.' It is doubtful even in the earlier model that science was quite that supreme. However, there is little doubt that in a risk-benefit management model, science occupies a broader spectrum of shared advisory space containing numerous kinds of knowledge, expertise, evidence, and values. This complex spectrum is thus capable of spawning fact-value controversies that blend scientific judgment with other forms of evaluation in regulatory decision making.

A second feature of the effort to transform a regime to one based on the risk management concept is that the central legislation governing the TPP (or Health Canada) does not yet explicitly endorse this concept. The TPP mission is in one sense therefore a step ahead of its full legal base. Some of this catch-up problem is found in the larger debate at Health Canada about new drug legislation and about how much of the law should be one overall act as opposed to several sectoral acts. The expression of the new paradigm is mainly found in an effort to devise a 'risk management framework.' This is being done, in various draft forms, both within the TPP and at the level of the Health Protection Branch (HPB) and of Health Canada as a whole. For the TPP, such a framework is needed to ensure that there is a basis for integration among the various product review directorates, but also in the regulation and policy-making process. The development of a risk-benefit management framework is being based on earlier efforts in other countries and on evolving debate within the department (Somers et al., 1991; Health and Welfare Canada, 1991). It is also being influenced indirectly by independent literature on risk and regulation (see Adams, 1995; Ratzan, 1998; Viscusi, 1998). The HPB had itself provided, in 1993, a guidance framework, but then it saw the need to strengthen it for a number of reasons: to encourage a more holistic approach, to encompass all hazards within its mandate, to develop a population health focus, and to encourage choice among multiple risk management strategies.

In one sense, throughout the 1990s, the main elements of a risk management system were becoming clarified. As discussed in Chapter 1, the new paradigm had to analytically, organizationally, and politically deal with: risk assessment, risk management per se, and risk communication (see also Health Protection Branch, 1997: 34). While descriptions of the above tasks and elements can extend to many pages of drafting and can both clarify and cover over deep controversies, the translation of these elements of action, information, and advice is, like all regulation, easier said than done.

The role of science in this broadened model of regulation and risk-benefit management is also altered by changes in the sources of scientific information. It is suggested that the older model and era of regulation was anchored around traditional sources such as epidemiological investigations, toxicological studies, and clinical trials. But more recently, and in the context of the risk-benefit management model, other sources and types of scientific information have come into greater use, including: biological markers, molecular epidemiology, new toxicological assays, in vitro assays, genetics, structure activity analysis, surveillance, and population health surveys.

Finally, as the previously discussed Gagnon study and Medical Devices Review Committee emphasized, science in the risk management model and era involves a far wider sharing, dependence, and exchange of scientific and professional information and knowledge among experts outside the TPP and outside Canada. These and related issues are best seen through a closer look at the drug review and medical devices review approval processes.

Science in the Review and Approval Process: Drugs and Medical Devices

As we have already seen, there are differences in the drug review process compared with the review process for medical devices, differences to which we will pay increasing attention below. But it is the drug review process that has generated the widest degree of political and economic attention in recent years.

Drug Review

In the 1990s in particular, the U.S.- and European-led global pharmaceutical and biotechnology industry has exerted pressure on national regulators to enhance the efficiency of the regulatory systems. Some of this pressure has crystalized recently around an effort by the independent, U.K.-located, primarily industry-funded, Centre for Medicines Research International (CMRI) to develop agreed benchmarks or 'league tables' for the approval times of various national regulators. Several countries including Canada (through the TPP) are cooperating in this effort through information exchange. In this regard the CMRI process has led to the need to identify what the key milestones are in the drug review process. Without such agreement, one could not compare data on approval times. The agreed eleven potential milestones (depending on the country's system) are listed below and also serve as a useful way to look at the TPP review process:

1 Marketing authorization application (MAA) or new drug application (NDA) submitted.
2 Valid submission accepted for review
3 Start of scientific assessment
4 Submission of scientific assessment reports
5 Review of MAA/NDA by advisory committee
6 Regulatory authority requests additional information
7 Response from sponsor
8 Assessment of response
9 Regulatory authority grants authorization (or not)
10 Regulatory authority notifies sponsor
11 Licensing authority issues product licence.

The TPP's system broadly corresponds to most of these milestones, although there are some parts of particular stages that contain either slight Canadian differences or which do not apply at all. Chief among the latter is the fifth milestone stage involving the use of an advisory committee. For the TPP process, the final three milestones are essentially one (milestone 10).

Before looking at selected milestone elements as they affect the science base of drug review, it is useful to note the reported changes in approval performance. First, a 1997 CMRI report concluded that 'over the 1990s, improvements have been seen in overall review times for a number of authorities including Germany, Spain, Australia, Canada and the USA' (CMRI, 1997: 13). Indeed, Canada's position in these rudimentary league tables looks quite good in terms of level of improvement. But the report also shows that only six milestones were identified as being applicable to the review processes of all nine countries being studied and 'only one milestone is routinely recorded by member authorities' (ibid.: 12).

Coincident with these international developments and pressures, the TPP was committing itself to the publication and use of performance reports and targets. Indeed such systems were part of a reinvented government strategy across the entire Government of Canada (Aucoin, 1997; Doern, 1994). Following initial efforts to both cut the backlog and speed approvals, the Drug Directorate did succeed in cutting average approval times in half. This was the performance change that garnered the approving comment from the CMRI. The TPP's own reports deal with a range of measures with the 1997 report indicating the following:

1 The number of notices of compliance (NOCs) granted on first review has increased to 82 (48 per cent) in 1997 from 49 (35 per cent) in 1996. The number of notices of non-compliance (NONs) requesting further company information decreased from 133 in 1996 to 64 in 1997.

2 There has been a 10 per cent increase in 1997 across the program in the total backlog of new drug submissions (NDS) and their amendments (ANDS). The report indicated that this disappointing increase 'must not be viewed in isolation but rather in conjunction with the greater emphasis and success of approving submissions on first review' (TPP, 1998: 4).

3 The median approval times for the 172 new drugs (pharmaceuticals and biologicals) in 1997 was 19.3 months compared with 21.2 months in 1996 and 23.2 months in 1995 (ibid.: 5).

4 The TPP has set targets for each submission type and class, but the 1997 report indicated that 'most established performance targets were not met in 1997' (ibid.: 5).

These and other targets and data in the reports are an important feature of the new culture of the TPP, and they also reveal both the complexity and problems of transition. Most of the performance characteristics deal with issues of speed of approval. These are clearly important concerns to business but also to parts of the health and consumer lobby which seek the faster availability of drugs. But equally, these indicators say little about other aspects of the *quality* of the actual reviews. Even under the best of circumstances, the task of assessing the quality of reviews will be difficult, and a consideration of quality inevitably goes back to the question of the science, but not exclusively so because regulating quality is always problematic and is usually linked to professions and knowledge groups (Dewees, 1983). Some of these qualitative dimensions can be seen from several glimpses into the approval process as provided by Gagnon's report and as revealed in recent comments by TPP officials. Inevitably also these take us back to the different milestone steps already outlined.

First, the quality aspects of the process, including science and risk, begin within the firm sponsoring and researching the new product. The crucial relationships of scientific exchange are between the firm's technical people and the drugs reviewed in the TPP as the formal approval process begins. Indeed, there are likely to have been discussions well before the formal application arrives. It is easy to underestimate the importance of a firm's internal review processes. But the TPP-centred risk regime is crucially dependent on it, and firms have their own concerns and disciplines. These will centre on profit, return on investment, and proprietary information, but also on producing an efficacious and safe drug that enhances the reputation and market position of the firm and that does not subject it to unwanted liabilities and costly litigation.

Second, once an application for a new drug enters the TPP review process, the question of the reviewer's role emerges. Gagnon stressed that the pre-1992 regime focused on *de novo* review that was the product of the thalidomide debacle of the late 1960s. In that process, the underlying assumption was that a regulator's reviewers should trust no one else's judgment, neither the sponsoring firm's nor other countries' regulators. But Gagnon also argued that this model could no longer hold, given the volume of new drugs, their greater complexity, and the new patterns of regulatory reform and scientific peer exchange that were evident in Europe and elsewhere in the early 1990s. Many of the core reviewers of the Pharmaceutical Assessment Directorate were naturally suspicious of these claims, in part out of normal institutional inertia when a new world has to be faced, and in part out of a view that *de novo* was still the best approach. In addition, inherently low morale as a result of other kinds of cutbacks in government and fewer opportunities for professional development and career progression may also have coloured reviewers' assessments of Gagnon's views. Gagnon discussed these issues at length, but he also argued that a new regime would have to include, as in Europe, a greater reliance on the use of outside experts and networks of experts.

To return to the milestones, one implication is that such outside experts would have to be in the review process itself where (as in milestone 5) some broader form of advisory committee review would be needed. It would appear that the Canadian drug review process has not yet adopted this strategy. It is constructing and using more outside advisory scientists and medical resources in the larger policy, regulation-making, and standard-setting processes, but there has been no *systematic* acceptance of outside experts in the core drug review process. In a presentation to a parliamentary committee, the TPP's director general, Dann Michols, noted that there are now five expert standing committees to advise the TPP on overall regulatory and policy matters. Michols also indicated that the TPP contracts with university staff and private physicians for the evaluation of submissions but only 'from time to time if we do not have that exact specific expertise on staff' (Standing Committee on Health, 1998: 2.)

Thus, there is still some caution about this opening up of the review process. Some of the caution is the result of the complexity of overall changes to the TPP, but some is also because both the agency and its minister ultimately may be reluctant to put its everyday trust in a larger array of outside, including international, experts, given that the latter's role is still episodic, part-time, and less aware of the combined technical-political realities that a responsible minister senses and faces. Thus, in the same hearing referred to above, the TPP's director strongly defended the competence and dedication of his core scientific staff, in part because in earlier stages of the hearings on natural medicines, witnesses had questioned the TPP's competence. Michols stressed that of the 575 professionals in the TPP as a whole, 550 have science degrees and that 'we are one of the most competent drug and medical device regulators in the world' (ibid.: 3).

There is also natural caution in relying too much on international processes regarding drug approvals. Largely this stems from strong concerns about national sovereignty, particularly because any minister of health, especially when something goes badly wrong with a drug, cannot be put in the position of having to say, in effect, that decision or approval was made by the Americans or the British and we (Canada) just accepted their judgment. However, as Gagnon anticipated, and as events have since shown, there is a growing likelihood that a globalized drug product review process will evolve whereby big global multinationals will simultaneously submit one agreed dossier (that is, agreed as to format and kinds of information) to several national regulators. One country may well then take the lead in some form of initial evaluation. At some point, however, all countries will insist that they have a right and need to make a final decision on the ultimate approval of that drug in their country. This is certainly the Canadian position. At the same time, as such a system evolves, there will in some way be a greater division of scientific expertise and evaluative resources in the approval process. This brief mention of the international process, of course, focuses on the premarket approval process. There is also an even greater impact from the sharing of scientific information on the postmarket surveillance side. This is not discussed in any detail in this chapter, although it must be stressed that the TPP's resources in this aspect of its work have increased markedly in the past five years.

Consider, finally, in these glimpses of the drug approval process, the overall image of the new regime conveyed at the previously mentioned parliamentary committee. The TPP director general, anchoring his comments on the provisions of the Food and Drugs Act, stressed: 'Generally on the drug side – and this is a comment that has been made by a couple of your witnesses – we do not ban substances. Our role is to approve products. What we do is to analyse a product or submission from a manufacturer who wants to put a product on the market; determine whether or not there is sufficient evidence to prove benefit, to prove safety, to prove quality and effectiveness of the product; and then we approve the product' (ibid.: 2).

The emphasis here on 'products' is a necessary reminder of what is legally at the core of the drug review mandate, whereas the onus put on the 'approval' mission is appropriate to the new political economy of drug regulation. There is an emphasis on speed and an assumption of approval subject still to a science-based but more risk-benefit oriented model of analysis than was the case in the 1970s and 1980s. The pressures come from business, but in contrast to the 1980s' agenda and its build-up of pressures, there is also a pressure from health lobbies and consumers who want new products available sooner rather than later. Thus, in the same testimony, Dann Michols indicated that he and his management team at the TPP cannot take responsibility for anything that has happened outside of the past five years: 'The entire management team has changed in that period of time. The organization has changed. All of the regulatory frameworks have been reviewed and renewed. We have done this in conjunction with advisory panels and consultation mechanisms, with all stakeholders' (ibid.: 3).

Medical Devices Review

Some of the key features of the medical devices realm have already been sketched through our earlier review of the 1992 Medical Devices

Review Committee Report: the greater need for premarket review; the far greater historic reliance (compared with drugs) on postmarket surveillance; the growing variety, number, and complexity of medical devices in use; and the more complex web of science professionals working with patients that are at the heart of this science-based regulatory activity. The situation regarding science in medical devices is in some respects different because of differences in the underlying area and because of greater progress being made in the past half-decade compared with the drug review realm. Several key points can be noted in this regard.

First, both the 1992 review study and pressures for international harmonization have produced new regulations that came into effect in July 1998. The set of basic rules has been consolidated by the TPP to a far greater extent than has been the case for drugs (where changes to parent statutes are needed and slower to achieve). Second, premarket review has increased, with some 300 implantable devices being reviewed annually. As was the case in the earlier 1990s, 80 per cent of these are made abroad (mainly in the United States) leaving about 20 per cent made in Canada. Some 4,000 to 5,000 notifications are made of other devices being marketed. Greater surveillance of these is occurring, but only now is mandatory reporting of problems with devices required. Third, there had been a review backlog in the early 1990s, but this was smaller than that for drugs and had been eliminated by 1995. Partly because of this, average review times (and targets) are now at sixty days. This performance is among the best in the international league tables.

The Medical Devices Directorate has about sixty-five staff based in Ottawa and twenty-five in regional offices. It is hiring up to fifteen new professionals, which will boost its Ottawa contingent to eighty. Its scientific staff cluster around a mixture of medical, engineering, and science disciplines, including particular strengths in areas such as biomaterials and electromagnetic interference. About ten are engaged in research while the rest function directly in the review and surveillance roles. The policy and regulatory network of this core group extends out increasingly to a trade-driven and international standard-setting world of fellow professionals. These include the electrical and mechanical professional networks of the International Standards Organization. Within Canada, the core medical and science-engineering staff of the Medical Devices Directorate also has to relate on a daily basis with a network of medical doctors and professionals.

Because of these core characteristics and the nature of the medical devices business, it is undoubtedly the case that the medical devices realm had less of a regulatory 'cultural distance' to travel in the larger transformation of the TPP from a traditional science-based regulator to a risk manager. There was less premarket review and hence fewer entrenched habits of *de novo* review. There was a greater familiarity with the very notion of risk-benefit thinking. In a sense, medical devices had always been regulated with a lighter touch within an explicit risk-benefit framework. But the new directorate had to struggle nonetheless against considerable institutional inertia both to get rid of its considerable review backlog and to recruit, train, and develop attributes in the review process that were not innate in the previous era. Thus, for some reformers at the TPP, the problem was often less that of managing the science and more that of managing the scientists, especially through the need for quality control and assurance procedures.

The role of science in the regulation of medical devices must also be related to the general posture and level of pressure from industry and from the health lobby. Greater pressure for regulatory efficiency was coming from both sides of the interest group terrain and in this sense was directionally similar to that for drug review. But the intensity of pressure was considerably less. The Canadian part of the medical devices industry was small and consisted of small firms. They had concerns about backlogs but these were resolved, albeit with strenuous institutional difficulty. Moreover, these small firms were not as able or willing to pay user fees as were the big drug companies to get greater regulatory efficiency. On the health and consumer lobby sides there was more pressure for access to devices and to strengthen the provisions for compassionate access, but this pressure was nowhere near that for drugs or even natural medicines.

The Medical Devices Directorate has been somewhat slower to establish an external science advisory committee, perhaps because it is more networked to start with. It is, however, engaged in the larger Global Harmonization Task Force and is involved in initial confidence-building meetings and joint product reviews with the U.S. Food and Drug Administration. Indeed, there is a sense in which the United States is more important for medical devices than for drugs, largely because most devices are made there and are imported into Canada. This was evident in the 1992 review report where the U.S. model became the norm for reform. In contrast, in his report on drug review

Gagnon was more impressed by reforms in Europe and saw the U.S. drug review process to be as flawed as Canada's (U.S. General Accounting Office, 1995).

Conclusions

The first major conclusion flowing from the analysis is that the TPP has transformed the regulatory regime for therapeutic health products. There can be little doubt that it has moved away from its former reliance on the traditional drug review model and has adopted the risk-benefit manager paradigm, philosophically and organizationally. In doing so it appears to have developed across a much larger organization a more integrated sense of its mission. Overall, it is engaged in more postmarket evaluation and monitoring and has opened up its own processes to a wider array of scientific input. In other words, in broad directional terms, the risk-benefit manager model can be defended as a needed change, given the changing nature and diversity of the global and national market in therapeutic products and given the pressures of both business and the complex health lobby.

At the same time, however, the difficulties of managing and communicating risk have become more complex, and it is not clear that ministers have an increased comfort level with being risk-benefit managers as opposed to cautious safety regulators. The Krever Commission's influence (which we have not examined in this chapter) is undoubtedly contributing to some of this caution, particularly because in blood regulation Krever stressed the need for the precautionary principle to be paramount. But overall, ministers are taking more risks, as are consumers. There is a therefore a need to communicate this increased exposure to risk to consumers and citizens.

With respect to the nature of the science base in both the older and newer paradigms, the main conclusion is that the science base (defined differently in terms of core competences in different product areas) is crucial to both paradigms, but that it is by definition situated differently in each. It was never quite the case in the old regime that 'science was science was science' and was therefore supreme in any absolute sense. It was extremely important but a slow or inefficient drug approval process may well have been slow not because science was supreme but rather because the process was simply slow and overloaded. But science in a risk-benefit management model is bound to occupy a larger shared decision-making space, first because risk and benefit involve both objective and subjective judgments and second because the science is itself now more pluralistic. That is, the science base involves a wider range of competences and tools of analysis, and the addition of more postmarket monitoring involves potentially wider ranges of opinion and also wider sets of values about risk and benefit.

The chapter also shows that when looking at any science-based regulatory body as a real *institution*, as opposed to a theoretically imagined one, it is crucial to appreciate the different subrealms of regulation within such an entity. The analysis of the TPP makes it clear that science in drug review is different from science in medical devices because the underlying scientific and technical competences cluster differently in the two areas. This is also the case in other areas of the TPP mandate not examined in this chapter. The natures of the markets for drugs and for medical devices are different and so are their underlying lobbies and interest groups. Thus, again, the relations between science and other players must necessarily be different.

Last but not least, the chapter shows that much greater attention has been paid to the speed of regulatory approvals, to international league tables, and to efficiency as a whole. These are important and needed features of what is undeniably an increasingly globalized regulatory and risk-benefit managerial regime. Efforts to devise a comparative basis for performance are important but they have yet to supply any satisfactory way of comparing the quality of assessments. The quality of assessments and review still depends ultimately, but more begrudgingly than thirty years ago, on some form of trust of scientists and professionals by citizens, consumers, and patients.

References

Abraham, John. (1995). *Science, Politics and the Pharmaceutical Industry.* London: UCL Press.

Adams, John. (1995). *Risk.* London: UCL Press.

Aucoin, Peter. (1997). *The New Public Management: Canada in Comparative Perspective.* Montreal: McGill-Queen's University Press.

Auditor General. (1987). *Drug Regulation.* Report of the Auditor General of Canada to the House of Commons. Ottawa: Minister of Supply and Services.

Canada. (1997). Commission of Inquiry on the Blood System of Canada (The Krever Inquiry). *Final Report*. Ottawa: Minister of Public Works and Government Services.

– (1998). *1998–89 Estimates (Part III), Health Canada*. Ottawa: Government of Canada.

Centre for Medicines Research International (CMRI). (1997). *1997 Annual Report*. Carshalton, Surrey: author.

Dewees, Donald, ed. (1983). *Regulating Quality*. Toronto: Butterworth.

Doern, Bruce. (1981). *The Peripheral Nature of Scientific Controversy in Federal Policy Formation*. Ottawa: Science Council of Canada.

– (1994) *The Road To Better Public Services*. Montreal: Institute for Research on Public Policy.

Eastman, H.C. (1985). *Report of the Commission of Inquiry on the Pharmaceutical Industry*. Ottawa: Minister of Supply and Services Canada.

Foot, David, with Daniel Stoffman. (1996). *Boom, Bust and Echo*. Toronto: Macfarlane, Walter and Ross.

Gagnon, Denis. (1992). *Working in Partnerships: Drug Review for the Future*. Quebec City: Laval University.

Health and Welfare Canada. (1988). *Departmental Response to the Recommendations of the Working Group on Drug Submission Review*. Ottawa: Drugs Directorate, Health and Welfare Canada.

– (1989). *The Economics of Canada's Pharmaceutical Industry and Principles of Cost Recovery*. Ottawa: author.

– (1991). *Health Protection and Drug Laws*. Ottawa: Minister of Supply and Services.

Health Protection Branch. (1997). *Draft Risk Management in Health Protection: Revised HPB Risk Management Framework, Phase II Report*. Ottawa: Health Canada.

House of Commons. (1994). *rbST in Canada*. Report of the Standing Committee on Agriculture and Agri-Food, issue no. 13, Thursday, 24 March.

Industry Canada. (1996a). Sector Competitiveness Frameworks, *Bio-Industries*. Ottawa: author.

– (1996b). *Biotechnology: What Is It All About?* Office of Consumer Affairs, *Consumer Quarterly*, 1(3): 1–4.

Kennedy, W. (1991). *Risk Determination: Pharmaceuticals. Canada and Selected National and International Programs for the Analysis and Management of Risk*. Ottawa: Canadian Public Health Association.

Lexchin, Joel. (1992). *Pharmaceuticals, Patents and Politics: Canada and Bill C-22*. Ottawa: Canadian Centre For Policy Alternatives.

Medical Devices Review Committee. (1992). *Direction for Change*. Ottawa: Minister of Supply and Services.

Mehta, Michael D. ed. (1996). *Regulatory Efficiency and the Role of Risk Assessment*. Kingston: School of Policy Studies, Queen's University.

National Advisory Council on Pharmaceutical Research. (1992). *Time to Act: A Strategy for the Development of a Growing Sector: Pharmaceutical Research*. Ottawa: Health and Welfare Canada.

Picard, André. (1998). *The Gift of Death: Confronting Canada's Tainted Blood Tragedy*. Toronto: Harper Perennial. Updated edition.

Ratzan, Scott C., ed. (1998). *The Mad Cow Crisis: Health and the Public Good*. London: UCL Press.

Somers, E., M. Kasparek, and J. Pound. (1991). 'Drug Regulation: The Canadian Approach.' *Regulatory Toxicology. Pharmacology*, 12: 214–23.

Standing Committee on Health. (1998). *Evidence*. Proceedings of Thursday, 26 Feb. Ottawa: House of Commons.

Stein, K. (1987). *Working Group on Drug Submission Review: Background Discussion Paper*. Ottawa: Drugs Directorate, Health and Welfare Canada.

Therapeutic Products Programme (TPP). (1997a). *Policy Development in the Therapeutic Products Programme: A Guideline*. Bureau of Drug Policy and Coordination. Ottawa: Health Canada.

– (1997b). *Strategic Framework for the Therapeutic Products Programme 1997–2000*. Ottawa: Health Canada.

– (1998). *Annual Drug Submission Performance Report*. Ottawa: Health Canada.

U.S. General Accounting Office. (1995). *FDA Drug Approval: Review Time Has Decreased in Recent Years*. Washington: author.

Viscusi, W. Kip. (1998). *Rational Risk Policy*. Oxford: Oxford University Press.

9 The Canadian Food Inspection Agency: Modernizing Science-Based Regulation

MICHAEL J. PRINCE

The Canadian Food Inspection Agency (CFIA), which came into being April 1997, is the lead governmental bureau in Canada devoted to the regulation of animal, food, and plant health as well as consumer safety in regards to the labelling and packaging of food products. As a recent innovation in public administration and science-based policy making, the CFIA warrants a close look as a science-based regulatory organization. This involves consideration of the role and nature of scientific knowledge and research supplied by natural scientists as well as technical and professional personnel in support of food policy making and related regulatory functions.[1]

My analysis and findings divide into five parts. First, I briefly examine the context and impetus for the creation of the CFIA. While a number of factors contributed to and influenced its birth, the main forces shaping the agency's formation were twofold: the general belief that food inspection was a core role of the state that ought to remain within the public domain; and the pressure from central agencies within the federal government, driven by the fiscal agenda of deficit reduction, to achieve savings by consolidating inspection activities housed in several departments. Second, I describe the mandate and priorities of the CFIA and, in the third part, its relationship to the larger food safety policy community. Much more than a single-purpose agency, the CFIA has a range of responsibilities and powers beyond inspection. The agency is not really at arm's length from the government, but it does have elbow-room in certain aspects of financial and personnel management.

Fourth, I explore the role of science in four stages of the food regulatory process: policy and standards setting; evaluating and approving new agricultural products; inspection, compliance, and enforcement; postmarket monitoring of products and risk communication to consumers, industries, and other governments and agencies. The CFIA is moving away from a traditional approach to regulation, hands-on inspection by different levels and agencies of government, product by product, towards an inspection system across commodities that relies more on intergovernmental partnerships and on industry responsibility for quality controls, with government inspectors auditing those controls based on scientific assessments of acceptable risk. This shift in direction and philosophy is apparent, in varying ways and degrees, in the Hazard Analysis Critical Control Point (HACCP) system as implemented in fish processing, the Integrated Inspection System (IIS) initiative, and the Modernized Poultry Inspection Project (MPIP). In the fifth part, I draw some concluding observations.

Political Impetus and Context for Establishing the CFIA

The idea of an integrated federal food inspection agency is far from new. Before the CFIA was established, the concept of a single inspection system had been languishing in Ottawa's corridors of power for over a quarter of a century (Beaver, 1997). If one factor triggered the creation of the CFIA, it was the imperative of reducing the federal deficit. While the logic for integrating federal food inspection activities had been examined and endorsed by a number of reports for more than twenty-five years, neither the administrative wish nor a sustained political will existed. This changed with the fiscal crunch imposed on the federal public service by the Liberal government through their Program Review and budgets in the mid-1990s. Certainly other factors are important and can be thought of as tailoring the response to the restraint agenda. Reforming food inspection was mentioned in the 1995 and 1996 federal budgets in terms of placing inspection operations on a more commercial basis to reduce budgetary requirements while maintaining service and protecting the public interest.

This commercialization and more affordable government were to be achieved by streamlining arrangements and sharing more responsibilities with industry for regulation and inspection and by moving towards more cost-efficient operations by reducing overlap and duplication within the federal government and across levels of government. This latter point is tied to the Program Review exercise the Liberals began in 1994, with a focus on organization forms and modes of service delivery, influenced partly by the New Public Management or NPM (Kernaghan, 1993; Aucoin, 1997) and to the work the federal and provincial governments had already started on moving towards a national inspection system. This intergovernmental work on a national inspection system took on greater symbolic importance, following the October 1995 Quebec referendum, as a way of renewing the federation and promoting national unity (Moore and Skogstad, 1998).

The political impetus for creating the CFIA was not that there was a science deficit within the federal bureaucracy for managing risks and food safety, but rather the federal government faced a serious financial deficit. A central argument for creating a single federal agency was that the government would realize significant efficiency gains. It was estimated that, in 1995, across the departments of Agriculture, Fisheries and Oceans, and Health, $430 million and 5,100 full-time equivalents (FTEs) in staff were devoted to food safety inspection and regulation activities. There had already been some cuts made in these areas under the Program Review and in the budgets. In creating the CFIA, further annual savings of $44 million were estimated, beginning in 1998–9, from consolidation and rationalization in communications, informatics, enforcement, and administrative overhead in the food safety system. This amount was separate from any new funding that might derive from additional cost recovery (Doering, 1996a).

A second important factor shaping the creation of the CFIA was the pervasive belief within the food safety policy community that the federal inspection and regulation functions ought to remain within the federal government domain. In contrast to the contemporary rhetoric of deregulation, downloading, outsourcing, and privatization of state activities, food inspection was regarded to have a fundamentally essential public interest and benefit. This sentiment was generally shared by federal politicians, consumer groups, industry associations, and all the provincial governments.

CFIA's Mandate, Mission, and Objectives

We should not be misled by the name of the Canadian Food Inspection Agency. It is much more than an organization concerned with food or with only inspection. Like other regulatory agencies, the CFIA's legislative mandate confers on the agency multiple functions and considerable discretionary powers; this is a feature of Canada's regulatory style (Doern et al., 1999). As the agency's name suggests, the activities of the CFIA centre on inspecting the food supply and administering and enforcing several pieces of legislation and related regulations and orders. The inspection function includes domestic and import inspection, export certification, quality assurance, registration of facilities, and audit activities. Besides inspecting food, there are inspection services concerned with fish and animal and plant health. The CFIA is also responsible for managing the quarantine system and a network of laboratories and research centres across the country. Agency research extends to understanding consumer needs and concerns in relation to food safety awareness. The agency has important policy-making and consultation functions with various groups in its policy community, including negotiating trade arrangements and developing international trade standards.

The CFIA legislation basically creates the agency in which all federally mandated food and fish inspection, quarantine services, and animal and plant health services are now housed. These responsibilities were previously located in four departments – Agriculture and Agri-Food Canada, Health Canada, the Department of Fisheries and Oceans, and Industry Canada. The legislation sets out the CFIA's responsibilities, corporate structure accountability regimes, powers, and reporting framework.[2] Government officials determined it would not be possible in the time available for creating the agency to consolidate all federal statutes dealing with food safety and inspection into one law. Hence, the approach centred on forming the organization, and consolidation of the various laws is at present a work in progress. The CFIA legislation contains amendments to the enforcement provisions and penalty structures of the federal statutes relating to food and fish and animal and plant health that are now enforced and/or administered by the agency.

The CFIA is responsible for the administration and enforcement of the following eleven acts:

- Agriculture and Agri-Food Administrative Monetary Penalties Act
- Canada Agricultural Products Act
- Canadian Food Inspection Agency Act
- Feeds Act
- Fertilizers Act
- Fish Inspection Act
- Health of Animals Act

- Meat Inspection Act
- Plant Breeders' Rights Act
- Plant Protection Act
- Seeds Act

The CFIA is additionally responsible for the *administration* of provisions of the Food and Drugs Act as they relate to food (excepting provisions that deal with public health, safety, or nutrition); and for the *enforcement* of the Consumer Packaging and Labelling Act and the Food and Drugs Act as they pertain to food. In addition to this legislative authority, the agency is responsible for more than thirty regulations mainly concerning commodities and agricultural products, and some seventeen orders, most dealing with cost-recovery fees. The CFIA is active in regulatory reform. The agency has more than thirty current and future initiatives on reviewing and amending existing regulations and developing new regulations (CFIA, 1998a: 18–22).

In the 1998–9 *Estimates* and its own *Corporate Business Plan*, the CFIA has described its mandate, mission, and objectives in the following terms. The agency's mandate is 'to enhance the effectiveness and efficiency of federal inspection and related services for food and animal and plant health.' Its mission is succinctly stated as 'safe food, market access, consumer protection.' The mandate and mission are expressed in terms of three objectives: '(1) To contribute to a safe food supply and accurate product information. (2) To contribute to the continuing health of animals and plants for protection of the resource base. (3) To facilitate trade in food, animals, plants and their products.' For the period 1997 to 2000, the *Corporate Business Plan* identifies four priorities for the agency. Closely reflecting the mandate and mission, the priorities are effectiveness and efficiency of the inspection system, domestic and international market access, consumer protection, and, intergovernmental cooperation. Under each priority is a set of key strategies and planned actions over the next few years. I will briefly discuss the four priorities in terms of which regulatory stages of the food safety regime each priority emphasizes, as well as which notions of science and risk are apparent.

Enhancing the efficiency and effectiveness of the inspection and quarantine system is the first priority. Strategies to implement this priority include reforming legislation and inspection tools, and improving service standards and the management of facilities. These strategies relate to the processes of making policy and setting standards, enforcement and compliance, and financial and human resource management. Science has a direct and growing input to this priority, as the agency's *Corporate Business Plan* notes: 'The evolution of new inspection methodologies is changing the approach taken to inspection around the world. The focus is increasingly oriented toward the audit of industry activities, supported by strong compliance and enforcement tools. As such, the CFIA will develop an Integrated Inspection System, which is an all-encompassing science-based system, focussed on areas of risk to health and safety, economic fraud, and trade access' (CFIA, 1997a: 3). Under the IIS approach, which I discuss in the fourth part of the chapter, industry is to assume more responsibility for the inspection of products and processes, and the role of government inspectors becomes one of auditing and verifying the industry's performance. Agency resources for inspection and setting standards are to be allocated on the basis of maximizing risk reduction. Considerations of science capacity and risk management also condition the agency's thinking on the pursuit of alternative delivery of inspection services. The agency's plans state that 'the CFIA will explore and implement options for the delivery of Agency services, provided risks can be adequately mitigated. These options will be implemented only if it can be demonstrated that they are cost-beneficial, involve no increase in liability, present no conflict of interest situations, have no negative impact on trade, and allow the CFIA to retain the core expertise it needs within the Agency' (CFIA, 1998a, 9).

The second priority deals with facilitating trade in food, animals, and plants and their products in Canadian and global markets. This relates directly to the policy-making, standard-setting, and product-review and -approval processes of regulatory regimes. The CFIA strives to achieve this priority, in large part, through participation in regional and international standard-setting organizations, and through participation in the negotiation of trade arrangements, such as at the World Trade Organization (WTO), that recognize equivalent Canadian requirements for agricultural products. The aim is to resolve issues of technical market access and reduce the costs of meeting trade requirements by influencing international trade standards. Whether these aims are achieved in international fora is shaped by economic and political factors, but also by methodologies of risk analysis and scientific evidence.

214   Michael J. Prince

Consumer protection as a priority of the CFIA relates to two processes of regulation. One is compliance and enforcement. Consumers
are expected to take responsibility for the proper care, handling, and
preparation of food in their homes; and firms and the agency itself are
responsible for ensuring that food labelling is accurate and informa-
tive for consumers. Postmarket monitoring and reporting is the second process connected with consumer protection. Here the agency
commits to work with provincial, territorial, and municipal governments, as well as industry councils and consumer groups 'to develop
a comprehensive approach to the identification of food safety issues
and the communication of such information in a meaningful way to
Canadians,' and as well 'encourage rapid disclosure of food and animal and plant health problems ... [and] develop a coordinated approach to product recall and emergency response' (ibid.: 10–11). At all
stages of the food chain, science underpins the identification, management, and communication of risks to the public.

The fourth priority relates, in the short run, to achieving closer integration of inspection services across jurisdictions and therefore realize
some efficiencies and savings; and, in the longer run, to working towards a Canadian food inspection system. This would truly be 'big
science,' extending the food safety regime across multiple orders of
government and sectors of the economy in Canada. Ultimately, this
priority affects all the stages of the regulation, although the focus in
recent years has been on developing national codes for certain sectors,
such as the dairy and meat industries (Moore and Skogstad, 1998).
Part of the rationale of the CFIA is nation building in the sense of
being the organizational vehicle for forging a pan-Canadian system of
food inspection.

Bilateral and multilateral strategies are actively under consideration
in the search for greater intergovernmental cooperation on food safety
policy. The CFIA has the authority to empower provincial public servants to use federal inspection and quarantine powers, enter into agreements with one or more provincial governments to provide services
within the CFIA's mandate, and to create, with one or more provincial
governments, corporations to carry out related activities in an integrated way (ibid.: 11). Such initiatives certainly have an impact on the
processes of managing financial and human resources in this regulatory regime, not to mention the nature of intergovernmental relations
in Canada.

The Food Policy Community

With the creation of the CFIA, federal responsibility for regulating virtually all agricultural products, including agricultural products of biotechnology, lies with the agency.[3] The CFIA includes what used to be the Food Production and Inspection Branch of Agriculture and Agri-Food Canada (AAFC), along with parts of Health Canada, Industry Canada, and the Department of Fisheries and Oceans (DFO) that deal with the quality, safety, and inspection of food products. The amalgamation of these activities and programs into a single agency makes the CFIA the lead federal body in the food policy community.

Establishment of the CFIA also reinforced the differentiation of federal powers between the minister of AAFC and the minister of health. Through the CFIA, the agriculture minister retains responsibility for establishing animal and plant health standards and providing supporting inspection activities. The CFIA conducts all federal food inspection activities, while the health minister is responsible for establishing policies and standards relating to the safety and nutritional quality of food sold in Canada. Health Canada is further responsible for undertaking a systematic and independent audit of the food safety components of the food inspection program of the CFIA to verify its compliance with Canadian health and safety standards. This separation of the 'steering function' in Health Canada (standard setting) from the 'rowing function' in the CFIA (inspection) was done to enhance food safety and to clarify the checks and balances nature of the federal system; as well it was explicitly an effort, influenced by the language of the reinventing government movement, to enable the CFIA to become more entrepreneurial and corporationlike (Doering, 1996a, 1996b).

Some responsibilities are still shared between the CFIA and Health Canada. With respect to product labelling, the CFIA is responsible for issues not related to safety, such as consumer fraud, while Health Canada is responsible for required labelling related to health and safety issues such as allergies and nutritional composition. Crisis management is another example. A general memorandum of understanding between the two organizations provides that while the CFIA has primary responsibility for the management of food safety emergency situations, Health Canada agrees to make available at short notice its research and testing facilities, as well as to provide expert advice in situations of, or leading to crisis management. In addition to Health

Canada and the AAFC, the CFIA works with a number of other federal departments. These include Fisheries and Oceans, Industry Canada, Foreign Affairs and International Trade, Natural Resources Canada, and Environment Canada.

Beyond the federal government, food safety is a shared responsibility in constitutional, societal, economic, scientific, and international terms. Under the Canadian constitution, both the federal and provincial governments have jurisdiction to set and enforce standards for the health and safety of food and to ensure that product information provided by firms is sufficient and accurate. In reality, territorial governments and municipal governments are also active in this policy field, adding further complexities and issues of gaps and overlaps. Since 1993–4, a joint steering committee composed of the Federal/Provincial Agri-Food Inspection Committee, representing agricultural portfolios, and the Federal/Provincial/Territorial Food Safety Committee, representing health portfolios, along with representatives of DFO and of the Association of Supervisors of Public Health Inspection of Ontario, have been developing and implementing a blueprint for a Canadian food inspection system. This national system would, in the words of the joint steering committee, 'embody sound scientific risk-based principles of health and protection, responsive consumer information, efficient use of resources, commonality of interest and approaches to issues, complementary and/or universal legislation and regulations, and the rationalization of services' (Canada, 1995: 2). At the federal level, to assist this process, is the Canadian Food Inspection System Implementation Group, a precursor to CFIA and a group still associated with the agency's activities. In addition, there is a Canadian Federal-Provincial System Implementation Group working on the development of national codes. The strategic directions contained in this blueprint show this to be a policy community closely connected to and affected by other policy sectors and wider issues of federalism. The blueprint has been endorsed by all senior governments in Canada and has resulted, to date, in a National Dairy Regulation and Code as well as progress continuing on a Meat and Poultry Regulation and Code, and on a Food Retail and Food Services Regulation and Code. Consultations are also ongoing between federal and provincial governments on the regulation of agricultural products of biotechnology, with provincial support of the leadership role of the federal government in this area.

Other domestic actors within the food policy community are government central agencies and legislatures, businesses and industry councils, consumer groups, farmers associations, social movement organizations like environmental and animal rights groups, researchers and scientists at universities and private laboratories, risk management specialists, the mass media, risk communication experts, the general public, and specific groups of the lay public such as a particular community or age group. The list could be extended, but the point has been made. A vast number of groups have interests in food safety and food inspection, offering a range of beliefs, opinions, and types of knowledge, and seeking to influence policy discussion and governmental decisions. A review by the CFIA of the guide to food labelling and advertising, for instance, has involved direct consultations with over forty organizations from the food and beverage industry alone, most of which are well-organized national associations. Other organizations, such as the Canadian Institute of Food Science and Technology, the Canadian Society of Allergy and Clinical Immunology, the National Institute of Nutrition, the Crop Protection Institute, and the Canadian Animal Health Institute, among others, reflect the research, science, and technology bases of this policy community.

An array of foreign and international institutions influence, and are influenced by, the Canadian food policy community. Institutions of foreign governments, especially in the United States and in the European Union, exercise a direct power over Canadian food policy and regulatory affairs. In the United States, these include the Food and Drug Administration, the Departments of Agriculture and Commerce, the Federal Trade Commission, the North American Freed Trade Agreement, and Congress, as well as governors and even state police.[4] The international state has also grown as has the influence of scientific and risk professionals in the international organizations to which Canada belongs. As part of the United Nations, these include the Food and Agriculture Organization (FAO), the World Health Organization (WHO), and the Codex Alimentarius Commission (CAC). The CAC has several subsidiary bodies and advisory expert committees dealing with methods of analysis and sampling; food additives and contaminants; food hygiene, and pesticide residues, among other topics. A joint FAO/WHO expert consultation was held in Geneva in 1995 focusing on the application of risk assessment of food hazards, and a second such meeting was held in Rome in 1997 on the application of risk management to food safety matters. The meetings exchange ideas and information on practices and are leading to the development of a shared terminology and set of principles on effective risk analysis.

The WTO is another actor in the policy community. World trade requirement that countries have a clear assessment of their animal health status, for purposes of animal disease control and research efforts, prompted the formation in 1996 of the Canadian Animal Health Network (CAHNet). The network has members from CFIA's science division, producer groups, veterinary schools, veterinary practice, and provincial veterinary services, and they gather intelligence on animal health and disease. Internationally, the federal government, with the CFIA playing a major part, has responsibility for negotiating agreements to protect the interests of consumers and producers in Canada.

Science in the Regulation of Food

A look at four stages of the regulatory process (see Chapter 1) offers further insights on the role of science and scientists in food policy making and regulation within the federal government. The four stages to be considered are policy and standard setting; product assessment and approval; inspection, enforcement, and compliance; and, postmarket monitoring of products and risk communication. This survey reveals that the regulation of food is, to a large extent, a science-based process, and that the CFIA is reliant on the expertise of internal staff and of other departments, industries, universities, and international bodies for technical knowledge and policy-relevant information.

Policy and Standard Setting

In the parlance of new public management (NPM), creating the CFIA enabled the division of the steering and policy-making function and the rowing and regulation function of the food safety system. The CFIA became responsible for the enforcement and/or administration of several federal laws that regulate foods, animal and plant health, and related products, as well as economic fraud and trade requirements. Health Canada's role as the primary policy maker and developer of regulations and guidelines for food safety and the nutritional adequacy of foods was reaffirmed, along with responsibility for risk assessment, research, and the audit of CFIA's inspection activities related to food safety. In policy and practice, however, there are still overlaps and interconnections between CFIA and Health Canada. The two organizations are in the federal food safety boat together; at times, both are sometimes steerers and at other times, rowers. Overall, though, Health Canada is closer to the stern of this regulatory boat.[5]

In the area of human health and safety, the CFIA has a complementary role to Health Canada in developing regulations and guidelines for food safety and in serving as a national authority for food safety issues at the international level in the development of conventions and codes of practice. In the animal and plant health area, CFIA is responsible for policy and standard-setting activities, except those activities directly related to trade and commerce. With respect to the priorities of market access and consumer protection, the CFIA has responsibility for designing standards for such matters as advertising claims, composition and the listing of ingredient, and codes of practice for animal welfare. The CFIA serves as the national authority, while recognizing the roles of AAFC and DFO, in the establishment of bilateral technical trade protocols, like mutual recognition of meat inspection with the United States, and also at international agencies like Codex and the Organization for Economic Cooperation and Development. Furthermore, CFIA officials negotiate import and export conditions and standards for dairy, fruit and vegetables, and meat and poultry products.

Product Assessment and Decision Making

The product assessment and decision-making stage of the regulatory process includes four elements: policy design considerations, review criteria and guidelines, information bases and analytical activities, and the reporting of decisions. Policy design refers to the purposes of agricultural regulation, the range of products regulated, and the tools and activities of regulating. The purposes of food inspection programs are safety, accuracy, and marketability via equivalency of standards. That is, to protect consumers, animals, and the environment; to ensure products make accurate performance and contents claims; and to promote the market access of Canadian agri-food products into other countries. Pursuing these goals involves monitoring the compliance of products imported, exported, or processed in federally registered establishments for safety, wholesomeness, and accurate representation in accordance with domestic and international quality and safety standards. Agri-food products regulated and inspected by the CFIA include meat and meat products, shell eggs and processed egg products, fresh fruit and vegetables, dairy products, processed fruit and vegetables, honey and maple products, veterinary biologics (animal vaccines, toxins, antisera, and diagnostic kits), fertilizers, livestock feeds and seeds, and certain genetically modified micro-organisms.[6] Whether the agricultural products have been produced using conventional methods or by the newer technologies of genetic engineering – for example, plants with novel traits created from the transfer of genetic material from one plant to another – the CFIA applies the same regulatory requirements.

Depending on the product, its origins, and intended use, the agency employs a range of control measures. For potentially hazardous imported commodities, for instance, control tools include permits, testing, environmental safety assessments, quarantine, and inspection. For new products, such as biofertilizers and livestock feeds, the tools of approval, registration, or licensing may be necessary prior to commercial production and sale. For approved products, control measures include food safety inspection and quality assurance monitoring, including for packaging and labelling standards. Monitoring programs are done also through the registration and inspection of establishments, licensing of dealers and operators, inspection of processes, and the testing for biological and chemical contaminants.

The CFIA's safety-based approach to regulating agricultural products includes determining whether a risk assessment is required, performing a risk assessment, implementing risk management, and administering the pertinent regulatory measures. When evaluating products, the CFIA follows principles that are similar, though not identical, to those used by other governments and international authorities. These principles include:

1 Build on current legislation administered by the CFIA, where possible, rather than creating new laws to govern new products that are developed.
2 Focus on product characteristics rather than the method of production. This allows the regulation of many products of new biotechnology processes to be carried out under existing legislation.
3 Regulate on a case-by-case basis. To determine the data and studies needed to demonstrate product safety, products are evaluated individually. As new types of products become more

familiar, it may be possible to reduce regulatory requirements or provide an exemption from regulation in some cases.

4 Establish safety levels and standards for each product on the best scientific information.

5 Safety is defined, not as the complete absence of risk, but rather as the level of acceptable risk, in light of the probability and magnitude of any adverse effects for each product.[7]

In this preregulatory review process, three key questions are asked of each new agricultural product. First, is this product similar to other products that are already in the market? Second, is the product substantially equivalent to other products that have already been approved? Underpinning these questions is the concept of familiarity, the knowledge that a certain product is similar to other products with traits and usage that are already understood and accepted. Third, for familiar and substantially equivalent products, does the product or commodity require regulation under existing laws? In the case of a product that is not considered substantially equivalent, perhaps because it has some new qualities, involves new techniques, and/or poses a new potential hazard, a risk assessment will be undertaken by the CFIA. Guidelines for each category of agricultural products are developed by agency evaluators in concert with industry and university experts. Extensive public consultations were held before the guidelines to regulate products of biotechnology were established, based on criteria drafted by advisory committees comprising members from consumer and environmental groups, universities, and government.

Consider the assessment criteria for determining the environmental safety of plants with novel traits (PNTs). A PNT is a plant variety with characteristics 'that demonstrate neither familiarity nor substantial equivalency to those present in a distinct, stable population of a cultivated species of seed in Canada and that have been intentionally selected, created or introduced into a population of that species through a specific genetic change' (CFIA, 1994: 1). The environmental safety of a PNT is assessed in terms of its potential:

- To become weeds of agriculture or be invasive of natural habitats in Canada
- For gene flow to wild relatives whose hybrid offspring may become more weedy or more invasive

- To alter plant pest potential
- Negative impacts on non-target organisms, that is, whether toxic to humans, other vertebrae, and insects
- Impacts on biodiversity
- For development of resistance to conventional chemical insecticides.

Such an assessment involves examining the agronomic characteristics of the PNT – plant vigour, growth, fertility, time to maturity, flowering period, and seed yield. Field testing PNTs in Canada is also subject to a CFIA regulatory directive that sets out the specific information required for making an application to do a field test and the field trial requirements and protocols (CFIA, 1995). The proponent of the new product is required to provide the necessary information for the assessment process. This can include results of laboratory tests, field testing of new plants or animal testing, and comparative information from other products. The company that has developed the product and is submitting it for approval bears the costs of conducting research trials and collecting the information needed by the CFIA regulators to evaluate the product's safety. The next steps are:

1 CFIA regulators then take the information, and based on scientific knowledge, expertise, previous experience, and access to up-to-date scientific information, evaluate the product for its safety. If CFIA regulators find that what has been provided is insufficient, they will require further studies or information. During the assessment, CFIA regulators compare the characteristics of traditionally derived products with those of the new products. The product will only be approved if it has been determined, after the evaluation, to be safe for humans, animals, plants, and the environment. In addition, should new information become available, the regulations they work with allow all decisions to be reconsidered.
2 If regulators do find that they do not have enough information to make a regulatory decision, they will not approve the product.
3 Research permits are granted for the field testing of genetically modified micro-organisms and naturally occurring micro-organisms following review by the CFIA and its advisers in Health Canada, Environment Canada, and the Canadian Forestry Service (ibid.: 2, 4).

Given the agency's reliance on the provision of evidence by firms, it is critical that CFIA regulators have access to the most current scientific knowledge from different sources. The food and animal and plant health programs receive support from the agency's own laboratory services. These services include *microbiology centres* that assess the microbiological safety of foods and respond to consumer complaints and illness; *food centres* that provide analytical services related to foods, feeds, fertilizers, and seeds; *animal and plant health centres* that engage in diagnostic testing of standards, technology development and transfer, laboratory accreditation to about 130 government and private laboratories servicing the agri-food sector, and scientific analysis of animal diseases and plant pests; and *fish inspection laboratories* that provide technical expertise to support the development and operation of Quality Management Programs carried out by industry, and do chemical, microbiological, and physical analyses on fish and fish products (CFIA, 1997a: 3).

In addition, CFIA regulators and program professionals acquire and exchange information and advice by participating in their wider 'epistemic community' (Haas, 1992) of knowledge-based experts with recognized competence in the domain of food safety and risk analysis. This community is composed of natural scientists and other professionals, is transnational in scope, and has a relatively shared set of beliefs on policy goals and instruments, causality, and notions of validity. With respect to food hazards, CFIA regulators access current knowledge, 'through scientific and academic libraries, international and national data bases, scientific journals and conferences and through contact with individual experts around the world. Canadian regulators participate in a number of international fora, where up-to-date scientific information, expertise and experience is shared' (ibid.: 3).

The federal regulatory system for agricultural products of biotechnology has been criticized for poorly communicating to the public about how it regulates and about the possible risks associated with biotechnology (Powell and Leiss, 1997). The CFIA has acknowledged this critique on its web site and addressed this criticism, along with others, about the regulatory system. When PNTs are allowed to be released into the environment, a 'Decision Document' is issued in both official languages and is made publicly available by mail and through the agency's web site. This topic raises wider issues, beyond the scope of this chapter, dealing with the interplay of scientific data, confidential business information, and effective communication to stakeholder groups and the general public.

Inspection, Enforcement, and Compliance

Aspects of the inspection, enforcement, and compliance activities of the CFIA are illustrated by the following vignettes:

- The CFIA operates a detector dog program at the Vancouver, Toronto, and Montreal international airports. Before becoming full-time canine inspectors, the dogs must complete a 12-week training program. When the dogs are on duty, working up to seven flights a day, they find three times as many smuggled products than would otherwise be detected.
- In light of public health concerns around bovine spongiform encephalopathy (BSE), a fatal disease in cattle that arose in Britain in 1995–6, and a subsequent WHO request that all countries ban the feeding of some rendered animal products to cattle, sheep, and goats, the CFIA amended regulations to implement such a ban and introduced new labelling requirements. Though Canada is recognized as free of BSE, the agency's chief of Red Meat Inspection Programs has said, 'these regulations are necessary to safeguard Canada's animal health status and maintain domestic and international confidence in the safety of Canadian animal products' (CFIA, 1997b).
- As of July 1997, the CFIA's Animal Health Division has required that all horses entering or re-entering Canada from the United States (except Alaska) be examined by a CFIA veterinarian. This rule of mandatory examinations was introduced in response to a viral disease, vesicular stomatitis, affecting horses in New Mexico and Colorado. This regulation is part of a larger set of protocols used to prevent and control the entry of foreign animal diseases into the country.
- The importing of honeybees from mainland United States into Canada has been banned since 1987, a prohibition that was extended until the end of 1999. The prohibition is designed to prevent the incursion of a varroa mite into Canada that feeds on the larvae and pupae of the honeybee. An infestation almost always results in the death of the infected colonies. The media notice on the extension of the ban observed that 'honey produc-

tion was worth more than $69 million to Canadian honey pro-
ducers in 1996. It has been estimated that honeybee pollination
contributes approximately $500 million annually to agricultural
production in Canada' (CFIA, 1998b).

These little regulatory stories point out (1) the use of different inspection and enforcement methods (detector dogs and their handlers, meat
inspectors, agency veterinarians, and import bans overseen by CFIA
regulators); (2) the range of agricultural products covered (smuggled
goods like foreign birds and snakes, mad cows, unhealthy horses, and
killer honeybees); (3) the mixture of issues and values involved (human health, animal welfare, and consumer confidence); and, (4) that
domestic and international science, government, and markets are in-
terconnected. All four stories reflect a traditional style of inspection
and enforcement, a state-centred style relying on government employees to exercise coercive public powers over others.

Upon its creation in 1997, the CFIA inherited several inspection
programs that regulated different agricultural sectors and products in
different ways and means. The current regulatory arrangements can
be said to fall into two broad categories of food inspection: the traditional and a transitional or modernized type. The CFIA is working
towards a transformational or integrated approach, the IIS.

In the traditional approach, the federal (and/or provincial or municipal) government sets the policy, regulations, and standards to be
met. Industry is expected to meet the standards and maintain records
to demonstrate compliance with policy. Agency inspectors are present
on-site, either full-time or at periodic visits, to inspect the products
and premises and records. Sectors that still operate under this approach include red meat slaughter, red meat processing, shell eggs,
and processed eggs. In a typical federally regulated meat facility, there
are four or five inspectors doing close, hands-on, carcass-by-carcass
inspection, and there is always a veterinarian present while the 'kill
floor' is operating. The role of the inspectors, then, are to be regulators
and enforcers, focusing on product physical defects. The role of industry is as producers and subjects of the regulatory process. In general,
the CFIA's plan is to move away from the 'poke-and-sniff inspector'
to more the 'auditor of industry's risk assessment system' (Doering,
1996a), but it cannot move that quickly in certain sectors, such as the
meat industry or perhaps the poultry industry. Canada sells about $3
billion worth of meat to the United States each year, and there is a

need to have an inspection system that is seen to be equivalent to theirs. The Americans are uncertain about Canada moving to a hazard analysis system and reducing the frequency of inspections and the number of inspectors. In their meat and poultry plants, the Americans have *added* the Hazard Analysis Critical Control Point (HACCP) system onto the other more traditional inspection and enforcement methods. From the land of reinventing government this is not the kind of additive reform that the CFIA wants to adopt to become a more nimble agency working in greater partnership with industry. However, the concerns of unionized inspectors within the CFIA and the trade considerations with the United States are clear constraints on fast action in particular sectors.

The Canadian poultry industry is an example of a sector undergoing interesting changes in inspection, from the traditional model to presently a transitional phase, and likely moving towards the transformational approach over the next decade.[8] Into the 1980s the Canadian and American national poultry inspection systems relied on government inspection of every carcass through the manipulation and visual examination for external, internal, and visceral defects. Inspectors were essentially quality controllers, and once carcasses were past their inspection stations, little if any process controls or further assessments were done by the inspectors or the plant operators. In the 1980s the Americans introduced the streamlined inspection system (SIS) in poultry processing plants. The SIS had four key features: the concept of process controls; the transfer of responsibilities for food quality and safety to the plant operators; the role of government inspectors becoming one of verification of the plant's compliance through tests on each shift; and, if a loss or control or a perceived trend towards losing control became apparent, the operator had to initiate a process action. Finished product standards were set and a company-designated employee would be responsible for an hourly monitoring with respect to trimmable dressing and processing defects.

The SIS was implemented in Canada on a voluntary basis by chicken abattoirs and, over the 1995–7 period, AAFC and the CFIA designed and implemented the Canadian Poultry Inspection Program (CPIP), which builds on and extends the SIS approach. Under CPIP, on top of the trimmable defects, the plant operator also assumes the responsibility for the detection of internal cavity defects. The CPIP was introduced as a voluntary program in April 1996 and was operational in 85 per cent of the broiler production and is being implemented in turkey operations. The goal is to have CPIP as a mandatory system by April 1999. Less prescriptive than the traditional model, this approach has industry conduct its own risk analyses, and government inspectors audit detection processes done by trained and accredited employees of the plants.

Work is being done as well on a pilot project, the Modernized Poultry Inspection Project (MPIP) which would incorporate HACCP plans, one plan covering prerequisite programs, such as the premises and personnel training, the other dealing with food processes within the establishment. A feature of the MPIP, which goes beyond the CPIP, is a pathogen-reduction component designed to evaluate the process performance through regular sampling for *E. coli* and Salmonella. The process performance is stipulated in the U.S. Department of Agriculture Pathogen Reduction and HACCP rule.[9] Canadian authorities have decided that similar sampling and testing approaches be adopted here. One pilot project testing the MPIP has been under way since September 1997, and one or more additional pilots are planned. A second pilot has been delayed because the cooperation of inspectors was not assured. The impacts of MPIP are several, spanning the farm level, the abattoir, the CFIA, and the consumer. This entails more information about the products being provided to processors by the growers; the training of plant employees to monitor the critical control points and to detect any visual defects; the introduction of mandatory bacteriological testing; and the continued presence of CFIA inspectors, though fewer than before, and an agency veterinarian on site. Affected inspectors are to be redeployed to other duties within the agency. The goals of the MPIP are to reduce microbiological pathogens in raw poultry products and to convert the inspection system to more of a science-oriented approach.

There are other examples of the transitional or modernizing approach to inspection but which space limits does not allow us to examine. One is the Quality Management Program (QMP) introduced in 1992 in Canada's fish processing industry. More generally and beyond the traditional and modernized inspection systems, the CFIA is also developing an integrated approach to inspection, enforcement, and compliance, called the IIS. The objectives of the IIS are to reinforce the CFIA's mission of safe food, consumer protection, and market access, by creating a more streamlined, uniform, open, and integrated inspection system. The CFIA is seeking to create a common approach and set of principles to agri-food inspection across the various inspection systems currently delivered by the different program groups in the agency. One aim is to avoid inconsistent impacts on industries and consumers, another is to build on the science-based approaches already in effect.

Postmarket Monitoring of Products and Risk Communication

This final stage of the regulatory process ties directly to matters of consumer protection and, in terms of the IIS, relates to the final links in the food and food products continuum. With the changing policy direction of food inspection, using fewer inspectors on-site checking products and expecting more self-regulation by industry, postmarket monitoring becomes even more critical, especially given media attention and public anxieties about food safety (Powell and Leiss, 1997; Campbell, 1998). Food labelling, of course, is one key way of informing consumers about products. Discussions on the labelling of genetically engineered foods have been under way at the international level for the past four years. Countries are divided over whether to introduce mandatory labelling of all foods produced using genetic engineering. This debate shows that the international food policy community is more than a network of scientists with a common style of reasoning (Haas, 1992), and includes competing interests and perspectives among industries, governments, consumers, and environmental groups. Risk communication is another aspect of this stage of regulation. A part of the risk analysis process, risk communication involves the 'exchange of information and opinion on risk among risk assessors, risk managers, and other interested parties' (Agriculture and Agri-Food Canada, 1996: 3). For example, the CFIA's Office of Biotechnology develops communication and consultation strategies with respect to the concerns of stakeholders and serves as a contact point for the dissemination of information on biotechnology.

The CFIA's food recall process demonstrates the scientific and the regulative nature of this stage of the inspection system. In its first year of operation, the CFIA managed 164 food recalls. Food recalls are classified according to the degree of health hazard posed to the public. Of the 164 recalls over the April 1997 to April 1998 period 46 (or 28 per cent) were Class I – reasonable probability that use of, or exposure to the product would cause serious health consequences or death; 104 (or 63 per cent) were Class II – health consequences would be remote; and 14 (or 9 per cent) were Class III – a situation in which the use of, or exposure to the product is not likely to cause any adverse health consequences. The extent and nature of these recalls, where 72 per cent had remote or lesser probability of adverse health consequences, underscore the precautionary principle of risk management in action. A product recall process has the following steps and actions: 'Once a decision has been made to initiate a recall, it is the job of the recalling company to assess the situation, notify the CFIA and provide specific information pertaining to the product. The Agency then analyzes the information and classifies the recall according to the degree of health hazard posed to the public. The CFIA and the company then advise a recall strategy that includes the recovery of the product and public notification as required. The CFIA always monitors the efficiency of the recall. For the CFIA and industry members, this product recall process helps to better safeguard Canada's food supply and protect the health and well-being of consumers' (CFIA, 1998: 1–2).

The CFIA regularly issues allergy alerts, warning consumers with an allergy to certain food items to not eat particular products that do not show those items on the list of ingredients. Peanuts, almonds, and other types of nuts are the most common undeclared foods in a product. For instance, fudge nut brownies topped with crushed peanuts rather than walnuts, as stated on the label, can cause a serious or life-threatening reaction in persons with a peanut allergy. In such a case, the product has to be recalled by the manufacturer. When issuing such an allergy alert, the CFIA states whether there have been any reports of illness and advises consumers that they may return the product to the point of purchase for a full refund. The CFIA also offers a point of contact within the agency for further information, and individual companies may set up a consumer information toll-free line to respond to questions about a recall.

Conclusions

The Canadian Food Inspection Agency represents the latest generation of science-based regulatory bodies in the Canadian federal public service. The ideas and language of 'reinventing government' and the new public management have influenced the organizational design and leadership philosophy of the CFIA. The origins and short history of the CFIA reveal also, however, real constraints and other contingencies involved in attempting to adopt NPM reform measures. Implementing a 'bottom-line' orientation is not easy nor especially desired by all the stakeholders in the food policy community. Reform ideas of privatization, deregulation, special operating agencies at arm's length from government, and greater cost recovery have not been adopted in this regulatory realm. While there may have been pressure from the Treasury Board and the Office of the Auditor General to increase user fees in the food inspection system, this was met with intense and vocal resistance by the key food industry groups. The result is that no new user fees will be introduced by the CFIA before 2000, with the emphasis instead on cost avoidance and reduction. The agency remains reliant on annual appropriations from Parliament for about 80 per cent of its budget. Thus, concerns for continued ministerial responsibility and parliamentary scrutiny tempered the design of the agency and the introduction of marketlike reforms (Prince, 2000).

Other influential political and economic realities have been the checks and balances between the CFIA and Health Canada in risk assessment and risk management; and international pressures for equivalency of standards and fair trade practices. The separation of policy making (steering) from regulating (rowing) in the federal food safety system actually predates the new public management discourse, and its experience shows that it is not possible nor likely desirable to totally shut off one of these functions from the other.

The CFIA has a statutory basis and an extensive range of legislative authorities and responsibilities. It has a workable organizational design as a departmental corporation, with elbow room in which to innovate on the administrative and management side. A major asset of the agency is its strong core of scientific and technical employees, reinforced by multiple linkages to scientists and scientific organizations across Canada and around the world. The CFIA has also benefited from the cooperative work of the federal and provincial and territorial governments on moving towards a Canadian food inspection system.. Like other science-based regulatory institutions in Canada and other nations, the CFIA is shifting away from the traditional paradigm of hands-on inspection by government officials located in various agencies and jurisdictions, examining products at only a few steps of the food continuum, towards a new paradigm of industry-managed systems, based on science and risk analysis, with government inspectors at all levels cooperating and serving more as auditors of industry's performance from the farm gate to the dinner plate. The acronym CFIA represents not only the agency's official name, but also its plan of modernizing the science-based regulatory process and changing from inspectors to auditors.

Notes

1 The research for this agency case study is based on several sources: discussions and interviews with 12 officials at the Canadian Food Inspection Agency; agency, governmental, and parliamentary documents; and literature on the new public management and on regulation. I wish to acknowledge the cooperation of all the officials, in particular, Dr Tom Feltmate for facilitating my meetings and access to materials. The agency's web site, www.cfia-acia.agr.ca is also a rich source of information.

2 The CFIA act's full title is, An Act to establish the Canadian Food Inspection Agency and to Repeal and Amend Other Acts as a Consequence. Statutes of Canada, 1997, Chapter 6. It is also available at the CFIA's web site: www.cfia-acia.agr.ca/english/actsregs/cfiact.

3 I use the phrase 'virtually all agricultural products' because at least two federal food programs remain outside the CFIA's mandate. The fish health program for aquaculture was part of the discussion on creating the agency but, because of the divided views within the federal bureaucracy and the industry, it remains at the Department of Fisheries and Oceans. The mollusc and shellfish water quality program delivered by Environment Canada was never part of the consultation process for creating the CFIA.

4 At the time of writing this chapter, the governor of South Dakota has posted state troopers around slaughter houses in his state to prohibit the delivery of pork and cattle from Canadian producers. Similar restrictions for livestock and grain have been introduced in Idaho, Minnesota, Nebraska, and North Dakota (Scofield, 1998).

5 On inspection activities, Health Canada has a complementary role in the investigation of food-borne illness outbreaks, and for veterinary drugs it has responsibility for registration and approval and for enforcement and compliance actions.

6 Microbes with pesticidal properties are regulated and registered by the Pest Management Regulatory Agency of Health Canada, while microbials used to increase crop yields or improve the physical condition of the soil are regulated by the CFIA.

7 This list is adapted from various sources from the Biotechnology Strategies and Co-ordination Office of the CFIA, available at: www.cfia-acia.ca/english/food/biotech/safety.html.

8 The following discussion is based on confidential interviews with CFIA officials and internal agency documents. Also see MacKenzie (1998).

9 As of January 1997, the USDA Pathogen Reduction and HACCP rule, or so-called Mega Reg, requires that all plants exporting directly or

indirectly to the United States have to test for *E. Coli* biotype I on an ongoing basis.

References

Agriculture and Agri-Food Canada. (1996). *A Risk Communication Policy*. Discussion paper for the Codex Alimentarius Commission of the Food and Agriculture Organization of the United Nations, Sarah Sheffield, Chief, Risk Management, Risk Analysis Unit. Ottawa: author.

Aucoin, Peter. (1997). 'The Design of Public Organizations for the 21st Century: Why Bureaucracy Will Survive in Public Management.' *Canadian Public Administration*, 40(2): 290–306.

Beaver, Tom. (1997). *Accountability of Alternative Service Delivery Organizations: The Case of the Canadian Food Inspection Agency*. Nepean: Canadian Food Inspection Agency.

Campbell, Murray. (1998). 'Fears about Food Safety on the Rise.' *Globe and Mail*, 13 April, A1, A4.

Canada. Joint Steering Committee of the Canadian Food Inspection System, the Federal/Provincial Agri-Food Committee, and the Federal/Provincial/Territorial Food safety Committee. (1995). *A Blueprint for the Canadian Food Inspection System*. Web site: www.cfis.agr.ca/blueprint.html

Doering, Ronald L. (1996a). *Evidence*. House of Commons Standing Committee on Agriculture and Agri-Food. 30 October. Ottawa: House of Commons.

– (1996b). *Alternative Service Delivery: The Case of the Canadian Food Inspection Agency (CFIA)*. Nepean: Canadian Food Inspection Agency.

Doern, G. Bruce, Margaret M. Hill, Michael J. Prince, and Richard J. Schultz, eds. (1999). *Changing the Rules: Canadian Regulatory Regimes and Institutions*. Toronto: University of Toronto Press.

Canadian Food Inspection Agency. (1994). *Regulatory Directive Dir98-08: Assessment Criteria for Determining Environmental Safety of Plants with Novel Traits* (Plant Biotechnology Office). Web site: www.cfia-acia.agr.ca/english/food/pbo/dir9408e.html

Canadian Food Inspection Agency (CFIA). (1995). *Regulatory Directive Dir95-01: Field-testing Plants with Novel Traits in Canada* (Plant Biotechnology Office). Web site: www.cfia-acia.agr.ca/english/food/pbo/dir9501e.html

– (1997a). *Corporate Business Plan: Priorities 1997–2000*. Web site: www.cfia-acia.agfr.ca/english/corpaff/html

– (1997b). *News Release*. 'Canada enacts regulation to enhance BSE prevention,' Ottawa, 5 September.

– (1998a). *Estimates 1998–99, A Report on Plans and Priorities* Minister of Agriculture and Agri-Food. Web site: www.cfia-acia.agr.ca/english/corpaffr/b98-99_e.html
– (1998b). *Media Notice*, 'Canada Extends Ban on Importation of U.S. Honeybees.' Ottawa, 5 March.
– (1998c). *Contact* 'Food Recalls.' Ottawa: author.
Haas, Peter M. (1992). 'Introduction: Epistemic Communities and International Policy Coordination.' *International Organization*, 46(1): 1–35.
Kernaghan, Kenneth. (1993). 'Review Article: Reshaping government: The Post-Bureaucratic Paradigm.' *Canadian Public Administration*, 36(4): 636–44.
MacKenzie, Anne A. (1998). 'Food Safety in a Changing World.' Presentation to the Agricultural Institute of Canada Conference, Ottawa, 5–7 July.
Moore, Elizabeth, and Grace Skogstad. (1998). 'Food for Thought: Food Inspection and Renewed Federalism.' In Leslie A. Pal, ed., *How Ottawa Spends 1998–99, Balancing Act: The Post-Deficit Mandate*, 127–51. Toronto: Oxford University Press.
Powell, Douglas, and William Leiss. (1997). *Mad Cows and Mother's Milk.* Montreal: McGill-Queen's University Press.
Prince, Michael J. (2000). 'Banishing Bureaucracy or Hatching a Hybrid? The Canadian Food Agency and the Politics of Reinventing Government.' *Governance*, 13(2): 259–76.
Scofield, Heather. (1998). 'Politics Name of the Game in Border Battle on Hogs, Cattle.' *Globe and Mail*, 23 September, B1, B12.

10 The Pest Management Regulatory Agency: The Resilience of Science in Pesticide Regulation

IVO KRUPKA

Protecting people and the environment from risks associated with pesticides raises some unusual and interesting public policy issues that do not have exact counterparts in other areas of science-based regulation. These issues relate mainly to the public's regular and involuntary exposure to pesticides and the deliberate use of pesticides in the environment. The issues also relate to the particular configuration of economic and political or public stakeholder interests associated with pesticide regulation.

During the past fifteen years or so, the political influence of stakeholders, the development of global markets, and budgetary pressures have led to extensive legal, organizational, and procedural changes in pesticide regulation in most member countries of the Organization for Economic Cooperation and Development (OECD). This chapter highlights changes in the framework for pesticide regulation in Canada and considers some of the impacts of these changes on the underlying science. The chapter is divided into five sections. The first section provides background on pesticides and on basic issues in pesticide regulation. The second provides an overview of the main processes in pesticide regulation. The third describes the key features of the interdepartmental regulatory system that existed before the Pest Management Regulatory Agency (PMRA) was established in April 1995. The fourth analyses three main political and economic factors that shaped the Canadian pesticide regulatory system during the past decade – the 1989–90 Pesticide Registration Review, international harmonization, and budgetary pressures, and the related introduction of cost recovery. The concluding section comments on the resilience of science in the face of the political and institutional pressures and events examined.

Pesticides and Their Regulation

Pesticides include a wide variety of chemical agents, biological control agents (including insects, bacteria, viruses, and fungi), and electronic and mechanical devices designed to control pests (PMRA, 1998; Bosso, 1988, 1987). Pests that are the target of pesticides include weeds, animals, insects, bacteria, viruses, fungi, and other organisms found in the environment.

At the margin, there will always be some arbitrariness in distinguishing between pesticides, veterinary drugs, and pharmaceutical products. For example, in Canada, certain chemical agents deposited in aquaculture fish pens to control sea lice are considered pesticides, whereas in the United States they are considered veterinary drugs. The same active ingredients may be used in pesticides, veterinary drugs, and pharmaceutical products. Pesticides are typically applied to the environment or topically, rather than taken internally, as are many pharmaceutical products and veterinary drugs. In some countries, such as Australia, the same authority regulates pesticides and veterinary drugs. Among the arguments favouring such an arrangement are the similar requirements for balancing risks and benefits and somewhat similar issues of involuntary exposure to residues in food.

Some organisms are both pests and pesticides. In reality, the definition of pest is arbitrary, and some organisms considered harmless or even lovable by some people, have become statutory targets. Control of the muskrat (identified by its Latin name) is one of the key objectives listed in an opening section of German pesticide legislation. The kangaroo, an agricultural pest, is Australia's national symbol. The main piece of U.S. pesticide legislation is the Federal Insecticide, Fungicide and Rodenticide Act (FIFRA). Casual observation around Canada's national capital region and a perusal of local by-laws support the conclusion that dandelions are no longer official pests in this area.

The first recorded uses of pesticides extend back more than 2,000 years. Today, pesticides are commonly used in a wide variety of settings such as farms, forests, aquaculture enclosures, pulp and paper and lumber mills, water purification plants, hospitals, homes, gardens, swimming pools, parks, golf courses, oil wells, and electric power line and railway rights of way. In Canada, agricultural pesticides constitute roughly 85 per cent of the $1.5 billion pesticides market (1998).

Regulation of pesticides in Canada initially addressed fraudulent claims regarding their effectiveness. The earliest federal statute relating to pesticide regulation was the 1927 Act to Regulate the Sale and Inspection of Agricultural and Economic Poisons. In the postwar years, the target of pesticide regulation shifted slowly away from fraud towards health and environmental protection. The 1969 Pest Control Products Act, the current foundation for federal pesticide regulation, marked a major shift in legislative focus to health and environmental concerns. Since 1969, the increasing prominence of health and environmental concerns has been reflected principally in changes to administrative arrangements and procedures in the pesticide regulatory process, rather than in adjustments to legislation (Castrilli and Vigod, 1987).

The main constitutional foundation for pesticide regulation, as for other federal health and environmental protection activities, is the criminal law power. This rather blunt instrument, that requires proof 'beyond a reasonable doubt,' is not well suited to the probabilities and subtleties associated with science-based regulation.

The principal reasons for regulating pesticides today relate to the limited options for protecting people and the environment from the risks associated with their use. Unique aspects of these risks arise from the public's routine, involuntary exposure to pesticides contained in virtually all food and drinking water, and their deliberate emission into the environment. While most food contains at least minute traces of pesticides, in many cases such traces are undetectable by normal means. Until relatively recently, one might have expected that northern Aboriginal peoples who gain sustenance from their natural environment would not be exposed to pesticides. Long-range atmospheric and oceanic transport of persistent organic pollutants, including some pesticides never used in Canada or banned many years ago, has resulted in strong concentrations of pesticides and other contaminants in fish and mammals consumed by aboriginal peoples in the Canadian north (see Indian and Northern Affairs Canada, 1997).

The reasons for regulating pesticides go beyond those for regulating therapeutic products, where human exposure is voluntary, and for regulating substances that could harm the environment. Acute health problems attributable to pesticide exposure are relatively rare, at least in most OECD countries (Canada, 1995). Health concerns associated with pesticides tend to centre on long-term effects that are very difficult to attribute to specific products or events. The opposite tends to be true with therapeutic products for people where adverse reactions are generally acute. In addition, physicians usually prescribe such products and can monitor their effects. One consequence is that it is easier for individuals to seek redress for health problems attributable to pharmaceuticals or medical devices through normal legal channels than it is for people seeking redress for health problems attributed to pesticides. The notable exceptions, such as the protracted cases involving tainted blood and defective breast implants, prove the rule.

The types of benefits associated with pesticides vary with their uses. In agriculture, for example, arguments for pesticides include economic benefits derived from their contribution to increasing the supply of safe, low-cost food for a growing world population. Similar arguments are advanced for pesticide use in forestry – abundant, durable, attractive, competitively priced, wood and wood products. In gardens, parks, and golf courses, aesthetic considerations are seen as important benefits of pesticide use. In hospitals and homes pesticides are commonly used to protect health by controlling pathogenic bacteria and disease-carrying insects. The use of pesticides to control purple loosestrife in wetlands or zebra mussels illustrates their potential benefits to the environment.

In general, persons who seek direct economic benefits from pesticides (for example, farmers and foresters) constitute a much smaller, and sometimes different, group from those who assume the bulk of the related risks – the public (the public also derives economic benefits in the form of lower food prices). By contrast, a person who uses therapeutic products seek personal benefits from them and also assumes the risks (Leiss and Chociolko, 1994).

Key political interests in pesticide regulation include users such as those involved in agriculture and forestry, pesticide manufacturers, and public interest advocacy groups concerned with health and environmental protection. These often-conflicting interests tend to be represented by relatively few groups, each with a focused pesticide agenda. Examples of leading Canadian organizations involved with pesticide issues are the Canadian Federation of Agriculture, the Canadian Horticultural Council, the Crop Protection Institute (representing pesticide manufacturers), the Canadian Manufacturers of Chemical Specialties, the Canadian Environmental Law Association, the World Wildlife Fund, the Sierra Club, the Consumers' Association of Canada, the Canadian Medical Association, and the Canadian Public Health Association. In most governments, such interests are often aligned with senior ministerial portfolios having goals that often conflict. The goals of agricultural and forestry, and other portfolios related to industry, for example, regularly conflict with the goals of the health and environmental portfolios. Few regulatory systems are characterized by such a configuration where a few, focused, conflicting political interests are aligned with a few major governmental portfolios.

Overview of the Pesticide Regulatory System

The general description of pesticide regulation that follows, while based on the Canadian system, also reflects the systems established in most OECD countries. The primary activity in pesticide regulation is the evaluation of data on individual pest control products to determine whether these products are safe and effective and have value. Evaluating data about safety includes making informed assumptions about how a pesticide will be used in the real world, the skill and behaviour of users, and the role and effectiveness of governmental and private sector inspection, monitoring, compliance, and other systems that complement pesticide regulation.

Some of these complementary systems can have a significant impact on pesticide regulation. For example, environmental legislation, policies, and programs have been instrumental in precluding the registration of most products characterized as toxic (as defined under the Canadian Environmental Protection Act), persistent, and bioaccumulative, and identifying for cancellation registered products with such characteristics. General reductions in monitoring activities by federal and/or provincial environmental authorities can affect pesticide regulatory decisions about the range of uses for a pesticide or the rates at which it may be applied.

Premarket phase

No pesticide may be sold or used unless it has the required regulatory approval – a registration – or falls into an exempt (low-risk) class. The typical process begins in a company's laboratory with the discovery of a chemical or biological agent that may have pesticidal properties. A candidate product then undergoes extensive studies that provide data about any associated health and environmental risks, as well as its economic and social value. Typically, many candidates are found, but few are chosen. The studies are undertaken in the light of the data that regulators require as part of the applications that companies must submit when seeking to register a pesticide. For a major new product, this study phase may last several years, typically generate voluminous data, and may cost well in excess of $100 million. One application submitted to federal regulators several years ago, was accompanied by data contained in 175 two-inch, three-ring binders. Some other applications are said to have weighed more than a ton. The substantial investment in data is protected in most countries with policies and laws designed to prevent the registration of products not supported by an original database. A company that applies to register a product that is equivalent to one already registered has two main choices – duplicating the studies that supported the registration (thereby incurring similar costs), or proving to the regulator that it has permission of the registrant to use his/her studies to support the new application. The latter course usually requires the new applicant to pay compensation to the registrant. Pesticide regulators have devoted substantial time devising and managing data protection policies and programs. In addition to data protection, patents may have been obtained to protect registrants' products. These regimes have inhibited openness and transparency in pesticide regulation because of their preoccupation with the proprietary nature of the data.

Experts in the regulatory agency evaluate the data to determine whether the applicant's claims about the safety, efficacy, and benefits of the product are justified. Regulators do not, as a rule, undertake studies of their own in relation to specific applications.

The information required to assess the economic and social benefits that a product may generate is inherently more difficult to define and obtain. For example, the benefits of a product are partly a function of the extent of its use and its price, neither of which can be forecast accurately until after the product reaches the market.

The definition of the data required by the regulator and the techniques for using them to assess risk are largely the product of an international consensus among experts in such areas as human and ecological toxicology and risk assessment. Such experts typically include university and industry scientists, as well as scientists from pesticide regulatory agencies, health, environmental, and other governmental organizations.

The proposed regulatory decision reached by regulatory authorities may be issued for public comment before a final decision is made. Under the Pest Control Products Act, the authority for most regulatory decisions is the minister of health.

Postmarket phase

In most OECD countries, including Canada, the regulatory authority retains responsibility for ensuring that a registered pest control product is used as directed and that it continues to meet evolving regulatory standards. This responsibility does not currently have an exact counterpart in the therapeutic products regulatory process. The reasons for this include the clinical trial process used for therapeutic products that can identify problems before the product is approved, the acute nature of most adverse reactions associated with therapeutic products, and the role that physicians and pharmacists can play in prescribing, dispensing, and monitoring. By contrast, it is generally more difficult to simulate situations that could identify the type of longer-term health and environmental problems that are of particular concern with pesticides. Moreover, there are normally no monitoring roles in the pesticide system equivalent to those of physicians and pharmacists in the therapeutic products system.

In Canada, responsibility for the postmarket safety relating to pesticides is shared mainly among federal, provincial, territorial, and municipal authorities concerned with health, safety, food, environmental, agricultural, forestry, and fisheries issues. Registrants also have responsibilities for their products, including reporting adverse effects. Registrants and their associations may also take the initiative to promote pesticide safety. For example, one of the associations representing major registrants instituted programs for recycling pesticide containers and ensuring adequate warehousing standards.

Normally, a registered pest control product, used as directed, should not give rise to action under such statutes as the Canadian Environmental Protection Act, Migratory Birds Convention Act, Food and Drugs Act, or provincial, territorial, or municipal legislation. In cases where pesticides are not applied properly, where the conditions of use have not been appropriate, or where there is evidence of an unforeseen hazard, health and environmental problems may come to light through monitoring activities. For example, pesticides may be found among pollutants whose clean-up is normally called for under the Canadian Environmental Protection Act. Kills of migratory birds, which have come to the attention of officials of Environment Canada's Canadian Wildlife Service, have provided the main evidence for cancelling a registered pesticide. Inspectors of the Canadian Food Inspection Agency may discover food products with pesticide residues above the relevant maximum residue limits.

If the problem has arisen because of the improper use of a pesticide, corrective action may be taken under the Pest Control Products Act, other federal statutes such as those mentioned above, as well as provincial, territorial, or municipal legislation. The choice of action and legal instrument tends to be made on pragmatic grounds, such as the availability of appropriately qualified staff at the site of the infraction.

Since pests tend to be local or regional problems, their management falls primarily within provincial or municipal jurisdiction. Each province and territory has a pesticide regulatory group as part of its department of environment, except in Manitoba, Saskatchewan, and Prince Edward Island, where such groups are part of the agriculture department. Relying on the federal regulatory system to ensure that registered products are safe and effective, provincial regulators focus on the safe and effective *use* of registered pesticides. Provinces may add restrictions on the use of registered pesticides but may not relax the terms of registrations. A Federal-Provincial-Territorial Committee on Pest Management and Pesticides helps to address issues of common interest. A growing number of municipal authorities have also enacted by-laws and taken other action to reduce risks associated with pesticides.

Part of the regulatory authority's postmarket responsibilities are fulfilled through systematic reviews of the safety of older registered products against current regulatory standards. It is clear that some pesticides, such as DDT, whose risks were considered acceptable years ago, are not considered acceptable today in most parts of the Northern Hemisphere. DDT is still widely used in Mexico, Central and South America, Africa, and many parts of Asia. The reason is simple; its use prevents many deaths even while exposing people and the environment to risks. Likewise, some pesticides considered safe today might not be considered safe in the future. Most OECD countries have re-evaluation programs of one sort or another, although such programs often face a tough challenge competing for resources, which are typically stretched to the limit handling new applications. In addition to systematic re-evaluation, special reviews may be undertaken when significant problems come to light with registered pesticides.

The balance between premarket and postmarket controls is determined pragmatically. For example, it is conceivable that new environmental or health protection legislation and programs could influence, to a greater extent than is now the case, some of the kinds of data and procedures required for evaluating applications for pesticide registration. This could lead to new classes of prohibited products, thereby possibly reducing some of the reliance on prevailing postmarket controls. Conversely, assuming adequate resources and good federal-provincial cooperation, relatively greater reliance might be placed on the monitoring of health and environmental impacts than is now the case, thereby reducing some of reliance on prevailing premarket controls.

Overall, the key challenge is to balance assessed health and environmental risks, on the one hand, and forecast economic and social benefits, on the other, to produce a regulatory decision that establishes both a level of risk acceptable to the public and a level of benefits acceptable to users.

The assessment of risks follows scientific principles, and in this way provides clear reference points to help decide on the levels of risk acceptable to the public. In the final analysis, however, decisions about what the public will regard as acceptable are substantially a matter of judgment, and judgment about what the public is likely to regard as acceptable – whether it be risks or other matters – is ultimately a political decision. The 1980 Ontario decision to ban the pesticide 2,4, 5-T, even though it had been registered by federal authorities, is an example of political authorities deciding that the public would not agree with the judgment of regulators about the acceptability of the risks associated with this pesticide. In other words, pesticide regulatory decisions, although science based, are significantly political in that they rest on an assessment of largely incommensurable factors of vital public interest.

This overview suggests that the science involved in pesticide regulation does, indeed, correspond to the characteristics of science-based regulation described in Chapter 1. Pesticide regulators typically do not conduct or direct research but they *do* support some of the most important functions of government – health and environmental protection.

While it is by no means evident that pesticide regulators need to have their own laboratories or research budgets; they do need to be in a position to influence research that relates to their responsibilities (Salter, 1988). For example, much of the environmental science that supports pesticide regulation is substantially less developed than the science relating to human toxicology. This suggests that pesticide regulatory authorities need to be able to influence the environmental research agenda so that environmental science can eventually be applied to pesticide regulatory decision making with the same level of confidence as human toxicology.

From time to time there will also be requirements for research to support specific regulatory needs. In the late 1970s, for example, Health Canada scientists took the initiative to develop the techniques for assessing and managing pesticide risks to bystanders. Such risks had not been previously assessed. Pesticide regulators need to have adequate means to commission or at least guide specific research needed to support their responsibilities.

Like other regulators, those concerned with pesticides need to be able to identify the qualifications they require of the university graduates they hire and the means to provide them with specialized training and development. They also need to have adequate means, including participation in conferences, to keep abreast of scientific developments and contribute to general knowledge on pesticides and their regulation. As will be suggested later in this chapter, the current cost-recovery regime is not well suited to providing adequate support for the development and maintenance of a strong science foundation for pesticide regulation. This can be seen as one of the dimensions of the concept of the 'science deficit' discussed in Chapter 1.

In addition to its science foundation, there is a major component of pesticide regulation concerned with essentially political considerations. This underdeveloped component of pesticide regulation is arguably much more significant than in some of the other regulatory areas, such as therapeutic products regulation, discussed in other chapters.

Canada's Pre-1995 Interdepartmental Pesticide Regulatory System

Before the establishment of Health Canada's Pest Management Regulatory Agency in April 1995, experts in Agriculture Canada, Health and Welfare Canada, Environment Canada, and Forestry Canada reviewed data accompanying applications for registration. (In 1993, pending the enactment of the relevant statutes in the wake of a major governmental reorganization, the names of these departments were changed respectively to Agriculture and Agri-Food Canada, Health Canada, and Natural Resources Canada. Environment Canada's name remained unchanged.) The minister of agriculture was the regulatory authority under the Pest Control Products Act. The Pest Control Products Regulations identified a senior official in Agriculture Canada as responsible for exercising much of the minister's day-to-day responsibilities on his behalf.

The interdepartmental system resembled the older model, characterized as 'science in the (secret) service of policy,' and discussed by Leiss in Chapter 3. Each department applied its own particular culture to assessing risk and its conclusions were, for the most part, confidential. Agriculture Canada was responsible for reviewing those parts of the data that reported on the efficacy and benefits of the product, as well as for coordinating the overall registration process. Since a review of efficacy data not only helps to determine whether the product is likely to work as claimed, but also how much product is needed to do the job, efficacy data are referred to in the evaluation of health and environmental data. Evaluations of efficacy data can normally be completed much more quickly than evaluations of data on health and environmental effects.

Officials of the Health Protection Branch (HPB) of Health and Welfare Canada reviewed the data that reported on risks to people. The determination of risks to people included assessments of their probable exposure to pesticides as consumers of food and drinking water, applicators of pesticides, and as bystanders. HPB's role also included making regulations under the Food and Drugs Act, concerning 'maximum residue limits' (MRLs) that define the maximum level of pesticide residues allowed in food. Evaluations of the data on health effects typically took more time than any other part of the review process.

HPB had a structured process for determining its advice to Agriculture Canada on whether products should be registered or allowed to remain on the market. In essence the process was to subject the conclusions reached by HPB scientists to a form of internal scientific peer review before communicating them to the pesticide regulatory officials at Agriculture Canada. Most often, HPB's advice did not explicitly say whether the product should be registered or kept on the market. Some scope was usually left to Agriculture Canada officials to interpret the advice.

Environment Canada's role was to review the data that reported on risks to the environment. The department had its own process for integrating the conclusions of the various officials concerned (including the Canadian Wildlife Service) and communicating them to Agriculture Canada. Forestry Canada reviewed applications for forestry products in much the same way as Agriculture Canada reviewed other products, that is, with the focus on efficacy. Health and Environment evaluated the risks associated with forestry products in the same way as for other products.

Under the interdepartmental system, Agriculture Canada, the focus of constant pressure from agricultural and other interests to register pesticides, was in the unenviable position of having to badger Health Canada and Environment Canada to complete their evaluations. Within Health and Environment, timeliness was less important than being completely satisfied that risks associated with pesticides could be kept to acceptable levels. By the late 1980s, it could be said that no major pest control product could be registered without the concurrence of Health Canada and Environment Canada, even though Agriculture Canada was the regulatory authority.

The disadvantages of the interdepartmental process included an inconsistent perspective on risk that corresponded to the varied expertise and diverse mandates and values of the main departments concerned and the inability to manage the overall regulatory process efficiently. There was no effective system, for example, even to track progress on an application, let alone to establish and meet timelines to complete the registration process. Many major pesticide companies employed experts to track the progress of their applications in the departments concerned. In one instance, where the author was involved, a company provided a report, complete with detailed graphs, documenting the evaluation process for one of its products and the time it took to reach a regulatory decision. Such information was not available within the federal regulatory system.

This arrangement did have an advantage, however, that has since been lost. Ultimately, from the Cabinet perspective, the arrangement reflected the main political interests at play in pesticide regulation: those of the main users (agriculture and forestry); those of the pesticide manufacturers; and those representing health and environmental concerns. Thus, the ministers representing these interests – and their officials – could normally speak on behalf of these interests essentially without compromise. No single minister or public service organization had to reconcile the divergent interests associated with pesticide regulation, as is now the case.

Under current arrangements, it is doubtful that the ministers who no longer have responsibilities for pest management regulation would be as willing to engage in vigorous debate on pesticide regulatory issues as they were in the past. They no longer have the expertise within their departments to support them in such debates, and it is more convenient to point their stakeholders in the direction of the minister responsible for pesticide regulation, the minister of health.

Focusing responsibility in one minister also increases the possibility of the classic problem of 'agency capture.'

Political-Economic Pressures for Change

The 1989–1990 Pesticide Registration Review

In the mid-1980s, pressure from many quarters to reform the pesticide regulatory system (Bosso, 1987) led to the establishment of the multi-stakeholder Pesticide Registration Review (Hill, 1994). Farm groups were concerned primarily that pesticides available to their U.S. competitors were often unavailable in Canada and that in Canada pesticides were generally more expensive than in the United States. They also felt that their competitive disadvantages would be compounded within a few years by tariff reductions on agricultural products expected as a result of the GATT discussions of the period, along with the strong possibility of a free trade agreement with the United States.

Pesticide manufacturers claimed that the time and cost associated with registering pest control products in Canada were substantially greater than in the United States. They suggested that this deterred applications for registering products in this country (especially products for the small-acreage, high-value horticultural sector) and that this would compound farmers' concerns about the availability of pesticides used by their competitors and trading partners.

Environmental groups, some other public interest advocacy groups, and unions were concerned that the registration process was not sufficiently rigorous or sufficiently focused on health and environmental protection. They indicated that the public, who assumed most of the risks associated with pesticides, had little opportunity to influence the shape or outcomes of the pesticide regulatory process. They suggested that the regulatory system should focus on promoting the safe and effective management of pests, in addition to performing the classic role of ensuring that the individual pest control products were safe and effective. These same groups also saw a conflict of interest between the minister of agriculture's responsibilities as the regulatory authority under the Pest Control Products Act, and the minister's responsibilities to support the economic and other interests of agriculture and related industries. The Alachlor case, which brought many of these issues to the forefront of political discussion, exposed senior pesticide regulators to unaccustomed tough public scrutiny (Hoberg, 1990; Hill, 1994).

In April 1989, the minister of agriculture announced the establishment of a multi-stakeholder review. The purpose of the review was stated as follows: 'Recognizing the principles of sustainability, the purpose of the Review Team is to formulate recommendations for the Minister of Agriculture to adapt the registration process to changing policies and conditions with a view to ensuring the efficient federal regulation of pest control products that minimize the risk of harm to health, safety and the environment while meeting the needs of stakeholders' (Pesticide Registration Review Team, 1990).

The decision to use a multi-stakeholder review team to reform the pesticide regulatory process and the way the team ultimately reached its fragile consensus is instructive (Versteeg, 1992). A good deal of time was spent on the composition of the Pesticide Registration Review (PRR) team because it was thought that, in the final analysis, only a report enjoying stakeholder consensus could lead to reform. For all practical purposes, any of the key stakeholders could stall reform because they stood a good chance of enlisting 'their' minister to support their veto. This was particularly true of stakeholders representing the interests of farmers, the pesticide industry, and environmental groups.

After more than eighteen months of work that included cross-Canada public hearings, the PRR team submitted its report to the minister of agriculture in December 1990. All team members signed the report except the representative of the Canadian Labour Congress, whose minority position, which included calling for a ban on virtually all pesticides by 1998, was appended to the report. Nonetheless, the chairman, executive secretary, and the members of the PRR team deserve a great deal of credit for reaching an unparalleled, if incomplete, consensus on major reforms involving issues that are normally the source of strong divisions among the key stakeholders.

The PRR report focused on issues of particular concern to the present chapter. The PRR team envisaged a comprehensive reform of the pesticide regulatory system including enactment of a new statute that would embrace a new philosophy of pest management. The statute would establish an independent Pest Management Regulatory Agency reporting to the minister of health and a Pest Management Promotion Office (PMPO) reporting to the minister of agriculture.

The new philosophy would have marked a radical departure from the case-by-case approach to pesticide regulation that still prevails. The essence of the new philosophy was to go beyond evaluating the safety and efficacy of products and consider the safest and most effective way to manage pests. For example, a new product, assessed as safe and effective, might not be approved if, in the judgment of the new agency, adequate means already existed to manage the target pests. A significant aspect of the proposed approach was to create systematic, downward pressures on pesticide use. In addition to pesticides, there are, of course, other ways to control pests. Examples include crop rotation to reduce the availability of a long-term food supply to particular pests, and mechanical and hand control. Integrated pest management (IPM), the strategic use of several methods of pest control, including pesticides, is designed to reduce reliance on pesticides.

The proposed role of the PMPO was to work towards 'the integration of pest management with the broader goals of environmental sustainability' (PRR Team, 1990: 7). This was to be done largely through promoting good pest management practices and reduced pesticide use, supporting research, and monitoring decisions of the proposed new agency.

Other key elements of the reform included the adoption of legislated timelines to govern the evaluation of applications for registration; cost recovery tied to timelines; the publication of proposed regulatory decisions for public comment before they are finalized; public access to the data on which registration decisions are made; the appointment of data advisers to provide independent scientific opinions on decisions relating to the data required by the regulatory authority; the establishment of a Canadian Pest Management Advisory Council to the minister of health; and the establishment of a Standing Federal-Provincial-Territorial Committee on Pest Management. The PRR team advised the government to designate the new head of the proposed agency without delay and envisaged that they (or other knowledgeable stakeholders) would advise the new head on the implementation of their report.

In retrospect, the multi-stakeholder approach to reviewing the pesticide regulatory system may be seen as supporting the shift away from the older model referred to in Chapter 3. The shift is from the relatively narrow perspectives on risks and related regulatory approaches shared largely by regulators and the economic interests most directly concerned, towards a broader perspective that corresponds more closely to public concerns. Early in 1991 the government established an interdepartmental process to review the PRR team's recommendations which culminated, in February 1992, in a public response to the recommendations. The government accepted the overall thrust of the PRR recommendations, but did not accept its recommendation for a new agency, much less a new statutory regulatory agency.

The government chose instead to establish an Interdepartmental Executive Committee (IEC) of assistant deputy ministers from the departments of Agriculture, National Health and Welfare, Environment, and Forestry to manage the regulatory system. A new Pest Management Secretariat was established to coordinate the management of the regulatory system under the direction of the IEC. Organizations represented on the PRR team were invited to constitute an Interim Canadian Pest Management Advisory Council to advise on the implementation of the government's response to their recommendations. The council was established in March 1992 and held six meetings over the next three years. The Standing Federal-Provincial-Territorial Committee on Pest Management, co-chaired by the executive secretary of the Pest Management Secretariat and a provincial official, was established at the same time.

The IEC and the Pest Management Secretariat made a number of attempts to establish a management framework that would monitor progress in each department, define timelines for evaluating pesticide applications, and reallocate resources as necessary. Despite some signs that such a system might work, its failure was not surprising at the time, and is certainly not surprising in retrospect. In essence, there is no system for reallocating resources interdepartmentally except through the normal or exceptional processes sanctioned by the Cabinet and its management committee, the Treasury Board.

By mid-1993 the Pest Management Secretariat was developing options for a pest management regulatory agency under Health Canada, along the lines of a Special Operating Agency. A campaign commitment of the Liberal party that won the October 1993 general election, was to implement the recommendations of the PRR team on an urgent basis. This provided impetus for the idea of a new pesticide regulatory agency that had been rejected by the previous government.

The Liberal government announced its plans to reform the pest management regulatory system in February 1995, and the new Pest Management Regulatory Agency under Health Canada was established on

1 April 1995. An Order in Council of the same date transferred responsibility for the Pest Control Products Act from the minister of
agriculture and agri-food to the minister of health. The process of
consolidating pesticide regulatory staff into the new agency from the
four departments concerned began immediately thereafter.

When the PRR review was launched in 1989 there was little, if any,
support among federal pesticide regulators for a multi-stakeholder
reform process. Many senior regulators tended to view themselves –
with substantial justification in many cases – as competent scientists
firmly dedicated to the public interest, and especially to the protection
of people and the environment from risks associated with pesticides.
The notion that recommendations of stakeholders, constituted almost
exclusively of non-scientists, should reform the pesticide regulatory system was incongruous, if not repugnant, to some of the senior regulatory
officials, who considered such a process as a threat to good science.

International Harmonization of Regulatory Approaches

Until the last few years, pesticide regulation made little sense from a
global perspective. If a company wanted to market a pesticide in several countries, a common practice, it would need to submit voluminous data for evaluation by pesticide regulators in each of the countries where its product was to be sold. By and large, the fact that a
pesticide was already registered in one country did not alter the fact
that essentially the same data would need to be evaluated in the other
countries where it was to be marketed. Moreover, the studies required
by various countries were not necessarily uniform. Since climate, soils,
pests, and crops may differ from country to country, the data required
to assess environmental risks and product efficacy might differ correspondingly. Significant differences also existed, however, in data requirements for assessing risks to human beings – who are, after all,
pretty much the same around the world. National differences in approaches to evaluating data and reporting results further compounded
the challenges to international harmonization.

From a global perspective, then, pesticide regulation was grossly
inefficient. Resources for health and environmental protection were
being misallocated to replicate evaluation of applicants' data. The use
of modern, often safer, pest management technology was delayed,
while older, less safe technology remained on the market. The costs to

pesticide manufacturers were unnecessarily high and this in turn translated into unnecessarily high costs to users.

The global inefficiency of pesticide regulation was particularly frustrating for Canadian farmers who could not see why a pesticide registered in the United States or Europe could not also be more or less automatically registered in Canada. Similar frustration existed in most European Union countries.

As the twenty-first century begins, pesticide regulation has become far more harmonized internationally. Initially, in Canada, international harmonization was a hard sell, particularly among some of the scientific experts involved in pesticide regulation. Arguments against harmonization included unspecified concerns about erosion of national sovereignty, the thalidomide case, the anticipated lack of public confidence in foreign regulatory processes, and the reluctance of scientific experts to 'sign off' on evaluations performed by others. Environmental groups, who predicted that it would lead to a lowering of health and environmental standards, also often resisted international harmonization. (The drug Thalidomide was approved for use in many countries, including Canada, on the strength of reviews of the relevant data in a European country. The fact that thalidomide use had such unfortunate consequences, and that Canada and other countries had not conducted their own evaluations of the relevant data, has often been put forward as an argument against international harmonization in health and environmental protection.)

Under the auspices of the Canada–U.S. Free Trade Agreement, the North American Free Trade Agreement, the OECD, and some other international organizations, Canadian pesticide experts have worked with their international counterparts towards substantial harmonization of the scientific foundations of pesticide regulation. A significant level of harmonization has been achieved between the Canadian and U.S. pesticide regulatory systems over the last five years. Part of the credit is due to the stakeholder groups on both sides of the border – particularly agricultural groups – who provided much of the drive to get the process under way and sustain it.

In 1993 senior staff of the Canadian Horticultural Council (CHC) were successful in stimulating U.S. agricultural groups to join them, along with Canadian and U.S. pesticide manufacturers, in putting pressure on pesticide regulators on both sides of the border to organize meetings of the Technical Working Group on Pesticides. The Free Trade

Agreement (FTA) contemplated the establishment of a number of technical working groups in each major sector covered by the agreement. The technical working groups were charged with developing the details for implementing the FTA. Unlike other FTA technical working groups that began meeting soon after the January 1989 agreement came into force, the Technical Working Group on Pesticides did not get off the ground because federal officials thought that the PRR team's 1990 report should first be completed and digested. The first meeting was held in the summer of 1993.

Three achievements of the Technical Working Group stand out. The first, the 'parallel review project,' was designed to identify similarities and differences in the way that Canadian and U.S. pesticide regulators evaluated the data accompanying applications for major new products. This was an essential first step towards generating mutual confidence in one another's approach to pesticide regulation, particularly its scientific aspects. A major chemical company volunteered to have one of its applications used in the project. The U.S. and Canadian regulators reviewed essentially the same application independently, and compared notes as they went along. This was a painstaking exercise calling for a great deal of professionalism and patience on both sides. In the end, the two groups of regulators could document in detail the way that each approached the registration process of a major new product. The evidence showed that similarities far outweighed differences and that the differences could be eliminated or accommodated.

The second achievement, the 'joint review project,' was a logical extension of the parallel review project. In the light of experience with the latter project, both the U.S. and Canadian regulators made some adjustments in the way that they did business so that they could divide the work of reviewing a major application between them. This meant that, together, they could bring to bear a much larger pool of expert staff on applications made simultaneously to each regulator, and thus complete the work more quickly than if they worked independently. This joint review process still leaves the door open – at least theoretically – for each regulator to reach a different final conclusion. Each regulator depends on the other, however, to carry out specific parts of the work in accordance with agreed procedures and standards.

The parallel review project and joint review project have effectively addressed concerns about sovereignty in decision making and ministerial accountability. If the minister of health is called to account on a 'joint review' decision, he or she can say with authority that the part of the registration process carried out by U.S. officials was undertaken in accordance with the same procedures and quality control as in Canada, and by staff with comparable qualifications. It is as if the work were done in Canada by Canadian regulators.

The third achievement was the development of a common Canada–U.S. map identifying similar zones on both sides of the border in which to carry out 'residue trials.' These trials allow for the study of pesticide residues resulting from various rates at which a product is applied. Before the map was created, a company applying to register a pesticide in both Canada and the United States would have had to duplicate residue trials on each side of the border. Now that the map has been developed, such trials, carried out in any zone common to both countries, are regarded as valid by both Canada and the United States, thereby reducing both the time and cost to market. Work is continuing to map common ecological zones that would permit certain environmental impact studies to be carried out in the same fashion.

When the FTA Technical Working Group's activities were subsumed under NAFTA institutions, some of the work begun by Canadian and U.S. regulators was extended to their Mexican partners.

In addition to their activities in the Technical Working Group on Pesticides, Canadian regulators were also active on related international harmonization fronts with U.S., Australian, and other foreign regulators. They also continued to be involved in various international fora such as the OECD and the CODEX Alimentarius Commission of the Food and Agricultural Organization and the World Health Organization. The upshot of much of this activity is broad agreement among Canada, the United States, Australia, and the European Union on the substance and form of the information that applicants must submit to register various types of pesticides. The broad agreement achieved is the result of painstaking work and international negotiation to define in detail the extensive scientific studies that applicants must undertake to demonstrate the safety and efficacy of specific types of products. There is also broad agreement on such matters as the way data are to be evaluated and the form of the reports on studies, including how they are to be summarized and cited in bibliographies.

Canadian stakeholders were active both directly in some of the meetings of the international organizations mentioned above and indirectly through their involvement with a number of international associations. The extensive interaction between stakeholders and regulators associated with the pesticide regulatory system provided a strong foundation for international action.

As a result of the progress achieved on international harmonization, Canadian regulators and their foreign counterparts may need to review only a report of the evaluation and a summary of the data that they require to support an application for registration, rather than the entire voluminous package. All of the detailed information still needs to be submitted by the applicant, but Canadian regulators may not need to review it unless, for example, questions arise in the course of reviewing the report and summary that can be answered by reference to the raw data.

The particular form of international harmonization that has been achieved in pesticide regulation effectively answers the two-pronged question, 'Who determines the science underlying pesticide regulation, and how is the determination made?' Given the international nature of science, it may be said that the data required by pesticide regulators to make registration decisions were always determined largely by an informal international consensus among the various scientific experts concerned with pesticide regulation.

Today that consensus appears to have been taken to a relatively high common denominator through the conscious efforts of pesticide regulators, mainly in OECD countries. One of the dynamics at play is that domestic pressures favouring strong health and environmental protection in some of the larger countries such as the United States, Germany, and the United Kingdom tend to be translated into correspondingly strong international standards. When interest in higher health and environmental standards flags in a few influential countries, that interest is usually maintained or increased in a few other countries. Usually the pressure for higher standards prevails. Since the key players in the international pesticide fora include senior health and environmental scientists, there tends to be a form of 'cultural resistance' to downward pressure on standards emanating from commercial or political interests.

Whether commercial interests tend to favour lower health and environmental standards is not so clear. However, high health and environmental standards are often sought by wealthy, powerful countries as a form of non-tariff barrier against food and other imports, particularly from low-cost producers.

In 1993 a highly respected, senior pesticide regulator suggested in a prediction to the author that it would take a new generation of scientists to accept the use of international reviews of pesticides as the basis for Canadian decisions. This prediction was amply supported by the glacial progress achieved towards international harmonization in pesticide regulation between the submission of the 1990 PRR team's report and the first meeting of the Technical Working Group on Pesticides in 1993. Nevertheless, four years after the prediction, most OECD countries were using the reviews of foreign regulators as the basis for their own regulatory decisions.

The foregoing observations suggest that the science underlying such decisions is at least as good if not better than that previously applied. For the moment, the overall result of international harmonization is that the 'global inefficiency' that characterized pesticide regulation only a few years ago has been substantially reduced. While much of the drive came from economic interests, the new international architecture of pesticide regulation is largely the product of regulatory scientists.

Budgetary Pressures and Cost Recovery

Budgetary pressures in Canada and most other OECD countries, and the related popularity of cost recovery, particularly over the past five years or so, have generally supported good management at the PMRA. It is less clear that cost recovery has supported good science, at least in the way that it has been applied in the agency.

In response to the PRR team's 1990 report, the government made a public commitment to add over $81 million between 1991–2 and 1996–7 to the pesticide regulatory system. If added to departmental A-base budgets, this would have increased overall pesticide regulation funding to more than two and a half times prevailing levels (Pest Management Secretariat, 1994). By the time the PMRA was established, a substantial portion of the promised funds had evaporated, and the proportion of the agency's budget that had to be provided from cost-recovery revenues grew commensurately (PMRA, 1997).

Even though efficiency is an uncontroversial goal, particularly because it serves economic, as well as health and environmental protection interests associated with pesticide regulation, it was not successfully pursued on a system-wide basis before the establishment of the PMRA. A common view among senior pesticide regulators during and after the PRR review was that there was not much wrong with the regulatory system that the infusion of substantial resources could not fix. In the absence of an effective management framework, however, the infusion of additional funds makes little sense. This was evident to stakeholders, who pressed for clear indications of a new, strong focus on efficiency when the PMRA's management and cost recovery frameworks were being developed in the summer of 1995.

Unfortunately, fractious stakeholder relations have marked the introduction of cost recovery in the PMRA. Few, if any, participants in the development of PMRA's cost-recovery regime – whether from the agency itself, or outside – regard the process as satisfactory, and the PMRA is not generating the revenue it considers it needs to do its job. This, in turn, is seen as a threat to the PMRA's scientific capacity. An explanation for this state of affairs seems to lie with the way that cost recovery was introduced, rather than with the suitability of cost recovery as a source of funding for the agency.

Some of the approaches to cost recovery adopted by federal agencies, including the Treasury Board, seem ill-advised in retrospect. The Treasury Board's identification of deficit reduction a major goal of cost recovery, for example, seems to have undermined the prospects for effective stakeholder relations when cost recovery was introduced in many agencies, including the PMRA. Perhaps identifying deficit reduction as a goal of cost recovery was considered a way to pre-empt debate and opposition to this particular form of revenue generation. Anticipated arguments against cost recovery to fund health and environmental protection activities could be overridden by the absolute priority attached to deficit reduction at the time. For regulatees, however, this sort of approach provided ammunition for arguments that cost recovery was simply a cash grab, accompanied by disingenuous consultation.

One consequence is that regulatees, often acting in concert, strengthened their resolve not to pay up. An indicator of this resolve and the mistrust associated with it can be found in the extensive, detailed provisions (often in regulations) of many agencies, defining procedures through which regulatees may appeal cost-recovery charges. The development and negotiation of such rules of the cost-recovery game, explicitly supported by Treasury Board policy, have consumed a great deal of time for both administrators and regulatees and have reinforced adversarial postures.

A more discriminating approach, undertaken in close consultation with stakeholders, might have generated as much or more revenue from cost recovery than has been realized and provided the basis for better managed, transparent regulation.

When the PMRA was being established there was an opportunity to undertake an independent, comprehensive, base-line analysis of the resources provided to the agency, as well as its management structures. This would have been useful for internal management purposes, including the introduction of cost recovery. Such an analysis might have provided stakeholders with some confidence that they knew exactly what they were being asked to pay for and how they could contribute to improved management. At the same time, the PMRA would have had an opportunity to identify the resources needed to equip the agency with a solid scientific capability and to explain to stakeholders and others concerned why they were essential to effective and efficient regulation.

The specific rationale for cost recovery for the PMRA (rather than the government's generic approach with its prominent deficit reduction goal) could also have been developed as the starting point for consultations with stakeholders. This could have been done straightforwardly because the PRR review team had itself recommended the establishment of a cost-recovery regime. A good case can be made for charging applicants and registrants fees for the services associated with the processing of applications and for the benefits associated with registration – even without becoming mired in arguments about private good and public good. Independently of the commercial value of a pesticide registration, there is good reason to charge for the cost of processing applications. The potential commercial value of a pesticide registration provides the basis for user charges. Under current rules registration provides a substantial degree of exclusivity as well as a government 'guarantee,' that the product is safe when used as directed. The guarantee is valuable, not only domestically but also in the export of goods treated with pesticides.

Finally, the range of possible approaches to cost-recovery charges might have been expanded to include approaches used successfully in the United Kingdom and Australia, among other OECD countries, that charge registrants a small percentage of their sales revenues.

The foregoing observations are not put forward as a critique of how the PMRA implemented cost recovery. Like many other agencies, the PMRA's efforts to introduce cost recovery were caught in larger political conflicts over which it could not be expected to have much influence. The observations are intended to illustrate that cost recovery can be an appropriate source of funding for the agency, and that cultivating effective relations with stakeholders is an essential ingredient to a successful cost-recovery scheme.

In the final analysis, if the PMRA is to have an adequately funded science base, the nature of that base needs to be defined more clearly than it has been to date. For example, given the recent and anticipated progress in international harmonization, what sort of in-house scientific expertise does the PMRA need to fulfil its mandate now and in the future? What sort of outside expertise can it enlist or buy to support its goals? What is the best way to ensure an adequate level of expertise over the longer term? What role should the PMRA seek to play domestically and internationally to ensure that it has access to the scientific and other expertise it needs to fulfil its health and environmental protection mandate? In particular, how should it seek to influence domestic and international research agendas? These are examples of questions that tend to get buried under the weight of daily operational pressures, stakeholder tensions, and trying to meet the payroll. They are also questions that scientific regulators have preferred not to debate outside their own community. Such a debate is likely to be essential in addressing the science deficit discussed in Chapter 1.

Conclusions: The Resilience of Science in Pesticide Regulation

This chapter has argued that the forces for change associated with the Pesticide Registration Review and international harmonization that have strengthened the Pest Management Regulatory Agency's science foundation. The PRR was an important force in making pesticide regulation more transparent. Transparency offers the possibility of demonstrating publicly the importance of science in identifying risks to health and the environment, assessing their severity against established reference points, and taking action to manage the risks.

The efficiency associated with international harmonization liberates scientific resources that might otherwise be applied to needless replication and tends to support higher, rather than lower standards of health and environmental protection. It remains to be seen whether international harmonization will evolve further towards the recognition of some foreign regulatory decisions.

Cost recovery, as it has been applied generally within the federal government and specifically within the PMRA, appears to be more of a threat than a support to good service. The pressure for efficiency associated with cost recovery can support an effective allocation of scientific resources, but if the basic level of resources for scientific activities is under constant threat, the quality of science is bound to deteriorate. The answer, however, is not necessarily to increase appropriations; funding for it could come from cost-recovery revenues.

A fundamental question is what kind of expertise does the PMRA need? Developments over the past decade or so suggest that the PMRA's tendency is to operate along the lines of the older model discussed in Chapter 3. This suggests that PMRA's answer would be characterized by a high priority accorded to maintaining a sizeable, high-quality, in-house scientific staff capable of addressing the growing and increasingly complex range of scientific issues associated with pesticide regulation. A lower priority would be attached to expertise in economic analysis, public consultation, and the management of external scientific expertise.

The way in which the federal pesticide regulatory system has changed over the past decade or so supports the maxim that bureaucratic institutions cannot reform themselves. The main forces for change – the Pesticide Registration Review, international harmonization, and cost recovery – all originated from outside the federal pesticide regulatory system and were all initially resisted by senior pesticide regulators. The external shock administered to the system by the Alachlor Review Board process, keenly felt by senior pesticide regulators, did not seem to be perceived as a harbinger of the coming change. This suggests that some of the general forces described in Chapter 1 did not have much impact on the former pesticide regulatory system and have not yet made a strong impact on the PMRA.

Such general forces are not, of course, criteria for evaluating the quality of pesticide regulatory staff nor of their overall effectiveness. There is good reason to believe that Canadian pesticide regulators rank high internationally in terms of their scientific expertise. Moreover, compared with other regulatory regimes that protect our health and environment, the small number of significant pesticide-related problems in Canada in recent years suggests that the approach to regulation adopted by the PMRA and its predecessors has met its principal goals.

References

Bosso, Christopher J. (1987). *Pesticides and Politics: The Life Cycle of a Public Issue*. Pittsburgh: University of Pittsburgh Press.
– (1988). 'Transforming Adversaries into Collaborators: Interest groups and the Regulation of Chemical Pesticides.' *Policy Sciences*, 21(2): 224–36.
Canada. (1995). House of Commons Standing Committee on Environment and Sustainable Development. *It's about Your Health! Towards Pollution Prevention*. Ottawa: Public Works and Government Services Canada.
Castrilli, J.F., and T. Vigod. (1987). *Pesticides in Canada: An Examination of Federal Law and Public Policy*. Ottawa: Law Reform Commission of Canada.
Hill, Margaret. (1994). 'The Choice of Mode for Regulation: A Case Study of the Canadian Pesticide Registration Review 1988–1992.' PhD dissertation, Department of Political Science, Carleton University.
Hoberg, Jr, George. (1990). 'Risk, Science and Politics: Alachlor Regulation in Canada and the United States.' *Canadian Journal of Political Science*, 13(2): 116–29.
Indian and Northern Affairs Canada. (1997). *Canadian Arctic Contaminants Assessment Report*. Ottawa: Minister of Public Works and Government Services.
Leiss, William, and C. Chociolko. (1994). *Risk and Responsibility*. Montreal: McGill-Queen's University Press.
Pesticide Registration Review Team. (1990). *Recommendations for a Revised Federal Pest Management Regulatory System: Final Report of the Pesticide Registration Review Team* (PRR Report). Ottawa: Minister of Supply and Services.
Pest Management Regulatory Agency (PMRA). (1997). *Guidance Document on Pest Control Product Cost Recovery Fees*. Ottawa: Health Canada.
– (1998). *Registration Handbook for Pest Control Products under the Pest Control Products Act and Regulations*. Ottawa: Health Canada.
Pest Management Secretariat. (1994). *Government Proposal for the Pest Management Regulatory System*. (Government Proposal). Ottawa: Pest Management Secretariat.
Salter, Liora, (1988). *Mandated Science*. Boston: Kluwer.
Versteeg, Hajo. (1992). *A Case Study in Multi-Stakeholder Consultation: The Corporate History of the Federal Pesticide Registration Review or How We Got There from Here*, vols. 1 and 2. Ottawa: Canadian Centre for Management Development.

11 Fisheries and Oceans Canada: Science and Conservation

DANIEL E. LANE

This chapter examines the role of science in the regulatory regime of the Department of Fisheries and Oceans (DFO) Canada with a focus on its Science Branch. Science-based regulation in fisheries refers to the direct use of the knowledge and research provided by research scientists, biologists, and technicians within DFO trained in diverse disciplines related to marine, freshwater, and oceanographic analysis of Canada's ocean and freshwater resources. This scientific capacity is required to carry out the mandate of the department, as embodied in the Fisheries Act of Canada, for the conservation and sustainability of Canada's marine and coastal resources that are exploited commercially and for recreational use.

The chapter presents three major thrusts in its analysis of DFO's science-based regulation of Canada's fisheries resources: (1) recent controversies in the role of science in DFO; (2) the evolution of change within DFO regarding the development and use of scientific advice; and (3) the changing nature of commercial fisheries regulation and its effect on the institutional structure of DFO.

Recent controversies and concerns about the regulation of the fisheries in Canada have centred on Canada's scientific capacity for 'managing the oceans' and the independence of science from operational decision making and political bureaucracy. These controversies raise a number of issues about how science-based fisheries regulators function and how they might be organized in a more effective manner that is consistent with transparency and public trust (Viscusi, 1998).

Crises in the status of fisheries resources, domestic and worldwide, have precipitated a rethinking among fisheries scientists regarding their fundamental methodology and approach to assessing the status of fish resources. This rethinking has resulted in a broadening of DFO science into wider views of interdisciplinary systems approaches, risk management, and precautionary approaches to decision making under uncertainty.

Fish stock collapses and the coincident fiscal crises of the mid-1990s in all areas of government services have engendered more interdependence and a demand for increased participation in decision making among DFO clientele (fishermen, processing companies, non-governmental organizations or NGOs, the oceans industry, and the public), who are now subject to increased fees and significant change in the application of regulatory services by the DFO.

Overall, this chapter provides a critique of the practice of science within the Department of Fisheries and Oceans with respect to: the use of stakeholder information, client cooperation, and compliance with regulations; approaches to risk assessment, risk management, and the communication of scientific advice; changes in the funding and efficiency of DFO scientific research; and the adequacy and accountability of the DFO's scientific and technical capacity to provide the best available scientific information and advice in a timely fashion.

The chapter is organized into five parts. First, the mandate of the DFO is reviewed. Second, recent issues in science and policy are presented. The third section examines the peer review process and fisheries decision making. The penultimate section notes organizational aspects of fisheries science within DFO. Conclusions follow regarding the anticipated evolution of fisheries science and fisheries regulation in DFO.

Mandate, Structure, and Functions of the DFO

According to departmental documents, the broad objectives of the DFO are to undertake policies and programs in support of Canada's economic, ecological, and scientific interests in the oceans and inland waters; to provide for the conservation, development, and sustainable economic utilization of Canada's fisheries resources in marine and inland waters for those who derive their livelihood or benefit from these resources; to provide safe, effective, and environmentally sound marine services responsive to the needs of Canadians in a global economy; and to coordinate the policies and programs of the Government of Canada respecting oceans' (Canada, 1998b: 6). The mandate of the DFO is enunciated in the Fisheries Act of Canada. The Fisheries

Act first became law in 1868 and for over 125 years has provided the Canadian government with policy goals in the management of renewable water resources. These goals, broadly stated (Laubstein, 1987) are the conservation of Canada's fish resources, the development of commercially viable Canadian fisheries, and the distribution of fish resources among Canadians who benefit from these resources.

The Fisheries Act is currently under revision with significant changes being proposed under Bill C-62 (Canada, 1998a). The current legislation is interpreted by the DFO and its minister into operational policies. These policies are carried out through the mechanisms of scientific research programs; stock assessment; maintenance of habitat and other measures for stock conservation and growth; the determination of annual total allowable catch (TAC) limits; the suballocation of the TAC into harvesting rights for licensed fishermen through annual management plans; subsidization programs for disadvantaged fisheries workers and their families; and the operational management (that is dockside and at-sea monitoring and enforcement of regulations) of the fishery throughout the fishing season.

The Fisheries Act of Canada is a powerful piece of legislation. Under its auspices, the minister of fisheries and oceans retains the ultimate authority and responsibility for decision making on all matters pertaining to the conservation and protection of the resource. In the words of Senator John Stewart of the Senate Committee on Fisheries and Oceans: 'My impression is that the Minister of Fisheries within his jurisdiction has more power than any other minister of the Crown, certainly more than the Minister of Agriculture. He has all these species. It is an industry. He is running a socioeconomic system. By reason of the way that the department evolved, I wonder if some of the ministers were ever fully seized of what a tremendously big responsibility has been imposed on them, but I am saying the department has not had a chance to perform the job which we think it ought to have performed, because the task was never properly defined' (Canada, 1998c: 5:17).

In attempts to meet its broad mandate, fisheries management in Canada has historically been driven by biological considerations resulting from the human impacts of stock exploitation for economic gain. The post–Second World War activities of government-led fisheries science agencies, in response to the need for more precise information about renewed exploitation, was to expand the existing scientific research infrastructure. The result, evident in many developed nations including Canada, is the existence of centrally controlled, publicly funded, fisheries agencies with major emphasis on the scientific research function (Anderson, 1988).

Since 1977, and the extended jurisdiction of coastal nations' fishing zones, Canada assumed greater responsibility for offshore marine resources (MacRae, 1980). On the Atlantic, in response to this increased responsibility, the Canadian Atlantic Fisheries Scientific Advisory Committee (CAFSAC) was established 'as a forum for appropriate scientific debate on methodology and the development of scientific advice' (Canada, 1978). CAFSAC inherited its management system from the International Commission for the Northwest Atlantic Fisheries (ICNAF) founded in 1950 through the joint efforts of the United States, the United Kingdom, and Canada. ICNAF was the first international fisheries agreement to specify conservation objectives (for example, maximum sustained catches), along with a slate of conservation measures to achieve them (for example, closed areas, size limits, gear restrictions, and total catch limits). Measures to achieve management objectives were made 'on the basis of scientific investigations' (ICNAF, 1968), and biological research was to be used as the sole basis of recommendations (for example, on total catch limits) to the international members. Economic, social, or political considerations were not permitted to influence the scientific advice (Iles, 1980). In later years, the effectiveness of the existing regulatory measures were challenged by arguing that scientific investigations should allow not only for biological-based analysis, but also for economic and technical considerations in decision making (Templeman and Gulland, 1965).

Fisheries science is defined as the application of science including biological research to fisheries problems (Wooster and Miller, 1988). Fisheries science is synonymous with fisheries biology (Magnuson, 1991) and has been characterized by the disciplines of fish biology (and ecology) and population ecology (stock assessment, resource evaluation). These disciplines have established a large literature and a strong scientific methodology. The employment of professionals in this field (mainly in the public service) is in the tens of thousands worldwide, and in North America has approximately doubled in each decade since 1940. The field is supported by several major international organizations, including the International Council for the Exploration of the Sea (ICES) established in 1902 and based in Copenhagen, Denmark; the North Atlantic Fisheries Organization

(NAFO) established in 1978 and headquartered in Dartmouth, Nova Scotia; the Fisheries Committees of the Food and Agricultural Organization (FAO) of the United Nations (based in Rome since 1951); and the Society for Conservation Biology, to name but a few. As well, there are hosts of national fisheries science organizations, for example, the American Fisheries Society established in 1870 and based in Bethesda, Maryland, since 1971, and the Australian Society for Fish Biology. In Canada, the Canadian Conference for Fisheries Research (CCFFR) holds annual conferences attracting academic and professional marine and fisheries scientists from across the country. Scientists at DFO play a significant role in international fisheries science bodies such as ICES and NAFO. There are also more than 120 relevant academic and professional journals linked to fisheries science (Royce, 1984).

Apart from fisheries science, other activities of the DFO include fisheries strategic policy and economic planning, operations and management (industry liaison, and monitoring and enforcement), corporate services, and since 1996–7, the Canadian Coast Guard. Fisheries operations or fisheries management are dependent on scientific advice above all other considerations in the decision-making exercise. The fisheries management focus is more directly associated with the regulation function. Fisheries operations are tasked with the design, justification, and administrative control of fisheries systems (Hilborn and Walters, 1992; Parsons, 1993). It deals with the interaction between the resource and its use. Fisheries operations, in contrast to fisheries science, has not developed a standardized methodology.

DFO operations management activities tend to be staffed by 'mobicentric' civil servants. In short, they tend to move horizontally among other government departments without necessarily acquiring career ties to the fisheries agencies. Science staff, on the other hand, with their highly specialized training in biological techniques and research, are much less mobile. Consequently, there is maintenance of stability, corporate memory, and growth within the science branch that is not prevalent in other branches of the DFO. Although movement across functions within the fisheries organization is encouraged, it is minimized by the narrow disciplinary knowledge base that defines each functional group. Figure 11.1 presents a summarized version of the Department of Fisheries and Oceans of Canada organizational chart (not including the Canadian Coast Guard, amalgamated with DFO in 1996–7).

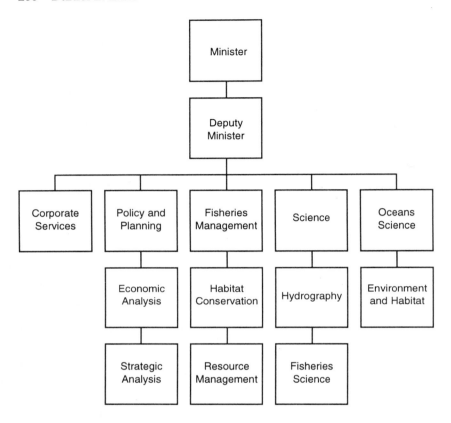

Figure 11.1 Simplified Department of Fisheries and Oceans organizational chart defined along five functional disciplinary lines (excluding Coast Guard)

DFO is a decentralized federal government department whose organizational structure is characterized by a functional arrangement of a fisheries institutions built historically along disciplinary lines. DFO has one assistant deputy minister for each functional area (that is, science, policy, fisheries management, oceans, and corporate affairs) responsible for eleven 'business lines' corresponding to the priorities and goals of the department. These priorities include:

• Conservation – managing and protecting fisheries resources

Table 11.1. Annual resource profile, main estimates of budget (000s $) and personnel (FTEs)

Branch	Budget 92–3	Budget 93–4	Budget 94–5	Budget 95–6	Budget 96–7[a]	Budget 97–8[a]	Budget 98–9[a]	Ave (SD) % 92–8
Science[b]	229	205	196	213	211	178	191	26(3)
Operations	304	481	310	481	325	224	203	41(7)
Policy	30	41	53	11	4	78	27	5(3)
Corporate	227	229	217	192	274	170	203	28(4)
Totals	791	956	775	897	815	650	769	100

	FTEs 92–3	FTEs 93–4	FTEs 94–5	FTEs 95–6	FTEs 97–8[a]	FTEs 98–9[a]	Ave(SD) % 92–8
Science[b]	2210	2133	2010	2145	1948	1916	37(3)
Operations	2597	2506	2619	2499	1423	1367	38(6)
Policy	138	229	280	86	–	–	2(2)
Corporate	1208	1207	1101	1097	1403	1341	22(5)
Totals	6182	6075	6010	5827	4574	4624	100

Note: FTEs are full-time equivalent positions.
[a]Does not include Canadian Coast Guard.
[b]'Oceans,' a separate functional area since the 1998–9 fiscal year, is included in 'Science.'
Source: Fisheries and Oceans Annual Estimates, 1992–3 to 1998–9.

- Habitat protection – contributing to the protection of the marine and freshwater environment
- Scientific research – understanding the oceans and aquatic resources
- Safety – maintaining marine safety
- Sustainable maritime industries – facilitating maritime commerce and ocean development.

The impact of federal Program Review and downsizing can be seen in Table 11.1 taken from annual main spending estimates for DFO. Although the annual budget of the department has been negatively affected in recent years, it is noteworthy from Table 11.1 that the Science Branch has been able to maintain a relatively fixed share of total budgets and human resources (as measured by FTEs or full-time equivalent positions in the department) throughout the period since 1992 when other activities were more severely affected.

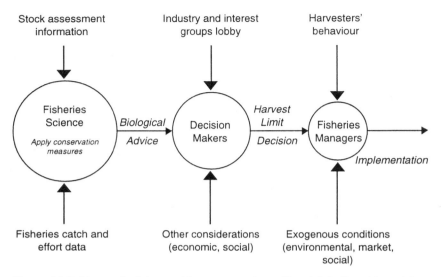

Figure 11.2 Linear decision-making process for setting total allowable catch (TAC).
Source: Lane and Stephenson (1995).

Recent Issues in Science and Policy

This section describes recent issues affecting DFO, in particular as they relate to the Science Branch of the organization. These issues include (1) the place of science in the governance and decision-making process of the department, (2) the methodology and application of science in practice, (3) the public debate over the control and use of science, and (4) the accountability of the science branch towards meeting the regulatory goals of the department.

Governance and Decision Making

The decision-making processes of fisheries management within the department mimics the disciplinary structure of the organization. The influence diagram of Figure 11.2 illustrates a simplified version of the decision-making process for setting annual TACs for commercially exploited stocks (primarily groundfish). This process, especially prior to 1993, has been characterized as a linear, reductionist decision-making process, whereby each of the participants contribute independently to the final decision (Lane and Stephenson, 1995). Since 1993 many groundfish stocks, now reviewed at arm's-length by the Fisheries Resource Conservation Council (FRCC) in Atlantic Canada, are managed under moratoria.

As long as the conflicting goals of stock sustainability and commercially viable exploitation are satisfied, the operation and equilibrium of the fisheries decision process are not challenged. Eventually, conflicts can be expected to arise in this system from exogenous factors that directly affect the stock status, the economic viability status, or both simultaneously. When a relatively stable situation is disturbed, conflicts arise, and trade-offs *must* occur between stock conservation and socioeconomic viability.

In the late 1970s, after extended jurisdiction and the promise of abundance that followed, the fisheries in Canada experienced unprecedented growth (Munro, 1980). This period culminated in the global economic malaise of the early 1980s with high interest rates, rising costs, and rampant inflation. The fisheries crisis of this period had nothing to do with stock status and everything to do with sector economic performance (Kirby, 1982). A decade later, in 1992, the crisis was one of stock collapse. In such instances, the participants in this system converge on the minister as the ultimate authority to influence the conservation versus exploitation trade-off in one direction or another, all with equally valid positions. Once this political conflict mechanism has been triggered, the pressure on the system will not likely dissipate even in the event that the system returns to a more generally acceptable equilibrium.

Traditionally, achieving policy and regulatory goals in DFO were dependent on command and control regulation based on scientific advice through a significant and centrally located science branch with headquarters in Ottawa – at a significant distance away from both coasts. As a consequence of Program Review and the associated Treasury Board edicts, a new approach characterized by 'alternative service delivery' and 'partnerships' has arisen that has eroded the command approach (Shane, 1998). These concepts are expressed in the Fisheries Act changes proposed in Bill C62 (Canada, 1998a).

Market-based approaches involve some privatization through property rights (for example, individual quotas) and deregulation of some services. As well, an array of arrangements between the regulators and stakeholder participants also develops including more diverse methods of funding regulators through fees for service and contracts and monitoring and auditing by third parties. The privatization issue is one of great concern in Canadian fisheries. Canada has been unable to decide – from the policy level down to the grass-roots local community level – whether or not the fisheries are essentially a business venture or predominantly a regional social welfare scheme. At the present time, the Senate of Canada and the Standing Committee on Fisheries and Oceans is writing its report on privatization and quotas in fisheries. The House of Commons Committee is similarly reviewing proposed changes to the Fisheries Act and holding highly charged political discussions on the pros and cons of alternative fisheries management regimes. Finally, the minister is dealing with a recent lawsuit by inshore (fixed gear) fishermen who claim that quotas now awarded to nearly 50 per cent of active fishermen on the Atlantic are outside the jurisdiction of the minister under the prevailing Fisheries Act and should therefore be ruled illegal.

On the positive side, the market-based approaches invite enhanced participation by stakeholders and a desire to attain increased responsibility for individual actions. However, for DFO, these implied changes in governance carry no formal responsibility accruing to fisheries participants. Instead, the ultimate authority for the conservation and protection of fisheries resources remains with the minister. Until such time as this incompatibility of partnerships without responsibility is resolved, the minister and the department will remain open to attack from all sources. Consequently, stakeholders' pleas continue for the government's need to define the exact definition of partnerships for delivery and implementation of operational policy.

The Role of Science

Federal fisheries science-based regulation refers to a group of regulators who rely on objective scientific and technical expertise to (a) set standards and develop operational rules; (b) handle and assess individual cases or applications within such rules or standards; and (c) ensure overall compliance. For changes to the existing scientific approaches to occur, it is necessary to know how the science is acquired and used.

In the free-spending expansionary days of the early 1970s, in the then newly formed Department of Fisheries and Oceans under Minister Roméo Leblanc, scientific research activities were funded freely through unencumbered A-base funding. These funds enabled DFO scientists a large degree of freedom to define their own programs of work in much the same way that university professors carry out their independent research activities. B-base funding, or contract work for a third party, carries with it the stigma of working for fees on issues that may not be purely objective, for example, waterway approval in environmental assessments for oil or lumber companies.

In the 1990s the process of Program Review in 1993–4 and the need to consolidate funding and cut spending by government departments eroded the earlier freedom of extensive A-base funding. DFO science directorates and individual research scientists became a much more dependent (like their counterparts in the universities) on fees for service than ever before. To an entire generation of senior scientists who shunned practical encumbrances, this 'prostitution of science' has been a bitter experience and one that detractors have been quick to add has a detrimental impact on doing real or pure science.

The stock catastrophes that have closed down a large proportion of the Atlantic groundfishery since 1992, and the difficult circumstances today with the Pacific salmon fishery, have left the science community and the public reeling in efforts to understand the complexities that led to these unexpected disasters. In very recent years, science has embarked on research into studying full ecosystem effects in order to understand environmental impacts on stock status. As well, the undetected nature of apparent abrupt environmental change has led science to a revised analytical methodology that embraces uncertainty and risk in decision making. Internationally, the concept of the precautionary approach has been considered as a solution to dealing with the stochastic variation of fisheries systems (Garcia, 1996). This methodology has been evolving for several years, yet a clear notion of the operational concept of the precautionary approach has not generally been described.

The poor record of compliance to fishing rules and regulations has also been a difficult lesson for Canadian policy makers. The courts, as the policy interpreters, have been unclear on the orientation of the right versus the privilege of fishing. In many cases, and despite evidence to the contrary, the courts have been sympathetic to the independent fishermen portrayed as scratching out a living on the inhospitable coastline versus the awesome bureaucratic presence of the policing DFO. In response, revisions to the Fisheries Act emphasize exercising the minister's power of issuing licences in questions of non-compliance. As well, boards of arbitration – rather than the criminal courts – involving representatives of the fishery are tasked with assigning penalties to alleged violators.

Finally, the separation of science from operations management in the institutional arrangement (Figure 11.1) makes it very difficult for science to develop an integrated, multidisciplinary regulatory policy. The science-led stock assessment process stands out as an example of the need for further integration. Currently, assessments are carried out annually on fish stocks on the basis of research vessel surveys and aggregated commercial landings data. This process is crucial to the scientific advice for determining global catch limits on stocks, however, it does not integrate the wealth of fishermen's data and observations at a different scale corresponding to the spatial–temporal definition of the fish harvest activity.

Science and Bureaucracy

Questions of who carries out fisheries science, and the degree to which the research is accepted and/or challenged towards building fisheries policy, have become major issues in DFO science circles. In 1996–7, when the Canadian Coast Guard became part of DFO, the department reorganized into five distinct autonomous regions: Pacific, Central and Arctic, Newfoundland, Laurentian, and the Maritimes. The regions inherited the responsibility for scientific advice on fish stocks within their region. Previously, scientists from the entire 'zone,' that is, the complement of coastal regions, got together in peer review to analyse, discuss, and develop consensus on stocks status.

In 1998, the scientific evaluation of cod stocks in southern Newfoundland (in NAFO geographical division denoted as 3Ps) hit a snag when there was a conflict of opinion between Newfoundland scientists and other zonal scientists. That spring a 'zonal meeting' among fisheries scientists was convened to assess and make recommendations on the 3Ps cod stocks. Newfoundland scientists who prepared the stock assessments for presentation at the meeting were confounded by highly variable stock status indicators. These indicators were interpreted optimistically, spurred on by pressures from local fishing interests to reopen stocks that were felt to be relatively plentiful from their on-the-water observations. However, a second group of institutional scientists were adamant that the optimistic interpretation of the data was essentially incorrect and that more conservative measures should be applied. This regionalization of science signalled a breakdown in the processes of peer review and consensus building. Consequently, the recommendations to the minister were held up to the point that all parties involved clearly suspected that something was awry. In the end, the regional science view prevailed in the compromise position that was ultimately presented by the minister. However, it is not clear what impact the internal debate has had on the future development of scientific consensus on stock status.

On the issue of the relevance of scientific research, events played out recently in the Canadian media regarding science and politics (Hutchings et al., 1997a, 1997b; Doubleday et al., 1997; Healy, 1997) have signalled a schism among the science community within DFO and even further afield. Hutchings et al., called for a new institutional structure that would remove fisheries science from alleged 'political and bureaucratic influence in government fisheries science' (1997a: 1198). They reported particular cases where senior science managers allegedly misinterpreted scientific work in order to appease their political taskmasters to the detriment of stock conservation.

In the cases in question, there have been suggestions for removing the fisheries science branch completely from its bureaucratic environment to create a completely separate and independent (from public policy decision making) body that would carry out pure science and act uniquely on the issue of stock conservation. Typical responses of this type have been termed 'the republic of science' by its dissenters. The empirical evidence prior to and since the recommendations of the Lamontagne Committee on science policy in Canada (Lamontagne, 1973) indicates that the Canadian public may not be well served by such a costly, non-coordinated arrangement (de la Mothe and Paquet, 1994). It is difficult to imagine that the current public appetite for a freely funded 'republic of fisheries science' would be an option.

The Summit of the Sea held in St John's, Newfoundland, 3 to 10 September 1997, provided a global perspective on the importance of our oceans. The penultimate session, as a last-minute addition to the summit, was titled 'Forum on Fisheries Science in Relation to Fisheries Management.' It promised to bring to a head the raging debate carried on in the media maelstrom surrounding the Hutchings et al. (1997a) article about the place of science in fisheries decision making. In the end, the great debate fizzled. While scientists tend to be polarized in the call for independence of researchers from 'managers,' the practical aspects of scientific advice and timely decision making are necessary requirements for ongoing and effective management of our fisheries. It is instructive in the context of the extremely complex, uncertain, and interdisciplinary environment of the fisheries to consider systemic options for integrating – not further isolating – science into the practical realm.

Accountability and Review in Science

The concepts of public trust and transparency are tied to basic forms of accountability, the publication of relevant and timely information, and opportunities for participation by stakeholders and citizens. These are also linked to the issue of managing risk and communication of advice to clients in need of the information.

This issue follows from the recent performance of fisheries science connected to the groundfish collapses of the Northwest Atlantic. Similar difficulties experienced worldwide have prompted fisheries scientists to make efforts to embrace the uncertain environment for estimating stock status in which they operate. This includes well-established methodologies for the assessment of risk (Smith et al., 1993; Lane and Stephenson, 1998) and the operationalization of the precautionary approach. While these initiatives are important and overdue, they are being treated as the purview of the fisheries science function and principally stock assessment estimation. It is important to integrate these procedures within the multiple objectives of the fishery to provide the appropriate balance required for effective decision making. The adoption of stochastic modelling methods will demand an extension to existing data requirements according to a much less aggregated procedure than is currently practised. These data needs will take the form of local observations about the fishery conforming to models at a disaggregated scale of spatial–temporal definition. The collection of such data will require the direct participation of fish harvesters and processors, and in so doing will provide them with further opportunity to contribute to the management of the fishery.

Recent reports of the Senate Committee on Fisheries and Oceans, the House of Commons Committee, and the Fisheries Resource Conservation Council continually point out the need for more participation of, and communication to, stakeholders of science-based information. In turn, this increased participation will induce a willingness to understand how science is being used for decision-making purposes. Consequently, the shift of modelling practice from aggregate, deterministic, 'black box' approaches to smaller-scale, spatial–temporal, probabilistic models will strengthen the feedback and accountability link from DFO to stakeholders.

Peer Review and Decision Making in DFO Science

In fisheries, science-based regulation is dependent on the direct use of the knowledge and research supplied by fisheries scientists and technical personnel from diverse scientific disciplines. Thus, for the DFO, science is central to both the older model of traditional science-based regulation and to the integrated risk management model. However, as the above issues point out, there are serious questions within DFO regarding (1) the funding for DFO science; (2) the use and interpretation of the scientific advice by decision makers; (3) the appropriateness of the scale of scientific research and its integration with other fisheries considerations; and (4) making scientific information accountable to management results.

Central to all of these points is the process of scientific peer review. The dismantling of CAFSAC in 1992 and the regionalization of the department since 1996 have disrupted the well-established institutional arrangements across the Atlantic region to carry on the scientific peer review process. As a consequence, and noting as well, the context of media and public pressure for more openness, stock collapse, and Program Review, the peer review process itself is in danger of breaking down. In spite of the schism in science as a result of the alleged bureaucratic muddling within DFO by so-called science managers, insiders and critics unanimously support the peer review process and the sanctity of the consensus position arising from open debate. However, the calls by the critics for further independence from science suggest that the public should act as the mediator in the interpretation of scientific information. This idea, critics believe, would protect the scientist from bureaucratic manoeuvring and pass on the responsibility of decision making to a higher court, for example, the minister. Given the recent events of the 3Ps stock evaluation, and the imagined shouting matches among science directors regarding the polarized view of appropriate advice, it is clear that institutional guidelines are required to restore peace between the warring science factions and re-establish the primacy of the peer review process and the consensus position.

In the traditional model of fisheries science, science is supreme. In the new governance model, science is paramount but not supreme. The call for renewed independence of fisheries science (that is, budgetary independence as well as independence from bureaucracy) is a reaction against this inevitable shift. Rather, the decision-making process must learn how to integrate DFO science with other related fields (for example, socioeconomics and administrative efficiencies). There are two aspects to this adjustment: (a) the development of an integrated framework for decision making in fisheries management, and (b) an institutional arrangement in support of integrated decision making.

In making decisions to resolve fisheries management problems, the process must follow the logical steps of a structured decision-making approach. This process treats complex problems in a structured way by detailing: (1) the problem definition, specific objectives and constraining factors, (2) the generation of alternatives for problem resolution, (3) the evaluation of the potential effectiveness of alternative decisions in relation to the stated mission of the organization, and (4) tracking and feedback response to the actual versus anticipated impacts of the implemented decisions (Lane and Stephenson, 1995). The following paragraphs outline these major elements of the fisheries management decision problem.

The fisheries management system is complex. It includes (1) the fish stocks of interest and the ecosystem and physical environment in which they exist; (2) description of the fishery sector and the dynamics of fishing and processing operations; (3) social implications of the fishing sector including income and community impacts; and (4) fisheries administration and the costs of management. In order to manage this complex system, controllable elements of the system must be differentiated from uncontrollable elements, that is, outside the realm of management.

Controllable elements of the fishery system include those variables that may be manipulated as direct or indirect controls on the system, for example, decisions on annual aggregate TACs, gear and vessel quota suballocations, the capacity and type of fishing effort and intensity, temporal and spatial distributions of harvesting (for example, area closures and gear restrictions), and measures designed to improve or restore ecosystem health and habitat enhancement.

System elements that are uncontrollable include exogenous environmental effects, dynamic predator-prey interrelationships, annual stock-recruitment behaviour, natural mortality, intraseasonal stock distribution (migration patterns), stock interannual growth, catastrophic events, political expediencies and agenda, and exogenous market impacts.

In general terms, the problem facing decision makers is how to use the controllable elements of the fisheries system in order to achieve specified anthropocentric, value-based objectives within the confines of system constraints, for example, resource sustainability.

Fortunately, the complexity of the system guarantees that there will be many alternative options for developing fisheries management decisions through the manipulation of controllable elements. The challenge of decision analysis is in the creative development and evaluation of these alternatives. This requires an integrated multidisciplinary perspective. Moreover, in the context of changing, dynamic settings, and in the interest of strategic, long-term sustainability, decision makers must commit to continuous improvement from examining the impacts of past decisions. This requires a commitment for the monitoring and feedback of results into future decision making and ongoing adjustment and tuning of decisions towards meeting clearly specified management objectives.

Current conditions and prespecified restrictions contribute to defining system constraints. In particular, biological considerations that quantify and define 'conservation,' and explicitly take into account limits on the rate of stock growth, represent constraining factors in the fisheries system problem (Wooster, 1988). Biological constraints are primary to the fisheries management decision problem, and their determination constitutes a major role for fisheries science. Decisions that do not achieve prespecified targets will require an adjustment to be made in the direction and our understanding of the ability to manage the stock. Conversely, decisions that achieve the milestones and strategic targets would be evaluated as successful.

Figure 11.3 illustrates the dynamics of a decision-making process designed to take into account important integrated aspects of the system. This process features the activities of the management team in developing and evaluating decision alternatives and in tracking the anticipated versus actual results of past decisions taken.

The participants in fisheries decision making include the fishing industry (harvesters and processors), government central agency representatives (including fisheries scientists, economists, fisheries management officials, and fisheries officers), community stakeholders, and other interested parties (environmental agencies and non-

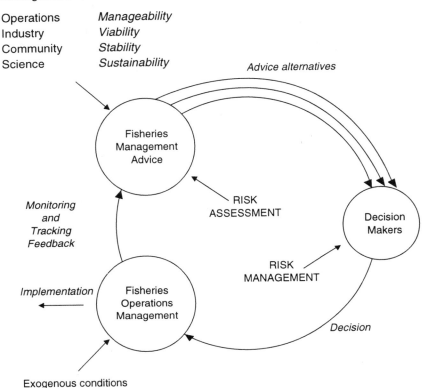

Management team

Operations   *Manageability*
Industry   *Viability*
Community   *Stability*
Science   *Sustainability*

Advice alternatives

Fisheries
Management
Advice

RISK
ASSESSMENT

Decision
Makers

*Monitoring
and
Tracking
Feedback*

Implementation

Fisheries
Operations
Management

RISK
MANAGEMENT

Decision

Exogenous conditions

Figure 11.3 Management team decision-making process (adapted from
Lane and Stephenson, 1995).

governmental interest groups). The diverse constituencies of these groups
must contribute to, and be represented in, policy setting at the strategic (longer term) as well as at the operational (intraseasonal) level.

Institutional Arrangements

Institutional reform has begun in DFO as part of larger developments
in the reinvention of government since Program Review. The DFO
must adapt to updated scientific methodologies to incorporate uncer-

tainty (dated methodology); a more demanding customer base (now being asked to pay for services as part of cost-recovery programs through increases in licensing fees, and fees for operations services, such as dockside monitoring or the observers' program); and pressure by the public (including the environmental lobby) to become more accountable for managing resources (fisheries catastrophes and high profile media reporting).

DFO as a function-based organization (Figure 11.1) with its associated linear decision process (Figure 11.2) is a flawed arrangement when it comes to dealing with the highly interdisciplinary, complex problems associated with the fishery. What is needed is to *construct* the new institution on the basis of what it must do to support effective interdisciplinary, real-time management, decision making, and conflict resolution, as described in Figure 11.3.

Organizations dedicated to the fisheries management process are defined by the formalized arrangements by which multiple parties share management functions and responsibilities. Within these arrangements there is a spectrum of stakeholder involvement, for example, from agency-dominated consultative organizations to formally empowered and participatory decision-making bodies (Sens and Neilsen, 1997). This is the manifestation of co-management through a generic form of industrial organization and formally defined and shared management roles of government and industry. Implementation of co-management organizations that are more than simply consultative requires considerable within-industry organization (Jentoft, 1989).

The organizational vision for the fisheries institution of the twenty-first century accounts for the interdisciplinary complexity of fisheries management. The organization must respond in an integrated fashion to the demand for interdisciplinary expertise. Such an organization will be constructed around the activities and output of the fishery itself. In as much as the fisheries operate on a regular, seasonal basis, management activities and interventions of the organization can only be expressed at the scale of in-season operations. Similarly, information from the fishery – and the in-season biological status of the ecosystem – can be attained at the level of ongoing seasonal harvesting. The role of in-season data collection is one responsibility that the fishing industry can coordinate and manage.

The DFO reorganization needs to be constructed from the bottom up, beginning with this lowest level of required decision making at the in-season level. Since the issues that arise at the lowest level in-

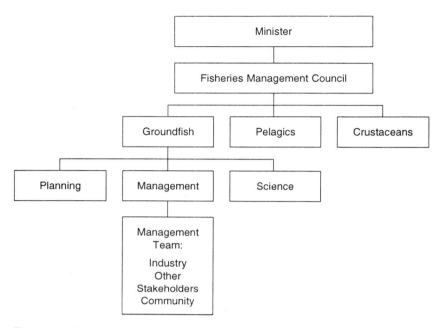

Figure 11.4 Fisheries management activity-based organizational structure with in-season decision making (Atlantic region).

volve the biology of fish stocks, the economics of the harvesting and processing sectors, the social structure, and administrative activities (for example, licensing and monitoring), then the organization must be composed of experts with the responsibility and autonomy to respond to these information needs in the context of each specific fishery. Figure 11.4 presents an example reorganization for the DFO constructed around the management of individual fisheries (for instance, groundfisheries, pelagic, and crustacean fisheries) and supported by dedicated, interdisciplinary management teams with joint expertise in science, planning, and fisheries management operations.

The organizational structure, as depicted in Figure 11.4, embeds the interdisciplinary decision-making arrangement through the existence of the management teams whose focus is on the issues and ongoing problems of each fishery. The management team in turn is responsible to a regional Fisheries Management Council, an independent decision-making body at arm's length from the minister of fisheries and oceans and made up of representatives from industry, NGOs, and civil servants in a decision support, advisory role (for example, the FRCC). It is the council, through the appropriate legislation, which would be ultimately responsible for the day-to-day decision making of the fishery and not the minister. The shift from a functional to an activity-based fishery management organization responds to the recognized need for more integration in fisheries management. A model of this kind is provided by the fast-moving high technology industry where autonomous, multidisciplinary project teams work together towards well-defined project objectives. Elsewhere, international institutions such as the OECD (1997) and ICES (1996) are investigating how to integrate all aspects of fisheries information into effective decision making for national and international fisheries issues. The Australian Fisheries Management Authority is a particularly good example of a legislated, industry-led fisheries management arrangement that has been successful (McColl and Stevens, 1997).

Conclusions

This chapter has traced recent developments in the transformation of fisheries science in the Department of Fisheries and Oceans from the traditional fisheries science-based regulation to a more participatory and integrated science-based management approach. It addressed in particular the need for change within DFO in several key areas. Regarding overall *governance*, the new Fisheries Act promises increased participation by stakeholders in regulation and decision-making issues. However, the minister of fisheries and oceans, backed by his extensive and predominantly science-based bureaucracy, retains ultimate authority over all issues related to stock conservation and protection. Real participation and enhanced responsibility by stakeholders can occur only with legislated autonomy to the regions and communities where fishing is most important.

The evolving role of science in DFO is requiring a more open, public scrutiny of the role and results of scientific research. This has forced fisheries science to extend its traditional methodology into the analysis of uncertainty and risk management approaches, systems integration, and multidisciplinary analyses. Scientific advice must become a more balanced component in a more widely peer reviewed process as an aid in fisheries management decision making. In the context of effective decision making, science must be more fully integrated in an activity-based institutional arrangement designed to support decision making and problem resolution in the fisheries. The existing separation of the Science Branch in DFO from other branches of the department is counterproductive to good fisheries management. Increased separation in the form of an independent fisheries science body would only further drive a wedge between scientists, social scientists, administrators, and the fishing industry, all of whom have a stake in and a potential contribution to make in improving management of our fishery resources. Furthermore, separation goes against the historical evidence in Canada and, more importantly, against the worldwide trend towards greater integration in fishery management.

Recent stock collapses such as those in the Atlantic fisheries have led some scientists and academics to state that fisheries simply cannot be managed (Ludwig et al., 1993). One reason for this view is that past science-based approaches have proven to be less than successful in attempts to meet unspecified goals. Alternatively, we can only know if we are capable of managing the fisheries through the coordinated activities of fisheries science, operations, and planning relative to specific dynamic targets for which decision makers are held accountable. This notion of management by objectives has never been effectively applied to fisheries and has kept the question of management capability an open one.

In brief, the DFO is one of the largest, most powerful ministries in the Canadian federal government. Today it is in a crisis stemming from its disciplinary organization and its inability to respond to the complex multidisciplinary management problems it faces. To survive, DFO must show a willingness to decentralize the command-and-control scientific regime and delegate real legislated authority and responsibility to its regional clientele.

References

Anderson, F. (1988). 'Policy Determination of Government Scientific Organisations: A Case Study of the Fisheries Research Board of Canada, 1963–1973.' PhD dissertation, L'Institut d'histoire et de socio-politique des sciences, Université de Montréal.

Canada. (1978). *Canadian Atlantic Fisheries Scientific Advisory Committee Annual Report 1977–1978*, vol. 1. Ottawa: Public Works and Government Services Canada.

- (1997). Canada's Oceans Act. http://habitat.pac.dfo.ca/mpa/OCEANS/ oacte.doc.
- (1998a). *Proposed Changes to the Fisheries Act.* http://www.ncr.dfo.ca/ communic/bill/c62/prov_e.htm.
- (1998b). 1989–1998 Estimates (Part III) Fisheries and Oceans. Ottawa: Public Works and Government Services Canada.
- (1998c). *Proceedings of the Standing Senate Committee on Fisheries,* issues no. 3 through 5. http://www.parl.gc.ca.

de la Mothe, J., and Paquet, G. (1994). 'Circumstantial Evidence: A Note on Science Policy in Canada. *Science and Public Policy,* 21(4): 261–8.

Doubleday, W.G., Atkinson, D.B., and Baird, J. (1997). 'Comment: Scientific Inquiry and Fish Stock Assessment in the Department of Fisheries and Oceans.' *Canadian Journal of Fisheries and Aquatic Sciences,* 54: 1422–6.

Garcia, S.M. (1996). 'The Precautionary Approach to Fisheries and Its Implications for Fishery Research, Technology, and Management: An Updated Review.' FAO Fisheries Technical Paper. 350/2. Rome: FAO.

Healy, M.C. (1997). 'Comment: The Interplay of Policy, Politics, and Science.' *Canadian Journal of Fisheries and Aquatic Sciences,* 54: 1427–9.

Hilborn, R., and Walters, C.J. (1992). *Quantitative Fisheries Stock Assessment: Choice, Dynamics, and Uncertainty.* New York: Chapman and Hall.

Hutchings, J.A., Walters, C.J., and Haedrich, R.L. (1997a). 'Is Scientific Inquiry Incompatible with Government Information Control?' *Canadian Journal of Fisheries and Aquatic Sciences,* 54: 1198–1210.

- (1997b). 'Reply: Scientific Inquiry and Fish Stock Assessment in the Department of Fisheries and Oceans.' *Canadian Journal of Fisheries and Aquatic Sciences,* 54: 1430–1.

International Commission of the Northwest Atlantic Fisheries (ICNAF). (1968). Report on the Working Group on Joint Biological and Economic Assessment of Conservation Actions. *Annual Proceedings of the International Commission of the Northwest Atlantic Fisheries 1966-1967,* 1794: 48-84.

Iles, D. (1980). 'The Natural History of Fisheries Management.' *Proceedings of the Nova Scotia Institute of Science,* 30: 3–19.

Jentoft, S. (1989). 'Fisheries Co-management: Delegating Government Responsibility to Fisheries Organizations. *Marine Policy,* April, 137–54.

Kirby, M. (1982). *Navigating Troubled Waters.* Report of the Task Force on Atlantic Fisheries. Government of Canada.

Lamontagne, M. (1973). *A Science Policy for Canada.* Report of the Special Committee on Science Policy, vol. 1, *A Critical Review: Past and Present.* Ottawa: Queen's Printer.

Lane, D.E., and Stephenson, R.L. (1995). 'Fisheries Management Science: The Framework to Link Biological, Economic, and Social Objectives in Fisheries Management.' *Aquatic Living Resources*, 8: 215–21.

– (1998). 'A Framework for Risk Analysis in Fisheries Decision-making.' *ICES Journal of Marine Science*, 55(1): 13–25.

Laubstein, K. (1987). 'Resource Allocation in Canadian Fisheries Management on the Atlantic Coast.' Department of Fisheries and Oceans Working Paper, September, Ottawa.

Ludwig, D., R. Hilborn, and C.J. Walters. (1993). Uncertainty, Resource Exploitation, and Conservation: Lessons from History. *Science*, 260: 36–7.

MacRae, D. (1980). 'Canada and the Law of the Sea: Some Multilateral and Bilateral Issues.' *Canadian Issues: Canada and the Sea*, 3(1): 161–74.

Magnuson, A. (1991). 'Fish and Fisheries Ecology.' *Ecological Applications*, 1: 13–16.

McColl, J.C., and R.A. Stevens. (1997). 'Australian Fisheries Management Authority: Organizational Structure and Management Philosophy.' In D.A. Hancock, D.C. Smith, A. Grant, and J.P. Beumer, eds., *Developing and Sustaining World Fisheries Resources. Proceedings of the Second World Fisheries Congress*, 655–60. Brisbane: CSIRO Publishing.

Munro, G. (1980). *A Promise of Abundance: Extended Fisheries Jurisdiction and the Newfoundland Economy*. Ottawa: Minister of Supply and Services.

Organization for Economic Cooperation and Development (OECD). (1997). *Toward Sustainable Fisheries: Economic Aspects of the Management of Living Marine Resources*. Paris: author.

Parsons, L.S. (1993). 'Management of Marine Fisheries in Canada.' *Canadian Bulletin of Fisheries and Aquatic Sciences*, 225. Ottawa: National Research Council.

Royce, R. (1984). *Introduction to the Practice of Fisheries Science*. Orlando: Academic Press.

Sens, S., and Neilsen, J.R. (1997). 'Fisheries Co-Management: A Comparative Analysis. In D.A. Hancock, D.C. Smith, A. Grant, and J.P. Beumer, eds., *Developing and Sustaining World Fisheries Resources: The State of Science and Management. Proceedings of the Second World Fisheries Congress*, 374–82. Brisbane: CSIRO Publishing.

Shane, B. (1998). 'Improved Performance Measurement: A Prerequisite for Better Service Delivery.' *Optimum, the Journal of Public Sector Management*, 27(4): 1–5.

Smith, S., J.J. Hunt, and D. Rivard (eds.). (1993). 'Risk Evaluation and Biological Reference Points for Fisheries Management. *Canadian Special Publication of Fisheries and Aquatic Sciences*, 120.

Stephenson, R.L., and D.E. Lane. (1995). 'Fisheries Science in Fisheries Management: A Plea for Conceptual Change.' *Canadian Journal of Fisheries and Aquatic Sciences*, 52(9): 2051–6.

Templeman, W., and J. Gulland. (1965). 'Review of Possible Conservation Actions for ICNAF Area.' *Annual Proceedings of the International Commission of the Northwest Atlantic Fisheries 1964–1965*, 15(4): 47–56.

Viscusi, W. Kip. (1998). *Rational Risk Policy*. Oxford: Oxford University Press.

Wooster, W.S. (ed.). (1988). *Fishery Science and Management: Objectives and Limitations. Lecture Notes on Coastal and Estuarine Studies*, vol. 28. New York: Springer-Verlag.

Wooster, W.S., and L. Miller. (1988). 'On Fisheries Science and Management.' In W.S. Wooster, ed., *Fishery Science and Management: Objectives and Limitations. Lecture Notes on Coastal and Estuarine Studies*, vol 28: 289–94. New York: Springer-Verlag.

12 Patient Science versus Science on Demand: The Stretching of Green Science at Environment Canada

G. BRUCE DOERN

This chapter examines Environment Canada as a science-based policy and regulatory institution. In concert with the book's overall purpose, it is an *institutionally* focused examination in that it tries to cover some basic realities that would confront the author or any reader of this book if we became minister or deputy minister of the environment tomorrow. Institutional analysis means that Environment Canada must be seen as an amalgam of laws, political and bureaucratic players, and organizations with cultures and histories, interacting with diverse interests with strong contending views about what has been done and what needs to be done about the greening of Canada in an increasingly interdependent world (Doern and Conway, 1994; Canada, 1998a). We are interested in it as science-based institution, but in the same breath we know immediately that it is more than a science-based entity.

Environment Canada is a complex and fast-changing institution, and thus the chapter must be seen as only a partial and necessarily selected look at its institutional make-up as a science-based entity.

Research for the chapter is based on the references listed as well as on numerous interviews with officials in Environment Canada and with other experts in the stakeholder community. My thanks are extended to these individuals both for the interviews and for commenting on earlier drafts of this paper. Thanks are also due to Ted Reed and Glen Toner at CRUISE for constructive comments and discussion. The chapter also draws on the author's earlier work with Tom Conway which resulted in a book on the history of the first twenty years of Environment Canada (Doern and Conway, 1994).

Some key features of overall change in its science roles and capacity are examined, and there is a brief case study or illustrative focus on science in the regulation of chemicals and on science in the wildlife realm and in the preservation of biodiversity. Institutional analysis shows very quickly that there are many kinds of pathways that science and scientists traverse in a regulatory institution depending on the inherent nature of the regulatory and policy function involved and on different substantive mandate areas. Many of Environment Canada's other science-based policy and regulatory responsibilities are not examined (for example, environmental assessment processes; weather services, environmental emergencies, and environmental reporting; field operations; and basic relations between the minister of the environment and other federal ministers and departments).

The chapter is organized into six parts. First, we set out the central thesis. Second , we sketch out the basic mandate and structure of Environment Canada. Third, we relate this mandate to the recent historical context of change, especially regarding developments in the past decade. The fourth section examines the general nature of the science and risk aspects of the environmental policy and regulatory realm. The fifth section then looks at the more particular dynamics of science-based input into the longer-established environmental protection area (with a focus on chemicals). The sixth section does the same regarding the more recent biodiversity conservation realm, an area linked with long-standing wildlife research but also going well beyond it. Conclusions follow about the state of the department's transformation as a science-based institution.

The Central Thesis: Patient Science versus Science on Demand

It is useful to begin an essay on science in Environment Canada with four basic facts: Environment Canada's mandate has been consistently expanding; public awareness of environmental issues and support for solutions, including a strong federal role, have been expanding; Environment Canada's science budgets and human resources have been cut by about 30 per cent since the mid-1990s; and the department has had twenty ministers in twenty-seven years of its existence. This is a summary recipe for a stretched-out, thinned-out science-based institution that ought to be in its prime, but is instead exhaustedly running just to keep up. Ministers come and stay, on average, for about fifteen months, and too often they find themselves having to play only the short game. Environment Canada's scientific and technical personnel (which constitute 70 per cent of the departmental staff) more often play the longer game but are buffeted between the environmental imperative for patient steady science and the political and administrative requirement for science on demand. The tension between patient science and science on demand is growing. The former is science that proceeds along venues or pathways that emerge from the actual conduct of research into matters of environmental priority, as judged by scientists. It is, in essence, a more anticipatory kind of science. The latter kind of science is one that has to respond to priorities from non-scientists including Cabinet ministers, national and local media, and other political interests. While all environment departments have had to carry out both kinds of science, science on demand is growing and displacing patient science.

The tension between patient science and science on demand, and the stretched nature of green science that results, is the dominant theme of this chapter. But the metaphor of an institution stretched to its limits may not evoke a negative image for everyone. Stretched may not suggest a thread-bare thin green science line but rather a taut alert elastic entity with enough give to be responsive to unforseen needs. Or it may simply suggest an agency that is delivering more environmental value for money underpinned by more efficient and effective science targeted on the most urgent environmental priorities. Thus, we need to look carefully at science in Environment Canada's recent evolution but also in a way that is cognizant of the limits of this brief chapter. Science-based regulation is our central concern, but it is clearly not the only explanation for why green science at Environment Canada is being stretched. Such other aspects have been examined in Chapter 1 and in other chapters as well.

Mandate and Structure

Environment Canada's mandate document begins with the statement that it 'is a science-based department with a mandate that covers preservation and enhancement of the quality of the natural environment, renewable resources (including water, migratory birds, and other non-domestic flora and fauna), meteorology, enforcement of the rules of the Canada–U.S. International Joint Commission, and coordination of federal environmental policies and programs' (Canada, 1998b: 7). Its statutory authority flows from major legislation such as the Department of Environment Act, Canada Water Act, Canada Wildlife Act, Canadian Environmental Assessment Act, Canadian Environmental Protection Act, and a number of other laws. The department and its minister also formulate policy and regulate jointly with other ministers and departments under the auspices of several other laws, including the Fisheries Act. Numerous regulations also flow from parent statutes, and the department's activities are driven by an ever-growing number of international agreements as well.

In all of this, the department says that 'science is the foundation' and 'sustainable development is the context within which Environment Canada carries out its environmental mandate.' The department goes on to describe its *mission* as one that will 'make sustainable development a reality for Canada. In order to help present and future generations of Canadians live and prosper in an environment that needs to be respected, protected, and conserved, we undertake programs to: reduce risk to human health and to the environment; provide weather forecasts and warnings and emergency preparedness services; and give Canadians the tools to build a greener society (ibid.).

Environment Canada describes its structure as being governed by a matrix management approach in that there are seven headquarters organizational units (and five regional operations) which are cross-cut by three business lines. The organizational units are responsibility centres that manage resources and are responsible for the delivery of results. Four of these are functional in that they deal with the minister and deputy minister, corporate services, policy and communications, and human resources. Three of the units are directly program-oriented services: the Atmospheric Environment Service, the Environmental Conservation Service, and the Environmental Protection Service. While science underpins each service, the broader research science and monitoring tends to reside in the AES and ECS, with EPS having a more operational science function tied to direct regulation. The business lines are broader groupings of activity intended to ensure that the department's activity is 'defined in a national context and delivered in a client-centred manner respecting regional differences; makes results the focus of departmental planning and reporting; and provides a shared strategic context for department-wide expenditure management' (ibid.).

The three business lines are currently described by the department as:

- A healthy environment: Canadians are concerned about risks to the environment from human activities, and the danger that these risks pose to human health and the sustainability of the environment. They expect that environmental risks will be understood, monitored and prevented or controlled.
- Safety from environmental hazards: The lives, property and livelihood of Canadians are threatened by naturally occurring and human-induced environmental hazards ranging from severe weather and airborne volcanic ash to oil spills and tire fires.
- A greener society: Through its third business line, the department seeks to reconcile environmental and economic interests, remove barriers to environmentally responsible action, and foster the capacity of all sectors of society to act on their environmental values and responsibilities. (ibid.: 8)

Science is said to underpin each of these business lines with science defined to include 'research, monitoring and assessment, technology and indicators development, and reporting activities' (ibid.).

With respect to this introductory portrait of the department, two further points deserve initial emphasis. Environment Canada is considered to be a science-based department in that 90 per cent of its expenditures are defined as science and technology, some 17 per cent of which is for the generation of new knowledge and technology (Canada, 1996: 5). The department's core staff is composed of approximately 4,400 persons, 70 per cent with science and technical backgrounds (defined broadly).

This bare-bones institutional description conveys, it may be said, too much of the organization-chart mentality. But the manner in which a science-based institution describes itself and fashions its basic structure is quite crucial. For our purposes it already suggests multiple pathways for science that will require integration and that can generate collisions and conflict over mandates within the department. A matrix of three main service organizations interacting with three business lines to deliver on results over a continent-wide territory suggests from the outset a very complex agenda and set of processes and management requirements. Keep in mind that little has been said of Environment Canada's regional operations, including several of its research institutes, nor of its complex and difficult science and policy relationships with other federal departments. These relations expand exponentially the more that the systematic policy approach of sustainable development is translated from words into action. This is because the decisions of these other ministries must be influenced at the very earliest stages of decision making.

The Recent Historical and Political-Economic Context

Environment Canada's current mandate, and the challenges of managing science in the past decade, must be placed briefly against the historical backdrop of the department and of environmental politics and economics. The pattern here is one of a double dose of 'rise and fall' in political fortunes and levels of basic political saliency in the context of a quite steady long-term growth trajectory in the underlying importance of environmental matters and of concern about sustainable development (Doern and Conway, 1994). The first dose of 'rise and fall' occurred in the 1970s and 1980s. Environment Canada enjoyed a decade of birth and expansion in the 1970s with a heady confidence in its mandate and science, backed by the growth of environmental non-governmental organizations (or ENGOs). From the late 1970s until about 1988, a long decline occurred largely evidenced by a policy of weak regulatory enforcement, deference to real or imagined provincial jurisdiction, and opposition within the federal government from resource departments and their allied business interest groups (Harrison, 1996; Brown, 1992; Hoberg, 1998).

The duration of the second dose of rise and fall, but starting from a higher base point in the longer-term trajectory, encompassed the last decade. Environment Canada's sense of place in national priorities reached its zenith with the announcement of the $3 billion Green Plan in 1990. This elevated position was underpinned by several contributing forces and ideas which included some newsworthy natural disasters in the late 1980s; the ascendancy of evidence and debate about global warming; and the articulation of the philosophy of sustainable development, first by the Brundtland Commission and then its endorsement by G-7 leaders at their 1988 Toronto Summit. A new federal assertiveness was in evidence during this period backed by opinion polls that strongly supported both the environment as a national priority and federal leadership. Arguably, this period peaked or ended with the Rio Earth Summit in 1992 but included the important acid rain agreement with the United States (Toner, 1996; Harrison, 1998a).

The most recent decline occupies the period since 1992. Cuts in the Green Plan began to occur almost immediately, but the dominant impetus for the decline in the environment as a perceived political priority came from the recession of the early 1990s and initiatives to manage the growing federal deficit. These initiatives took the form of a major governmental reorganization in 1993 and the introduction of Program Review in 1994. The cumulative consequences and effects of the latter's multiyear cuts extend right to the present. The net effect of the various phases of Program Review was that Environment Canada absorbed a cut of over 31 per cent in its budget and almost 23 per cent in its personnel (Canada, 1996: 4; Toner, 1996). The department had in 1993 just lost Parks Canada, which was transferred to the newly formed Department of Canadian Heritage, and it was also engaged in reorganizing its regional personnel into five integrated regions. The last period of decline was somewhat different from the first in that it was largely a resource decline but combined with major reorganization. Meanwhile, the department's mandate had in fact grown as had its statutory base. These enlarged responsibilities had emerged from the development of legislation such as the Canadian Environmental Protection Act (CEPA) and the Canadian Environmental Assessment Act as well as international obligations on matters such as global warming and biodiversity. Even today there is parliamentary activity to deepen the mandate through a revised CEPA in the context of continuing resource constraints. The head of the Commission of the Environment and Sustainable Development drew particular attention in his first report to Parliament to what he called a serious 'implementation gap' (Canada, 1998a).

In the overall process of dual ups and downs, the twenty ministers came and went, some contributing to, and some simply riding the environmental waves in whatever direction they were already going (Doern and Conway, 1994).

General Conceptions of Science and Technology in Environmental Policy and Regulation

As defined by Environment Canada, science includes research, monitoring and assessment, technology and indicators development, and reporting activities (Canada, 1998b: 8). For some science managers in Environment Canada, these kinds of science are compressed into two broad kinds, research science and assessment and monitoring, with the latter centred on the strict analysis of samples and other data. The former is cast as a less reactive kind of science than the latter in that it involves a process whereby researchers identify longer-term issues and problems and mount research programs to predict effects and ultimately to inform possible policy and regulatory responses. An example of this kind of research science is that which identified and tracked acid rain or, perhaps less well known, persistent organic pollutants (POPs). With the advantage of hindsight one can see that this type of patient research science can extend over a ten- to fifteen-year cycle, and, of course, it eventually will generate the need for ongoing science monitoring.

The assessment and monitoring, or second form, of science is ostensibly more routine. Or it may be needed to respond on demand to real and perceived environmental problems, events, spills, and other occasions when ministers or communities need information about such problems and about whether the government has it, in some sense, under control (politically, environmentally, or both). Scientific monitoring capacity is also needed for ongoing environmental indicators and reporting and accountability, and for informing citizens about the state of national, local, regional, and even neighbourhood environmental issues.

In the 1990s, as a whole, the nature of science in Environment Canada underwent five changes that affect the nature of both of these broadly defined kinds of science and of the relationships between the two. The first change is that science has to be conducted and managed with less money and fewer internal personnel. The second is that there is now a much more concerted effort to closely match science and policy. In short, there is more pressure for science on demand. This need flows from the hard budget constraint, but it is also the result of the expanded mandates referred to above and for accountability for performance in achieving results and meeting agreed priorities. The third change is that there is less 'freedom to roam,' as one Environment Canada scientist put it to me, in launching new research initiatives based on the instincts of scientists as opposed to the dictates of existing policies and commitments. In our terms, there is less room for patient science. The fourth change is that there is simply much more global science, both in the sense that the scale of the environmental problems are global and in the sense that modern computerized and internet technologies put Environment Canada scientists in touch on a daily basis with scientists and science throughout the world. The fifth change is that with regard to monitoring science there is a shift away from repeated measuring activity (such as regular measurements over a twelve-month period) to the use of statistical sampling approaches. Though this may partly stem from budget cuts, it also results from quite genuine views in compliance and monitoring theory (including financial auditing) that less routine and bureaucratic approaches can work just as well, especially in the information age.

All of these five changes are important and daunting enough and contribute to the caution about what 'stretched' green science means. But it is all layered on top of yet other features of science in the environmental realm that form part of Environment Canada's history, its current institutional memory, and organizational and cultural make-up. These elements do not simply go away, and they are each partly driven by inherent tensions within each element. These elements include the clean-up versus sustainable development concepts of environmental policy and regulation; the perceived historical need to 'out-science' other countries, especially the United States on bilateral problems as a counterweight to Canada's weaker political power; and the varying concepts of risk management practised, if not always enunciated, by Environment Canada.

The remediation versus prevention tensions are in fact long-standing in Environment Canada. The very definition of the department in 1970 centred around those who advocated a systemic resource management approach (the precursor to the 1980s sustainable development concept), versus those who saw the greater need being an 'end-of-pipe' clean-up approach. The latter won the day in the 1970s (Doern and Conway, 1994). When sustainable development emerged as an articulated concept in the latter 1980s, it gained a greater foothold. But there was still always a tension, often with new ministers – and remember there were *always* new ministers in the one every fifteen months average cycle – who wanted a tougher line taken with polluters. The sustainable development model is always more subtle, multifaceted, knowledge-based, and inchoate. It achieves by 'preventing,' which means that it ultimately trades in a world of non-events, that is, things that, happily, do not happen and that cannot be 'announced,' only obliquely 'reported on.' It does not make for good media-driven politics or the proverbial 30-second sound-bite. The more that Environment Canada becomes a sustainable development department, the more its science may become less explicitly noticeable, although still remaining essential. Meanwhile, science in support of end-of-pipe remedial regulatory action often has to be explicit, specific, or local, and it must be administratively causal science if blame is to be legally apportioned and assigned to firms or other polluters.

The desire to out-science may seem paradoxical given the greater than ever need for global sharing and cooperation in environmental science. But it has been an important part of the attitude towards, and pride in, science at Environment Canada. Given early bilateral problems such as Great Lakes pollution and acid rain, and given the asymmetry of political power between Canada and the United States, Environment Canada always felt that its counterweight to U.S. political might had to be very good science, indeed better science than the Americans might assemble. There was considerable sense in this view, and its legacy is still present in Canada's approach to other problems since then, even when these are increasingly multilateral and global in character. Canada's leadership on the science on ozone layer, which led to the Montreal Protocol, reflected this need for science as a crucial power base. To have a voice that will be heard at the growing number of international tables, a small or medium-sized country has to bring a good science-based view, or else it will simply not be a credible player in complex negotiations.

The third and final long-term element that characterizes science in Environment Canada is the department's varying views of risk and risk management. The views are varied in the sense that they are both stated and unstated and they vary across the department's mandate areas. In addition, Environment Canada's main interest groups, the ENGOs and business, also have diverse views about risk. In its early water pollution regulatory programs the preferred approach in Canada (and in many other countries) was to require firms to minimize end-of-pipe effluents consistent with the *best practicable technology* rather than to promulgate more precise standards regarding assimilative capacities in particular bodies of water. This was a strategy more akin to preventative risk management.

Interestingly, the above-quoted discussion of Environment Canada's purposes indicates its job is to help Canadians 'reduce risk' rather than manage risks and benefits. Environment Canada has adopted the precautionary principle as a concept from the Rio summit to underpin sustainable development. It is a feature of laws such as CEPA, especially regarding the screening of new substances. The precautionary principle is itself vague but in general implies that action is to be taken to prevent environmental damage even if there is uncertainty regarding its possible cause and possible extent. According to this view, 'The environment should not be left to show harm before protective action is taken; scientific uncertainty should not be used as a justification to delay measures which protect the environment' (Jordan and O'Riordon, 1995: 59). One implication of this view is that one does not need complete scientific proof to practice the principle. As Jordon and O'Riordon argue, the setting for the use of the precautionary principle may be more propitious in recent years because of a broad-scale critique about science in environmental policy and regulation. They argue that the 'science of assimilative capacity, predictive modelling and compensatory investment to offset the loss of ecological resilience is being challenged' (ibid.: 61). This and other criticisms have led to the view that 'at the very least, science should evolve into a more applied, interdisciplinary, format for coping with environmental threats, and that it should be seen as a tool for a more open and participatory culture of decision taking' (ibid.).

Environment Canada's main public statements stress the sustainable development concept rather than the precautionary principle, but they do imply a greater acceptance of the applied interdisciplinary nature of contemporary environmental threats and policy challenges. The department is careful, however, not to endorse the implied view that one does not need science. Even to engage in precautionary practices, one needs good science.

Environment Canada's most comprehensive philosophical statement about its overall science policy was arguably found in a 1996 document where it was tied to the broader federal government review of science and technology then being completed as part of Program Review (Canada, 1996). Environment Canada maintained that its approach to science was consistent with the federal government's seven principles concerning science and technology. First, it would increase the effectiveness of federally supported research and training through peer review and a market test of relevance. Second, it would increasingly capture the cost-risk and knowledge-sharing benefits of partnership with universities, business, and other governments. Third, it would emphasize preventative approaches and sustainable development, as discussed above. Fourth, it would adopt policies, practices, and regulatory approaches that encourage innovation. Fifth, it would extend information networks as part of the infrastructure of the knowledge economy. Sixth, international science and technology linkages would be strengthened. Finally, seventh, a greater science culture would be fostered.

As a mid-1990s statement, echoed by other statements since, these aspirations, while often quite problematical, are undoubtedly in keeping with the perceived realities of green science at the turn of the millennium. At least half of these statements would not have and did not find expression a decade earlier. But science in the overall departmental context is necessarily only the beginning. Environment Canada is also a holding company of diverse services and program providers and therefore has a number of different pathways for science to travel as it interacts with policy and is in turn influenced by it. We look at only two such micro-realms, one on environmental protection and regulation and the other the mixed old and new realm of wildlife conservation and the goal of enhancing biodiversity.

Science in Mandate Areas: Protection and the Regulation of Chemicals

Science in the Environmental Protection Service tends to serve a more direct regulatory role. This can encompass pollution in industrial sectors such as pulp and paper and automobiles (Schrecker, 1991; Harrison, 1998a). In this section, we look briefly at science in the regulation of commercial chemicals, not in the sense of evaluating them in any substantive way but rather in how science and science relationships have changed in the 1990s. The Commercial Chemicals Evaluation unit of the EPS has a core science evaluation staff of about thirty-five persons which in turn comprises part of a unit that has about sixty-five full time staff and another thirty or so contract or other term staff which also includes science personnel. Unlike some areas of scientific employment in the federal government, the core science staff is relatively young and has not suffered from people leaving the organization or staying only for brief periods.

Functioning largely under the provisions of the Canadian Environmental Protection Act, the regulation of chemicals is necessarily done in the context of a need to differentiate existing chemicals or substances from new ones. Hence, its longer history is one of regulating existing chemicals in a postmarket sense. But it also has a role in a form of premarket assessment of risk of new chemicals and substances. While the latter task is likely to be more conflictual with industry than the former, both have encountered difficulties, which is one of the reasons for the slow emergence, evolution, and consolidation of the CEPA regime. CEPA is a complex law; it is underpinned by detailed regulatory provisions ultimately involving several federal agencies. These detailed provisions are not dealt with at all in this chapter. (For discussion of the emergence and nature of CEPA, see Canada, 1995; Environment Canada, 1996; Schrecker, 1991; Doern and Conway, 1994.)

In an overall sense, the nature of the science-in-regulation task has been quite consistent over the past twenty-five years. The core science staff has to reach its control decisions on the basis of a review of all available relevant science effects of substances on the ecosystem. It works closely with Health Canada scientists, whose focus is on the human health aspects of this knowledge base. Since the thousands of existing chemicals in the economy have many well-known effects and a knowledge base that could be canvassed in scientific literature and through contact with scientists nationally and internationally, there is a sense in which this regulatory task is more routine than that for new chemicals. Frequently, however, the science may need to be mobilized to fill smaller gaps in knowledge. But, science here basically involved a volume of review of cases or assessments that was large on an annual basis as slight modifications to known chemicals and substances were made and approval sought.

In other respects, the science role in the chemicals area under CEPA is different in the 1990s. The general realm of new chemicals and of biotechnology products often means that there is less relevant ecosystem data and knowledge available. Moreover, there is a greater need to, and value in, utilizing modelling techniques regarding the composition of products and potential hazards. These newer realms have also been accompanied by the need to draw even more on the network of scientific knowledge in business, and internationally among fellow regulators. The chemicals branch and EPS generally has also had to add scientists with different science backgrounds to begin to deal with these areas.

The level of complexity of the science for these newer realms also increases. For example, the direct impact of metals in the environment is presenting more complex problems. The chemicals branch has to reach out to other parts of Environment Canada to obtain some of the new research that might be needed for this work. It has also reached out in the 1990s to universities, particularly through its own funding of, and support for, the Canadian Network of Toxicological Centres. The CNTC was initially funded at about $2.3 million, but this has recently been cut back. Among its priority areas of work are metals as well as basic work on concepts and practices in risk assessment. The chemicals branch has seen its budget cut from about $11 million to $8 million, but it has largely succeeded in avoiding cuts to its core science staff, which is regarded as its central and crucial asset. It has, however, had to cut other areas of expenditure which does limit its flexibility and capacity to deal with other issues.

Science in Mandate Areas: Wildlife and Biodiversity

The second mandate area to be given a somewhat closer look in this chapter is wildlife management and biodiversity. It is a part of the Environmental Conservation Service and hence, at first glance at least, it is not centred in a directly regulatory setting. Biodiversity as an environmental priority and as an area of environmental science very profoundly flows from international commitments through the international Convention on Biological Diversity, hereafter referred to as the Convention on Biodiversity (Environment Canada, 1994, 1998). Indeed, the convention had been a key priority of the federal government at the 1992 Rio summit, with Prime Minister Brian Mulroney taking a personal hand in pushing it forward. But in another sense it is also a very old and very local role for Environment Canada centred in its earlier work in the Canadian Wildlife Service (CWS).

The convention calls for the establishment by signatory countries of national strategies to attain three key objectives: the conservation of biological diversity; the sustainable use of its components; and fair and equitable sharing of the benefits arising from the use of genetic resources. The launching of the Canadian Biodiversity Strategy in 1993 was accompanied by an initial effort to appraise the science of biodiversity in Canada and in the department. The 1994 report supplies an initial baseline view of science in this realm (ibid.).

The report drew an immediate link between the concept of biodiversity and the earlier national Wildlife Policy for Canada endorsed in 1990. Biodiversity in the convention refers to the conservation of variety at three levels: 'The genetic diversity within species [whether or not this genetic diversity is apparent]; the diversity of species; and the diversity of ecosystems' (ibid.: 5). The 1990 Wildlife

Policy for Canada, supported by all governments in Canada, had already committed itself to 'maintain and enhance the health and diversity of Canada's wildlife, for its own sake and for the benefit of present and future generations of Canadians' (ibid.).

The 1994 report urged that Environment Canada and Canadian society as a whole have 'a more proactive strategy on biodiversity conservation' and try to avoid as much as possible 'being put in defensive no-win situations of the type: spotted owl versus lumberjack' (ibid.: 6). In virtually the same breath, however, the report then identified the dilemmas at hand. First, most decision making that affected biodiversity conservation was not the responsibility of the department. Second, the bulk of Environment Canada's past science was not directed at biological issues, and the latter would have to be greatly increased if the department was to play a leading role in the biodiversity issue. With respect to such scientific research, the report indicated, not surprisingly, that there were areas where Environment Canada had to set priorities and still other areas where it ought to encourage others. 'Others' referred to a host of sectors including forestry, the fisheries, agriculture, and biotechnology.

A Biodiversity Convention Office was set up to give focus to the new commitments, but the underlying issues of science in biodiversity are bound up in the longer-standing evolution and 1990s fate of the CWS, including its National Wildlife Research Centre. At one point in the late 1970s, the Canadian Wildlife Service had been a much larger operation (Conway, 1992). It has since been cut considerably, but the nature of these cuts are hard to track because of the different structure of regional operations in the 1990s and because of the usual problems in exactly how one is defining a scientist. The National Wildlife Research Centre in Hull has the oldest and arguably most out-of-date facilities in the Environment Canada science establishment. But science in this realm is also the most decentralized in the department, functioning in all regions in Canada. Indeed, the historic image of the wildlife researcher is quite literally that of the single lonely researcher in some distant and remote site in Canada diligently and competently carrying out his or her research, far away from the vagaries of Ottawa politics of the general or bureaucratic variety. It was in this respect a kind of mythical jewel in the crown of Environment Canada's science, a myth in the best symbolic sense of that word. It was also quite vulnerable to the cutting thrusts of various ministers, from the Blais-Grenier cuts in the mid-1980s to Program Review in the mid-1990s.

Thus, we observe the paradox that all the while that biodiversity was gaining ground as a political priority, wildlife science was being cut. It has been subject to more than cuts, however, and thus science in the full wildlife–biodiversity realm travels with its own mixture of science linked to policy and science disconnected from policy. As in all areas of federal science in policy and regulation, the paths and situations are numerous and exhibit situations of patient science and science on demand. Several examples will illustrate this diversity. First, there are some areas, such as that feeding into the mandate of the Migratory Birds Convention, where science has a fairly orderly link with policy makers, including the conduct of greater amounts of useful research on habitat. This is also an area where there is greater systematic collection of data. Second, in contrast, in wildlife research on toxic substances there is a much more crisis-oriented short-term demand feature to the research, sometimes responding to a specific ministerial and media concern or to local concern about why some species may be endangered. Third, biodiversity which, as we have seen, ought to be a major impetus for research, is caught up in the sheer daunting scope of what has to be done. The wildlife scientists, on the one hand, see biodiversity as something that they have always believed in, and, on the other hand, as a broad umbrella concept that makes it simply another word for environmental sustainability. But they also have to confront serious problems in the adequacy of biological information management systems. These include systematic inadequacies in the collection, storage, accessibility, sharing, and use of biological data in Canada.

Without doubt the scale of issues to be managed and the kinds of science to be conducted are enormous. The challenge can be likened to the problems that had to be faced decades ago by those officials who had to design the science, monitoring, and analysis of weather systems to provide basic weather forecasts and other information services. A federal biodiversity strategy has been established but it is not yet supported by extensive underlying knowledge. Scientists know the names of perhaps half of Canada's species. As a recent report points out, 'Although 71,000 species of wild plants and animals have been recorded in Canada, scientists estimate that 68,000 have yet to be discovered and named ... and of those discovered, approximately 97 per cent have not been studied in depth' (Canada 1998c, 13). Environment Canada has classified about fifteen ecological zones that relate to both species and habitat, but they have only begun to look at them. There is a very fragmented approach to methodologies and a serious lack of interoperability of data sets and systems of holding information.

Paradoxically, the United States, which has not signed the Biodiversity Convention, has arguably made a more systematic high-level start to dealing with this underlying need and have linked it to its wider work on information infrastructures (President's Committee of Advisors on Science and Technology, 1998). Nevertheless, the Convention on Biodiversity has made it clear how global these issues are and how no nation has anything but a tenuous grasp on the challenges and on the science needed. It is also clear that in the design of any science-based systems, both international networks and vast amounts of local knowledge will have to feed into the science and monitoring base. Thus, both Environment Canada as a whole and the small Biodiversity Convention Office know that they cannot possibly do all the science. They can lead in priority-setting about research and monitoring systems but partnership science, including community science, and knowledge, will be the far larger underpinning for the task at hand.

All of these paths and evolving changes generate challenging issues and choices about research management in the wildlife–biodiversity realm of ECS. It could easily be argued that there is a need for a more centralized science and research capacity to generate the critical mass of capacity to deal with the new international biodiversity imperatives. Biodiversity is also consummately local and regional, and thus the institutional pull here would be to reinforce the traditions of the decentralized CWS. Other quite particular partnership-based science and institutional choices are also coming to the forefront. For example, some discussions have occurred between the department and Carleton University and the University of Ottawa to possibly jointly manage the existing National Wildlife Research Centre. Several of the latter institution's scientists are already adjunct faculty members at the two universities and are engaged in supervising younger research students who are a crucial source of new ideas and new science efforts.

Regenerating science through these and other measures is seen as a priority, but it has to be promoted in the face of continuing hard budget constraints. The wildlife area of Environment Canada is absorbing the effects of a defacto Program Review III. For example, the delayed impacts of cost-recovery requirements are having an adverse effect as other parts of Environment Canada such as libraries or computer services) now charge the research units for activities that used to be free. When a scientist leaves, the person is often not likely to be replaced. Instead, the money is used to stay afloat. There are also concerns at the individual scientist level not only about job security but also about possible changes in the overall classification system for federal scientific personnel.

Conclusions

Through an examination of the current mandate and structure of Environment Canada set in the context of key features of its almost thirty-year history, this chapter has analysed the changing nature of the role of science in Canada's lead environmental policy and regulatory institution. As cautioned from the outset, the analysis has had to be selective and does not cover all of the important mandate areas of the department. Only two mandate areas were explored more closely, namely, chemical regulation centred in the Environmental Protection Service and wildlife and biodiversity centred in the Environmental Conservation Service.

Environment Canada's science capacity has been stretched and thinned in an almost self-evident aggregate fashion. The department's mandate and laws have been expanded by the federal government, and expectations about federal leadership remain high. The 'minister every fifteen months' phenomenon brings in ministers who want more done but who rarely stay long enough to have to worry in any consistent way about what gets done. They are without doubt interested in sustainable development, but they (along with the ministers of other departments) are also a part of the reason why there is a serious implementation gap. All ministers recognize that the science base is crucial, but the science base has been cut by 30 per cent.

The analysis has tied this aggregate pattern of the stretching of science capacity to twin pressures which we have expressed as the tension between 'patient science' versus 'science on demand.' Environment departments always have to manage this tension. But the latter is growing at the expense of the former. Environment Canada's science managers tend to express this tension differently, but many agree that in recent years science has had to lean, much more than in the past, towards satisfying policy demands, including quite short-term ones, rather than responding to agendas that are indicated and triggered by underlying research. The difficulty with resource shifts between these two kinds of science is that to be properly managed there is a very real sense in which environment departments need extra science resource slack, in short, a reserve capacity.

When speaking of such a reserve capacity to enable more patient science to be practised, several questions immediately follow. In terms of this chapter they can only be posed as further questions. Is there a case that such patient or more anticipatory science needs to be conducted in more arm's-length institutions tied to universities but with a capacity to feed into eventual policy and regulatory deliberations on a systematic basis? If so, how shall such work and institutions be funded including mixtures of taxpayer and user funding? Even beyond these questions, do the non-federal and non-governmental science resources and institutional capacities (business, university, community) in fact exist to be partners in this complex endeavour? For complex it already is, and it will undoubtedly increasingly be so. No environment department that is a *sustainable development* department can possibly do, or should do, all the science it needs nor will the science and related policy issues arrive in some orderly or linear manner.

The chapter has shown, illustratively at least, that science in policy and regulation at Environment Canada exhibits many complex paths and pathways, some of which are caused by historical inertia and some by the different non-linear character of environmental and eco-system problems. Science needs are different depending on the inherent tasks at hand such as underlying research, monitoring and measurement, and the production of environmental reporting. There are also broad differences among the three services, the EPS, ECS, and Atmospheric Environment Service and in the subelements within each. For example, science in the wildlife and biodiversity realm has seen major cuts while in the midst of making not just new commitments but in fact quite massive commitments in the internationally driven biodiversity agenda. In the realm of chemicals regulation, there have been resource constraints to be sure but the possible gap in science capacity seems on the surface to be smaller and the core science asset (the scientists) has been preserved.

As with other federal science-based departments and agencies, Environment Canada has had to extend its networks and linkages to outside scientists in Canada and internationally. Green science has always been international, but the more complex and global the nature of the science and the underlying ecological interactions the more that this internationalizing process has increased. There is evidence as

well in the two case areas looked at here of efforts to better institution-
alize relationships with universities to both broaden the research and
benefit from the training and research of younger scientists. These
links are fragile and stretched largely because resources and patience
of a scientific and institutional kind are needed, but are in short supply.

References

Brown, M.P. (1992). 'Organizational Design as Policy Instrument: Environ-
    ment Canada in the Canadian Bureaucracy.' In Robert Boardman, ed.,
    Canadian Environmental Policy: Ecosystems, Politics, and Process, 24–42.
    Toronto: Oxford University Press.
Canada. (1995). *Environmental Protection Legislation Designed for the Future:
    A Renewed CEPA*. Ottawa: Environment Canada.
–   (1996). *Environment Canada's Science and Technology: Leading to Solutions*.
    Ottawa: Minister of Supply and Services Canada.
–   (1998a). *Report of the Commissioner on the Environment and Sustainable
    Development to the House of Commons*. Ottawa: Minister of Public Works
    and Government Services Canada.
–   (1998b). *1998–99 Estimates: Part III Environment Canada*. Ottawa: Environ-
    ment Canada.
–   (1998c). *Caring for Canada's Biodiversity: Canada's First National Report to the
    Conference of the Parties to the Convention on Biological Diversity*. Ottawa:
    Environment Canada.
Conway, Tom. (1992). 'The Marginalization of the Department of the Envi-
    ronment: Environment Policy 1971–1988.' PhD dissertation, Carleton
    University.
Doern, G. Bruce, and Tom Conway. (1994). *The Greening of Canada: Federal
    Institutions and Decisions*. Toronto: University of Toronto Press.
Environment Canada. (1994). *Biodiversity in Canada: A Science Assessment*.
    Ottawa: author.
–   (1996). *Canadian Environmental Protection Act: Report for the Period April
    1995 to March 1996*. Ottawa: author.
–   (1998). *ARET: Voluntary Action on Toxic Substances Update*. Ottawa: author.
Harrison, K. (1994). 'Prospects for Harmonization in Environmental Policy.'
    In Douglas Brown and Janet Hiebert, eds., *Canada: The State of the Federa-
    tion 1994*. Kingston: Institute for Intergovernmental Relations.
–   (1996). *Passing the Buck: Federalism and Canadian Environmental Policy*.
    Vancouver: University of British Columbia Press.

- (1998a). 'Talking with The Donkey: Cooperative Approaches to Environmental Protection.' Paper presented to Annual Meeting of the Canadian Political Science Association, Ottawa, 1 June.
- (1998b). 'Promoting Environmental Protection through Eco-Labelling: An Evaluation of the Environmental Choice Program.' In D. Cohen and K. Webb, eds., *Exploring Voluntary Codes in the Marketplace*. Ottawa: Government of Canada.
Hoberg, G. (1998). 'North American Environmental Regulation.' In G. Bruce Doern and Stephen Wilks, eds., *Changing Regulatory Institutions in Britain and North America*, 305–27. Toronto: University of Toronto Press.
Jordan, Andrew, and T. O'Riordon. (1995). 'The Precautionary Principle in UK Environmental Policy Making,' in Tim S. Gray, ed. *UK Environmental Policy in the 1990s*, 57–84. London: Macmillan.
President's Committee of Advisors on Science and Technology. (1998). *Teaming with Life: Investing in Science to Understand and Use America's Living Capital*. Washington: author.
Schrecker, Ted. (1991). 'The Canadian Environmental Assessment Act: Tremulous Step Forward to Retreat into Smoke and Mirrors?' *Canadian Environmental Law Reports*, 5 (March): 192–246.
Toner, G. (1996). 'Environment Canada's Continuing Roller Coaster Ride.' In Gene Swimmer, ed., *How Ottawa Spends 1996–97: Life Under the Knife*. Ottawa: Carleton University Press.

13 A Question of Balance: New Approaches for Science-Based Regulation

BILL JARVIS

This chapter examines several overall new institutional approaches crucial to enhancing the openness and efficacy of science-based regulation in Canada. New approaches are necessary to react to the changing context for government, globalization, diminished public confidence, and fiscal constraint. Virtually all of the operations of government in Canada are caught up in this process of profound transformation. There is virtually no area of government activity that is not subject to intense scrutiny and assessments of the potential for change. Even the most stable and fundamental roles of government are being subjected to review (Aucoin, 1997).

Among the elements of public administration most resistant to change are the regulatory functions that the government undertakes to protect the health, safety, and environmental integrity of the community. The stability and predictability of these regimes have been seen as necessary characteristics of good management. The responsibility of government to act in these areas is not seriously challenged. Yet even here significant change is under way.

For the purpose of this chapter, science-based regulations are those regulatory functions that are based principally, though not necessarily exclusively, on the natural sciences (including medicine). It excludes those regulatory functions that are based principally on economics, institutional contexts, or law. For the most part, science-based regulations are in the domains of scientific activity dedicated to protection (especially health and safety) and stewardship.

This chapter was produced as part of a program examining issues of science and government at the Public Policy Forum. It was supported by Natural Resources Canada. The author wishes to thank all those who contributed ideas upon which this chapter is based.

The first part examines three dominant aspects of science-based regulations, in the current social and economic circumstances, that provide the motivation and context for change. In the second section, some of the essential principles of the changing approach to government are explored, particularly in the context of science-based regulations. Then a decision framework that emphasizes the balancing of competing interests and forces is put forward. In the next section, we suggest three areas that should be examined further by science-based regulatory agencies as potential sources of constructive change.

The chapter concludes by noting the complexity of the issues that influence new organizational and financing arrangements for science-based regulatory functions. In particular, it points to the need to examine opportunities on a case-by-case basis. For each discrete decision point, a balance must be sought, with a clear understanding of the intentions driving the proposed changes and of the signals such changes will give to those affected by the regulatory framework.

Key Aspects of Science-Based Regulations

Many of the principles for reforming government apply quite broadly across all elements of the relationship of government to citizens. Good models exist with respect to government relationships with citizens, for example, the categorization of government service recipients into voluntary users, entitled users, and compelled users (Farquhar, 1993). Yet, some aspects of science-based regulations, for example, those that look at new institutional forms and new financing arrangements, create special circumstances that must be addressed. The most important of these are:

- The commercial and economic aspects of the markets influenced by these regulations
- The nature of the public goods being addressed by these regulations
- The roles that scientific inquiry and information play in their development and operations.

It is no accident that these are closely linked to the three drivers for government change already noted, namely, internationalization, cost of government, and public confidence.

Commercial and Economic Potential

This first element relates to the role of regulations in the evolution of fast-evolving and internationally integrated technology markets. The clearest, but certainly not the only, expression of this is in areas such as biotechnology, where major efforts are under way to standardize, internationally, elements of national regulatory processes. The Organization for Economic Cooperation and Development (OECD) notes that 'global interdependence in economic, social and environmental spheres is reducing the effectiveness of governments when they act unilaterally. In response, governments of OECD countries are addressing common problems by creating cooperative arrangements linking supra-national, national and sub-national levels of government' (OECD, 1998). The intent of these changes is to serve the needs of, mostly, large multinational companies trying to get product to customer markets worldwide as quickly and as cost-effectively as possible, as well as to minimize the costs of regulations and to assure access to products as soon as possible for consumers. Three factors influence this process:

1 The speed of technological change ensures that those corporations who do not stay on the leading edge are quickly made irrelevant.
2 The portability of the capital – mostly knowledge and patents, often developed with significant government assistance, both financial and non-financial – partially disconnects investments from geography.
3 The corporate structure of the producing sectors is such that large economies of scale drive the markets to conditions where a few extremely large multinational companies control major product segments, creating monopoly or quasi-monopoly conditions.

The consequence of these conditions is to create competition, not between producing companies, but rather between national economies that strive to position themselves to take advantage of the economic potential of these emerging technologies. Where these corporations locate their research, development, and testing, as well as their production depends on a large number of factors. As these organizations adapt from being multi-national corporations to truly global corporations, they have strong interests in ensuring active representation in as many major markets as possible. We might observe here that major markets are mostly in OECD countries, where up to 80 or 90 per cent of sales of new, technologically advanced products occur. The national manifestations of these corporations are usually structured to be in competition with each other for research activities, world product mandates, and other transnational functions. In this context, these national branches are allies of the respective national governments in trying to enhance the allocation of corporate activities performed in their jurisdiction. They will perceive all elements of national competitive circumstances most clearly in relation to the situations faced by the other, competing, units of the parent corporation.

A key factor of national circumstances that can influence the location of corporate activity is the regulatory regime. Clearly, the more efficient the regime and the 'friendlier' it is to the research, testing, production, and marketing interests of the companies involved, the more the regime can be an element of comparative advantage in attracting (or sustaining) investment. The characteristics of the regulatory regime affect the competitiveness of the firm or product being regulated. Such characteristics include the service standards that ensure the timeliness of decisions; the transparency of the process; the cost of the process and of compliance; international credibility and acceptance of the national regulatory regime; and the regime's responsiveness to the rapidly evolving needs of industry. Such characteristics do not necessarily or normally mean the lowering of national standards. Large multinationals with quasi-monopolistic market power can engage in strategic behaviour to pressure countries to improve their regulatory regimes from the perspective of the companies. Fortunately, in most cases, these companies share the objective of having regimes that are effective and dependable at high, internationally acceptable standards of protection.

It seems inevitable that the regulatory requirements for the acceptance of new technologies will gradually become more homogeneous. The global structure of industry provides strong economic incentives for companies to press for harmonization. Their market power suggests that they are likely to have considerable success, especially where these changes are consistent with the fiscal objectives of the governments involved. National governments will have less individual say, and mutual recognition of regulatory testing and even approval is likely among governments. Companies will look to the most efficient and least onerous regulatory regimes that have the confidence of the international community to process their regulatory needs.

This emerging situation creates three new opportunities.

1 To become providers of first choice of regulatory services to the emerging industries regulatory authorities will strive to create a competitive regulatory regime. One could conceive of this as the creation of a new economic sector – the international regulatory services sector as a commercial enterprise.
2 Regulatory operations involve access to a considerable investment in human capital. This capital includes both expertise in the regulatory system as well as subject knowledge of the products and industries being regulated. Such capital can, under the right conditions, become an additional source of advantage. Providing access to this expertise in a consultative approach to the development of regulations can enhance the regulatory process both in terms of timeliness and effectiveness.
3 The regulatory system itself can become an important element of comparative advantage by providing reliable, timely, and effective regulatory services to the highest world standards. Lower regulatory costs can improve the competitiveness of domestically based regulated industries.

The business of regulation has the potential to provide significant economic opportunities for Canada. Furthermore, one could expect significant spin-offs from the successful commercial exploitation of regulatory comparative advantage. It would be associated with both an exportable service such as training, and the development of regulatory processes for other countries – especially those without the critical mass of resources and expertise necessary to produce their own regulations. The corporate interests developing the new technologies would find it more advantageous to locate in Canada to be close to those sources of expertise. Much of the commercial potential for the regulatory sector in globalized markets is influenced by increasing economies of scale of significant proportions. Location theory suggests that, once established, such sectors can create self-re-enforcing properties, establishing strong market position in 'growth poles' (see, for example, Arthur, 1990). This context creates a very complex set of relationships between the regulator and the regulated. There is little doubt that the domestic regulatory regime will have large potential economic effects. The important aspect of this discussion is to point out the multiple implications of any such change. Without a well-articulated set of objectives for all of the various possible consequences, including protection, commercial exploitation, and economic development, not only could some significant opportunities be missed, but, over time, the domestic implementation strategy could be rendered irrelevant by international circumstances.

The Public Good and the Damage Function

Any examination of the structure and financing of science-based regulations needs to give special consideration to the nature of the objective – or the public good – that the regulatory regime has been created to serve. This objective depends on the field of regulation. It is useful to look at regulations aimed at protecting the public from harm, for example, health and safety regulations, separately from those that are part of the management of resources held in common by the community under government stewardship, such as environmental regulations (Jarvis, 1998). This distinction is not always perfectly clear in real world applications. It is useful, however, for clarifying the intentions of regulations to separate those that protect the individual from those that protect the environment (while acknowledging that the latter may have consequences for the former).

The outstanding characteristic of regulation implemented to protect the public is the extreme nature of the risk function. Shortcomings in regulatory decision making can result in severe consequences for the citizens of the jurisdiction, including exposure to disease, serious injury, or death. Even where compensation is possible, it is not always, or even often, able to reverse or eliminate the harm done. A building that collapses causing injury or death, a drug that causes congenital deformities, or a regulated food product that causes severe illness or death, all result in consequences that cannot be undone.

Two other factors exacerbate the problems. First, the expectations of citizens in Canada are quite high with respect to performance in this area. The relationship between the public and the provider of government services is not 'mechanical': 'Expectations [are] formed on the basis of a value structure which also relates to the clients' perception of the role of government in society and, specifically, about the type of service expected from a normal governmental organization' (Zussman,

1991). In this case the values of Canadians include an expectation that the government will take responsibility for a wide area of the health and safety of its citizens. The reactions of Canadians to the Krever Inquiry into Canada's blood supply system and the subsequent hepatitis C issues are instructive in this regard. Error-free performance is not merely desirable for this activity of government – it is expected.

In application, too often, the risk premium is zero up to a certain point, after which it becomes infinite for all practical purposes. This leads to 'acceptable consequences' and 'prohibited consequences.' A much more flexible and responsive approach, where the transition between acceptable and prohibited is gradual and based on particular circumstances, would be very helpful and is in some cases under development.

The second complicating factor is the credibility of government science. On a multitude of issues, when it comes to personal health or safety, Canadians are often unwilling to accept scientific research that reports that certain products or processes are safe, even when the scientific consensus is strong (Powell and Leiss, 1997). The level of trust needed to sustain a rational regulatory context does not seem to exist.

For the stewardship side of regulatory responsibilities, the damage function is not as direct. Normally what is at stake is the integrity of resources held in common by the community. In the case of renewable (biological) resources, this can include the survival of a species or a stock. Nonetheless, the indirect damage to individuals and communities can be extensive. Communities that depend on communal resources (such as fish, forests, or rivers) for their economic well-being can be severely affected if decisions on the stewardship of resources lead to long-term damage to those resources.

All this results in a system of regulations where the tolerance for error is very, very low. Most errors are only evident in retrospect; some are apparent very quickly, such as food poisoning, but some take a long time to become clear, such as depletion of fish stocks. This differentiates this function of government from many other government activities. The tolerance of citizens to experiment with new ideas or new institutional forms in a search for improvements in efficiency and effectiveness is much higher for areas where the damage function is not beyond remediation, or where it can be offset by equivalent gains without severe damage to individuals. Inherent in institutional experimentation is the increasing risk of error. For science-based regulations, as a general rule, this risk factor has a very high premium.

The Need for Scientific Inquiry and Information

The science-based regulation process involves a wide variety of applications of science and the scientific method. These applications of science are characterized by their *importance* (the dominance of scientific aspects of the regulations in the decision processes); *diversity* (the large number of decision elements (or tasks) for which science is a necessary component; and *interconnectedness* (the requirement for information and advice from several different disciplines and institutions on particular questions).

Although the nature and the depth of the science differ somewhat for each regulatory application, the tasks for which science is required are roughly the same. They are:

- Policy definition. For each application of regulatory intervention, the initial development of the policy requires an assessment of the damage that might be done to citizens or to the natural environment by the product or process under consideration. New science leads to better understanding of these risk functions and hence to the continuing potential for new regulatory activities. Regulations to improve urban air quality, for example, may need significant input from air chemistry, atmospheric science, respirology and other health sciences, industrial and automotive technology, fuel chemistry, and transportation studies. For example, information on the chemical process that created smog (NO_x + VOCs + sunlight), the sources of these elements (emissions from combustion and other sources), the atmospheric conditions that kept the smog from dissipating (temperature inversions), the health effects on human populations, and the potential impact on the incidence and severity of smog episodes from various regulatory options (auto and industrial technology, traffic flow, fuel composition, etc.) may be required for an assessment of the appropriateness of government action.
- Public consultation. Normally, new or revised regulations are subject to public review, and it is important to have credible scientific expertise available to answer questions and explain the scientific basis for the proposed regulations.

- Risk assessment. Once the nature of the problem has been determined, and the need for government action decided on, the natural sciences need to be integrated with economics and social sciences to determine what the parameters of the regulations should be, based principally on assessments of the risks associated with the damage that might be done and the economic and social costs of taking action at various levels. Rarely is the scientific basis of regulation sufficiently clear and unambiguous to provide a basis for decision on its own. Some of our regulatory systems have been built on that basis, but both the complexity of the decisions required and the demand by citizens for participation have rendered such approaches less effective.
- Legislation and regulation. The drafting of legislation and regulations requires accurate interpretation of the scientific underpinnings. This means that detailed knowledge of the associated science must be an integral part of drafting the legislation and regulations. Otherwise the outcome flowing from the regulation may well distort, diminish, or fail to realize its original intention.
- Evidence for applications. When a new product or process or activity is proposed for approval under science-based regulations, a body of scientific evidence is necessary to assess whether the proposal meets the requirements of the regulations.
- Analysis of evidence. Once the evidence is available, an analysis of the evidence is normally necessary to check the integrity and completeness of the evidence in order to take a decision. While the initial data can come from a variety of potential sources, the regulatory process demands that the assessment be conducted in an impartial and disinterested context.
- Appeals. The scientific basis for regulatory decisions needs to be available and sustainable in the event that the any decision is appealed.
- Monitoring. The application of and compliance with regulations need ongoing monitoring. Measuring effluents or inspecting buildings, for instance, are normally seen as necessary aspects of effective compliance programs and require applied science and engineering activities.
- Performance assessment. Finally, continuing assessment of the consequences of the regulations is important in ongoing program evaluation. There is a need for a continuing stream of scientific

data to ensure that the objectives of the regulations are being met and that no unacceptable side-effects are identified.

Each one of these functions can, and should, be considered separately with respect to the institutional choices available. There is no overarching reason, except for functionality, that would dictate that these activities need to be done in the same organizational context. Conversely, creating separate agencies or agents for each task should not be seen as an end in itself. Clearly, some of the functions are closely related, providing functional advantages to close institutional ties. The choices remain open, and should be examined based on the issues and the decision framework (or their equivalent) to be described below.

The Context for Organizational Decision Making

The decisions on whether to maintain or to change the organizational context will be based on a large variety of issues specific to each regulatory activity. But three important aspects of science-based regulations will be common to most decisions. A common understanding of the differences between the public interest and private interests, and role of government in managing them, is the first basic underpinning. The feedback influence that funding choices will have on the effectiveness of regulatory functions is a second key issue. Third, a good understanding of the context in which the science is developed and communicated is a necessary condition for effective organizational decisions.

The Public Interest

The public interest, in this case, the protection of citizens and stewardship of common resources, and private interests, determined in part by access to markets and international competitiveness, are the yin and yang of science-based regulations. These two sets of interests provide the tension that forms the basis for policy choices in this area, as they do in many areas of public policy.

With respect to the government's role in the management of private interests, the economic literature, and the recent literature on public administration, provide good guidance to the basic framework for government action. Intervention in the marketplace should be avoided unless there is a demonstrable need, and a reliable public process that can satisfy that need, with net benefits to society. Where intervention is required, the cost of the intervention should be borne by the beneficiaries of that intervention where possible and practical. Governments should enable, and encourage, the realization of private interests where possible, subject to the necessary public management of monopolies or quasi-monopolies, externalities (costs borne by other parties), and adequate information for the effective exercise of individual choice. Of crucial importance is the understanding that the expression of private interest is by far the most important source of the creation of wealth for our community. In general, barriers to the pursuit of private interest are likely to reduce the overall wealth of the country.

Issues are more complex when there is a public interest involved. Inherently, the identification of the beneficiaries is often difficult or impossible. Who, for instance, benefits from a regulation that requires universal inoculation against a communicable disease? Presumably, the beneficiary is the person who did not contract the disease but who otherwise would have. The commercial supplier of the vaccine gets a direct benefit (a guaranteed market), but the intention of the regulation is not to further the suppliers' interests. Regulatory activity oriented towards the prevention of 'bad things' happening (health, safety, or many environmental regulations) can rarely find a process to attribute the costs to intended beneficiaries. There are exceptions such as air safety programs where travellers can be targeted through airport taxes, for instance. (These should not be confused with airport capital development charges that emerged recently in Canada. These provide a good example of a situation where the beneficiary is *not* the one who pays the charge. Capital charges at airports result in costs to today's travellers for benefits that will accrue to travellers in the future – after the new construction for which the charges are being collected. Such a charge would be impossible in a normally functioning market where active direct competition exists. Note the exemption from the charges by passengers in transit who presumably have options for stop-over points. In theory, only a monopoly, without regulation to prevent it, could result in such a charge.)

A key question is: How far is it possible to go in using market mechanisms to provide the public interests that are the intentions of science-based regulations (Schultze, 1977)? Market-based instruments have proved to be very effective in delivering policies efficiently, and they have become well accepted as the preferred models for government intervention. It remains important to differentiate the objective (the public good) from the instrument (the marketlike mechanisms). Therefore, where a public interest can be identified, and where a community believes it to be worth pursuing, there must be an agent acting for the community – that is, a government – to ensure its realization.

As Gilles Paquet (1997: 42) points out, 'The real fundamental danger in exploring alternative service delivery schemes is that it is very easy to lose track of the effectiveness imperative.' Efficiency can, in some circumstances, drive out effectiveness. The achievement of the benefits from incentive-based action, as described by Schultze (1977), while, at the same time, ensuring that the objectives for the public good are realized, requires careful design of government interventions. Schultze identifies four 'virtues of the market': (1) markets are a form of unanimous consent (under normal conditions); (2) markets reduce the need for, and cost of, hard-to-get information; (3) markets promote change; and (4) markets direct innovation into socially desirable directions (efficiency of resource use).

Funding Sources

One particular area where the issues of public and private interests impact on decisions for science-based regulation is the question of how the costs of the regulatory activity should or can be allocated. In recent years, an important element of the restructuring of government has been the expansion of the use of fee-for-service charges or user-pay policies. There are two separable, but not always separate, intentions for the introduction of cost-recovery policies. The first objective is based on well-established theory concerning the responses of people and institutions to economic incentives. How an activity is financed, and by whom, has important consequences for the efficiency and the effectiveness of delivery.

If the direct beneficiaries, that is, those citizens who benefit from the primary objective, of a government service (including regulatory services) must pay for the delivery of the service, they will ensure that they express their needs clearly, review the delivery options regularly to ensure efficiency, and try to ensure that they receive value for money to the greatest extent possible. For the deliverer of the service, where a part of the income received comes from recipients of the service, there will be a tendency to do what is possible to satisfy the beneficiaries' needs as effectively and efficiently as possible. Economic determinism asserts that deliverers of services will align their approach with the interests of the source of their revenue.

The other objective of cost recovery is management of the overall fiscal position of the government. In this case, the objective is to reduce the financial burden of program (including regulatory programs) delivery to the taxpayer as much as possible without (usually) defeating the purpose of the program itself. Political decisions focus on the trade-offs between the effectiveness of programs and the recovery of costs rather than on their intersection.

For programs intended to address a public good, a difficulty in the implementation of measures to achieve the efficiency objective is that it is not always clear who the intended beneficiaries are. These include, for different regulations, health, safety, and stewardship interests (mostly in the case of public goods) and economic development interests (mostly in the case of private interests). Four basic requirements for an effective cost-recovery policy that is intended to go beyond simply fiscal objectives are: (1) the careful identification of the real interests being served; (2) the allocation of full costs according to those interests; (3) the avoidance of 'regulatory capture' by financial dependence on a single interest for a significant share of total revenue; and (4) the maintenance of a competitive regime relative to the costs of similar regulations in other countries. These objectives can clearly be in conflict in some circumstances. One of the basic arguments of this essay is that the resolution of such conflicts cannot be effectively resolved by a blanket 'one-size-fits-all' policy. Rather, careful assessment of the options and their implications on all interests – and on the credibility of the regulatory regime itself – needs to be done on a case-by-case basis. Such an approach would normally require consultation with the interested parties, both to clarify their interests and to assure that the information on which the policy is based is robust.

It is usually easy to identify and consult with those who represent the private interests. It is much more difficult, however, to identify appropriate representatives of the public interest. This could result in an unintended bias in the source of funds and the operational context of the regulations. Conversely, regulatory bodies can find it is easier to raise revenues from identifiable targets (usually the private interests) when those sources are compelled users (Farquhar, 1993) of regulatory services and/or when there is pressure on the political process to resist user fees or additional tax revenues. These pressures and ambiguities create a difficult decision context for effective cost recovery.

There are many circumstances where the public interest and private interests overlap. That is, regulatory policies and operations that serve one set of interests also serve the other. For example, an effective and highly credible meat-inspection program can ensure the highest level of food safety for Canadians as well as provide assured access to foreign markets for Canadian meat producers. In such circumstances, the design of regulations can be relatively easily agreed on, but the allocation of costs according to who receives the benefits is correspondingly more difficult to determine.

The Science Establishment

The possibility of separating the scientific research activities from the operational aspects of science-based regulations provides some interesting opportunities. As already noted, there are a number of discrete science-related activities that can be examined for potential change. But, such opportunities must be balanced against some potential drawbacks. Before making the general case for institutional reform, it is worthwhile to identify three particular aspects of the science establishment.

A consideration that lies partly within the efficiency objective, but deserves some special attention, is the issue of scale. The scale of operation, and hence the scope of human and physical scientific capital, is of great importance in many scientific functions. Organizational decisions on the science aspects of these regulations must include the implications for maintaining a critical mass of human capital and achieving the economies of scale available to large and/or narrowly focused scientific establishments. As science interests have been quick to point out, from the time of Vannevar Bush's report to President Truman – which established a postwar orthodoxy with respect to the government's role in science – the scale, scope, and long-term focus of science argue strongly for significant government involvement in the creation and maintenance of an effective scientific establishment (Bush, 1945).

The credibility of the science, at each stage of the regulatory process, is a most critical ingredient for the success of science-based regulations. Perceptions are as important as the underlying reality. International acceptability will certainly depend on perceptions of the reliability and integrity of the science. Citizens' acceptance of the regulatory regime that protects their health, safety, and environment very much depends on the citizens' confidence in the scientific basis for decisions. For example, scientific views on forestry practices that come from a forestry industry association or from an environmental non-government organization (NGO), justly or unjustly, will be assessed only in the context of the interests of the source, and that source is unlikely to be perceived as neutral or disinterested. Similarly, if government views on the potential dangers of some new chemical, say, are provided from an industry ministry, they may be perceived quite differently from (perhaps even the same) information that comes from an environment ministry. The independence of the science from commercial or political interests is an important factor in its credibility.

The third key issue is the need for significant input from experts on the science for the development of policy. To fulfil this responsibility, a source of scientific expertise must be available and in close contact with the policy development. Furthermore, various streams of science information need to be integrated with social and economic perspectives to allow for informed decisions. The more remote and independent the science establishment is from the policy world, the more difficult it will be to establish effective linkages.

These factors must be considered when the case for or against specific institutional options is examined. The next section provides a more general framework for decisions.

The Essence of Decisions – Balancing Interests

Competing Interests

The commercial potential, or private interest, of science-based regulations provides a strong rationale for an intensive examination and transformation of the form and financing of the regulatory agencies and their functions. Canada needs to develop a long-term strategy that will maximize Canada's potential advantages in this emerging domain of economics. Without a comprehensive plan based on new and open thinking, Canada may well be left behind. However, the damage function, representing the public interest, seems to argue equally strongly for a very conservative approach to institutional change. Governments are, to some extent, hostage to the strong aversion to risk of their constituents on matters of personal health and safety and on issues that threaten to do significant damage to the environment. Change for the sake of change, or for purely fiscal reasons, may carry unacceptably high risks – personal, social, and political.

Finally, the variety of needs for scientific input suggests that one factor that is encouraging organizational reform is the increasingly interdisciplinary nature of the issues and the interaction of various disciplines. For purposes of public policy, the boundaries between scientific disciplines are less and less relevant. The need for a more inclusive approach to scientific and other information that feeds into regulations is now widely accepted. In addition, the credibility of the science needs to be maintained at a high level to satisfy the need for public confidence. The diminishing trust in institutions, including governments, suggests that new institutional approaches may help if they can be the basis for more open and transparent scientific information for regulatory decisions.

Decisions will have to be made on a case-by-case basis, trying to balance these competing forces. The key requirement is to ensure that all the relevant considerations are examined in such decisions. As illustrated in the next section, there is a rather large number of questions that should be asked, or options that should be examined, in the process of choosing new approaches to science-based regulation. They focus on the attributes that the agent or agents responsible for the regulatory functions must have.

Elements of Decision Making

The establishment of a new organizational form to manage science-based regulation will present policy makers with a large array of possible institutional arrangements. The list below is indicative of the choices that should be considered. It is useful to note that some of the choices are interdependent, but for most of the areas identified, a full spectrum of choices is available. The elements of choice are elaborated with the types of options to be considered.

Type of Institution
- Unit within department (for example, division or branch)
- Special purpose agency
- Cooperative venture (joint ownership)
- Non-governmental organization (not for profit)
- Commercial enterprise (for profit organization)

Source of Legitimacy
- Federal legislation
- Parallel federal and provincial legislation
- Departmental mandate (from minister)
- Industry and government agreement
- Contract for services

Market Position
- Competes with private sector service providers
- Monopoly provider of regulatory services
- Virtual monopoly (only provider with legislative authority)

Governance
- Departmental responsibility (deputy minister)
- Board of directors (advisory, quasi-judicial, recommends, reviews)
- Directors can be responsible for substance or administration or both
- Governing council (representing parties to contract)

Reporting/Accountability
From
- Deputy minister, executive head, board of directors, or governing council
to
- Minister(s)
- Prime minister through minister
- Parliament through minister

Scope of Minister's Responsibility
- Policy (development of regulations)
- Operational decisions under regulations
- Compliance
- Science for regulation
- Administration of agency

Procedures: Human Resources (HR)
- Subject to Public Service Staff Relations Act (PSSRA) and Public Service Commission (PSC) administration

- Subject to PSSRA but with local administration
- Separate negotiated HR regime
- Private sector HR status
- Remuneration and pension rules

Procedures: Finance and Audit
- Subject to Financial Administration Act
- Freedom regarding contracting, borrowing, rate setting, and/or financial controls
- Auditing by auditor general
- Private sector auditing

Source of Science
- In-house
- From regulated companies and intervenors
- Contract, that is, from universities
- Purchase from commercial vendors (including offshore)

Source of Revenue
- Appropriations from federal budget
- Costs covered by beneficiaries (that is, home owner pays inspection fee)
- Costs allocated to system users (annual charge to be in system)
- Fee for direct services (builder pays inspection fee)
- Endowment (revolving fund and interest income)

Disposition of Revenue
- To central revenue fund
- To agency budget (for discretionary spending)
- To outside funders (to reduce annual contribution)
- To reserve fund (to be spent when instructed)

Finding a Balance

The decisions made on the institutional basis for science-based regulations will all, in different ways, affect the essential trade-off being faced. Economic interests are served by speedy, predictable, and efficient regulation. Citizen engagement and trust, reflecting the high level of public concern for the areas under consideration and the increasing demands for citizen participation in decision making, require a time-

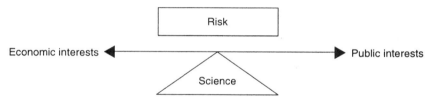

Figure 13.1 Science arbitrates interests subject to risk perceptions.

consuming, unpredictable, and often cumbersome process. On most of the critical elements of the decision processes, science is a necessary component of the arbitration of these competing interests. But, science is not, as we have seen in recent history (Powell and Leiss, 1997), sufficiently certain to be completely authoritative. It cannot provide unambiguous advice without an assessment and understanding of the risks involved, and the interpretation of those risks by all parties. For decision making, the science must also be combined with other goals and objectives of the regulatory system to provide a complete and robust context for the ultimate decision (see Figure 13.1; Jarvis, 1998). There are a variety of ways to look at the trade-offs inherent in this model. The core concept, which lies at the heart of any of these conceptual frameworks, is the notion of the public interest and the role of governments in identifying and serving the public interest.

Decision-Making Model

The public interest itself cannot normally be portrayed as a one-dimensional aspect of the decision-making process. The primary objective – protection – is nested inside a variety of attributes of the institutional framework. These attributes address issues of governance, effectiveness (and perceptions of effectiveness), cost to the society of obtaining the benefits, and other key objectives of the government of the day (in current circumstances, costs to the treasury cannot be ignored).

The effectiveness of science-based regulatory activities, that is, the delivery of the principle societal objectives, will ultimately depend on the capacity to satisfy all of these attributes. Each is, in turn, affected by the institutional framework within which the regulatory activities are undertaken. In a very simplified form, these characteristics can be grouped under the general areas of:

- Accountability: The Westminster system makes ministers accountable for their portfolios to Parliament, and hence to the Canadian public.
- Neutrality (credibility): The trust and confidence that the Canadian public, and external users of Canadian regulations, have in the regulatory system depend on the perception of disinterested (neutral) and effective process.
- Efficiency: The quality and quantity of product per unit cost – not necessarily the total cost or the effectiveness with respect to outcomes are important.
- Cost to the treasury: The financial burden that must be borne by governments from general tax revenues is taken into consideration.

The organizational options, although rich in detailed variety, can be grouped to represent the main generic options. These are departmental (in-house), stand-alone agency (with legislative base), non-governmental organization or voluntary sector, and private sector enterprise (including industry-led voluntary or compelled regulatory programs). These general categories can be used to demonstrate a decision-matrix for desirable organizational options for science-based regulations. In very abstract terms, accountability is strongest within the established accountability systems of normal government operations (Table 13.1). Departmental and ministerial accountability are clearly defined in precedent, regulation, and operational practice. Conversely, the more that the functions can be undertaken within a private sector environment, the stronger is the potential for cost minimization with respect to the public purse. Thus, Table 13.1 attempts to show a continuum of options for organizational form on the basis of each form's strengths and weaknesses against key criteria.

The decisions regarding form need not be taken, for any particular regulatory function, as an all-or-nothing proposition. The argument of this chapter is quite the opposite. Not only is it conceivable, it is desirable to separate the scientific activities on which the regulatory process is based from the operational or policy elements of regulatory activities for purposes of organizational decisions. Furthermore, each step of the regulatory process has different characteristics, and by extension different criteria for selecting an optimal organizational form. For instance, the policy development, and the writing of legislation and regulations, probably require direct and unambiguous political

Table 13.1. A conceptual decision-making framework

Criteria/form	Accountability	Neutrality (credibility)	Cost (to gov't) minimization	Efficiency
Department	✔✔✔✔	✔✔✔	✔✔	✔
Stand alone agency	✔✔✔	✔✔✔✔	✔	✔✔
Non-gov't organization	✔✔	✔✔✔	✔✔✔✔	✔
Private sector	✔	✔✔	✔✔✔	✔✔✔✔

accountability as the first priority. The assessment of submissions function, and the consultation function, need the perception and reality of neutrality and credibility. The development of evidence for assessment and regulatory decisions needs to be as efficient as possible to sustain competitiveness, and that may argue for the application of private sector options. In fact, this is the approach taken by many of Canada's regulatory agencies. Information on the proposed application of regulatory functions is the responsibility of the proponent, sometimes augmented by public or NGO information sources.

More detailed institutional decisions concerning form and responsibilities, as illustrated in the previous section, can also be taken in the context of this framework. Thus, for instance, financial authorities and the auditing function can and should be tailored, case by case, to the particular intentions of the organizational form. Specifically, the application of desired procedural changes, such as cost-recovery criteria, will have widely differing implications for the various aspects of the regulatory implementation process. Careful assessment is necessary in all cases to ensure that the universal pursuit of one or another of the key objectives does not, in fact, diminish the pursuit of other objectives where they are most important for an effective regulatory regime.

Options for Change – Three Proposals

The above discussions provide a mostly conceptual look at the issues of institutional change for science-based regulations. They provide the basis for a framework for decision making, as well as identifying some of the forces for change. Can this framework be used in real applications that deal with the problems and challenges that must be faced?

This section moves beyond the conceptual framework to examine real opportunities for change.

How should governments in Canada proceed? On a case-by-case basis, and subject to the criteria already noted, this chapter proposes three key areas of opportunity: (1) cooperation, (2) scientific authority, and (3) voluntarism. Each of these areas responds to some of the concerns and/or opportunities identified above. Provided that the development and implementation of change respects the need for balance and for comprehensive assessment, these suggestions can provide the basis for effective and productive change.

Cooperation

In many areas, complex systems of regulation are managed by diverse, sometimes competing, organizations. Where these organizations coexist within one level of government, a rationalization of regulatory programs along the principles that guided the development of the Canadian Food Inspection Agency should be examined. There, eighteen government programs from four departments were integrated into one agency. Not only did this create a critical mass of regulatory expertise in the area of food system regulations, but it also addressed issues of duplication and *gaps* in the exercise of federal responsibilities, as well as giving industry and consumers a single reference point for issues related to Canada's national food regulations.

The next logical step in coordination is the federal-provincial areas of common regulatory interests. On a small scale, agencies such as the Canada–Newfoundland Offshore Petroleum Board give examples of how joint responsibility can be shared through one agency. The harmonization of federal and provincial information requirements that are inherent in such an arrangement could provide valuable efficiency gains if the jurisdictional integrity of the actors can be sustained. To accomplish this, the federal government would need to take the lead. Establishing open-ended regulatory agencies, where other jurisdictions could opt-in, with carefully structured decision-making authority, could provide the basis for a step-wise movement to integration at the national level. As pointed out for the case of food inspection, 'the federalism problem ... is not (only) a case of eliminating costly duplication. Rather the task is to coordinate disparate regulatory systems and fill in gaps in the system.' (Moore and Skogstad, 1998: 131).

Cooperation, with the objective of harmonization and possibly integration at the international level, should also be carefully considered in light of the emerging trends in markets. Bilateral agreements can proceed step by step if agencies have the authority and the flexibility to undertake the necessary compromises for harmonization. The establishment of joint review processes, such as the ones being developed by the Pest Management Regulatory Agency, demonstrate the potential for progress. However, issues of sovereignty form a major impediment to the creation of international agencies with shared decision-making powers. Multinational harmonization may require the establishment of arm's-length agencies to negotiate a research consensus among nations. Only where there is a genuine bilateral desire for harmonization, with identified shared interests, are the prospects for successful harmonization worth pursuing (George Jack, personal communication).

Cooperation at all levels provides an opportunity to improve overall efficiency, as well as reduce costs to governments. Ultimately, successful implementation will require the development of new institutions where decision-making authority is shared by the parties according to their particular roles. The question of accountability of ministers for decisions taken by agencies with multiple reporting structures needs careful consideration. The risk of capture by the strongest existing international organizations (the major corporate interests), which poses a concern about the neutrality and effectiveness of the resulting process, must also be managed to the satisfaction of citizens.

Scientific Authority

Two propositions have been raised in this chapter: (1) Trust and credibility of the science base for regulations are essential elements of effective regulation; and (2) government science is no longer always viewed as neutral or disinterested. Organizational and/or financing options can be used to address this difficulty. As noted earlier, dependence on a particular source of financing can affect the independence, or at least the perception of independence, of the information put forward by scientific authorities.

A formal scientific review agency, serving many departments and agencies, as independent as possible from departmental budget decisions (and fluctuations) could help establish a framework for a more authoritative science review. It would be used as a supplement to the normal sources of science to regulatory agencies, whether in-house or externally based, when the science is challenged or when there is a specific need for an independent view. Such an agency need not have on-site expertise in particular fields of science. It would act more as an organizer of scientific review by Canada's experts in particular fields as requested by regulators or ministers when faced with challenges to the scientific advice arriving through normal channels. Such a separate agency (reporting through, not to, a central agency of the government administration) could resolve the difficult tension between the need for independent scientific assessments and the internal and policy needs for science for the operation of regulatory activities. The main scientific work would remain close to the policy areas, but with a fallback to the independent structure in the case of controversy. To be successful, secure and independent funding would be required. The incentive structure should be to sustain credibility, not to seek out more business or to benefit from higher levels of controversy.

Provided the incentive structure for both the new agency, and its potential users, is well structured, enhancing the authority of the science base for regulations is achievable. But, it would not be achieved immediately. Trust in the institution would build up over time. Unlike commissions of enquiry or other such one-off review processes, such an institution could build confidence over time on the basis of its performance. That is, a sort of 'confidence capital' could be built up.

Voluntary Approaches

Over the past decade the increased use of formalized consultation processes on issues of public policy has established a better understanding in all the communities involved of the needs and the potential for action of each of the main sectors. The openness of the relationship between business, government, and other sectors in Canada provides an opportunity to take some creative steps in utilizing the self-interest of companies to provide more effective and less costly regulatory regimes. Some examples of such approaches already exist (for example, through commitments of the chemical industry and the electricity-generating industry to environmental standards). Science-based regulatory processes could take advantage of such approaches provided that a sufficient degree of confidence can be established.

At the centre of such an approach is the implementation of an out-comes basis for achieving the intention of regulations rather than, or in parallel to, prescriptive approaches. Provided that the administrative and organizational overhead are not major costs relative to the overall costs of compliance, it is reasonably easy to demonstrate that a performance-based, self-administered program can minimize the costs of achieving the desired outcomes. Experience seems to show (although this is an issue that requires some further study), that not only is compliance less costly, but the standards achieved often exceed those that result from non-voluntary prescriptive measures. The reason for this is that, in a voluntary approach, the incentive for companies is to demonstrate the best possible achievement, whereas in a prescriptive, non-voluntary approach the incentive is to minimize the cost of achieving the prescribed levels. Successful implementation depends on a well-structured framework, including well-specified objectives, prescribed monitoring and reporting regimes, and mechanisms for verification of performance. For example, the New Directions Group, a multisectoral interest group, has developed eight criteria for credible and effective voluntary programs. These should be developed and implemented in a participatory manner; transparent in design and operation; and performance-based with specified goals, and measurable objectives and milestones. They should have clearly specified rewards and consequences regarding performance; encourage flexibility and innovation. They should prescribe monitoring and reporting requirements, including timetables, and include mechanisms for verifying the performance of all participants, as well as for continuous improvement for participants and for the program.

Problems remain. Accountability is difficult to manage, and the issue of free riders must be addressed. However, it is possible to envisage a two-tiered regulatory process whereby commitment to a voluntary approach, together with an auditable reporting system to the responsible minister, could exempt companies from a second tier prescriptive regulatory regime. Clearly, such a plan would not be suitable for all areas of science-based regulations. However, where achievable, it could improve efficiency, lower costs to the taxpayer, and provide increased effectiveness.

Such an approach must be developed by industry, and a necessary condition is that there be sufficient flexibility in the legislation to permit this. An industry-based institutionalization of such a program, through an industry association, for instance (as is the case for both the chemical industry and the electricity-generating industry), would be a necessary component. Virtually all costs except policy development and monitoring could be borne by the companies involved.

Finally, the system would need to pass the test of public acceptability. This would require significant investment in public relations, and it may prove to be impossible in highly contentious areas. In spite of the difficulties, the potential benefits warrant serious examination in many areas of science-based regulation.

Conclusion

This chapter has argued that, across a large number of dimensions, the rethinking of the institutional underpinnings and the financial basis for science-based regulations face competing tensions. Independence versus relevance, public versus private interests, efficiency versus effectiveness, among other trade-offs, are at the heart of decisions for reform. The issues are sufficiently complex and case-dependent that a prescriptive approach to reform is not only unwarranted, but inadvisable.

This does not suggest that reform is either unnecessary or impossible. On the contrary, to meet the emerging challenges of a more internationally linked and more publicly engaged context, continuous review and reform will be essential to achieve the greatest net benefits to Canadians. The analysis has explored some examples of areas where opportunities exist and should be examined. However, the chapter is not intended to be prescriptive in a simple fashion. Each regulatory function needs to be looked at on its particular merits. Change should be an ongoing process for science-based regulators with an expectation of continuously emerging new challenges calling for well-targeted reforms.

To be successful, such reforms will need to be informed by: (1) the intended consequences of the reform; (2) the potential unintended implications for the regulatory framework; and (3) a good understanding of the implicit and explicit signals to all participants that result from the reform. This can only be done with a case-by-case approach, based on political direction that includes all of the important aspects of the regulations. Ultimately, the resolution of the difficult trade-offs will require political decisions. It is absolutely essential that these decisions, just like the regulatory decisions themselves, be based on sound and complete information.

References

Arthur, B. (1990). 'Positive Feedbacks in the Economy.' In *Scientific American*, 65 (February): 92–9.

Aucoin Peter. (1997). *The New Public Management: Canada in Comparative Perspective*. Montreal: Institute for Research in Public Policy.

Bush, V. (1945). *Science: The Endless Frontier, Report to the President of the United States*. Washington: U.S. Government Printing Office.

Farquhar C. (1993). *Focusing on the Customer: A Catalyst for Change in the Public Service*. Ottawa: Conference Board of Canada.

Jarvis, Bill. (1998). *The Role and Responsibilities of the Scientist*. Ottawa: Public Policy Forum.

Moore, E., and G. Skogstad. (1998). 'Food for Thought: Food Inspection and Renewed Federalism.' In Leslie Pal, ed., *How Ottawa Spends 1998*, 127–52. Oxford: Oxford University Press.

Organization for Economic Cooperation and Development (OECD. (1998). *International Regulatory Cooperation*. PUMA Work on Regulatory Management and Reform Web Site (7/31/98). www.oecd.org/puma/regref/coopern.html

Pacquet, G. (1997). 'Alternative Service Delivery: Transforming the Practices of Government,' in D. Ford and D. Zussman, eds., *Alternative Service Delivery*, 31–58. Toronto: Institute of Public Administration of Canada.

Powell, D., and W. Leiss. (1997). *Mad Cows and Mother's Milk*. Montreal: McGill-Queen's University Press.

Schultze, C. (1977). *The Public Use of Private Interest*. Washington, DC: Brookings Institution.

Zussman, D. (1991). 'Government Service to the Public: Public Perception.' *Optimum*, 10: 22–4.

14 Central Agencies, Horizontal Issues, and Precarious Values: Coordinating Science Policy in the Federal Government

EVERT LINDQUIST and MARGARET BARKER

Science and technology (S&T) policy can be viewed as the quintessential horizontal policy and administrative challenge that confronts the federal government: scientific activity spans departments and agencies across the system, and it has always supported competing policy goals and been of interest to very different sectors of society. Moreover, we know that many of the boundaries that defined the traditional categories of scientific inquiry, as well as the borders of the institutions that sponsor that work, have been melting away. For a variety of reasons, then, considerable pressure has emerged for the federal government to better coordinate the activities of science-based departments and agencies (SBDAs) and to increase collaboration across traditional program, department, and portfolio boundaries. In March 1996, the federal government announced a new strategy entitled *Science and Technology for a New Century: A Federal Strategy* (Canada, 1996a).

Every policy area has its own complexities and institutional trajectories, but for those who study more general issues in public management, many of the themes presented by recent debates and initiatives on federal science and technology policy seem quite familiar. The purpose of this chapter is to explore how the central institutions of government have been mobilized and how they have contributed to recent initiatives in science and technology policy. We think that too often many of the broader developments in federal S&T policy have been analysed and evaluated on their own terms, without reference to larger developments in public administration. Conversely, we believe that there is insufficient understanding of how the central institutions do their work and how they contribute to the identification and resolution of problems in substantive policy areas.

What follows can be seen as an attempt to use recent developments in federal S&T policy as cases for discerning the ways in which modern governments and central agencies review, implement, and monitor policy regimes. This chapter has four parts. The first introduces an alternative way to conceptualize how science and technology policy is developed and then administered. It identifies two intersecting coordination challenges: one that is presented by the problems and opportunities inherent in furthering science and technology goals, and the other emerging from the full range of demands that governments must confront. We introduce a framework for analysing how central institutions can be organized to deal with such challenges, one that guides the rest of the chapter. The next three sections explore how the federal government and its central institutions were involved in recent efforts to review, implement, and then assess the progress made on science and technology policy.

We conclude that the case of recent policy making in science and technology illustrates well the new and different ways in which central agencies are involved in the affairs of the departments and agencies, particularly with respect to horizontal issues and performance management. However, we link this analysis to larger questions about the extent to which *Science and Technology for a New Century* can be viewed as a sustainable policy and administrative regime. We argue that science policy can be viewed as a 'precarious value' in politics and society in Canada and that therefore it is amenable to shifts depending on the whims of governments and on evanescent views about how public policy and public management ought to be handled more generally.

Two Coordination Challenges: Managing S&T Issues and Managing the Government

To properly analyse the issues and developments in the management of the current federal science and technology policy regime requires acknowledging that its very complexity and the pressures for its reform emanate from two general directions. First, there are the substantive challenges arising from S&T activities that must be balanced across the spheres of government, business, universities, and society. Second, there are the political, policy, and administrative challenges that confront the central institutions of government, which are responsible not only for balancing contending demands and views inside and outside government, but for providing leadership and guiding frameworks. Central agencies must grapple with substantive policy challenges like those presented by science and technology, but just as views evolve about how to deal with particular domains of public policy, they also evolve about how the centre ought to address such challenges and deal with other departments and agencies.

There is a big literature on the gaps, contradictions, and complexity of science and technology policy in Canada. The themes and issues are well known (O'Gorman, 1998), but little is said about the management challenge confronting institutions at the centre of government attempting to advise governments. Central agencies are confronted with the challenge of monitoring and coordinating a myriad of departments and agencies with diverse interests in S&T policy. They include the following:

- Departments with very different mandates but that invest substantial resources in scientific activities include Industry Canada, Environment Canada, Health Canada, Agriculture and Agri-Food Canada, Department of Fisheries and Oceans, Natural Resources Canada, Statistics Canada, and Department of National Defence
- Somewhat more autonomous agencies involved in science, research, and technology include the National Research Council, Natural Science and Engineering Research Council, Medical Research Council, Canadian Space Agency, and Social Sciences and Humanities Research Council of Canada
- The Department of Finance is directly involved because it controls tax policy expenditures on science and technology, and it sets parameters, along with the Treasury Board of Canada, on outlays for each department and agency
- Human Resources Development Canada and several regional development agencies such as the Atlantic Canada Opportunities Agency, Federal Office of Regional Development (Quebec), and Western Economic Diversification Canada administer funds to promote the development of skills in science and technology jobs, and some offer programs to encourage business to undertake and utilize research and development.

To further complicate matters, provincial and territorial governments also have their own array of programs to assist universities, hospitals, business, and other partners with research and its commercialization.

Many SBDAs not only manage their own scientific enterprises, but also support the work of researchers at universities and private sector entrepreneurs.

Governments and central agencies have to find ways to monitor, balance, identify, and bridge gaps in the activities of all of these actors. Transcending the particular needs of any one department, agency, or program is the problem of competing policy goals and difficult choices about where to invest scarce resources. Where S&T expenditures are concerned, should the federal government primarily seek to support pure or curiosity-driven science, economic growth, and commercial enterprises, or social goals such as improving health and managing risks such as pollution control? These questions have long vexed governments and their advisers from inside and outside the federal government. However, S&T challenges stand as only one bundle of issues with which governments must contend. One has to think of foreign policy, the national unity debate, health care reform, the question of child poverty, immigration policy, the closing of fisheries on the east and west coasts, and defence policy, to name only a few issues, to see the point. Even with the consolidated structures arising out of the June 1993 restructuring of the federal government, there are still twenty-three departments and over fifty additional agencies. It is a mind-numbing, higher-order level of complexity that confronts the prime minister and Cabinet ministers every day of the week.

For this reason governments created central agencies such as the Privy Council Office, Department of Finance, Treasury Board Secretariat, Public Service Commission, Departments of Justice, and Department of Public Works and Government Services – and other coordinating entities such as ministerial portfolios and ministries of state. These agencies assist governments in developing and then implementing their priorities, develop policy and fiscal frameworks within which all programs and initiatives must proceed, explore the intergovernmental implications of policy problems, develop cross-government views on public policy and administrative issues, filter and respond to demands from departments and agencies, coordinate and cajole departments and agencies to implement initiatives and to provide information, and serve as focal points for accountability. These central agencies are often the gatekeepers to Cabinet committees and the progenitors of rules and procedures guiding the activities and reporting of departments and agencies. However, central agencies and other coordinating entities can also provide leadership when it comes to identifying policy and administrative problems, and designing reforms to remedy the problems, particularly when the problems and remedies transcend the boundaries of departments and agencies.

The central institutions of government inevitably look powerful and concentrated when viewed from a distance in most systems (as is usually implied by the term 'the centre'), because of their responsibilities and proximity to Cabinet committees (Lindquist, 1996a, 1998a). However, practitioners know this image becomes more complicated and confusing if one works in or around central agencies or, alternatively, for parts of departments and agencies with regular dealings with the centre. Central agencies have broad spans of specific responsibilities including budgeting, policy and administrative reviews, machinery-of-government and alternative service delivery, a multitude of human resource issues, financial reporting, official languages, employment equity, intergovernmental relations, and real property management, to name only a few. Moreover, central agencies often *share* responsibility for developing, implementing, and monitoring administrative policies with the departments and agencies they seek to regulate.

Rather than evaluate the behaviour of entire central agencies, it may be more fruitful to identify the domains of responsibility held at the centre, which are usually the responsibility of specific, and often quite small, central bureaus (that is, units within larger central agencies), which stand at the nodes of networks of interested or affected departments and agencies across a public service, which may include officials in other central bureaus. As Lindquist (1996a: 227) has argued:

> This way of looking at central agencies is striking for several reasons. First, each network represents different spheres of substantive and administrative policy, and each has its own communities-of-practice in the public service across central bureaus, departments and agencies. Rather than take an organization-based view of central agencies and their influence, it suggests that we adopt a more functionally-based and knowledge-based view of specific clusters of tasks, and then explore how central bureaus related to those its seeks to influence, regulate or control across the bureaucracy. Second, it suggests that we should pay relatively less attention to the number and size of central agencies, and instead see institutional structures (i.e., such as a cabinet office or management board) as organizational 'baskets' for housing central bureaus and their responsibilities. Closer scrutiny of specific bureaus and their networks is war-

ranted in order to determine how each is managed, how they respond to evolving demands, and how they identify and adopt best practices. In short, this approach places less emphasis on formal structure, and more emphasis on capacities and learning.

This approach suggests that influence may obtain more from information, consultation, best practices, idea sharing, and pockets of expertise *not* at the centre, than from the formal approvals, pretransaction clearances, and limits dictated by central bureaus. It also anticipates that departments and agencies may possess greater competency and capacity than central bureaus. This suggests that, at times, the centre may be in 'catch-up' mode with some departments and agencies, even while playing an important role in assisting some others that are laggards. This approach also suggests that the relative capacities of central agencies may vary considerably by administrative or substantive policy domain. Each central bureau will have different tasks and authorities, and a unique basis for interacting with departments – and therefore the character of the network should change accordingly. For example, in the area of human resources, central bureaus usually delegate many tasks to officials in operating departments, monitor their activities, and help to organize councils across the system. In contrast, estimates divisions monitor and liaise with particular departments. They tend to interact with departments on a bilateral basis, and do not ordinarily facilitate the exchange of ideas and practices across programs and departments.

This framework, in effect, calls on observers to examine central agencies with a finer grain – to engage in what some might call 'differentiation.' However, if central agencies are indeed baskets of smaller bureaus, this points to the important question of integration; since departments and agencies must often deal simultaneously with different parts of each of the central agencies. From their vantage point the centre does not comprise three or four central agencies, but perhaps twenty or more central bureaus. Thus, even before one contemplates horizontal policy challenges such as science and technology, the matter of integration and the need to coordinate looms for practical and conceptual reasons, both for central agencies and for departments and agencies.

There are many ways to integrate and coordinate. Prime ministers have a crucial role flowing from their prerogative to design the Cabinet decision-making system, its committees, and processes, and to make decisions about the size and responsibilities of departments and ministerial portfolios. These are powerful tools, and they can be deployed not only to allocate political and bureaucratic responsibilities, but also to better coordinate across departments and portfolios. Such coordination can be achieved by assigning the task to a Cabinet committee (which could be created for this purpose), to a lead minister (perhaps with the assistance of a secretary of state), to a central agency or a central bureau (either of which could also be created for this purpose), or to task forces composed of officials from different departments and agencies. Coordination can also be achieved by requiring departments and agencies to report to lead agencies on new matters, either by utilizing existing reporting regimes or by creating new ones, and by having lead agencies provide horizontal perspectives on information.

These mechanisms can be used in various combinations, and they produce their own complexities for officials in central bureaus, departments, and agencies. Indeed, some caution must be exercised: there can be much coordination around an issue without remedying the underlying problems; consequently, it behooves leaders and observers alike to assess whether or not coordination produces meaningful change for programs and working-level officials. To adapt a phrase from Aaron Wildavsky, 'If coordination is everything, then maybe it's nothing.'

Outlining the possibilities for coordination can take us only so far. One way to deepen our knowledge of the issues, and to capture nuances, is to examine how a policy area like federal S&T policy evolves, and to review how the government intervened. Lindquist (1998a) suggests it may be useful to organize analysis around the phases of strategic review, implementation, monitoring, and evaluation 'although finer distinctions could be made,' and below we present preliminary observations and analysis on the management of S&T policy according to the general framework.

Strategic Reviews: Demands for a New Science and Technology Strategy

Many observers might contend that, because of the challenges posed by the information technology revolution, and the emergence of freer trade regimes, it was inevitable that a country like Canada would have to develop a new S&T policy during the 1990s. But identifying such secular pressures for a policy challenge usually fails to indicate why certain policies were adopted at particular times, and why they took the shape they did. Below we show that the federal strategy, *Science and Technology for a New Century*, arose as much as a result of domestic forces as external ones. Understanding how S&T rose to the top of the government's agenda also serves to illustrate the subtle roles and dance between central agencies and of de facto central agencies like the auditor general of Canada.

The first pressures emerged after several years of cuts to operating budgets and wage freezes in the public service. With few exceptions, the government of Brian Mulroney was unwilling to make major program cuts or to further increase taxes, which resulted in a burgeoning deficit. This affected all areas of government, with the important exception of the Green Plan announced in 1990, which at the outset called for the expenditure of $3 billion of new money, much of which found its way into science-based departments. However, in the February 1992 federal budget, the government eliminated what it believed were unnecessary agencies, such as the Science Council. Although the conventional wisdom is that basic science was cut more deeply in favour of applied research and other programs directly delivered to Canadians, it has been argued that, until 1994, the amount of basic research conducted inside the federal government and in the private and university sectors had not decreased, but that more applied research was being done on a collaborative basis with the private sector (Gualtieri, 1994). However, notwithstanding the activities of the National Advisory Board on Science and Technology (NABST) the government failed to produce a robust science policy for the country. This era culminated in the June 1993 restructuring of Cabinet and the public service by the government of Kim Campbell shortly before an election. It dramatically reduced the size of Cabinet, transferred and consolidated departments and agencies into new portfolios, and secured additional reductions in expenditures. The ultimate goal was to better position the public service to grapple with major expenditure reductions and subsequent policy change.

From an S&T perspective, the restructuring seemed promising initially. As Doern has described (1996: 75–6): 'Industry Canada incorporated a wider set of policy tools and mandates by absorbing areas such as consumer policy and business framework law, including competition policy, from the former Department of Consumer and Corporate Affairs, investment policy and research from Investment Canada, and telecommunications policy and research from the former Department of Communication and the minister also had to manage an enlarged portfolio or ministry as well as a department per se.' The new department was, briefly, called Industry and Science Canada, and was to be the lead within government on S&T policy matters, although most science in the government was carried out in agencies outside the department in the new portfolio and in other science-based departments (ibid.: 91, 97). The real question was: How quickly could the department coalesce as it took on major policy and administrative challenges?

These challenges arrived early in 1994 in the form of three review processes: the Science and Technology Review, the Program Review, and audits undertaken by the auditor general of Canada. The S&T Review was announced in the February 1994 budget as a cross-governmental initiative, led by Industry Canada, rather than a central agency. The review was not formally launched until June that year, and it involved regional public conferences, a national forum, several cross-governmental working groups, and a receipt of submissions (Canada, 1996b). NABST was also asked to prepare a report. The Program Review announced in the federal budget spanned all federal programs. It too began tentatively, and although it was depicted as an 'alternative delivery' process, it became driven by expenditure reduction targets as the deficit situation deteriorated (Greenspon and Wilson-Smith, 1996). Departments and agencies had to develop options generally consistent with these targets for a committee of ministers and a committee of deputy ministers, advised by Finance and Treasury Board officials (de la Mothe, 1996).

In the spring of 1994, the auditor general released a devastating critique of how government managed research and development activities (see Auditor General of Canada: chapters 9–11). The critique pointed to the lack of strategic context for S&T programs, poor management of professional development of scientists and staff, and insufficient interest on the part of Treasury Board in the problems and challenges of the scientific community. It called on the government to become more strategic and develop a government-wide approach. Such findings could not be ignored by a government depicting itself as supportive of knowledge and research and as an astute and hard-nosed manager of government programs.

Neither the S&T Review (March 1996) nor the NABST Report (June 1995) influenced the Program Review decisions on science and technology. Some observers lamented their delay (de la Mothe, 1996), but they had been deliberately de-coupled from the Program Review process once senior Industry Canada officials realized that decisions would be taken quickly and would be budget-driven. The Program Review decisions led to deep cuts to Industry Canada, reductions in its workforce by 20 per cent and in overall spending by 51 per cent over the planning horizon from 1994–5 to 1997–8, and substantially cut department-based S&T funding as well as locating the responsibility for S&T under the broader domain of micro-economic policy (Doern, 1996). The auditor general's report contributed to the perception of unfocused and poorly managed S&T programs.

From a planning perspective, it was probably appropriate that the final report of the S&T Review was delayed so that its authors could better assess the resource base from which a federal strategy would work. It was predicated on a commitment to a national innovation system and to the 'dynamic interplay' of science serving simultaneously in the interests of economic growth, quality of life, and the advancement of knowledge (Canada, 1996a). It provided a list of new priorities and pilot projects (but did not indicate where cuts were taken), and it indicated that the government would continue to emphasize alternative service delivery and partnership arrangements, as well as higher-quality science. The report was accompanied by the release of department and agency S&T action plans (Canada, 1996b), and included a commitment to prepare an annual report on S&T programs across the government. The report also announced new advisory and decision-making mechanisms, new management structures and processes for managing S&T programs across departments and agencies, and a new human resource management framework. Finally, it called for improved coordination among federal, provincial, and territorial governments, and a commitment to create stronger public interest in science, especially among youth.

The purpose of this chapter, however, is not to dissect the contents of the federal strategy, nor to determine which policy actors exerted the most influence on certain issues. Rather, our task is to shed light on how the government and central agencies recently handled the science and technology review. Let us begin by noting that the federal strategy emerged out of a very interesting confluence of events, having to do with the 1993 restructuring of the federal government, the arrival of a new Liberal government with an interest in the new economy, the decision of the auditor general of Canada to audit S&T programs, and a deteriorating federal deficit shooting to the top of the political agenda. One can imagine that, had one or two of these developments occurred at different times, or not at all, that the scope and timing of the federal strategy may well have been quite different. Some authors place emphasis on the role of chance, and the streams of people, ideas, and problems in policy debates and policy development (Kingdon, 1984). For example, if public interest in the deficit had occurred a year or more later, then a more policy-driven review and restructuring of federal S&T programs might have unfolded. Our point here is that no single minister, central agency, or department seemed to have decisive control over the process and its substantive outcomes.

Decisions that had considerable consequence for S&T programs were often taken by small groups of ministers and officials in closed and time-constrained processes. For example, the design of the massive June 1993 restructuring that created the Industry portfolio emanated from a small unit responsible for the machinery of government and senior personnel matters in the Privy Council Office. Because of its different focus, that process could not possibly have worked through the implications for science and technology policies and programs in the Industry portfolio and across the government, though Phase III of the process was later intended to address restructuring at that level. So, too, with the Program Review process: a small group of officials coordinated and vetted the submissions from departments and agencies to, first, a committee of deputy ministers, and later, to the committee of ministers. Notes from analysts in the Department of Finance, the Treasury Board Secretariat, and the Privy Council Office challenged and provided perspective on the submissions, but these notes were drafted by a handful of officials, often with only general knowledge of programs. Finance, of course, set and generally guided the agenda with notional targets and a fiscal framework, with profound consequences across the government, but Finance certainly did not have the capacity to micro-manage the decisions of the Program Review committee and their implementation by departments and agencies. In short, the strategy of the government and deputy ministers of central agencies was *not* to create alternative capacities to design and coordinate policy; rather, they set targets and time-lines that would challenge departments and agencies, and force decisions that ultimately would result in significant changes to policy and programs.

We want to draw particular attention to the role of the auditor general of Canada. His report precipitated concern at the highest political and administrative levels, even if it probably did not directly influence the Program Review decisions announced in February 1995. Indeed, many of the problems identified had been festering, and were known in R&D establishments in departments and agencies across the government, but these problems did not seize the attention of ministers during the late 1980s and early 1990s. Although the Office of the Auditor General is autonomous from governments and central agencies, it can put an issue high on the political agenda in dramatic fashion, and perhaps influence ministers in a way that senior officials in other departments and agencies cannot, even those well aware of, and sympathetic to, the problems in question.

However important the push from the auditor general, it was not decisive: the Liberal government had to take an interest in the matter, and in this instance S&T had champions in John Manley as minister of industry and Paul Martin as minister of finance. But an interesting question is: Why did the Science and Technology Review nevertheless proceed along with the Program Review? We believe there is a parallel here with the Social Security Review, which proceeded under the aegis of Lloyd Axworthy, at that time the minister of human resources development. Both issues dealt with themes of central importance in the Liberal's policy Red Book, and they were embraced within portfolios led by strong ministers. Subsuming the policy reviews into the Program Review process would not deal adequately with personal aspirations and the symbolic and political importance of the issues themselves. The decision to proceed with the S&T Review was also consistent with the prime minister's interest in department-led policy making, as well as with the early disposition of the government of Jean Chrétien to seek multiple sources of advice, as was the case with the early budget consultations and the Social Security Review. This, too, would explain the request that NABST also prepare a report on the future of S&T policy.

We want to argue that, aside from putting S&T management squarely on the agenda, the auditor general had an impact via the 'enlightenment function' of policy research (Weiss, 1977). He introduced themes, such as a focus on results, performance management, horizontal management, and producing better information for Parliament and citizens that would influence the S&T community in the medium term. Such themes, though a staple of the auditor general, were relatively new for Ottawa's science establishment. Nevertheless, they were adopted quickly by the government and deputy ministers as a sort of cosmology guiding planning and discourse. As such, any plan or report crafted had to deal squarely with these themes, regardless of the issues at stake and the direction that reform needed to take.

Implementing and Elaborating the Science and Technology Framework

The conventional wisdom is that it is one matter for public sector organizations to conduct reviews and to design policy frameworks and quite another to implement those strategies. Much has been written on the challenges of implementation that often involve changing or supplementing a strategy, but here we focus on the role of central agencies and how their bureaus implemented the federal S&T strategy. Although we cannot be comprehensive, we examine how the commitments for a human resources strategy and for improved coordination for S&T were implemented by the centre. For a qualitatively different facet of implementation, we examine the genesis and approval of the Canadian Foundation for Innovation.

Moving Forward on Human Resource Management in Science and Technology

As previously noted, when the new federal strategy, *Science and Technology for a New Century*, was released in March 1996, it was accompanied by a human resource strategy (Canada, 1996c). This was not surprising, given that human resource management was identified as a key issue by the auditor general and by the S&T Policy Review. How this document was prepared and then acted on reveals much about how the centre now works.

The framework document was prepared by Treasury Board Secretariat (TBS) officials, and informed by consultations with scientists and officials, union representatives, and the assistant deputy ministers of science-based departments and agencies. The steering committee, the Assistant Deputy Ministers (ADM) Committee for S&T Human Resource Management, was formed to oversee the project which had representation from the TBS, the Public Service Commission (PSC), the Professional Institute of the Public Service of Canada (PIPSC), other departments, and the National Research Council. To support the project, TBS formed an S&T unit with two officials and a scientist representing PIPSC and tapped into expertise from across the secretariat as needed. Accountability for the project was assigned to two senior officials: the deputy secretary of the human resources branch and the assistant secretary responsible for labour relations and human resource management. Despite the long-standing tensions over salary and benefits between the government and bargaining units, the human resource framework was endorsed by senior officials in the public service and by PIPSC.

Consultations and drafting of the framework led to agreement on several topics deserving more sustained analysis. Initially, five working groups were established to look at several issues: recruitment and rejuvenation; classification and compression; rewards, recognition, and incentives; management and scientific development and training; and workforce and mobility. Later, three more working groups were established on technologist support and development, scientific management development, and workforce demographic analysis. Although each group dealt with different matters, they had similarly diverse representation as the steering committee. Several pilot projects were initiated under the aegis of the project; several were department- or agency-based, or involved piggy-backing on existing programs, but tailoring them to meet science and technology human resource needs. Finally, two studies on best practices were prepared (Treasury Board, 1997; Public Service Commission, 1997), and a web site was established to provide a forum to discuss issues and best practices. Indeed, the web site is a cooperative effort of science-based departments and agencies, TBS, and PIPSC.[1]

One outcome of this process was to be a blueprint for human resource management for the science and technology functional community, in addition to the many initiatives noted above. Although it was intended that the blueprint be published in early 1998, this did not happen; however, there does exist a 'living' document maintained by the S&T unit in TBS that consolidates and provides updates on the status of various activities and circulates only inside the public service. The document has circulated in draft form inside the government and the auditor general for comment. It lists the progress and administrative policy changes that have been made (that is, such as changes in travel and conference policy, lifting the cap on appointment of senior scientists, and engaging union representatives). One stated reason for the delay is that the final blueprint will be contingent on the findings of the pilot projects, some of which have yet to be completed.[2] However, to date the process reflects a very different image than the conventional wisdom about how central agencies work: rather than dictating how policy should be altered, TBS officials have consulted, collaborated, and partnered with officials across the public service and with bargaining agents, although TBS clearly has the responsibility to implement particular administrative policy changes and to produce reports on aggregate results. All of this has been accomplished without erecting huge new bureaus.

Moving Forward with Coordination: Community and Portfolio Thinking

A principle theme of the auditor general's report was the lack of coordination of S&T programs across government. Although the interest in policy capacity and horizontal issues is vogue in Ottawa, the problem of coordinating across departments and agencies is hardly new in Canadian S&T policy. The Science Secretariat was created in 1964, and later the Ministry of State for Science and Technology (MOSST) in 1971, for precisely this purpose. When the Ministry of State for Social Development and the Ministry of State Economic and Regional Development were dissolved in 1984 by Prime Minister John Turner, MOSST was left untouched.

There are many ways for governments to coordinate or raise the profile of a horizontal activity. One way is simply to improve coordination and the flow of information across the bureaucracy. Up until the S&T Review, horizontal exchange of information and coordination among the SBDAs was the task of the Assistant Deputy Ministers (ADM) Interdepartmental Steering Committee on S&T, whose secretariat was based at Industry Canada. Along with other handicaps, this committee was unable to identify federal S&T priorities, since it had to arrive at decisions by consensus, and therefore was unlikely to have the ability to make priority decisions because such would require one or more assistant deputy ministers to concede that some of the activities in which they were engaged were not priorities (NABST, 1993: 13). The ADM committee, initially co-chaired by Industry Canada and Treasury Board ADMs, was revitalized as the federal strategy was developed. However, it remains an information-exchange forum, without a role in policy development and resource allocation. It is supported by approximately ten staff, complemented by another group supporting the Advisory Council on Science and Technology. In addition, the Committee on Senior Officials (COSO) created a subcommittee on science and technology to identify priorities and provide oversight for implementing the 1996 federal strategy, led by the deputy minister of natural resources, and it is supported largely by her own staff. The work plan is carried out by the revitalized S&T ADM HR Steering Committee on S&T, co-chaired by senior officials from Environment Canada and the TBS. This work has fed into the broader strategy for renewing the public service known as the La Relève initiative (Canada, 1998). Interestingly, the work of the ADM committee and the COSO subcommittee is not directly connected, and neither assumes the responsibility for developing policy and monitoring performance.

A powerful way for governments to support a horizontal priority is to commit valuable ministerial time to monitoring a program initiative. The federal strategy committed the Cabinet Committee on Economic Union (CCEU) to set aside time to review the state of S&T programs, to set new priorities, and to publish an annual report. One source of information, then, would be the draft version of an annual report, which would be produced by the working group of ADMs Steering Committee on S&T and vetted by the COSO subcommittee. Another source of independent advice is the Prime Minister's Advisory Committee on Science and Technology (ACST), which replaced NABST, and consists of individuals from outside the public service. ACST members are appointed by the prime minister, but the committee is chaired by the minister of industry. This group also prepares a report on priorities to be considered by the Cabinet committee, which can be informed by expert panels and is not made available to the public. The presumption is that confidential advice is more likely to be heard and considered by ministers. A third source of advice comes from the new Committee on Federal S&T Advisory Bodies (CFSTAB), whose members are drawn from the external advisory boards of SBDAs. Finally, the secretary of state for science, research and development, who assists the minister of industry by meeting with federal S&T advisory groups, also provides advice.

The prominent role of the ministry of industry and his department also points to another means for coordination: the ministerial portfolios assigned by the prime minister. The issues encompassed by science and technology have, for more than a decade, been closely related to industrial policy. In 1987, MOSST was placed in a new Department of Industry, Science, and Technology along with remnants of the former Department of Regional Industrial Expansion, which had lost its programs on regional development, in order to develop policies to better position Canadian business to compete in a freer trade environment (Doern, 1990). The Industry portfolio was further broadened in the June 1993 restructuring, encompassing an interesting array of science-based and regional development agencies (Doern, 1996). But portfolios can be groupings of convenience, and even the most powerful ministers may find it difficult to challenge and to coordinate agency heads, whose organizations usually have greater independence from the government. However, what changed during the mid-1990s was that the Program Review and February 1995 federal budget introduced expenditure reductions so dramatic for departments and agencies alike that their leaders had no choice but to work together more, beginning a dance not unlike the consolidation of large departments with distinct program areas (Lindquist, 1998c). More recently, however, this influence has worked in reverse: with the federal government generating a surplus, the minister of finance has resources to support new initiatives, and, as the next section demonstrates, he has been supportive of S&T programs.

Added to this was the increasing currency of horizontal issues management, as was indicated by the clerk of the Privy Council, establishing, in 1996, the Deputy Ministers' Task Force on Horizontal Issues. At the ministerial level, Treasury Board ministers also began to take more interest in horizontal issue management as part of their interest in shifting towards more of a management board role. This paralleled the elaboration of another, less high profile tool for coordination: the Treasury Board had started to request that departments and agencies submit business plans for review and approval in 1995. However, the second round of business plans submitted in 1996 also consisted of a requirement that Industry Canada and its agencies meet directly with the Treasury Board; the department and agencies each made single presentations, but they were not asked to prepare an overarching portfolio plan. In 1997 the new twist on business planning was that the Treasury Board sought to review portfolio plans, and the Industry portfolio was one of eight portfolios to be reviewed directly by ministers (Lindquist, 1998c). In short, there had emerged considerable political and bureaucratic incentive for leaders of the department programs and agencies comprising the Industry portfolio to begin marketing and thinking of themselves in portfolio terms. For example, an Industry Portfolio Forum on Science and Technology was held in March 1997,[3] and the following December representatives of science-based departments and agencies participated in a round-table on 'portfolio management' (Public Policy Forum and Consulting and Audit

Canada, 1997). Industry Canada has not been granted the authority to request information and data from SBDAs in the manner that TBS can under the Financial Administration Act, making it difficult to properly monitor the management and performance of S&T programs.

The notion that 'there is no one way to coordinate' has been taken in an interesting direction by the federal S&T strategy. Rather than select a mechanism or two from the 'menu' of coordinating devices, the government is utilizing many ways to coordinate. While this is bound to create the appearance of complexity and big government, as is the case with intergovernmental coordinating mechanisms, this may be the only sensible way to manage the interdependencies that inevitably exist in complex governance systems (Lindquist, 1999).

Canadian Foundation for Innovation: External Concertation?

The Canadian Foundation for Innovation was announced in the February 1997 federal budget, but was an idea developed by the Association of Universities and Colleges of Canada (AUCC), the Canadian Association of University Teachers (CAUT), and the National Consortium of Scientific and Educational Societies. In spring 1996 they sought to have research infrastructure included in the $6 billion Canada Infrastructure Works program launched in 1994 (Andrew and Morrison, 1995). The government marketed the program as a source of support for not only traditional economic infrastructure 'sewers and sidewalks' but also for infrastructure critical to building the 'knowledge economy,' although it had so far failed in this latter regard.

The original aspiration was not lost on the research community (Hough, 1997). As discussions over a potential extension of the infrastructure program proceeded, officials from AUCC, CAUT, and the consortium got busy. In a departure from previous lobbying practices, which tended to focus on members of parliament and relevant ministers, the coalition briefed a range of relevant, senior government officials involved in science policy, adding only those political actors who responded to invitations, in practice one minister and two secretaries of state. Meetings were held with officials at the assistant deputy minister and/or director general level from the main SBDAs, plus TBS and Finance. The partnership focused on three issue areas: academic research infrastructure, renewal of the Networks of Centres of Excellence program, and improved coordination of government science activities. It convinced the government that a focus on university research infrastructure was critical for Canadian science, politically timely, and made good economic sense. The coalition proposed that 20 per cent of the allocation for the rumoured Infrastructure II Program be dedicated to upgrading university research infrastructure.

The lobbying was successful, but this was accomplished by the Canadian Foundation for Innovation (CFI) introduced by the minister of finance in the 1997 budget, and not by means of the extended Infrastructure Works program. The CFI's mandate was to disburse $800 million over five years, while levering additional amounts from other levels of government and the private sector to bring the total infrastructure investment in university, college, hospital, and other public, non-profit research laboratories up to $2 billion. There were fears that the CFI would be construed as an intrusion into provincial jurisdiction, but this was not generally the case. Many provinces have responded with new programs to match the CFI effort.[4]

Because the granting councils (NRC and NSERC) have long had equipment and infrastructure awards under their purview, and they sponsored partnership programs in the past, the CFI is not necessarily the great departure from past experience that on first glance it might appear to be. However, it does show – along with Infrastructure Works and the Health Transition Fund announced in the February 1997 budget – the government's determination to develop national programs that reach out to a range of government and non-government actors. While CFI may reflect a science-based view of how to manage scarce resources as part of a 'national innovation system,' it can also be seen as reflecting a new cosmology of the government and central agencies that may apply increasingly to *all* policy and program sectors. This case also shows that the government seeks to move forward with relatively little in the way of hiring of permanent staff in government. Indeed, in contrast to the Infrastructure Works program, federal coordination of CFI will not proceed under the aegis of the Treasury Board, but rather under the minister of industry.

Implementation and the Centre: Organizational Parsimony and Engagement

We have briefly reviewed three case studies for exploring how the centre gets involved in implementing and elaborating a horizontal policy strategy. Our reviews of the crafting of the human resource framework, the introduction of coordinating mechanisms, and the arrival of the CFI concept should only be viewed as indicative of the range of issues that confront those responsible for implementing the S&T strategy. However, they do provide interesting evidence on how the centre operates, and under what circumstances in might operate most effectively.

Our cases suggest that the parsimonious or light organizing strategies utilized by central agencies in the 'upstream' efforts to undertake S&T reviews were also employed in the implementation phase. Generally, central agencies relied on steering committees and working groups that looped out across different levels of the public service, and included representatives of bargaining agents, with support by very small secretariats or bureaus located either in Industry Canada or in TBS. This approach thus directly taps into departmental and agency expertise and has the advantage of securing 'buy-in' from key constituencies. The other element of the strategy was to use *existing* processes – such as Cabinet committee deliberations on the emergent business planning regime, and the previously mentioned La Relève initiative – to review and bolster S&T implementation and to cultivate a portfolio sensibility in the Industry portfolio and among science-based departments and agencies across the public service.

The auditor general, in his 1996 follow-up review of the federal strategy, lauded the commitment underpinning this approach, but expressed concerns. He worried about having the same 'champions' and officials throughout the system taking on responsibility for coordinating and fully implementing the agenda. Although the auditor general was careful not to make the point directly, the implication was clear: Is the government allocating sufficient resources to move the agenda forward? This leads to a slightly different, but no less important, question: Is there a point beyond which coordination and many smaller initiatives will cease to yield benefits because of insufficient capacities in central bureaus and in departments and agencies?

Finally, we want to draw attention to the importance of political support inside and outside government in moving issues forward. The federal S&T strategy may appear to be a bold new plan, but observers familiar with the policy domain know that many of the solutions, such as those relating to human resource policies and coordinating mechanisms, were already known to officials. Many of the frustrations on the human resource front had emerged in previous exercises, but the solutions identified, such as the more flexible Universal Classification System, were not implemented. Before 1994 there were internal coordinating committees of officials, as well as NABST, to advise ministers and manage horizontal matters, but they were not actively used by the government. The cases reviewed above show the critical role of political engagement and leadership, even in domains of administrative policy (Lindquist, 1996b). There are many problems that challenge governments, and ministers and senior officials have only so much time to devote to them. Even if problems and solutions are understood at the working level, political leadership is required to pierce through the system and ensure that the issues are fully addressed. We believe that the case of the CFI also demonstrates that, if outside actors are well organized, and anticipate the constraints confronting ministers and their officials, as well as their objectives, they can significantly influence the elaboration of existing policy strategies.

Monitoring and Reporting on the Science and Technology Strategy

Performance management is now considered a crucial element of modern public sector management (Aucoin, 1996; Lindquist, 1998b). Like any plan, the federal strategy, *Science and Technology for a New Century*, has many ambitions. There are several questions, however, posed by its implementation and elaboration: Will elements of the plan get put in place in the time frames originally proposed? Even if properly implemented, will these elements achieve the desired objectives? How does the government monitor and gauge the success of such a complex set of undertakings? Can this be conveyed to members of Parliament, citizens, and the media in such a way as to ensure meaningful accountability? In this section, we consider the role of the auditor general and central agencies in the monitoring and reporting on progress on science and technology matters.

The auditor general of Canada has functioned, during the 1990s, something like a 'shadow central agency' on the S&T policy makers. Not long after *Science and Technology for a New Century* and *A Framework for the Human Resources Management of the Federal Science and Technology Community* (1996c) were published, the auditor general followed up with a report that evaluated the extent to which the federal strategy addressed the issues and gaps identified in its 1994 reports (Auditor General, 1996). The follow-up systematically reviewed the new strategy according to the recommendations contained in the 1994 reports and generally endorsed the federal strategy and framework, calling them an 'important accomplishment.' The auditor general approved the activities occurring at the department and agency levels, and the amount of collaboration proceeding across departments and agencies, between managers and bargain agent representatives, and between governments. However, the auditor general wondered about the myriad of committees responsible for advancing the science and technology agenda across boundaries and wondered who would be responsible. He called for an annual report for public scrutiny, not simply one for Cabinet review, and worried about systematic reporting, particularly with respect to results. Finally, he worried about the time of senior personnel to sustain implementation.

The government did publish an annual report on progress. The first report, *Minding Our Future*, was released in 1997 under the auspices of the minister of industry and the secretary of state for science, research, and development (Canada, 1997a). The report was generally organized around themes found in *Science and Technology for a New Century*. Aside from providing a few examples of recent initiatives by SBDAs and at the corporate level, *Minding the Future* does not systematically present data in such a way as to allow outsiders to evaluate how well particular SBDAs and SBDAs as a collective are doing with respect to several goals. Readers are instead referred to the first S&T plans of SBDAs and subsequent business plans. Oblique references are made to the difficult decisions flowing from the Program Review, but there is no account of the resulting gaps nor what activities were dropped or reduced.[5] Releasing the report seems consistent with the principles associated with performance management and transparency, but even knowledgeable observers would find it difficult to hold the government to account on the basis of the documents. In many ways, it is a restatement and update of the federal strategy.

Some documentation has accumulated on the projects relating to human resource management, as is evident from our analysis. In addition to the web site (which has not been updated for some time), an important accountability tool was to be the 'Blueprint for Human Resources Management,' which is not yet available for public consumption, but does exist in draft form. Otherwise, the main vehicle for accountability and reporting has been through the La Relève initiative which, until recently, proceeded under the auspices of a secretariat in the Privy Council Office and led by a deputy minister. In March 1998 all departments, certain functional communities, and regional councils reported on their progress with respect to plans for renewing and revitalizing their staff (Canada, 1998). The contribution from the science and technology community, about six pages, consisted of a general listing of the major initiatives launched under the plan released in April 1997, and was drafted by the TBS's S&T unit. Like *Minding Our Future*, the report on the functional community is not a systematic review of progress, but only outlines some successes and activities such as the pilot projects, the working groups, and the committees overseeing the process, as well as remaining challenges. It is written in such a way so as to demonstrate momentum on the basis of activity, but it cannot be construed as a report that reviews results, and it does not ensure accountability. We want to emphasize, however, that providing insufficient information and context is not only an S&T problem; it extends to department and agency business plans as well as aggregate requirements such as those on accounting for results that emanate from the president of the Treasury Board (Lindquist, 1998b).

The responsibility for monitoring and reporting on the progress of the federal strategy rests in the hands of several administrative committees in the public service. Responsibility for providing detailed data on progress rests with particular working groups as well as with departments and agencies that must report on programs as a normal management undertaking. The role of central bureaus, whether they be the S&T bureaus in TBS and Industry Canada, or the new bureau responsible for the Leadership Network and the La Relève initiative is to aggregate and report on those activities. Ultimately, these reports are to be reviewed by ministers and advisers as they adjust existing plans, develop new priorities, and make decisions about where to invest new resources. At this point in time, though, it seems that only the auditor general can monitor and delve into the material and ask tough questions about whether all of the activity and supporting institutional structures are making a difference in the S&T effort of the federal government and the national innovation system. Indeed, the auditor general issued yet another report on S&T management in December 1998. However, even the auditor general has limited resources and is grappling with budgetary constraints, and a deep focus on S&T management may be difficult to sustain.

Conclusions: Has the Federal Strategy Surmounted Precarious Values?

This chapter is an attempt to develop a perspective on how the government and central agencies have tried to better manage, coordinate, and report on science and technology across the federal government in recent years. Rather than focus on these issues simply as an S&T challenge, we portrayed them as a broader challenge that confronts governments and central agencies, and then introduced an analytic approach that captures the more subtle ways in which central agencies work, particularly with respect to horizontal policy and administrative issues, and the fact that governments often work through much smaller central bureaus to review, implement, and then monitor policies.

The case of recent S&T policy making by the federal government was used to explore how bureaus undertake this work. We discovered that the federal government is relying on a host of intersecting coordinating strategies, most of them at the administrative level (though variously centred in the Committee of Senior Officials, the Human Resources Branch of the Treasury Board Secretariat, Industry Canada, and with participation from the SBDAs and bargaining agents) and at the political level. The central bureaus involved in recent S&T policy at all stages and levels have been quite small, and they have levered the resources of SBDAs and other central bureaus. Perhaps, more importantly, we believe that the work at the administrative level, no matter how determined or well coordinated, would not have been sustained for long without the engagement of the Liberal ministers. We were intrigued by the contributions of the auditor general, which we cast as a 'shadow central agency' because of its important role in putting the problem of S&T management high on the agenda, and then monitoring the response of the federal government. This role is crucially important because, despite the commitment of working officials and the current government, there appears to be little outside interest in closely monitoring progress on the federal strategy. Indeed, we have argued that even if outside groups wanted to undertake such monitoring, it would be difficult to do so under the current reporting regime.

By way of conclusion, we wish to make two additional points that certainly deserve more research and discussion. First, the federal strategy, *Science and Technology for a New Century*, is very much a product of its times. The document and the entire strategy were crafted under the mantle of Ottawa's expenditure management system, with its current emphasis on the themes of alternative service delivery, business planning, horizontal coordination, as well as results and performance indicators (Canada, 1995). Those drafting reports on behalf of every department, agency, or functional community have considerable incentive to be congruent with the prevailing cosmology espoused by the government and the leadership of the federal public service. It is hard to believe that any major policy initiative launched during the 1990s would not have contained these elements as major components of its 'plot line.' The interesting question, then, is: 'Does the March 1996 strategy and *Minding the Future* tell us much about the substantive progress made to date about dealing with fundamental S&T problems, or does it reveal more about how the leaders of departments and agencies rhetorically align themselves with the government and leadership of the public service?

This view, while provocative, should not be that surprising, since decisions about science policy and administrative coordination at the federal level have always been reflected in larger currents in thinking. The Science Council was created not long after the Economic Council of Canada in 1963, and just before the National Council of Welfare in 1968. The design of these advisory bodies was predicated on the importance not only of independent advice based on policy research and consensus from different elements of society. The Ministry of State for Science and Technology was created in 1971, at the same time as the Ministry of State for Urban Affairs, under the premise that knowledge could underpin coordination across the system (Aucoin, 1979). The Nielsen Task Force on Program Review, which proceeded from 1994 to 1996, was not just about science and technology, but, like the Program Review from 1994 to early 1995, dealt with virtually all federal government programs, and it was more about expenditure reduction than improving policy. When MOSST was moved to the Department of Industry, Science, and Technology in 1988, it was part of a larger restructuring of government portfolios, a process repeated on a larger scale in the June 1993 restructuring (Osbaldeston, 1992). The dissolution of the Science Council proceeded along with the Economic Council, the Law Reform Commission, and the Canadian Institute for International Peace and Security. In short, the current emphasis in Ottawa on horizontal coordination and performance management in S&T policy reflects larger corporate themes that now prevail, and in this way repeat historical patterns, even if the themes differ over time.

This leads us to our second and final point. We have argued that much of the activity and motivation on the current federal S&T strategy at the bureaucratic level is contingent on political interest, since officials can only act within spheres of authority. However, even with such political and bureaucratic engagement, there are limits on the progress that can be made as a result of the amount of resources that can be allocated to S&T programs and to the limited public interest in S&T. Even if Canadians may generally be aware of the manifold ways in which S&T is changing their lives, this has yet to translate into a commitment nearly as powerful as to our health care system or to the environment. Without strong articulation of collective interest, it is difficult to see how political leaders can sustain their commitment, unless one believes that technological change and the demand for science are so inevitable that all governments will quickly find themselves dealing with the challenges.

We suggest that Canadian S&T policy displays many hallmarks of policy domains characterized by 'precarious values' (Clark, 1956). While the function continues to be demanded and receives considerable financial support from various quarters, policy is not the result of strongly held values in society about its importance. The history of successive attempts to coordinate and frame S&T policy at the federal level reinforce this assertion and poses sobering questions: Does *Science and Technology for a New Century* represent a watershed in the so-called national innovation system, one that has galvanized support in many quarters? Will the next government feel obligated to proceed with similar themes and programs, encountering not only a robust administrative regime but, also, a strong public interest in S&T, which, though not impervious to the ideas of a new government, has its own momentum? Or will the next government have to discover the importance of S&T once in power, and develop its policies and coordination strategies in accordance with the prevailing views on how public policy and public sector management should proceed?

Notes

1 A wealth of detail on these initiatives reviewed in this paragraph can be found on the web at http://www.tbs-sct.gc.ca/tb/hr/scitech/frm -home.html. For more on the working groups, see 'Established Working Groups.' Pilot projects include the following: the NWRI Inc. Pilot Program, the Green Corps Pilot Program, the AAFC Pilot Program, the Scientific Personnel Mobility Exchange Pilot Program, the People and Jobs Pilot Project, the Best Practices Web Site Pilot Program, the Interchange Canada

Pilot Program, the Career Assignment Program (CAP) Pilot Program, the Management Trainee Program (MTP), and the Scientific Personal Career Development Plans.
2 See 'Update and Response to Specific Auditor general Issues' available under 'Consultations and Communications' at http://www.tbs-sct.gc.ca/tb/hr/scitech/frm-home.html.
3 For the agenda and links, see *http://www.nrc.ca/conferences/stforum/agenda1.htm*.
4 For more details, see Henderson (1997: 4). On Quebec's involvement, see 'Quebec Creates Mechanism to Match CFI Funding but Proposals Must First be Approved by Province,' *Research Money*, 25 March, 1998, p. 3.
5 For example, see the concerns expressed in various articles in *Re$earch*, 11/12 (1997).

References

Andrew, Caroline, and Jeff Morrison. (1995). 'Canada Infrastructure Works: Between "Picks and Shovels" and the Information Highway,' in Susan Phillips, ed., *How Ottawa Spends 1995–96: Mid-Life Crises,'* 107–35. Ottawa: Carleton University Press.
Aucoin, Peter. (1979). 'Portfolio Structures and Policy Coordination.' In G. Bruce Doern and Peter Aucoin, eds., *Public Policy in Canada: Organization, Process, and Management*, 213–38. Toronto: Macmillan.
– (1996). *The New Public Management: Canada in Comparative Perspective.* Montreal: Institute for Research on Public Policy.
Auditor general of Canada. (1994). *1994 Report of the Auditor General of Canada.* Web site: http://www.oag-bvg.gc.ca/domino/reports.nsf/html/94menu_e.html
– (1996). 'Federal Science and Technology Activities: Follow-up.' In *Report of the Auditor General, September 1996*. Web site: http://www.oag-bvg.gc.ca/domino/reports.nsf/html/9615ce.html
Canada. (1995). *The Expenditure Management System of the Government of Canada.* Ottawa: Minister of Supply and Services.
– (1996a). *Science and Technology for a New Century: A Federal Strategy.* Ottawa: Minister of Supply and Services.
– (1996b). *Highlights of Departmental S&T Action Plans in Response to Science and Technology for a New Century.* Web site: http://canada.gc.ca/depts/science/english/highlt-e.html
– (1996c). *A Framework for the Human Resources Management of the Federal Science and Technology Community.* Web site: http://www.tbs-sct.gc.ca/tb/hr/scitech/fram-eng.html

- (1997a). *Minding Our Future: A Report on Federal Science and Technology 1997*. Ottawa: Industry Canada.
- La Relève Task Force. (1998). *First Progress Report on La Relève: A Commitment to Action, Detailed Reports March 1998*. Ottawa: Canada Communication Group Inc. Web site: http://lareleve.pwgsc.ca

Clark, Burton A. (1956). 'Organizational Adaptation and Precarious Values.' *American Sociological Review*, 21(3): 412–31.

de la Mothe, John. (1996). 'One Small Step in an Uncertain Direction: The Science and Technology Review and Public Administration in Canada.' *Canadian Public Administration*, 39(3): 403–17.

Doern, G. Bruce. (1990). 'The Department of Industry, Science and Technology: Is There Industrial Policy After Free Trade?' In Katharine A. Graham, ed., *How Ottawa Spends 1990–91: Tracking the Second Agenda*, 49–71. Ottawa: Carleton University Press.
- (1996). 'Looking for the Core: Industry Canada and Program Review.' In Gene Swimmer, ed., *How Ottawa Spends 1996–97: Life Under the Knife*, 75–6. Ottawa: Carleton University Press.

Greenspon, Edward, and Anthony Wilson-Smith. (1996). *Double Vision: The Inside Story of the Liberals in Power*. Toronto: Doubleday.

Gualtieri, Roberto. (1994). 'Science Policy and Basic Research in Canada.' In Susan D. Phillips, ed., *How Ottawa Spends 1994–95: Making Change*, 301–37. Ottawa: Carleton University Press.

Henderson, Mark. (1997). 'Canada Foundation for Innovation Opens Doors to Innovative Partnerships to Improve Research Infrastructure.' *Research Money*, 12 March.

Hough, Paul. (1997). 'Summary Notes of the National Consortium of Scientific and Educational Societies.' November–December 1996. Lobby, distributed by list serve to the Canadian Association of University Research Administrators (CAURA), 25 January.

Kingdon, John W. (1984). *Agendas, Alternatives, and Public Policy*. Boston: Little, Brown.

Lindquist, Evert A. (1996a). 'New Agendas for Research on Policy Communities: Policy Analysis, Administration, and Governance.' In Laurent Dobuzinskis, Michael Howlett, and David Laycock, eds., *Policy Studies in Canada: The State of the Art*, 219–41. Toronto: University of Toronto Press.
- (1996b). 'On the Cutting Edge: Program Review, Government Restructuring, and the Treasury Board of Canada.' In Gene Swimmer, ed., *How Ottawa Spends 1996–97: Life Under the Knife*, 205–52. Ottawa: Carleton University Press.
- (1998a). 'Strategic Review and Public Sector Reform: Reconceiving the Center.' Discussion paper for the 1st Meeting of the Country Experts

Group for the Project on Strategic Review and Reform, Public Management Group (PUMA) of the Organization of Economic Cooperation and Development in Paris, 16–17 May.

– (1998b). 'Getting Results Right: Reforming Ottawa's Estimates.' In Leslie A. Pal, ed., *How Ottawa Spends 1998–99: Balancing Act: The Post-Deficit Mandate*, 153–90. Toronto: Oxford University Press.

– (1998c). 'Business Planning Comes to Ottawa: Critical Issues and Future Directions.' In Peter Aucoin and Donald Savoie, eds., *Managing Strategic Change: Learning from Program Review*, 157–61. Ottawa: Canadian Centre for Management Development.

– (1999). 'Efficiency, Reliability, or Innovation, Managing Overlap and Interdependence in Canada's Federal System of Governance.' In Robert D. Young, ed., *Stretching the Federation: The Art of the State*, 35–68. Kingston: Institute of Intergovernmental Relations, Queen's University.

National Advisory Board on Science and Technology (NABST). (1993). *Spending Smarter*. Ottawa: Report of the NABST Committee on Federal Science and Technology Priorities.

O'Gorman, Erin. (1998). 'Science Policy: Surfing the Waves – An Examination of the Three Decades of Science Policy in Canada.' Paper prepared for the School of Public Administration, Carleton University, July.

Osbaldeston, Gordon F. (1992). *Organizing to Govern*, vol. 1. Toronto: McGraw-Hill Ryerson.

Public Policy Forum and Consulting and Audit Canada. (1997). 'Summary of Key Points and Background Notes and Discussion Guide on the Public Policy Forum Roundtable Discussion on Portfolio Management in Relation to Science-based Programs.' 9 December.

Public Service Commission of Canada. (1997). 'Human Resources Management of the Scientific and Technological Community in the Private Sector, Benchmarking Study.' July. Web site: http://www.tbs-sct.gc.ca/tb/hr/scitech/frm-home.html

Treasury Board of Canada Secretariat. (1997). 'Human Resource Strategies in Times of Change, An Inventory of Initiatives,' 2nd ed. Web site: http://www.tbs-sct.gc.ca/tb/hr/scitech/frm-home.html

Weiss, Carole H. (1977). 'Research for Policy's Sake: The Enlightenment Function of Social Research.' *Policy Analysis*, 3(4): 531–45.

15 Conclusions: New Institutions and Prospects for Change

G. BRUCE DOERN and TED REED

The central contribution of this book is that it is the first to offer a reasonably focused and comprehensive examination of Canada's science-based policy and regulatory regime. A reading of both the macro-issues in Part 1 and of the agency and institutional chapters in Part 2 clearly suggests that this complex and important regulatory regime is undergoing significant change. The more detailed and different levels of analysis provided by the macro-policy and institutional chapters have served as prerequisites for offering a further set of conclusions and observations about the nature of the new institutions now in place and the prospects for additional change.

Our overall conclusions focus on four salient features of institutional change. First, we look at regulatory fiscal costs and the need to avoid what we refer to as the *déjà vu* of realized risk; in essence, a de facto science deficit following, and partly caused by, the fiscal deficit. Second, we probe further the issue of the independence of science both within and outside the regime. Third, we examine the implications of a 'double pluralization' dynamic, a process that simultaneously involves the pluralization of science and the pluralization of interests, including those with claims to knowledge, if not claims to science. Finally, we look at the problem of communicating institutional risk mandates as perhaps the riskiest and most challenging business of all.

Regulatory Costs and Avoiding the *Déjà Vu* of Realized Risk

We start with a simple factual observation revealed by looking at key agencies. As Table 15.1 shows, there has been a significant increase in revenue generation by selected science-based departments and agen-

364   G. Bruce Doern and Ted Reed

Table 15.1 Comparison of external user charge revenues of selected science-based departments and agencies (SBDAs), 1994–7 (000s $)

	1994–5	1995–6	1996–7
Atomic Energy Control Board[a]	28,967	30,274	36,941
Canadian Food Inspection Agency[b]	20,810	27,269	34,127
Environment Canada	16,054	18,493	26,884
Fisheries and Oceans Canada	23,549	43,625	78,228
Health Canada – Medical Devices Program	0	113	1,390
Health Canada – Drugs Import/Export Licences	0	0	152
Health Canada – Drugs Product Master File	0	0	73
Health Canada – Foods Veterinary Drugs	0	0	929
Health Canada – Product Label Reviews	0	0	29
HC – Authority to sell drugs, product licences	2,490	7,094	6,679
Health Canada – Drug Evaluation Fees	0	3,532	17,844
Health Canada – (Non PMRA, for TPP)	2,490	10,739	27,096
Pest Management Regulatory Agency (SOA-HC)	0	353	293
Total: Selected science-based regulators	91,870	130,753	203,569
Last two years indexed to 1994–5 level = 100	100	142.32	221.58

[a] Now the Canadian Nuclear Safety Commission.
[b] For comparability, some figures have been restated to reflect changes in program reporting structure or additional information.
Source: Government-Wide Summary of External User Charge Revenues, Treasury Board Secretariat (1998), Government of Canada.

cies as a result of the implementation of a conscious policy of cost recovery within a general environment of aggressive fiscal constraint.

Table 15.1 shows a 42 per cent increase in revenues from cost recovery from 1994–5 to 1995–6, and a 55 per cent increase from 1995–6 to 1996–7 for six selected science-based regulators. Rapid alterations in the funding mix, through increased reliance on cost recoveries, and decreased reliance on parliamentary appropriations, can cause radical shifts in the behaviour of science-based regulators as well as impacts on their employees. This in turn can lead to what we have referred to in Chapter 1 as a science deficit and depletion of science reserve capacity.

The phenomenon known as Program Review has involved major reductions in expenditure levels for most affected federal departments and agencies, including a number of science-based departments and agencies (SBDAs), such as Environment Canada and Health Canada

Table 15.2 The funding mix of federal science-based regulators, 1994–9 (millions $)

Federal science-based regulators	1994–5	1995–6	1996–7	1997–8	1998–9
Atomic Energy Control Board					
Gross actual or planned spending	41.1	42.5	44.6	43.8	49.3
Respendable revenues	30.4	31.1	38.7	32.7	36.7
Appropriation in funding mix	26.0%	26.8%	13.2%	25.3%	25.6%
FTEs			395	409	430
Canada Food Inspection Agency[a]					
Gross actual or planned spending				345.8	355.9
Respendable revenues				43.1	47.4
Appropriation in funding mix				87.5%	86.7%
FTEs				4,555	4,556
Environment Canada[b]					
Gross actual or planned spending	753.4	707.9	634.0	618.7	631.0
Respendable revenues	37.7	47.2	52.9	70.6	71.6
Appropriation in funding mix	95.0%	93.3%	91.7%	88.6%	88.7%
FTEs	5,476	5,174	4,910	4,707	4,358
Fisheries and Oceans Canada					
Gross actual or planned spending	1,322.2	1,266.2	1,322.9	1,191.6	1,425.2
Respendable revenues	9.4	12.6	29.1	40.1	54.7
Appropriation in funding mix	99.3%	99.0%	97.8%	96.6%	96.2%
FTEs[c]	11,152	10,631	10,208	9,892	8,569
Pest Management Regulatory Agency – Health Canada SOA					
Gross actual or planned spending		21.2	25.9	23.1	25.7
Respendable revenues		0.4	0.3	7.4	7.7
Appropriation in funding mix		98.1%	98.8%	68.0%	70.0%
FTEs		327	326		
Therapeutic Products Program					
Gross actual or planned spending	67.9	72.3	51.0	60.7	76.8
Respendable revenues		10.6	24.8	35.5	34.7
Appropriation in funding mix		85.3%	51.4%	30.4%	54.8%
FTEs			646		688
Total Selected Federal Science-Based Regulators					
Gross actual or planned spending	2184.6	2110.1	2078.4	2283.7	2563.9
Respendable revenues	77.5	101.9	145.8	229.4	252.8
Appropriation in funding mix	96.5%	95.2%	93.0%	90.0%	90.1%
FTEs	16,628	16,132	16,485	19,563	18,601

Sources: Expenditures are from Public Accounts for Fiscal Years 1994–5, 1995–6, 1996–7, and 1997–8. Expenditures for 1998–9 are forecast in the 1999–2000 Main and Supplementary Estimates and Part IIIs (RPPs).

(continued)

(continued)
Table 15.2 The funding mix of federal science-based regulators, 1994–9 (millions $)

ᵃ Information for CFIA is from CFIA Annual Report and Performance Reports.
ᵇ In 1996-7 the Environment Canada Program includes CEAA as well as the Depart-
    ment. Other sources include Reports on Plans and Priorities (RPPs) and on
    Performance (DPRs).
ᶜ The FTEs for DFO for 1994–5 were estimated from Transport Canada data on FTEs
    for the Canadian Coast Guard using 1995–6 proportions of FTEs in CCG to DFO.
    Gross spending in 1997–8 and 1998–9 will be lower than for 1994–5, as expendi-
    tures for CFIA and PMRA have not been isolated to simulate these agencies'
    spending prior to their creation through consolidation. FTE information is taken,
    where available, from the DPRs, or TBS Public Service Employment Statistics.
    FTE = full-time employees (equivalents).

(Swimmer, 1996). Table 15.2 provides data on actual and planned gross
spending levels of six selected science-based regulators that reveals a
dampening down of the relative fiscal costs to the state as a result of
lower parliamentary appropriations, increased costs recoveries, or both.

The successive phases of the Program Review of Canadian federal
budgetary expenditure were in large measure necessitated by the size
of the federal deficit, but more particularly they resulted from a substantial increase in the level of annual interest charges on the federal
public debt. In 1993–4 annual interest costs on the public debt stood at
$37.75 billion, then jumped by $3.87 billion in 1994–5 and $4.81 billion
in 1995–6. This increase to $46.43 billion in total in 1995–6 was a 23
per cent increase in just two years. The immediate cause of this increase in federal public debt charges was the realization of the risk of
a significant jump in market rates of interest on a Canadian debt structure being held at a relatively short average maturity by historical
standards. This shorter average maturity structure of outstanding debt
contracts allowed the Department of Finance to lower its annual public debt charges for a time, in return for the trade-off of having to
accept an increased exposure to the risk of an adverse increase in
market rates of interest. The unfortunate realization of this debt management risk amplified the need for Program Review that much more.
Program Review then reduced the budgetary resources available to
many governmental sectors, such as the federal science-based policy
and regulation-making regime, partly to compensate for the realized
risk of rolling over a very sizeable federal short maturity debt.

In essence, rising interest costs on a burgeoning debt and deficit led
to acceptance of increased exposure to market risk that was then sub-

sequently realized. This in turn has led to systemic expenditure cuts that, other things being equal, entail increased exposures to risks in the particular sectors where expenditure reductions have been made, or where budgetary levels have not kept pace with the expansion of mandates. As the discussion in Chapter 1 on the science deficit suggested, fiscal risk is not the only risk faced by the state. Canada finds itself once again with the difficult-to-avoid prospect of suffering the 'déjà vu of realized risk,' only this time in respect of its underlying science capacity and science deficit, as understood in the above multi-faceted ways.

Thus, we see the distinct possibility of an inadvertent or unintentional construction of a science deficit along lines analogous to the fiscal deficit. Although, as we have argued, it took a couple of decades to properly appreciate and then to take decisive policy action on the fiscal deficit, it would be too dangerous – *it would be very risky business* – if policy learning on the science deficit were to take as long. With fiscal pressure straining science capacity in policy and regulation making having to do with the protection of human and environmental health, there will be an increase in exposure to risks that could otherwise be avoided in the presence of an adequate science capacity. As a result of continuing fiscal constraint, the balance between risk and cost in the federal regulation of human and environmental health will have shifted, by choice of the central political and economic executive, to an attenuation of the short-term fiscal costs to government of science-based regulation.

The trade-off so far has involved a higher level of cost to some regulated industries through the application of a policy of enhanced cost recovery, as well as unintended but real increases in the exposure of citizens and consumers to greater risks. Even where budgetary appropriations for science-based regulators have remained stable, expanding mandates and higher demand for regulatory services (for example, therapeutic products) and positive rates of inflation will have meant increasing levels of risk. Cost recoveries have been counterbalanced, it is argued by federal policy makers, in part by increased efficiencies resulting from consolidated institutional arrangements (PMRA, CFIA, TPP) and the creative application of new information technologies. The enhanced accountability and regulatory efficiency that a single institutional focus for regulatory risk management can introduce have in part mitigated the increased exposures to risk. These have also been somewhat contained through a considerable increase in labour effort from the management and employees of downsized SBDAs in the regulatory regime. The fact that such risks may not have yet been realized or are not readily visible does not alter the possibility of our experiencing *déjà vu* in the science-based regulation sector in the future, as occurred in the public finance sector in the not so distant past.

An example of the danger of trading off fiscal or industry cost for increased risk is apparent in the BSE case in the United Kingdom (examined in Chapter 4). The emphasis by Conservative governments on a policy of minimizing short-term costs to the Exchequer led to a very high level of exposure of the public to health risks that were in fact eventually realized. The eventual realization of such risks resulted in inordinately high costs to the Exchequer, to the relevant industry sectors, and to affected citizens and consumers. So a policy of short-term regulatory regime cost minimization actually led partly to the realization of very significant costs, as there was insufficient adjustment for possible risk, even in the face of contrary scientific advice.

A key lesson to be drawn from the BSE case is that while fiscal instability may threaten financial markets, public financial integrity, and household incomes, health and environmental risks can threaten citizens' lives, the profitability of whole industry sectors, and related tax revenue flows into government treasuries. A deficit in science and risk management in this particular regulatory regime is arguably more critical or acute than the fiscal deficit, yet the struggle to correct the fiscal deficit became the dominant public policy objective of the past decade or so in Canada. The higher priority being accorded to fiscal stability at the cost of stability in the protection of human and environmental health and safety is a very risky business. While the high potential costs if these latter risks are realized is understood abstractly at the centre of government, a tragic realization of these particular kinds of risks would communicate only too clearly the binding nature of the risk–cost trade-off in science-based policy and regulatory regimes.

The data on increased user fees and overall trends in spending on science policy and regulation making contained in Tables 15.1 and 15.2 can, of course, be subject to different interpretations other than the links we draw regarding the *déjà vu* of realized risk. Bill Jarvis's chapter shows that user's fees as such can be justified in theory provided that they are accompanied by a careful look at 'public goods' science versus science and regulation that is seen as a private chargeable benefit. But the evidence suggests that Program Review was more a political juggernaut to offer up spending cuts rather than a series of considered judgments concerning public goods versus private benefit science and science capacity (Swimmer, 1996).

The Independence of Science and the Choice of Venue

A key debate emerges in this book about the independence of science and the choice of venue that maximizes such independence. This is largely in response to the case advanced by William Leiss (in Chapter 3). Leiss argues that over the past fifty years or so there has been too much emphasis on science and too little on risk management in government and that the latter is entirely paralyzed by, and cannot solve, the problems encountered at the science–policy interface. Powell's account (in Chapter 6) of the Guatemalan raspberries case implies a similar position. This overall view sees risk management as part of the regulatory black box, with a range of inputs, including science, going into the box and with regulatory decisions emerging from it. Seen from this perspective, there is a strong requirement for improving transparency in the process of risk regulation and for science to be located and conducted outside of government as much as possible.

Leiss sees the need for a rational institutional process with a formal set of rules; that is, regulatory procedural rules. In such a regulatory process, all inputs would go into the risk management decision process box that need to go in, and the box would be made clear or transparent through the specification of the appropriate decision-making rules. He then argues the need to separate science from government through self-contained or complete agencies, and he suggests that the science policy regulatory process should be moved to arm's-length expert panels in order to encourage the science portion. An example of this latter institutional arrangement provided by Leiss concerns the primitive state of knowledge about radiation from mobile telecommunications technologies such as digital and PCS telephony. According to Leiss, government needs to separate the risk management process from political intrigue and involvement, so that science is not manipulated by other interests and to other ends in the regulatory risk management process, the main purpose of which is to protect human and environmental health and safety.

Another example provided was that of the manganese-based fuel additives case, where there was never a proper risk assessment undertaken in the federal government. As Leiss observes, given the need for an out-of-court settlement, there must certainly be better ways to do science-based regulation. He draws the conclusion that government needs to open up its risk management process to dialogue, as the Health Protection Branch of Health Canada has indicated it will be doing over the course of the next few years. Through separation at arm's length from government, Leiss wants to increase the *transparency and weight* of science in the risk management decision-making process, which itself needs to be rationalized and rendered more transparent and accountable through the institutional arrangements of formalized rules and stand-alone regulatory decision-making bodies.

This view, which is also inherent in several of the chapter on agencies and institutions, sees the challenge of risk management today as utterly different from that in previous periods. This is because risk management itself now includes the application of science, and because the public is demanding to see inside the black box and to know the specific reasons for particular regulatory decisions. There is also the fact of increasing demand for regulatory services, as pointed out by Doern (in Chapter 8) for the case of much higher volumes of applications for the approval of therapeutic products. This altered nature of the risk challenge is one reason for the development of new institutional arrangements for science-based regulation.

Leiss envisages a new division of labour in the regulatory process. Science, which is viewed as a rigorous and mature process relying on the system of peer review at arm's length from regulatory decision making, would best be done outside of government. This would be accomplished by means of an enhancement of the role of the universities, leaving government to concentrate more time and resources on the underdeveloped function of risk management that encompasses the risk–benefit and cost–risk trade-offs lying at the heart of policy and regulation-making processes. Leiss does not identify whether industry or government or both would provide the financial resources for such enhancement of university-based capacity for generating the essential science inputs for the federal regulatory process. The level of funding and the mix of funding sources, as well as the location or venue of science-based activities destined for input into regulatory processes, conditions the degree of 'independence' of science, either from any one governing coalition or from any single societal sector, such as industry.

Thus, the purpose of the proposed new division of labour is to leave little wriggle room for government. It would then be very hard for it to avoid having to forthrightly and openly address the central tasks of risk management that are increasing in strategic importance with our increasing dependence on science and technology. Forcing the state to better manage risk in the regulatory process is intended to vastly improve the capacity of government to make higher-quality decisions about risk, and to be inescapably and visibly responsible and accountable for taking the hard cost and risk trade-off decisions.

Other chapters have revealed determinants that act to constrain the full realization of this model for a new division of labour in the regulatory regime, or the separation of the production of scientific inputs in the universities from risk management decision making within government. One such determinant was the view taken by Millstone and Van Zwanenberg (in Chapter 4) that new kinds of risk emerging in food production chains actually demand greater rather than less reliance on the strong administrative accountability that can be found in typical departmental lines of authority. This position is grounded in the interaction of short term market forces with their diminutive effect on risk management vigilance in matters of human and environmental health protection, by firms competing for survival and profit.

Institutional arrangements of society evolve for many reasons, but three very important considerations that can help to explain the location and particular structure of institutional activities are the factors of cost, reward, and risk. For example, an investment portfolio takes on structure (variety of instruments) as a result of decisions taken over time to diversify against risk, to reduce transactions and other costs, and to secure return or yield as a benefit of investments. Similarly, institutional arrangements within government can serve to check and balance various interests so as to reduce the risk of significant error or instability in governance that could be highly negative to the wider society. Alternatively, institutional arrangements may be selected so as to minimize fiscal costs such as through the consolidation of organizational units involved in regulation or to make the most of perceived opportunities.

Thus, one can safely assume that the existing institutional pattern for the production and funding of science-based regulation will have something to do with reducing risks to voters, costs to taxpayers, costs and risks to regulated entities, and of increasing benefits to the various parties involved. This empirical idea of costs, risks, and benefits as interacting factors that positively explain the existing structure of how work is carried out in the regulatory regime contrasts with Leiss's normative approach. This has to do with how he thinks the regime should be structured in rational or logical terms, given the overriding objective of having governments focus on questions of risk management.

Papers by the Professional Institute of the Public Service of Canada (1995) have made the simple but very fundamental observation that regulatory institutions are productive organizations with a workplace and a workforce. These organizations produce or make risk-benefit and risk-cost decisions as agents. Professions of scientists can in turn become interest groups themselves, a fact more than borne out by individual scientists 'going public' against the way the rbST case was handled. Chapter 8 on the TPP pointed out that science is the foundation for risk management, that science-based regulation is especially dependent upon knowledge and research, and that there are a variety of ways in which science is actually used in the regulatory process. Such variety is needed in all similar regulatory agencies on the front line of such a requirement for scientific capacity.

One key reason that favours the location of science-based activity in regulatory institutions close to government is the fact that scientific knowledge and personnel are essential factors of regulatory production. The relative net benefits to governing coalitions from producing the science inputs to regulatory production internally rather than contracting them out involve some calculus of the comparative levels of political support, fiscal cost, and regulatory performance. With fiscal pressure and the need to generate more economic activity in Canada throughout the 1990s, the regulatory pendulum has been set in motion by central authorities towards short-term cost minimization. This process has been *partially compensated* through: (a) cost recovery from regulated sectors combined with new organizational forms and an increased voice for non-public financial contributors; (b) innovation in the regulatory process through the use of information technology, increased labour effort on the part of regulatory personnel, and increased reliance on the level of self- or market-based regulation; and (c) a belated realization by the centre of the need for increased 'bio-risk vigilance.'

The question of the location of science activity is necessarily tied up with the stability of funding. Fiscal pressure is straining science capacity, thereby increasing risk. As a result of a continuing hard budget constraint in SBDAs combined with cost-recovery policy, the locus of governance of science activity has been subtly shifting. Central re-source allocation agencies that have reduced the resources available to policy- and regulation-making SBDAs, in some cases very deeply, have in effect been making cost-risk trade-offs in human and environmen-tal health and safety matters without adequate reference to science. What is particularly troublesome about such central decision making is that it appears to exhibit repeated failure in policy learning, exem-plified by the accumulation of a science deficit in a manner akin to our unhappy experience with fiscal deficits.

A dominant force shaping the evolving structure of the regulatory regime is the combination of the technologies for organizing and com-municating scientific and other types of information that are cen-tral to policy and regulatory decision taking in the federal bioscience regulatory regime. As science and technology evolves and transforms the general economic processes of production, regulatory production processes associated with governmental authority must also evolve and be transformed. In addition to general changes in the nature of the productive process in all organizations, there may be new science and technology more specific to the domains of bioscience and its regulation that will serve to radically change the regulatory policy path and the future character of regulatory agencies.

Human and environmental health and safety regulation goes to the very core of the function of government, a role that involves a respon-sibility, and a duty, to provide for the physical security and protection of its citizens from threats to their physical health and well-being. Arguably science-based regulation falls into that core category of ac-tivities that one would call an 'inherently governmental function.' In-sofar as regulation of such high public policy importance cannot cred-ibly be designed, produced, and delivered without a guaranteed first call on the necessary science capacity, then government will have failed to adequately perform its absolutely fundamental, long-standing func-tion of protecting the physical security and well-being of its citizens.

Leiss has expressed the view that government should not be in-volved in science risk management because of the uncertainty of sci-ence, which he describes as the natural state of scientific inquiry. Rather, government should arrange for science input to regulation making to be undertaken by independent arm's-length science panels. The ratio-nale for this suggested institutional arrangement is that government, as such, cannot resolve scientific controversies. But authors in other chapters, such as those on the CFIA and Environment Canada, rebuff this position. They suggest that the theory of risk, in the presence of insufficient scientific knowledge, is not robust enough to be helpful in decision making. Regulatory practitioners rely heavily on the application of science in the regulatory process, but whenever this is not possible, they must rely upon softer judgments. In those cases, such as the protection of human health in the area of food consumption, where existing science-based risk management theory may not be able to help, quite difficult regulatory decisions have to be taken nonetheless. Indeed, such situations may actually call for *more* government science not less. There may be unintended consequences that cannot be foreseen, which introduces uncertainty, or risk that is not yet capable of quantitative characterization. Regulatory practitioners point out that regulators, such as the CFIA, have a requirement for their own scientists. A good example of such a requirement for in-house capacity can be found in the area of forensic science, even though industry might prefer that such agencies not have their own science capabilities.

It is evident that an important role of science activity in policy and regulatory decision making is to yield knowledge and information that will help to reduce risk and uncertainty. Science can help to clarify, through objective methods, who wins and who loses. It can provide a foundation and a setting, or mediation framework, through which consensus can be sought. High-quality science is needed for good policy and regulatory decision making, and institutional arrangements and policy processes should help to insure that decision makers have access to such science. Science in turn involves peer review, publication, and conformity with the long-established *methods* of science. Here the role of science is integral to the process of governing itself, providing both the knowledge foundation and the frame for governance. In part this is because some of the methods of science are incorporated in the methodological processes of both public policy formation and public administration, which are increasingly reliant upon information technology and collective processes for gathering, analysing, and using factual information.

Regulatory practitioners also argue that science is strategically important to policy and regulatory decision making. If so, it is imperative to have senior officials in policy and regulatory management positions who have backgrounds in science. A key role for science in government that argues against its separation from the state has to do with the degree of structure or direction that it can provide and the longer-term focus and strategic research cycles that science, not politics and economics, can provide. Thus, regulatory science must identify the exact nature of hazards, what technical solutions exist, if any, whether such solutions are practical, and how they can be incorporated and drafted into statutory law, regulations, or standards. This is not a set of diverse skills and experiential knowledge that one will find readily available in universities, or contractually available from the private sector, in a *timely* fashion. This involves research that is related to pressing issues or imperatives of the day, and anticipatory research utilizes expertise that is strategic in character.

Several chapters show that there are also mechanisms designed to seek outside advice from external science panels, on matters such as HIV, blood regulations, input on drug reactions, and so on. A second type of external committee is the expert working groups formed to provide advice and guidance on such matters as organs (safety for transplantation) and safety standards (Canadian Standards Association). Such committees may be ad hoc advisory panels, such as those on calcium channel blocker drugs or advisory panels representing stakeholder groups. Consumers are also represented on such committees and not just scientific experts. The increasing demands for more efficient and faster drug approval processes also requires science to be more, not less, accessible to the regulator.

Another reason for holding regulatory decision-making organizations close to government is the requirement, particularly in product or case approval processes, for the protection of commercial secrets and information that must be kept confidential under law or regulation. As our framework in Chapter 1 suggests, science in an overall product approval subprocess operates in a much more intensive decision-making space and higher volume of activity compared with overall regulation making.

The model of separation of science input for regulation from the regulatory institution, whether inside government or an independent (once removed) regulatory body, is claimed by many practitioners not to be a workable model. This claim is based on the fact that since the regulator has a statutory responsibility to regulate, without a science base it would be in danger of trying to regulate without the necessary scientific inputs or information. This would include science for the compliance and enforcement of existing federal regulations, which a federal agency can be sued for not legally upholding. As Dennis Browne and his colleagues have shown (in Chapter 5), governments have a responsibility to protect their populations with regulatory agencies being responsible to the public through government. From this perspective there is a legal rationale as to why good government science is very important. Such science needs to be sound and unbiased, as it is increasingly difficult to secure objective or unbiased scientific advice outside government, since the ties between university researchers and industries have been increasing. Browne points out that between 1985 and 1995 industry relationships with the universities have increased ten-fold, and that 90 per cent of life science companies have a relationship with academic researchers.

While this trend is understandable and is very positive for facilitating technological and industrial innovation, we are losing a very valuable resource – independent academic science, which in the universities can be influenced by increased reliance on private funding. This trend poses a difficulty for Leiss's proposed division of labour, as it is imperative that science inputs into the policy and regulation process be unbiased and independent. The combination of Browne's point about the introduction of bias into the university through corporate funding, Leiss's argument for reliance on the universities for science inputs, and industry calls for independent science reviews together point to credibility problems in the separation argument. Perhaps the best that can be achieved in the area of 'independence' or 'unbiased' science in the context of the regulatory regime is for a diversified funding mix for the science activities involved through the design and construction of the institutional arrangements in the regime in a balanced way. There is some urgency that we get these institutional arrangements right, since as we move into the biotechnological century, it is going to become increasingly difficult to regulate science and scientists themselves.

The human resource aspects of the science-based regime are also entwined in the federal merit system which still seeks legally and in practice to ensure that system-wide merit criteria and procedures are applied in the recruitment, promotion, pay, and career process. These principles and procedures often, but not always, collide with the need for particular regulators to attract, pay, and maintain the kinds of scientists that they need for the front-line regulatory and risk–benefit analytical tasks. These issues, as we have seen, are linked to new organizational forms and to issues of how independent a particular science-based regulatory body is, or should be allowed to be.

The Double Pluralization Dynamic: Science and Interests

A third feature of institutional change for the science-based policy and regulatory regime as a whole emerges from what can be called a dynamic of double pluralization. Science is itself more pluralistic and so is the structure of other social and economic interests. This produces a double interaction effect. Some of this was first hinted at in Chapter 1, in our discussion of the framework for science-based regulation and its subprocesses and science paths. The subprocesses for regulation making, postmarket monitoring, and overall compliance all exhibit this dual pluralization dynamic.

On the science side of this dynamic, one must begin with the observation that scientists are often remarkably unscientific about their own profession and changing division of labour. They appear to lack a collective appreciation of the sociology of science and of its basic shape and nature at the start of the new millennium, especially its growing pluralization. Science, as an organized social and intellectual enterprise, has never been simple or monolithic but always pluralistic in some sense: however, the growing degree of pluralization is extensive and some of its key features need to be highlighted.

Merton's basic framework on the sociology of science is still immensely useful both in capturing the core norms of science and hence its bedrock pluralism. The principles of communalism, universalism, disinterestedness, originality, and organized scepticism are central to the social system of science as represented by the research scientist and the basic researcher (Merton, 1973; Storer, 1966; Grove, 1990). Implicit in this set of characteristics is the core notion that science is above all about evidence and measurement and the ability to distinguish good evidence from bad evidence (Gribbin, 1998). Subsequent analysis has had to amend these norms and the way they coalesce when scientist-practitioners find themselves lodged within complex bureaucracies, be they corporate, governmental, or academic.

Science is more pluralistic in three ways that transcend these different overall institutional settings. First, the nature of the discipline structure of science is changing, which in turn alters how scientists label themselves and how others see them. Added to the early disciplines of physics, engineering, chemistry, and biology one now sees a proliferation of newer disciplines, subdisciplines, and interdisciplinary fields. This pattern can easily be seen by comparing a typical university calendar from the late 1970s with one from the late 1990s, or by comparing the names of branches of science-based regulatory bodies over a similar period. It can also be found in the emergence of new scientific journals. Indeed, often one of the definitions of an 'established' or 'prestigious' journal and 'second line' or emerging new journal is that a new subdiscipline or transdiscipline is being borne in the latter's challenge to the former. Some of this pressure for differentiation and stratification emerges from the sheer growth in the number of the world's scientists but it is more than that. Specialization of disciplines and subdisciplines is both a reflection of innovation and a cause of it. It is also present, in a different way, in the pressure from within professions by subgroups to obtain self-regulating status and recognition. Disciplines and subdisciplines must inevitably construct their own kinds of discourse and language both to communicate new kinds of knowledge and to separate themselves from the larger lay public and from other cognate disciplines.

A second feature of the pluralization dynamic arises from the partial breakdown of the earlier post–Second World War model of the spectrum of scientific activity (Gibbons et al., 1994; Crow, 1994). The main presumption was that basic or pure research, even when driven by curiosity, broadly drove the *later* applied research and development phases. But for at least the past fifteen years an alternative to this presumption has been offered by other evidence and experience that shows interactions as being much more complex, and indeed with causal links often being reversed, and more subtle. In short, the pathways to science-based innovation are multiple and complex. The new institutional linkages and partnerships between industry and universities are partly forged on the basis of this new and deeper understanding of the many avenues to innovative research and development activity. They also create legitimate opposition centred on what this means for the independence of researchers and for science and research as a public good (Lee, 1996; Etzkowitz, 1996).

The role of science in regulation, and in risk–benefit management is also more pluralistic because of changes in the sources of scientific information. It is suggested that the older model and era of science-based regulation was anchored around traditional sources such as epidemiological investigations, toxicological studies, and clinical trials. More recently, and in the context of the risk–benefit management model, other sources and types of scientific information have come into greater use, including biological markers, molecular epidemiology, new toxicological assays, in vitro assays, genetics, structure activity analysis, surveillance, and population health surveys. These newer sources and techniques are breaking down boundaries of competence among traditionally defined scientific disciplines and are reflected in generational differences in the backgrounds of scientists in government and outside it. This evolution also leads to a far wider sharing, interdependence, and exchange of scientific and professional information and knowledge among experts in Canada and internationally.

All of the above aspects deal mainly with the growing pluralization of science *within* the changed social system of science. They do not in themselves say anything about other interests and players with whom scientists are interacting, except that they will find the realm of science itself to be increasingly more complex. Nor do they address issues concerning the modes of communication of scientific information. For example, they do not focus on the crucial issue as to how much scientific input is communicated *verbally* and in person within government, as opposed to in writing, let alone via the ubiquitous Information Highway.

As for the pluralization of other interests, the evidence of growing pluralization is found across the chapters of this book, both those dealing with macro-policy and those with agencies. But the evidence begins in the larger realm of political analysis, which for many years has observed the rise of special interests and the weakness of institutions that might aggregate such interests (Pal, 1997). It also emerges from the growth of the new public management or reinvented government, whose very essence is to look for and seek out different categories and subcategories of customers and clients rather than serve only powerful producer groups (Aucoin, 1997; Flynn, 1997). Additional evidence is provided by some of the consequences of governing in the information age. The Internet changes interest politics and interest formation profoundly (Stanbury and Vertinsky, 1995). Groups and subgroups can form and communicate less expensively and more quickly than in earlier eras because computer communications technology has drastically changed the economics of individual and collective action.

In many of this book's chapters the growing pluralization of interests is clearly in evidence. Trade regimes and global trade imperatives bring the structure of interests *within* other countries ultimately into

Canada's *domestic* deliberations. The structure of interests surrounding the TPP and Health Canada in general is now much more complex than before. This is true not only in the regulation of drugs and medical devices, where new health coalitions and networks of doctors and patients now exist, but also in areas not covered in this book, such as in interests forming around natural foods products (House of Commons, 1998). The discussion of biodiversity (in Chapter 11) indicated links to diverse national and international groups who hold strong views about the resources of the ecosystem. The analysis of the fisheries clearly shows the emergence of diverse fishery interests who want a say in the processes through which science is examined and decisions about conservation made.

These changes also mean that, almost by definition, there are more combinations of views about what constitutes appropriate independence for science and what constitutes usable knowledge. Biodiversity draws on local and Aboriginal knowledge that may be as suspect as mainstream science, but which compels respect as experiential knowledge. The same is true for the previously mentioned natural foods lobby. Groups opposing biotechnology also exhibit a growing pluralism (Canada, 1998). In all of these developments there is, of course, a considerable potential for an anti-science ethos to emerge that takes on a modern version of *ludditism* or an irrational fear of technology. Such an ethos can also be reinforced by prior regulatory failures that may have undermined the level of the public trust. Views that are critical of science or which raise serious issues about the limits of science also come from quite serious and respectable quarters (Horgan, 1996; Barrow, 1998).

There is, however, no mistaking that a double pluralization dynamic is at work and that this affects the way scientists and interests see each other and interact with one another. Such a phenomenon leads readily into our final point about the difficulty that the state has in communicating science-based policy and institutional mandates in this new kind of policy and regulatory world.

Communicating Mandates: The Ultimate Risky Business?

We began this book by observing that the renewed and concerted national attention given to science in government in Canada was the product of media exposure in 1997–8 to several controversies. These included the collapse of fish stocks in the Atlantic fishery, the issue of tainted blood and the failure of the blood regulatory system, the independence of science in the Health Protection Branch at Health Canada, and issues raised concerning nuclear reactors utilized in electricity generation in Ontario. These controversies have developed alongside a global set of concerns that included the U.K.'s BSE or 'mad cow' disease debacle, the cloning of Dolly the sheep, and the new technical and ethical imperatives of biotechnology. We noted how previous decades had had periodic episodes where science-based controversy had emerged on the Canadian political-economic agenda. But we also suggested that what was different about the new millennium cluster of controversies and concerns was that they began to raise issues about the science-based policy and regulatory regime of government as a whole. They also began to grapple with issues as to how risk is assessed, managed, and communicated in a government-wide context.

This flurry of concern in the late 1990s was immediately followed by federal efforts to repair the breach in public confidence. Advisory scientific bodies were immediately created and a macro-Council of Science and Technology Advisors established. Research was commissioned on 'best practices' and guidelines on how scientific advice should be structured in policy formation and regulation. While important, this flurry of concern is partially misleading and distracts from the larger instances of institutional change that in fact stretch (as our chapters show) back through the decade of the 1990s. These changes include:

- The consolidation of federal authorities respecting the regulation of pesticides into a single separate operating agency, the Pest Management Regulatory Agency, and the transfer of ministerial responsibility for its functioning from the Minister of Agriculture to the Minister of Heath
- The creation of the Canadian Environmental Assessment Agency separate from the federal Department of the Environment (Environment Canada) charged with the management of environmental assessments of proposed developments that trigger federal regulatory authority and interest in environmental impacts of development initiatives, and of the Office of the Commissioner of the Environment and Sustainable Development reporting to Parliament under the aegis of the Office of the Auditor General
- The establishment of the Therapeutics Products Programme as a component of the larger Health Protection Branch at Health Canada as a result of the amalgamation in 1997 of the formerly

separate Drugs and Medical Devices Programmes of Health
Canada, with a mandate to ensure that drugs, medical devices,
and other therapeutic products in Canada are safe, effective, and
of high quality
- An important review and reform of the processes, procedures,
and institutional arrangements for producing and using scientific
information and advice in management decision making in
respect of the offshore fisheries in the Department of Fisheries
and Oceans, primarily in response to the catastrophic failure of
the East Coast cod fishery
- The consolidation of a number of disparate federal authorities
over food inspection and safety matters into a hybrid departmen-
tal-commercial Crown corporation, the Canadian Food Inspection Agency, largely in response to fiscal pressures for increased
efficiency in food inspection but also to satisfy the public policy
imperative for clear accountability in matters of food safety
- An update and overhaul of the Atomic Energy Control Board
which regulates, licenses, and inspects the acquisition, use, and
disposal of radioactive materials in Canada such as those used in
the generation of energy, to be replaced by the Canadian Nuclear
Safety Commission with increased emphasis on safety along with
the traditional considerations of national security.

These changes reveal a more complex trail of change triggered, as
we have seen, by the realization of large risks in debt management,
deficit politics, globalization, the new public management, and new
views of risk and risk–benefit management in science-based regulation. Our agency chapters in Part 2 have examined these changes using our framework in different ways, but final institutional attention
needs to be drawn to two of their aggregate institutional features,
both of which raise dilemmas about the political communication of
mandates.

One feature about aggregate change is that changes in the pesticides
and food inspection fields have involved shifts away from the agricultural ministerial domain to the health domain. Thus, Canada, through
its new institutional reforms in the area of food inspection and pesticide regulation have moved to overcome one of the key institutional
shortcomings in the U.K. regulatory administration that entered as a
contributing factor into the BSE case. In part this was because the
agricultural domain was seen as being too agriculture producer domi-

nated with perceived too little weight given to human and environmental health considerations. Agriculture Canada had in fact become
Agri-Food Canada in 1993, and thus its internal politics had itself
changed, but nonetheless it is important to note the shift in regulatory
domains towards Health Canada. Meanwhile, this latter department's
Health Protection Branch was consolidating its various arms of risk
regulation under the Therapeutic Products Program. It also eventually
succumbed to pressure from the natural foods lobby and established
in 1999 a separate regulatory body for this aspect of health and food
(House of Commons, 1998).

All of this suggests that Health Canada was becoming more and
more of a super-department for the management and regulation of
risk. As a result it is facing the increasingly difficult task of trying to
project an integrated view of risk regulation to the political community and to its own disparate *ensemble* of regulatory units. These changes
raise serious problems for communicating specialized mandates in the
wider institutional setting of one-stop shopping at super- or supra-
institutions. Health Canada's centre of gravity for these tasks is still
called a health 'protection' branch. Nevertheless, the nature of the
activities within the branch is shifting in the direction of activities
to be found in risk-benefit management organizations. Within each
sub-unit (for example, drugs versus medical devices versus blood)
risk–benefit can mean different things or at least occur in different
combinations of activity. This poses a fundamental problem in the
basic communication of risk and regulatory mandates, and science
in government cannot help but be affected by such disjunctures and
contradictions.

Some related problems also exist in the case of Environment Canada.
While it has not been loaded up with newly *transferred* agencies into
its ministerial realm in the manner experienced by Health Canada, it
has been subject to continuous mandate expansion. Additions in the
areas of biodiversity and other internationally mandated tasks, including parts of the climate change file, have been thrust upon it, but
without adequate levels of funding.

Environment Canada shares with Health Canada a fundamental
problem of communicating risk mandates in that, like its health counterpart, it is effectively seeking a risk–benefit and risk-prevention
mandate rather than just an older-style protection and remediation
mandate. The problems facing the environment are so cross-cutting
and government wide that to be truly effective the department and its

minister must in effect call on, and are extremely dependent on, the cooperation of other ministers and agencies, not to mention industry and the public. It is for this reason that Environment Canada wants and needs to reach out more in partnership than its earlier 1970s-born environmental protection persona indicated. This is more than just a trivial word game of 'What's in a name?' Science-based regulation and risk management ultimately cluster in very important ways in the eyes of the public around health and green ministries, but the most fundamental messages about mandates are themselves a very risky part of the politics of science-based policy making and regulation.

Once again the four concluding institutional aspects examined here suggest the need for different levels of analysis of Canada's changing science-based policy and regulatory regime. Juggernaut-like fiscal politics can produce the *déjà vu* of realized risk in science regulation, and resource provisioning to the science regulators in the regime needs to be re-evaluated in those terms. Views of the independence of science need to take into account the new complexities of risk, including challenges to the authority of science, but also the practical realities of the institutional subprocesses of regulation set out in our framework in Chapter 1. The double pluralization of both science and the structure of interests has to be taken as a *given* in taking stock of what kinds of interests overall take part in the enlarged politics of risk–benefit management in Canada and internationally. Last, but not least, disjunctures in communicating basic mandates about core health and environmental ministries are likely to grow as Canadians pay even more attention to the government's management of risky business and to the politics of protection.

References

Barrow, John D. (1998). *Impossibility: The Limits of Science and the Science of Limits*. Oxford: Oxford University Press.

Canada. (1998). *Renewal of the Canadian Biotechnology Strategy: Roundtable Consultation Document*. Ottawa: Industry Canada.

Crow, Michael M. (1994). 'Science and Technology Policy in the United States: Trading in the 1950 Model.' *Science and Public Policy*, 21(4): 202–12.

Etzkowitz, Henry. (1996). 'Conflicts of Interest and Commitment in Academic Science in the United States.' *Minerva*, 34: 259–77.

Flynn, Norman. (1997). *Public Sector Management*, 3rd ed. London: Prentice-Hall Harvester Wheatsheaf.

Gribbin, John. (1998). *Almost Everyone's Guide to Science*. London: Weidenfeld and Nicolson.

Gibbons, M. (1994). *The New Production of Knowledge*. London: Sage.

Grove, Jack. (1990). *In Defence of Science*. Toronto: University of Toronto Press.

House of Commons. (1998). *Natural Health Products: A New Vision*. Report of the Standing Committee on Health.

Horgan, John. (1996). *The End of Science*. New York: Broadway.

Lee, Yong S. (1996). 'Technology Transfer and the Research University: A Search for the Boundaries of University–Industry Collaboration.' *Research Policy*, 25: 843–63.

Merton, R.K. (1973). *Sociology of Science*. New York: Macmillan.

Professional Institute of the Public Service of Canada. (1994). *Lifting the Silence*. Ottawa: author.

– (1995). *Science and Society*. Ottawa: author.

Stanbury, W.T., and Ilan B. Vertinsky. (1995). 'Assessing the Impact of New Information Technologies on Interest Group Behaviour in Policy Making.' In Thomas J. Courchene, ed., *Technology, Information and Public Policy*, 381–401. Kingston: John Deutsch Institute, Queen's University.

Storer, Norman W. (1966). *The Social System of Science*. New York: Holt, Rinehart and Winston.

Swimmer, Gene (ed.) (1996). *How Ottawa Spends 1995–96: Life under the Knife*. Ottawa: Carleton University Press.

Treasury Board Secretariat. (1998). *Government-Wide Summary of External User Charge Revenues*. Ottawa: author.

Studies in Comparative Political Economy and Public Policy